THE DEVIL AND MARIA D'AVALOS

Victoria Hammond is a full-time writer and art historian, and has worked as a Director of the Shepparton Art Gallery and Guest Curator at the National Gallery of Victoria. An award-winning author, she has written several art catalogues and sponsored histories in addition to the critically acclaimed *Letters from St Petersburg* (Allen & Unwin, 2004), and *Visions of Heaven: The Dome in European Architecture* (photographs by David Stephenson, Princeton Architectural Press, 2005).

THE *Devil* & MARIA D'AVALOS

VICTORIA HAMMOND

ALLEN&UNWIN

First published in 2007

This project has been assisted by the Commonwealth
Government through the Australia Council, its arts
funding and advisory board.

Allen & Unwin
83 Alexander Street
Crows Nest NSW 2065
Australia
Phone: (61 2) 8425 0100
Fax: (61 2) 9906 2218
Email: info@allenandunwin.com
Web: www.allenandunwin.com

National Library of Australia
Cataloguing-in-Publication entry:

Hammond, Victoria.
    The devil and Maria d'Avalos.

    ISBN 978 1 74114 685 1 (pbk.).

    I. Title.

A823.4

Text design by Tabitha King
Set in 11.5/15 pt Garamond by Bookhouse, Sydney
Printed and bound in Australia by Griffin Press

10 9 8 7 6 5 4 3 2 1

To Stefania

On Death of the Two Most Noble Lovers,
Maria d'Avalos and Fabrizio Carafa

Weep, O Graces, and you too bewail, O Loves,
the cruel trophies of death and the cruel spoils
of the beautiful couple whom death enviously
takes from us

Weep, O Nymphs, and strew blossoms on this
couple, their moist leaves painted with old
lamentations

Weep, Erato and Clio, for this horrible event,
and scatter with mournful sound your
bitter complaint

Weep, sad Naples, clothed in mourning,
for the dark fate of beauty and of virtue

Torquato Tasso, 1590

The tomb of Maria speaks to a pilgrim

It seems to me that I hear who she is, o wanderer,
who under my stone is sealed. Know that she was
the most beautiful Maria d'Avalos, resplendent
not only on earth but in heaven

She had three illustrious husbands; the third
one gave her death. And here she lies under
the earth. Let this suffice as an example to
blind lovers. The rest is already known by all
the world.

Anonymous poet, Naples, 1590

CONTENTS

PREFACE

Late one night, unable to sleep, I turned on SBS television. To the accompaniment of hauntingly doleful music came the seductive voice of the German filmmaker, Werner Herzog, narrating his documentary on the sixteenth century Italian composer, Carlo Gesualdo, Prince of Venosa. It was just beginning. As Herzog's camera roved through decaying palaces and he interviewed Neapolitans and Gesualdo aficionados, the story of the most famous murder in the history of music unfolded. I was riveted.

Herzog is obsessed with characters of rare genius: visionary, isolated individuals whose loves go tragically awry. Carlo Gesualdo fitted the bill perfectly. A composer of genius, nephew of a pope and a saint, and, for the last sixteen years of his life, madman—or so it was alleged—the contradictions in his temperament and talents were of Shakespearean complexity. His murder of his wife, Maria d'Avalos, and her aristocratic lover was operatic in its details: a chilling mix of cold calculation and frenzy. Its aftermath was no less dramatic.

Yet Herzog's film contained tantalising fragments of another, equally compelling story, that of Maria d'Avalos herself—her legendary beauty, her three husbands, her affair with 'the handsomest and most accomplished nobleman in Naples', and her status as the victim of what appeared to be a classic southern Italian *onore* killing. Who was this Neapolitan woman who haunted Herzog's *Death for Five Voices*. Was she, as he suggested, the sitter for Leonardo's *Mona Lisa*? When I began reading about Gesualdo and the murder soon after, other puzzles in the story intrigued me. Why, for instance, did her lover have the same surname, Carafa, as her first husband? And then there was the city of Naples itself, capital of the vast Spanish empire during Maria d'Avalos's lifetime, and a focal point of bitter wars between the French and Spanish for domination of the Italian peninsula that erupted sporadically over the course of three centuries. What role had this then richest and most dangerous of cities played in her life? There was nothing for it but to go there to try to discover if, after more than four centuries, any traces of Maria d'Avalos remained.

Only in Italy could I have discovered what I did. The splendid palaces, castles and churches where the dramas of Maria d'Avalos's life were played out, and which form the settings of several chapters in this book, still exist in Naples or the wider Campagna region. These buildings have endured for more than five hundred years. Visiting them was like collecting the individual pieces of a jigsaw, for at each I encountered generous Italians who would provide me with yet another piece of the puzzle.

My research in Naples was in part a series of fortuitous encounters. On my very first day there, to escape the teeming rain, I hastily entered a hotel in the Spaccanapoli district, for I knew Maria d'Avalos had lived in the area at one point. The hotel was on the fourth floor of a building characteristic of Naples' historic centre. Its dark lower storeys, with their massive stones, were medieval; floors had been added during the Renaissance when many of these buildings had been converted into palaces; and over the centuries other conversions and additions had been made, so that walking up the stairs of these wonderful buildings is like travelling through time. The owners of the hotel were, as luck would have it, architects. They had an affectionate knowledge not only of the history of their own building, but of many others in Naples, so with their help and that of their friend, the superb architect Stefania Salvetti, it was only a matter of days before I was familiar with every palace in Naples that Maria d'Avalos had inhabited. In the face of this generosity, and the locals' intense interest in Maria d'Avalos, who remains a legend in Naples—her ghost is said to haunt Palazzo San Severo—my initial qualms that I may have embarked on a fool's errand evaporated.

From the outside, enormous Palazzo d'Avalos, on its hill overlooking the celebrated Bay of Naples, still epitomises the classical grandeur of Renaissance palaces, its tall palms adding a characteristic southern Italian exoticism to its façade. But to go inside the palace is to experience the ravages of five hundred years. My progress up several flights of marble stairs was uneventful until I reached the wide landing that led to the top floor. The balustrades and railings had long since disappeared, but this was not why I hesitated. I stood there contemplating the void on either side of the staircase; there was simply nothing there, only a yawning blackness bridged by the pale marble steps. Above me a door opened, and the current Prince d'Avalos beckoned, telling me it was perfectly safe to proceed. As this dignified, middle-aged man led me through a series of nobly proportioned rooms—empty but for the occasional set piece: a pair of gilt baroque chairs, a table with legs fashioned as writhing serpents, an exquisite vase—he sadly explained that part of the palace had collapsed. The famous d'Avalos art collection—the prince's ancestor had been the patron of the great Venetian painter, Titian—was stored out of harm's way on the first floor, along with other precious heirlooms and artefacts pertaining to the d'Avalos glory days. What would happen to it all when he could no longer prevent his beloved palace from being converted into a shopping complex? His family history was a terrible responsibility, a burden. The gentle prince dreamed of a saviour in the form of a rich American.

There was one room that had not changed since the time of Maria d'Avalos. Proudly, he showed it to me. It was the ballroom and it was indeed miraculously intact. The sunlight streaming through the tall windows, the stucco cherubs and garlands of its airy, sky-blue walls and ceiling, gave it a feeling of weightlessness, so that this perfect room seemed to float in some unassailable realm above the timeworn fabric of the rest of the palace. We then sat down in a large olive green room with a beautiful quatrefoil ceiling, bare but for a small table and chairs and a Steinway grand. Prince Francesco d'Avalos, a noted musician and composer, had just completed an opera about Maria' d'Avalos. He presented me a copy of the d'Avalos family tree. It dated back to the birth in 838 of Igniquez d'Avalos, captain of the king of Navarre's army. Only later, when I matched the names and dates on the family tree with various histories of Naples in the period 1400–1600, did I understand the prominent role his illustrious family had played in the history of the Italian peninsula. This, then, was Maria d'Avalos's family.

In the remote township of Gesualdo, having inspected the ruined, frescoed rooms of Gesualdo Castle courtesy of the local *comune*, I stepped out into the snow to be greeted by a leonine figure in a flapping black overcoat, flying up the hill towards me. 'Come to my house. I have things to show you.' Who was he? Professor Annibale Coglione, Italy's Gesualdo expert. News in sleepy Gesualdo travelled fast. The professor was born in Gesualdo and had devoted his life to the study of its famous namesake. It is a researcher's dream to encounter a scholar who readily shares his knowledge, and Professor Coglione was that dream. He was completing another book about Carlo Gesualdo, centred on a scandalous incident that involved a witch. To my amazement he gave me a copy of his manuscript. This enabled me to include the little-known affair in this book's final chapter. The professor also gave me a copy of the letter written to Maria d'Avalos at Ischia in 1586 by her Aunt Antonia, Princess of Sulmona, which is reproduced, in translation, in 'The Nuns' Cemetery' chapter.

There were other memorable encounters, among them one with Felice, the docent of the church of San Domenico Maggiore, who, as he illuminated the painting of the Carafa family which hangs in the church's Carafa chapel, pointed to the face of Maria d'Avalos and murmured, *dolce, cosi dolce*, sweet, so sweet. It was he who introduced me to the significance of the Carafa family, as illustrious as the d'Avaloses.

The Devil and Maria d'Avalos is a fiction based on historical facts. These facts include members of the d'Avalos family, their relationship to each other and their role in historical events in Naples and beyond; Maria d'Avalos's relationships with and those between Federigo, Ferrante, Fabrizio, Beatrice and Marc Antonio Carafa; Maria d'Avalos's relationships with and those between the members of the Gesualdo family; the Clarisse nuns and the Nuns' Cemetery at Castello Aragonese; the d'Avalos and Carafa families' defiance of Spain's attempts to introduce a court of the Inquisition in Naples; Carlo Gesualdo's marriage to Leonora d'Este, their son Alfonsino, and the fate of the d'Este kingdom in Ferrara; the Duchess of Andria's purported 'vision' of the murder and her subsequent fate; the murder of the Duchess of Malfi, Giovanna d'Aragona, and her kinship with the Piccolominis and d'Avaloses. Other 'real' characters are Alfonso

Gioeni, Sylvia Albana, Laura Scala, Pietro Bardotti and the priest, Alessandro. Carlo Gesualdo's murder of Maria d'Avalos and Fabrizio Carafa is based on the circumstances of the actual murder, which took place on 16 October 1590, as recounted by witnesses in the report of the proceedings of the Grand Court of the Vicaria.

The Leonardo da Vinci painting referred to in Chapter One and later is the *Mona Lisa*. While the identity of the sitter for this painting has spawned a veritable industry outside of Italy, the Italian historian and philosopher, Benedetto Croce, was convinced that she was Costanza d'Avalos, and many Italian art historians adhere to this view. The painting mentioned later, *Pala per perdona*, hangs in the chapel of Santa Maria delle Grazie in the township of Gesualdo. I should add that Gesualdo Castle is currently being restored, under the auspices of the Gesualdo *comune*. The painting of Alfonso d'Avalos by Titian mentioned in Chapter Three is held by the Prado Museum, Madrid. Its companion piece, *Portrait of Alfonso d'Avalos with a Page*, also by Titian, signalled the inception of the standing state portrait and thereby revolutionised portrait painting. It was purchased by the Getty Museum in 2004 for US$70 million. The painting I mention of Maria d'Avalos's grandmother, Maria d'Aragona, as Venus was also painted by Titian.

Among the many Neapolitans not yet mentioned, and to whom I owe thanks for their assistance and the pleasure of their company, are Gaetano and Alessandra D'Auino, Leonardo Campobasso and Raffaelo Falchini. I am also thankful to the staff of Naples' Biblioteca Nazionale, a Borgesian paradise, and to Magica Fossati.

Of the many books about Carlo Gesualdo, I make special mention of *Gesualdo: The Man and His Music* by Glenn Watkins, with an introduction by Igor Stravinsky.

Once again, it has been a pleasure to have the encouragement and support of the team at Allen & Unwin. I am especially grateful to Jo Paul and Catherine Taylor. Particular thanks are due to the editor of the manuscript, Julia Stiles, for her enthusiasm and intelligent comments and suggestions, which improved the story immeasurably. I greatly appreciate a grant from the Literature Board of the Australia Council, which enabled me to travel to Italy and to commence writing *The Devil and Maria d'Avalos*.

One

CASTELLO ARAGONESE

Maria d'Avalos stood on the waterfront, her black mourning clothes flapping in the wind. She'd returned to her city—the world's richest and most vicious—only momentarily. Sailing ships were arriving with cargoes of nutmeg and cocoa beans; others were noisily preparing to set sail again, their holds crammed with maize or bolts of silk. Maria's eyes were restless behind her dark veil; they lingered briefly on a richly dressed merchant who wore pearl earrings, the curly-haired ruffian who was eyeing him, and a family bidding a tearful farewell to a departing passenger, before returning again and again to an imposing palace with regal palms that stood high on a hill overlooking Naples' celebrated bay. She lifted her gloved hands and drew back her veil. A fisherman paused in the act of sorting his catch and stared at her boldly. Never had he seen such eyes. She appeared not to notice; instead, her startlingly beautiful face broke into a smile as she caught sight of her daughter Beatrice approaching through the crowd. The child, small for her nine years, was perched on the shoulder of a tall guard and stared about her in fascination. A sturdy, frowning servant woman followed close behind them.

'Mama, I saw a monkey climbing a mast,' called Beatrice excitedly.

'Then you've been well entertained,' smiled Maria, indicating for the guard to set her daughter down. 'Sylvia, tell the captain we're ready to leave.'

'Yes, my lady,' said the servant, and hurried over to the barque that was to ferry Maria and her party of servants and guards across to the island of Ischia. Maria drew her daughter to her and pointed up the hill to the terracotta-coloured palace with its green shutters. 'That is Palazzo d'Avalos. Do you remember it?'

She wasn't surprised when the child shook her head. It had been six years since they'd left Naples for Messina, and the only memory Beatrice had of her birth city was a dim recollection of lost happiness on that long-ago day when she and her mother had departed Palazzo Carafa and the protective circle of her father's family.

'Why can't we go to the pink palace now?' asked the child. 'Why must we go to the island?'

'Because it's what your grandfather has decided,' replied Maria.

'Why has he decided it?'

'Come, we must go. I'll tell you on the ship.'

As they sailed out of the harbour, the captain skilfully negotiating a passage through the confusion of vessels, Maria sat aft of the barque, watching Naples slowly recede. She considered what simple answer she might provide to Beatrice's question, one that concealed from the child her mother's sense of being banished from Naples to be a virtual prisoner on Ischia while her family negotiated with the Vatican her proposed marriage. Maria's second husband, the Sicilian Alfonso Gioeni, Marquis of Giulianova, had died only three weeks ago and her illustrious family had lost no time in entering into arrangements for her third marriage. The negotiations with Pope Pius, however, might take months. She knew her sense of banishment was foolish, symptom of a deeper sorrow and her impatience to return to the city she loved. The reasons for her enforced sojourn on Ischia were clear to her: aristocratic pride and a centuries-old habit of protectiveness, particularly of such a prize as a d'Avalos daughter. To return to Naples a widow, her future uncertain, would be unwise, dangerous even, for among the many who would scheme to marry her were those who might resort to rape, and if such vile dishonour were to befall her, then her only hope of marriage would be to her violator.

The re-entrance of Maria d'Avalos into Neapolitan society must be a triumphant one, and it was as if fate had conspired to make it so. Two unexpected deaths had followed one after the other: that of her cousin, Luigi Gesualdo, heir to the princedom of Venosa, and that of Alfonso

Gioeni. Luigi's death had resulted in his younger brother Carlo becoming heir to the Gesualdo estates, and hence a most desirable prospect for marriage. Desirable only in the worldly sense of such things, that is, not in a way that gladdened Maria's heart.

She cast her private feelings aside, well knowing that as the official betrothed of the young Prince of Venosa, she would be esteemed and envied. And if Pope Pius did grant the dispensation necessary for her to remarry during her period of mourning, then he would also be granting what she had longed for during those six unhappy years in Messina: a return to Naples and its way of life.

How to explain all of this to Beatrice?

Her daughter stood windblown on the side of the ship with Laura, Maria's maid, her grey eyes fixed on the twin peaks of unpredictable Vesuvius, snowy white in the winter sun. 'Could the mountain erupt now and bury us all?' she asked.

'No, no. It would mumble and grumble deep inside and we'd have time to get away,' Laura assured her.

'That's not what Poppa Alfonso said. He told me that the last time it happened the earth just opened up and swallowed houses and people, and rivers of fire turned everything to flames, and by the time it was finished the whole city was rearranged.'

'Poppa Alfonso was exaggerating,' said Maria, concerned by Beatrice's preoccupation with death and destruction. 'People who aren't from Naples like to tell such frightening stories. It pleases them to think that a city as beautiful as Naples must also be dangerous.'

'Are you dangerous?' asked Beatrice.

'Of course not. Why would you ask such a question?'

'Because everyone says you're famous for your beauty.'

'You know very well I'm not dangerous. You're being too clever again, Beatrice.'

Maria frowned. Was it possible that her daughter had heard the salacious gossip that her first husband, Federigo Carafa, had died of, as they put it, an excess of connubial bliss? She prayed not. Beatrice was Federigo's daughter. And what of Alfonso's sudden death? Had that, too, become a subject of spiteful rumours?

'Why are we going to the island?' asked Beatrice.

'Because your mama's family owns this beautiful island and Grandpapa d'Avalos wishes you to see it. A long time ago the King of Naples gave it to the d'Avalos family because one of them was a great hero who saved the king's life in a battle with the French. After that it became famous throughout Italy because it was attacked by French warships and your great-great-aunt Costanza d'Avalos fought them off and became a heroine.' Although she'd simplified the facts, Maria was telling her daughter the truth.

'A *woman* fought them off? By herself?' Beatrice was enthralled.

'No, not by herself. She'd shown the people of Ischia how to use weapons to ward off pirate attacks, so when the French attacked unexpectedly they were prepared and she led them as an army.'

'How did she know how to use weapons?'

'She was trained in warfare by her father and brother who were great military commanders in the king's army.'

'Why didn't *they* fight off the French?'

'Because they were fighting elsewhere. In any case, Costanza was the Governor of Ischia and it was her duty to defend it.'

'The governor.' This seemed both odd and thrilling to Beatrice. 'How did she become a governor?'

'See that dark fortress over there with the two towers?' Maria pointed back at Castelnuovo, the Kingdom of Naples' seat of government. 'Alfonso d'Avalos, who had previously saved the king, was tying to recapture it from the French. His army succeeded but he was killed. So, to honour the d'Avalos family, the king gave Ischia to Alfonso's brother and sister, Inico and Costanza. Shortly afterwards, Inico died, so Costanza became Ischia's sole governor. She lived on the island and ruled over it for fifty years. And you and I are going to live in Costanza's enormous castle for a while, so you see it's exciting to be going to Ischia.'

The prospect of Ischia did suddenly seem less grim. Maria found she enjoyed telling this slice of family history to Beatrice, for in doing so she was recapturing her old sense of pride in her family, and hence in herself. Alfonso Gioeni had been a possessive husband. In Messina, far from her relatives, her d'Avalos identity had been subsumed by her status as his wife. As they sailed toward Ischia, she was struck by a curious, unexpected sense of coming back to herself.

'When did Aunt Costanza die?'

'About forty years ago.'

'Who's the governor now?'

'Your Uncle Ferrante, but he lives in Milan. Come Beatrice, it's getting too cold to be standing out here. Let's go below deck and have a sleep now so that we'll be awake when we approach Ischia. The castle looks wonderful from the sea, like something in a painting, and you'll want to see it.'

The barque skimmed across the Tyrrhenean Sea toward the two islands that flanked the entrance to the Bay of Naples: larger but dangerously volcanic Ischia to one side, and on the other Capri, the safer island on which the Roman Emperor Tiberius had re-established his holiday resort, abandoning the more beautiful Ischia.

The sun was beginning to set by the time they reached Ischia. Heading for the offshore island that formed its eastern tip, they sailed around the coastline, passing lines of cliffs and wide sandy beaches. Marble ruins of Roman resorts marked the sites of hot thermal springs that gushed amidst the woodlands. Maria's eyes searched for the most intact of these ruins, remembering the day Federico Carafa had laughingly peeled off her cumbersome clothes and they'd plunged hand in hand into a sulphurous pool and blissfully idled away a soporific afternoon in its steamy vapours. She'd been fifteen. She recalled the details of that day with such clarity it seemed barely believable that it was ten years ago.

Massive Castello Aragonese came into view. As they drew closer, it towered above them on its great rock, the steep craggy outline darkly silhouetted against the steely sky. Each time Maria saw its complex of buildings afresh, stacked and sprawling across the uneven rock as if they'd grown out of it, she was reminded of the castello's relationship with events of the past: the ancient Greek fort on the west pinnacle; the medieval fortified walls, narrow-windowed, stark and watchful; and the arched colonnades and domed cathedral built by the Angevin French. She turned her smiling face to her daughter's and was met with a frown. Beatrice did not like the castello. Its looming darkness seemed ominous to her.

Maria pointed to the high Greek fort. 'That's where your Aunt Costanza stood raining down arrows and directing cannon fire,' she said, hoping to impart a sense of the romance of the place to her daughter.

But Beatrice was cold and fretful. Maria gave her over to the maid, Sylvia, as she always did on such occasions.

As they walked along the causeway that connected Castello Aragonese to the main island, Sylvia beckoned to one of the guards. 'Run ahead, quickly now, and make sure the rooms are prepared, fires lit and food ready.'

Mules carried them up narrow spiralling lanes to the d'Avalos apartments near the top of the castle. As they journeyed upwards they passed occasional shops and dozens of little houses where much of Ischia's population of 1700 lived. Roughly clothed Ischians stood in their doorways, arms folded, curious about the procession. These days, their d'Avalos overlords did not often come to stay among them. The Ischians thought well of them nevertheless; they felt safe within the walls of the castle, protected from the attacks by Barbary pirates that had plagued them for centuries. A few of them waved. Maria lifted her veil and waved back. When they saw it was Donna Maria Dolce—sweet Lady Maria—they responded enthusiastically, cheerfully waving and crying out greetings. They remembered her, remembered her last visit with her young Carafa duke, laughing and running about and getting up to all sorts of tricks, providing them with more entertainment than they'd had since old Princess Costanza's day.

Halfway up, the procession passed a convent established by Maria's aunt, Beatrice. Her namesake, thin little body cushioned against Sylvia's copious one on the mule, let out a cry of revulsion: 'Mama, what's that horrible smell?'

'I don't know, darling, but the sea air will blow it away soon,' answered Maria, not daring to tell her what it was and praying she would never find out, although given Beatrice's curiosity and her habit of sneaking off by herself, that was unlikely. She must warn her not to go near its source. This, Maria now realised, was what had made her dread coming to Ischia. The smell was far worse than when she'd last been here, understandably so. Then one had got used to and almost forgotten it. Now it was a lingering stench that faded only when they'd climbed far higher.

Sylvia need not have troubled to send the man ahead. The Clarisse nuns, devoted to the d'Avalos women, had been told of Maria's arrival and had prepared the d'Avalos apartments very comfortably. Candles glowed; fires blazed in the great hearths; meat, bread, fruit and wine were laid out on tables in the various rooms; and clean beds awaited. At the sight of all this Beatrice's mood improved, although she was nearly asleep and, after eating an orange and a few mouthfuls of bread, she went off with Sylvia to her bed.

Maria was pleased to have been given Costanza's spacious, richly curtained and carpeted bedchamber. She had never slept in it before; on previous visits it had been occupied by her parents or one of her aunts.

Maria, too, ate little and after Laura undressed her was soon in the enormous Spanish bed surmounted by the d'Avalos coat of arms. For six days her party had travelled along the wild southern coastline of plunging cliffs and lurking brigands. They'd made overnight stays in the country houses of relatives and friends, and even, once, at an inn. She was exhausted. Waiting for sleep to come, she lay quietly, with the end bed curtain open, staring into the flames.

Had it really been less than a month since Alfonso had lain beside her? She had not absorbed the fact of his death, yet it already seemed distant. She moved into the middle of the bed and stretched out her limbs luxuriously. A forgotten feeling of peace descended upon her. It seemed not such a bad thing after all, her being marooned here for weeks or months. It would allow her to rest and recuperate, perhaps even regain something of her old zest for life.

After six years of claustrophobic marriage, her thoughts were at last free to roam as they pleased. 'What are you thinking?' Alfonso had asked her numerous times each day. Even in the dark he'd asked it, as he'd lain beside her and she'd thought him asleep. 'The garden,' she'd replied, or 'The sun on the sea,' or 'The taste of oysters', omitting the fact that it was not their garden her mind lingered on, not Messina's sea. The taste of oysters she forever associated with the occupant of her secret thoughts, Federigo, who'd sometimes sensuously, playfully slipped them from his mouth to hers in a long kiss. Federigo *was* the sun on the sea. That in any case was how she liked to imagine him, as having been absorbed into the ether after his death and being, somehow, everywhere. She knew it was childish, only a daydream; but the one remnant of true happiness she'd had since his death eight years ago was the memory of her three years with him, and the daydream made the memory more vivid.

Her grief had still been raw when she'd married Alfonso. The one thing she remembered from their first weeks of marriage—aside from the physical revulsion she'd eventually schooled herself to overcome—was his saying to her on their wedding night, 'Though you are already plucked, it was but a callow, irresponsible boy who plucked you, so I am willing to overlook it. Now you will know a real man.'

She'd had an urge to burst out laughing in his fleshy face, the arrogance of this aging man, and her urge to laugh had intensified as Alfonso had fumbled and sweated, as clumsy as Federigo had been artful, so that at last she'd been able hold it back no longer and it had broken out disguised as mounting cries of pleasure, her face contorted in the dark, tears streaming from her eyes. Alfonso, the fool, had been well pleased with himself. Never again. Never again would she have to perform these pantomimes of pleasure. The heady sense of liberation she allowed herself to experience at last brought with it such a feeling of guilt that she covered her face with her hands.

In the first months of their marriage she'd understood and forgiven Alfonso his possessiveness. Maria's fair colouring added an irresistible aura to her beauty. In a country dominated by dark-haired people, where artists painted saints or goddesses as fair or auburn-haired to convey their ethereal nature, Maria's tawny-blonde hair, green eyes and pale luminous skin endowed upon her a Madonna-like charisma. In Naples it had undeniably set her apart, but in Sicily males were riveted; even members of Alfonso's noble circle behaved foolishly in her presence. One night at a banquet in their palace, a drunken old prince had gone down on his knees in adoration before her. After helping him back on his unsteady feet, his embarrassed son had apologised to her profusely but then had not been able to resist taking her delicate hand in his and covering it with kisses. She'd withdrawn it with a smile that had been merely polite, though Alfonso had chosen to interpret it as invitingly seductive. There had been no more banquets at Palazzo Gioeni after that. Indeed there had been very few social gatherings at all in the splendid white palace, and Maria, accustomed to lively balls and concerts, had begun to find life dull and constricted.

In moving from Naples to Messina, it was as if she'd stepped from the heady pleasures of youth directly into a world of advanced middle-age. This was represented by Alfonso's interest—his only interest outside of her—in the restoration of ancient churches. He'd insisted she accompany him to meetings with church fathers on the selection of marble and the choice of architects and painters. This had at least given her some sense of participating in Messina's community life and she had admired Alfonso for expressing his faith in this useful way; the churches with their delicate tracery work were so old that their outlines were misted with the patina of the ages and she'd come to find them attractive. But then her pregnancies had begun. Alfonso had regarded her as a hothouse flower to be confined indoors at such times, so even her mildly interesting conversations with priests and architects had come to an end. Had any of the four children she'd borne Alfonso survived beyond infancy, her life with him might have been different. A son would have been a distraction, but as it was, the full force of Alfonso's passionate nature was vented upon Maria.

On that last day, she'd been in Palazzo Gioeni's extensive garden that sloped down to Messina's sickle-shaped bay, with her party of ladies and Sylvia in attendance. Alfonso had come across Maria asking one of the gardeners, who was neither young nor appealing, if he could border the rose beds with hedges of lavender as it filled the air with a delightful perfume. To the astonishment of the ladies and even Sylvia, he'd flown into a tumultuous rage. He'd grabbed Maria's arm, marched her inside and, ranting about the lawless sensuality of seductresses, had given her a resounding slap across the face that caused her to cry out in pain. Maria's look of perplexity as she drew her hand to her stinging cheek enraged him even more. Excrescences of rage like white pus had appeared in the corners of his eyes. At this nasty sight, Maria allowed the feelings she'd hidden from him for all those years to surface, and she bestowed upon him a look of such regal contempt that within moments he was frothing at the mouth. 'Sylvia, fetch the doctor, quickly,' she'd called, feigning concern, for she had truly wished him dead. The doctor arrived too late, and pronounced the cause of death as a fit of apoplexy, remarking privately to Maria that he'd often warned the marquis about his appetite for rich food. Only then had remorse set in.

Maria recalled Alfonso's choking red face, startled and emitting gurgling sounds in the moments before his death, and she squeezed her eyes shut and buried her face in the pillows. 'Federigo,' she murmured.

She could say it out loud now. And at the mere sound of that name, the image of Alfonso's convulsed face dissipated.

Maria opened her eyes. The tolling bells of the insubstantial nightmare she'd just awoken from went on tolling. Befogged by the dream's sense of dread, it was a minute or two before her mind grasped where she was and recognised the sound as the bells for early morning mass.

It was still dark outside. There'd been a squall during the night but now the wind had died down. She lay in her warm bed staring at the glowing coals and felt pity for the Clarisse nuns, already up and dressed and making their way to the chapel in the cold dawn.

She rose, pulled aside the curtain, opened the window and sniffed the air. The day promised to be fine, but that nauseating smell was still faintly detectable. It came from the nuns' cemetery. Maria shuddered. The sisters went there to pray every day. How they endured it was a mystery, for the vile stench had been suffocating ten years ago; what it must be like now was unimaginable.

She closed the window, climbed back into bed and drifted into sleep again, thinking that she must soon explain to Beatrice the origin of that reek or the poor child would discover it for herself.

An hour or so later she awoke to the touch of a little hand gently running its fingers through her long, reddish-blonde hair. Beatrice had inherited her father's light-brown colouring and she loved her mother's golden hair. Maria reached out, closed her own hand over her daughter's, and opened her eyes. They looked into each other's eyes, the mother and the daughter, smiling, silent. They sometimes did this. It brought Maria a sweet, sorrowful feeling of peace, for to hold his daughter's hand like this was to hold all that was left to her of Federigo, and to look into Beatrice's grey eyes, his steady eyes, offered a trace of those hours when fifteen-year-old Maria d'Avalos and nineteen-year-old Federigo Carafa had lain on their bed together, eyes locked in a kind of ecstasy, each entranced with the beauty of the other.

'I told her not to wake you, Donna Maria,' said Sylvia, bustling into the room.

'It's all right, Sylvia. Just fetch our chocolate.'

The authority Alfonso had entrusted to Sylvia had added a formidable air to her already stern appearance. Many trembled before her and it secretly pleased Maria that she could not always discipline Beatrice. The child would listen patiently, looking quietly at the woman with her father's steady gaze, and then calmly march off and do what she'd intended to do all along.

'I hate this place,' said Beatrice. 'It smells.'

'Yes it does, and I must tell you why.'

'You said you didn't know.'

'That was because I didn't wish to speak of it, but you're such a brave girl that I decided it was better that you know.'

'Why does it smell?' Beatrice had no patience with flattery and conventional niceties.

'Many sisters of God live at the castle. Your kind Aunt Beatrice, after whom you are named, built a convent here. Before that, the sisters lived in a monastery at the top of Mount Epomeo on the main part of the island.' Maria hesitated. Best not to tell Beatrice that Mount Epomeo was subject to earthquakes. 'Your aunt brought them here so they could be closer to the people of Ischia and help them.' Beatrice was becoming impatient with these details, so Maria drew in her breath and took the plunge. 'The smell is from their cemetery. It's different from other cemeteries because it's a part of the nun's faith to confront the realities of death and the mortality of the flesh.'

'Can I see it?'

'No, Beatrice. You can't go there. It's a sacred place, only for the nuns.' Maria sighed. That had been the wrong thing to say. It would make Beatrice even more curious. She grabbed the child by the shoulders. 'That smell has unhealthy miasmas. It will make you ill if you go there. Do you want to become ill? Do you want to become sick in your mind as well as your body? You must not go near that place. I want you to promise me.'

Beatrice was a perceptive child—she understood her mother's morbid fear of losing her. 'All right, Mama, I won't go. I only wanted to see what death looks like.'

'We've had enough of death, Beatrice, you and I, and you think too much about it. I want you to forget about death on earth and think only of how the soul flies up and lives on in Heaven. From now on we are going to think only about life. Soon we'll go to Naples and have a happy life there. Life and happiness. Do you understand, Beatrice?'

'Yes, Mama,' said Beatrice quietly and without conviction.

Winter settled in. Gloomy clouds amassed over the island, misting the sombre outlines of the ancient towers on the pinnacle. Rain pelted down for days at a time, creating streams that gushed down the narrow sloping alleys between the castle buildings. Maria and Beatrice were confined indoors, and even here it was as if the thick stone walls oozed damp.

One evening Maria instructed Sylvia to build a roaring fire in the large library, an octagonal-shaped room with circular windows and heavily carved Spanish furniture. Maps and rich tapestries lined its walls. Cabinets spilled with books, manuscripts and letters containing the history of the d'Avalos family's glory days.

Sylvia performed her task efficiently but grudgingly. The maid had been employed by Alfonso early in their marriage. Maid in name only, for in practice Sylvia had been Maria's watcher, shadowing her whenever she left the palace, and reporting her movements back to jealous Alfonso. Maria had grown so used to this swarthy, heavy young woman dogging her steps, she'd come to regard her almost as a protector. With Alfonso dead, Sylvia had fallen from grace and her role was now unclear. She was well aware that Maria kept her on only out of the goodness of her heart, knowing she had no family to turn to, but, accustomed to Palazzo Gioeni with its army of servants, Sylvia nevertheless resented performing the menial tasks necessary for Maria's comfort at the castello. Alfonso's jealous nature had infected even his servant, for Sylvia was resentful of Maria's personal maid, Laura Scala.

'You can go to your room now,' said Maria. 'I won't be needing anything more tonight.'

Sylvia hesitated. She'd grown used to being with Maria every minute of the waking day. 'You'll need me here to put more logs on the fire, my lady.'

'I can do that myself. Leave a pile of them stacked on the hearth.'

Sylvia's hands flew to the sides of her head. 'Whoever heard of a lady tending her own fire? You might set yourself alight.'

'I'm not so careless. Go and make another fire in my bedchamber. You can tend that until I come up. Tell Laura to stay with Beatrice until she is asleep and then to come here.'

Sylvia thudded logs from the firebox onto the hearth, saying, 'Don Alfonso said I must always take care of you, Donna Maria.'

'Don Alfonso is dead.'

Sylvia gasped at such sacrilege and crossed herself, looking heavenward with an expression of mournful piety. The woman had a natural gift for theatrics that sometimes made Maria want to laugh. 'He watches over us from above, Donna Maria.'

The idea of her possessive husband still watching her from beyond the grave made Maria's throat constrict, causing her to speak more sharply to Sylvia than she meant to. 'He'd be the only one watching over you if it weren't for my father the Prince of Montesarchio, who puts a roof over your head. Now go.'

'I am grateful to your father the prince,' muttered Sylvia unconvincingly as she trounced from the room.

Maria sank into a tapestry chair by the fire and stared into the flames. She felt a little guilty at speaking so sharply to Sylvia. She must tell the woman not to keep referring to Alfonso and Messina. She must explain to her that she wished to focus on the future, not the sorrows of the past. Sylvia knew very well that Maria's life in Messina had been a cycle of pregnancy, birth, death and sorrowful burials, Alfonso's jealous rages mounting in concert with his disappointment as each of their four infants succumbed to malaria, to cholera, to infant fever. He'd grieved over the boy, his heir; Maria grieved over all of them: Antonietta, Alfonsino, Marianna and Francesca, those perfect little babies, innocent and smiling at first, before their tiny faces grew hot and tormented, and their fragile bodies began writhing with the agonies of fever. Each year a new grief had been heaped on top of the old, until it had become her permanent state of being. She realised to her dismay that she had grown accustomed to grief. And yet she had become so used to hiding her secret thoughts that outwardly she seemed serene. Now this cycle was broken at last, though Messina would not begin to fade from her mind until her life began afresh in Naples. And that meant marriage to the young cousin she hadn't set eyes on for six years. She wondered what Carlo was like now. He'd been such a disquieting child. Full of gaiety one minute, performing with the musicians at his father's court or excitedly preparing for a hunting trip, then gloomy and silent the next, retreating into his own world, like a flickering flame in a fitful wind.

Maria rose from her chair and began pacing about the room, agitated. She threw a log on the fire and sparks flashed, Sylvia's warning along with them, causing her to draw back in panic. She was loath to give Sylvia the satisfaction of even a scorch mark on her dress, for to control Sylvia was to have some control over her own life.

She searched the shelves for something to read. It would calm her mind. The library had been well stocked by Costanza. What a dreary place Ischia had become in comparison with what it must have been when Costanza presided over her lively court. Maria opened drawers crammed with poems and letters. So many signatures of names that had since become famous: Enea Irpino, Michelangelo Buonarotti and Ludovico Ariosto, whom Castello Aragonese had inspired to write his great epic poem *Orlando Furioso*. If only Maria could be in such company now. And they were all addressed either to Costanza or to Vittoria Colonna, who had lived with Costanza at Ischia and had become a famous poet herself before her death. Vittoria had been the adoring wife of Maria's great-uncle, Ferrante Francesco d'Avalos, commander of the imperial Italian army and victorious general of the historic Battle of Pavia in 1525; and after his death Vittoria had written her numerous sonnets to no one but him. Maria empathised with Vittoria in this, understanding the dolorous pleasures of a life spent in reminiscence of a beloved dead husband. Wasn't Maria's own chief pleasure to fly in her thoughts to Federigo?

Maria gathered together a pile of the most interesting-looking poems and returned to her chair by the fire, drawing up a little table and arranging them on it. Perhaps, she thought, remembering the pleasure writing had once given her, reading these lines by superior poets would inspire her to write some verses of her own during this temporary lull in her life.

She smiled at a pleasant thought, a vision of her writing poetry in the women's apartment of the Palazzo San Severo that was perhaps to be her new home, and Carlo Gesualdo off in some other part of the palace practising his lute or cembalo, each pursuing separate but complementary activities. Perhaps their marriage would be like this. It was possible: word had it that Carlo was still obsessed with music. But of course now that he was to become the Prince of Venosa, she'd be given no rest until she'd produced him an heir. She well knew that her reputation for fecundity, as they described it, was the chief reason she'd been chosen as his wife, that and the wish of her machinating male relatives to establish an alliance with the powerful Gesualdo family.

The thought of coupling with Carlo brought a sardonic little smile to her face, for she still regarded him as a strange child. Now that he was a man, would she find him attractive? It was impossible to know. She prayed that there would be no more need for pretence, as there had been with Alfonso. Only to desire Carlo a little would be sufficient, for she'd been expertly tutored by Federigo in how to give pleasure as well as take her own. She pictured the way Carlo bent over his lute, delicately plucking its strings with his inordinately long fingers, rapt as if making love to the instrument, and her smile lost its sardonic edge. With Carlo it would at least be sweet young flesh again, not decaying and faintly odorous as Alfonso's had been. She returned to the pile of carefully copied poems and lost herself in reading.

After a while there was a gentle knock at the door. Laura came in and joined her mistress by the fire, saying, 'I hope I haven't kept you waiting, my lady. Beatrice has been restless these past nights and though I read to her as she asks, she interrupts to talk of everything under the sun and it takes a long time for her to settle. Now, at last, she has fallen into a sound sleep.'

'I'm afraid Beatrice won't settle until we return to Naples. You have too many duties here, I know,' said Maria, noting that Laura was, unusually, looking rather untidy; long strands of curly hair had escaped her tight chignon. Maria was fond of Laura and had grown into the habit of chatting with her on the long, lonely evenings. The girl had been well educated in a convent so was able to converse intelligently about matters close to her mistress's heart; she had been with Maria for ten years and was the one person with whom she could spend hours reminiscing about Federigo. She had in fact been engaged for her by Federigo's mother, Maddelena Carafa, and this link with her first marriage and the Carafa family contributed to Maria's fondness for her. Unlike Sylvia, she had been properly trained as a lady's maid. A quiet, attractive girl with almond eyes and masses of curly brown hair, she came from a good but impoverished family. Federigo had told Maria that this was due to the family's estates having been seized by the Carafa pope, Paul IV, and that Maddelena had brought her into their household out of a sense of guilt.

'The days are long here,' said Maria, 'but you must do as I do and tell yourself every morning and every night that we will soon be back in Naples.'

'I do, my lady, and I also pray that your third marriage will be as happy as your first.'

Maria looked at her in surprise, a little taken aback by such a blunt remark. 'That's kind of you, but I confess I have little idea of what life with Carlo will be like.'

She leafed though the pile of poems and found a cycle written by Enea Irpino from Parma, saying, 'Let us entertain ourselves, Laura. Just now I was reading a poem written to my Aunt Costanza, whom I've told you about. Do you remember?' Laura nodded. 'I should tell you that my family, to commemorate her victory over the French, commissioned a portrait of her by the famous painter, Leonardo da Vinci. One of her many admirers wrote this description of the painting. Shall I read it to you?'

'That would be most enjoyable,' said Laura sincerely, knowing that Maria loved to read poetry aloud, and liking the sound of her clear, rather high-pitched voice with its melodic rhythms.

'This is my lady alive,' began Maria, smiling and repeating the first line as if it especially pleased her.

This is my lady alive
this is the lovely mouth, whose words
so sweet and gentle are formed by Love.
These are the eyes, brimming with noble zeal;
this is the lovely neck and breast, where is figured
by Heaven its own immeasurable beauty.
That good and famous painter, who depicts
so much beauty under the modest veil,
overcomes art and vanquishes himself.'

'I should like very much to see that painting, my lady. Is it here?'

'No, I don't know what's happened to it. I remember seeing it at home as a child, but then it disappeared. I should like to see it again myself. Being here among Costanza's things has made me curious about her.'

'It would seem your Aunt Costanza was very beautiful,' said Laura.

'You would think so from the poem, but she was not. It was the painting itself that was beautiful. I can't recall its details but I do remember that the face had a wonderfully gentle, mysterious smile. But Costanza herself was typically Neapolitan looking, dark and rather swarthy.' Maria stared into the fire. 'Yet how much more rewarding and interesting her life was compared to mine.'

'You are but twenty-five, my lady, so we can't yet know what life has in store for you. In Naples men will not see only your beauty and behave as if they are dazzled by it rather than your good nature and virtue, so it will not be the burden it was in Messina. Perhaps it will attract the good fortune it deserves once again.' It was only after they'd gone to Messina that Maria had begun confiding in Laura, and the girl had witnessed how Alfonso's initial adoration had festered into the frenzied jealousy that had made their lives a misery. What Laura liked about her mistress's face was its angelic sweetness, something that was normally associated with mere prettiness rather than Maria's fine aristocratic features.

'To be loved as Federigo loved me is all I hope for, Laura, although I know that's like asking for the moon and the stars.'

'Perhaps not. Your cousin Prince Carlo is much younger that you, is he not?'

'Yes, he's barely nineteen.'

'In that case he will not play the stern husband-father as the marquis did. Such a young man is likely to be in your thrall.'

'You know, Laura, that is exactly what Costanza did, held men in her thrall. Yet it had little to do with beauty. I've been sitting here thinking tonight'—she did not add that Laura could not imagine the pleasure this gave her after having had her every thought sternly supervised. 'On reading through these poems I've come to see that the men in Costanza's life, and she had numerous lovers, remained worshipful of her because of the power she wielded over them.'

'What kind of power, my lady?'

'A king's gift of an island, a fiefdom. I've been asking myself why my life is so different from my great-aunt's.' Maria had in fact reflected on these questions as if they might hold a key to some future, dimly imagined liberty. 'Costanza made Ischia the creative hub of a brilliant court, while for me, as you can see, it's a cage, although some may consider it a golden cage. Costanza was subject to the will of no man, while I must do my family's bidding. Costanza was also widowed young, but the d'Avalos family's schemes to arrange an advantageous second marriage for her were futile. Costanza had no need of marriage because she was independently wealthy. She governed Ischia and that allowed her to command her place in the world. That is what I mean by power, Laura, a rare opportunity indeed for a woman.'

'It is, my lady, but it seems to me a frightening one. Is it not an unnatural thing for a woman to lead an army?'

'Do you mean because of the responsibility it would entail?' asked Maria. Laura looked bewildered so she didn't wait for an answer. 'It seems so. But perhaps it is not if that woman were trained in warfare, as Costanza was.'

'Such a strange thing is beyond my imagining.' Laura shook her head in perplexity. After a moment she said, 'May I ask you something, my lady?'

'Yes, Laura.'

'Do you think you would have had the courage to do battle with the French navy?'

'If I'd been trained in the arts of warfare, you mean?'

'Well, yes, I suppose you would have to be,' replied Laura uncertainly, having no idea what would be required for such an impossible task.

Maria imagined herself high on the battlements, skirts and hair flying, and the thought filled her with excitement and fear. Which was probably what Costanza herself had felt. 'Perhaps I might, Laura. Federigo used to say I was like an innocent child when I first married him. He delighted in teaching me the ways of the world and as I loved my tutor so well I was a willing pupil. From Alfonso, I learned only things I would rather not have known, but it is those very things that have transformed me from a girl into a woman. I've begun to understand that only since his death. On that last day, before he died, I resolved never again to allow my spirit to be crushed as he crushed it.'

'I doubt your young cousin Carlo will be so inclined, my lady.'

Maria sighed. 'I'm not so sure.' She laughed softly and added, 'Perhaps Cousin Carlo will prove to be the French fleet that fate has in store for me.'

Two

THE NUNS' CEMETERY

During the third week the clouds scuttled away, opening up the sky to a bright clear blue. Beatrice was like a little cat in the way she liked to perform an overall inspection of any new territory she found herself in and Maria spent the first welcome sunny day meandering through the castello's self-contained world with her. They explored its thirteen churches, its winery and terraced vineyards and vegetable gardens. Stretching across the summit behind the ancient Greek fort was an ornamental park. In the late afternoon, weary from walking, they rested there. Beatrice disappeared into a jungle of exotic green succulents. Maria sat at the far edge of the park on a marble bench under shading palms, breathing in the perfume of citrus trees and lavender. She looked across the chiffon sea at Naples far, far in the distance. She fancied she could see Palazzo d'Avalos on the riviera at Chiaia, its vastness reduced to a pink speck.

Beatrice's serious little face emerged between thick trunks in the middle of the park and she ran to her mother.

'There's a secret garden in there,' she said without excitement. 'It's not very nice.'

'Why? What's there?'

'Just big old strange trees and things. There's a fountain with awful gargoyles. It doesn't work. Everything's dark and furry green.'

'It sounds rather frightening,' said Maria.

Beatrice silently looked out to sea. 'It is,' she finally admitted.

'Shall we explore it together?' Maria asked, knowing that this was what Beatrice wanted and taking her hand as she rose.

'I'd like you to see it,' replied Beatrice.

It was a minute or two before Maria could find space enough to squeeze through the thick trunks in her wide skirts. Followed closely by Beatrice, she picked her way through the foliage and deep shadows until she came to a clearing with a marble fountain and benches. The marble had turned green with lichen. The watery green succulents had grown so tall they created a giant umbrella of weird forms.

'All this must have been planted long ago,' said Maria, looking around her.

'Do you think Aunt Costanza planted it?'

'Perhaps, but it seems so old I'm inclined to think the Angevin French might have created it when they had control of Ischia.'

'Do you like it here?' asked Beatrice, sitting on one of the marble benches with her back to the fountain and peering into the gloom.

'Yes, I do,' answered Maria, joining her. She looked up at the eerie overhanging tentacles and prickly fruits, withered on their branches now that summer had passed. 'Your father had a Spanish friend who'd been to South America. This place reminds me of his description of the jungles there. Dark and secret but bursting with life.'

'Poppa Alfonso told me about jungles, but I think that was Africa. He said they're full of chattering monkeys and screeching birds and roaring beasts and the noise is deafening. This place is too silent. I don't like it. It's interesting to look at for a few minutes because it's very different to any garden I have ever seen, but I don't want to stay here. I feel as if there's something lurking behind those trees, watching us. Let's go, Mama.'

'There's nothing there, Beatrice, and it's not like you to be afraid,' said Maria, rising.

'Look!' exclaimed Beatrice, running into the gloom.

Maria followed her daughter. She found her standing beside an enormous red cactus flower, long and pendulous with thorny spikes.

'Beatrice, you clever, sharp-eyed girl, what have you found? What an extraordinary flower.' Maria placed her hand under the flower to lift it and take a closer look, murmuring, 'It's hard to say whether it's ugly or beautiful.' Suddenly she withdrew her hand with a cry and examined her finger. Blood oozed from it and dripped onto her dress.

'Oh, Mama, it's attacked you!' cried Beatrice, throwing her arms around Maria's waist.

'It's all right, darling. It's just a prick. Flowers don't attack people.' She sucked her finger, not telling Beatrice that the spike had penetrated deeply and her finger was beginning to throb. 'Sylvia will give me something to put on it.'

'I told you this place wasn't very nice,' sad Beatrice. 'Let's go now.'

In the following days, Maria came to sit in this exotic jungle while the nuns gave Beatrice her lessons. She wended her way up the steep lanes followed by a straggle of four or five of the castle cats, each with one gold eye and one blue. She loved the experience of sitting in the green filtered shadows, feeling solitary, suspended in time, as she watched the cats sniff around. She brought Laura there once or twice, but found that conversation broke the spell of being there, of being hidden in some unknown place unmarked on any map.

Laura had accompanied Beatrice to the convent schoolroom and left her there. Beatrice sat waiting for Sister Speranza. Today was Latin. She hated Latin, all that tedious rote learning. The forbidden region of the castello beckoned; an hour or so to herself without nuns and servants poking and prodding at her thoughts.

She slipped from the room, nobody in sight, and crept down the stairs and out into the sunlight. A twisting narrow lane she hadn't yet explored led off to one side, and she turned into it, heading downhill. All she had to do was follow the smell.

What did death look like? Human death. She'd soon know. Mama had kissed her little brother and sisters in their coffins, but she hadn't been allowed to see them. The only death she'd witnessed was that of a bird, Arlecchino, the raucous macaw Poppa Alfonso had given her for her name day when she was five. He'd insisted the parrot be kept in its cage. Arlecchino had brightened her days at Messina. She'd spent hours each day teaching him to talk and he was very smart. 'BEET-RICE OPEN THE CAGE,' he'd screech, bobbing up and down manically on his perch whenever he heard Poppa Alfonso's carriage departing, knowing this meant that Beatrice would release him. 'Poppa's getting fat,' he'd confide as he sat on her shoulder. Just before her ninth birthday, he'd waddled over to her as she sat reading a book and made a listless attempt to fly onto her shoulder. She'd picked him up and tickled the side of his head. He liked that. 'Keep it up,' he'd squawk. But on that day he'd looked up at her, given a little sigh, and gone still. She'd put him on the bed and lain beside him for the rest of the day, stroking his bright feathers and feeling his body grow cold and stiff. She'd felt very sad. He looked the same but he just wasn't there any more. She hadn't seen his soul leave his body but she knew he'd flown off somewhere else. Darling Arlecchino. She missed him terribly.

The lane ended at a narrow flight of steps. Descending them, Beatrice drew out a kerchief and held it to her nose. She found herself on a high wide terrace that offered a panoramic view of part of the main island: a beach with pale yellow sand, woodlands rising up behind it and Mount Epomeo beyond, running through the centre of the island like a green spine. The sunny beach was tempting. No, she'd see out her plan and go to the beach another day, as a reward perhaps.

To her left was an unadorned stone building with a narrow entrance. She walked to it, hesitated for just a moment, and then entered the darkness. Immediately she reeled back out. The sickly stench was overwhelming. Waving the kerchief in front of her face to dispel the reek she resolved that she was going to have to be very brave. She'd no idea what she expected to see, dead nuns in their habits in open coffins lined up in rows perhaps. But in that brief moment she'd spied a tiny vestibule that contained only a wooden crucifix and steps spiralling down into blackness. Would she be able to see down there? Anticipating that the smell was going to get much worse, she took gulps of air as she chanted to herself, 'I will not turn back. I will keep going down. I am Beatrice Carafa and I fear nothing.'

She plunged through the entrance and began a careful descent down the steep winding steps, hand against the cold stone wall to steady herself. She stopped halfway down, nauseated by the fetid stench, clutching the kerchief to her mouth and nose. Six steps on she glimpsed a faint light beyond. She had been secretly hoping that it would be dark so that she'd have to turn back. 'I will not turn back. I will keep going down.' She travelled five more steps and found herself in a claustrophobic chamber, dimly illumined by candlelight. She hesitated there, noting two candles in sconces and two crucifixes, placed on either side of the entrance to another chamber. In the silence, the sound of a single drip resonated eerily.

Gagging on the excremental air, Beatrice briefly took in what she could of the room beyond. The entrance framed a candle burning in there. Its flame was perfectly still. There was something about the unnatural stillness of that flame and the sickly grey quality of the light that hinted at the nature of what was in the chamber. Another echoing drip, louder this time.

Beatrice passed through the entrance. At the scene before her, she entered into a trancelike state of terror. She took it all in, desperate to flee yet somehow unable to, unaware that urine was trickling down the insides of her trembling legs. In the gloom, rotting corpses of nuns in various stages of decomposition were seated on ghastly stone thrones. The hideous things seemed to move, so maggot-ridden were the tatters of slime-grey flesh putrefying on their skeletons. Bits of disintegrated black fabric were all but absorbed into their foul flesh. Under the box-shaped wimples that they still wore, their half-rotted faces were like terrible screams. One of them had only one glutinous eyeball remaining. The drip sound again. Beyond terror now, in some transcendent but still cognitive state, Beatrice noted that urns had been placed under the hollow-seated thrones. The sound was the bodily fluids from the corpses dripping into the urns. At this latest horror, Beatrice became aware that she was choking. She managed to stagger back though the entrance way and across the adjoining chamber before she collapsed at the foot of the stone steps.

Maria stood at the bedroom window holding an alabaster statuette, examining it in the light. She'd discovered it in a niche hidden behind a curtain. Waiting for Laura to come in and dress her, she turned it around and around. It was very old, Hellenistic or ancient Roman perhaps, a pagan goddess of victory with outstretched wings. Its transparent draperies accentuated rather than concealed its breasts and mound of Venus. Maria's fingers traced the curves of its half-smiling lips, its sightless eyes, the tight waves of its coiled hair, its splendid wings. The niche she'd discovered it in was gilded with gold leaf and placed at eye level like an altar. She wondered if Costanza had secretly worshipped it as a personification of female power. She put the Victory on a ledge so that the sun illuminated it from behind, and stared at it, thinking it strange that divine wings always reminded her of her poor little babies. Last night she'd had a terrible nightmare in which they'd appeared. It had begun as an eerily lucid vision of Palazzo Gioeni, perched high on the amphitheatre formed by encircling Mount Pelortani. The palace glittered white in the bright sun, its golden interiors visible through its many open windows. Then the sun was eclipsed, and the interiors darkened. Wispy white ghosts of the dead appeared at the windows. All of them, her four babies, all dead, and then Alfonso, too. But there had been something else, something even more dreadful that had caused her to wake with sobbing screams. Closing her eyes, she struggled to remember what it had been, but the terrible details eluded her.

There was an urgent rapping on the door. Maria, startled, hurriedly grabbed the statuette and hid it under the bed.

'Come in.'

It was Laura, looking distinctly pale. 'It's Beatrice, my lady. We can't find her. Sister Speranza reported to me just now that she didn't show up for her lesson this morning. It's a mystery to me because I took her to the schoolroom myself. I took the liberty of reprimanding the sister for not letting us know sooner and I'm afraid she's very upset . . .'

'Call the guards,' exclaimed Maria, rushing from the room, her sense of dread no longer the stuff of nightmares.

'Sylvia has already done so,' said Laura, running behind her. 'They've gone off to search the castle. The sisters have joined the search. They've put out an alarm.'

Maria flew to Beatrice's room. It was empty. She stood there wringing her hands, heart thudding with fear, not knowing what to do. 'Sylvia,' she cried out.

'She's gone off with the guards, my lady,' said Laura.

'Haven't I told her to wait for my instructions before she acts?' shouted Maria, feeling the need of Sylvia's sturdy presence for once.

'I'm here, my lady,' said Laura, gently placing her hand on Maria's arm. 'Let us try to think where Beatrice would go.'

Yes, I must use my wits instead of standing here helplessly, thought Maria. Where would Beatrice go? She might be anywhere. She might have climbed up on a high wall and fallen into the sea. She might be sitting in the shade somewhere calmly reading a book, blithely unaware of the distress she was creating. One never knew with Beatrice. Maria pictured the layout of the castle, following her daughter's slight form in her mind as she surveyed its alleyways and chief attractions. Suddenly she cried out and rushed from the room, Laura behind her.

Running in the direction of the wine cellars, she spied a guard questioning the vintner's wife in the cellar doorway. 'Guard, follow me,' she cried as she sped past. A group of gardeners on their way home to take lunch with their families stopped and looked in consternation at this extraordinary vision of the beautiful one running in her dressing gown like a woman possessed, golden hair loose and wild.

'What's the matter with La Dolce?' they shouted to the vintner's wife.

'Her little Beatrice has gone missing,' the woman replied. 'Have you seen her this morning?'

They shook their heads. Within moments other Ischians joined them and they stood clustered around the cellar doorway.

'Our poor young lady had just lost another husband and now her daughter has disappeared.'

'The only child left to her.'

'An albatross has been wheeling about here. It's an ill omen.'

'Beauty like hers is always dogged by ill fortune.'

'The Devil's galloping behind her and he rides a fast horse,' proclaimed a sage, crossing himself. The rest of them followed suit.

Maria and Laura reached the nuns' cemetery. En route they had been joined by guards, nuns and curious Ischians, along with Sylvia muttering about the stench and how could the child endure it.

'Down there, quickly,' Maria said to the guard. 'The rest of you keep back.'

'No, in God's name!' exclaimed the mother superior stepping in front of him. 'This place for is the sisters only. I will—'

'Seize her!' commanded Maria. 'Go!' she shouted to the guard.

The astonished mother superior found herself restrained by two burly men-at-arms. Sylvia followed the guard down and Maria let her go. She couldn't go herself. Federigo, daredevil as always, had once led her down there. Those foul miasmas. Those unspeakable . . . *things*. Would Beatrice survive it? Would she be alive? To go down there alone! Maria should have ordered the nuns to bar the entrance. Knowing Beatrice's insatiable curiosity, why hadn't she thought to do this? Why? Why? The mother superior was glaring at Maria, outraged. The frail woman wouldn't have had the strength to carry Beatrice back up those stairs; she should have had the wit to realise this. Maria prayed that Beatrice was still alive. She began to cough from the foul stink.

'Fetch some water,' Laura ordered a guard. 'Not from here,' she added, wrinkling her nose in disgust. From the well higher up.' She put her arm around her mistress's trembling shoulders. Only Maria, Laura and a few sisters remained right outside the entrance. The guards and Ischians had backed away, holding their hands to their noses.

The guard emerged with Beatrice limp and ashen in his arms, Sylvia panting behind. Maria flew to her daughter, still not knowing whether she was alive or dead, breaking into sobs at the sight of the deep cut on her left temple and its long trickle of congealed blood. What had happened to her down there?

'She's breathing, she's alive,' said Sylvia.

Maria sobbed with relief.

'Move,' shouted Sylvia, pushing the guard. 'We must get her to bed straightaway.'

The murmuring crowd pushed forward to look. A few of the men slyly looked at Maria's snowy décolletage, her dressing-gown open, the shape of her nipples visible beneath the flimsy white nightgown.

'Make up your potions, Sylvia . . .' began Maria.

'I know,' replied Sylvia, running ahead.

Beatrice writhed in Maria's large bed, screaming that the flames in Hell had gone out. 'The dead sisters are in Hell,' she sobbed. 'They're meant to go to Heaven. They're screaming to get out. There's been a mistake.'

Maria tried to enfold the hysterical child in her arms as she made yet another attempt to get out of bed. 'I *must* go to the garden,' she cried, rubbing her nose frantically. 'It's that putrid smell. It's stuck in my nose. Only the sea wind will make it go away.'

'Sh. Sh. Sylvia will make it go away,' comforted Maria, wondering why the woman was taking so long.

'Sylvia can't do anything. I *have* to be in the wind.'

'Yes, yes she can.'

Maria, all too familiar with the symptoms of fever, placed fresh vinegar-soaked cloths on Beatrice's forehead, carefully avoiding the bandaged wound on her left temple. The doctor had been and gone. After speaking with the guard who had carried Beatrice out of the crypt, he'd told Maria that Beatrice had probably fainted and struck her temple on the sharp edge of the bottom step as she'd fallen. He'd bled the child as she stared at the ceiling and ranted that she mustn't close her eyes. Sylvia, who had absolute faith in her own inherited apothecarial skills, had fretted about Maria having allowed Beatrice to be bled, tactlessly pointing out that the child had gone from ashen to deathly pale afterwards and making Maria frantic about whether she had done the right thing.

Sylvia and a nun entered carrying steaming bowls of a sweet-smelling preparation made from herbs Sylvia had brought from Messina. The women placed them on either side of the bed. Sylvia went to place a cloth over Beatrice's head, which set the child thrashing about wildly.

'The mixture will make the smell go away, Beatrice,' reasoned Maria. 'You must inhale it.' But Beatrice was beyond reason. 'We will try later,' whispered Maria. 'She'll be inhaling some of the steam in any case.'

Sylvia nodded, then produced a phial from her pocket and poured some of it into a spoon. She swiftly tilted back Beatrice's chin and inserted the spoon into her mouth, causing the child to gulp it down before she knew what was happening.

'It's the drips, the black drips!' screamed Beatrice.

'No, my little princess,' cooed Sylvia. 'It's drops from Heaven. Our Lord has sent them down to you. You'll soon feel much better. Here, smell the spoon.'

Beatrice sent the spoon flying and turned her head away, raving that Hell didn't burn, it dripped.

'It will make her sleep,' Sylvia said quietly to Maria. Then she dropped into a chair, white-faced herself. She had gone into the crypt's inner chamber briefly, not out of curiosity but to acquaint herself with what Beatrice had experienced, and what she had seen there as she'd gagged on the foul air had raised the hairs on her sturdy back. No mortal should ever look on such an abominable sight. Oh that poor, poor child. She would never recover. The foul miasmas down there were enough to kill her; only the Lord Himself knew what evil contagion they carried.

Later that night, Sylvia decided, she would take some of her herbal opiate herself. For without it, she was sure she would never sleep soundly again.

The essence of springtime perfumed Maria's room. Sylvia and Laura sat silently in chairs by the cold hearth. Sylvia had put out the fire in order to keep Beatrice's temperature down, and as midnight approached the room grew icy cold. Beatrice had fallen into a deathly sleep. Her mother sat vigil over her, not daring even to change the cloths on her forehead lest she waken her. Suddenly she rose from her chair with a strangled cry. Laura and Sylvia ran to her. She waved them away and sank back into the chair, shaking. She'd remembered the rest of the nightmare. Palazzo Gioeni's windows with the wispy forms of the dead looking out from them, her four infants and Alfonso. There had been another window from which yet another insubstantial form had gazed. It had been Beatrice. Beatrice, too, had been dead.

Maria sank to her knees and prayed to the statue of the Virgin that Sylvia had placed by the bed. Ears strained to the sound of Beatrice's faint breathing, she concentrated all her will into her plea that her only remaining child not be taken from her. She eventually fell asleep there. Laura, loath to move her in case she disturbed Beatrice, placed a rug over her mistress and a cushion under her head and sat back down by the empty fireplace to wait out the night.

The next day Beatrice's fever worsened. Her frail body wracked by extremes of heat and cold, she threw off the covers one minute, dripping sweat, and the next huddled under them, teeth chattering. She ranted of drips, screaming faces, and a flameless Hell. When finally she emerged from her delirium, she refused to take food; the sight of it revolted her. 'It's rotting,' she'd scream whenever Sylvia brought soup or fruit near her. On the third day Sylvia began spooning watery broth down her throat, but the anguish this caused Beatrice led Maria to tell the servant to desist. And so Beatrice grew weaker and weaker.

The nuns prayed for her. Ischians fashioned talismans reminiscent of the Nativity figures they made for Easter and left them outside the entrance to the d'Avalos apartments. Over the days these piled up. One of them moved Maria to tears; she brought it into the room and placed it near Beatrice. It was a finely moulded pair of figures, Maria with brightly painted green eyes and pale orange strands of silk for hair smilingly holding the hand of a rosy-cheeked Beatrice whose dress bore the sacred emblem of a dove.

Beatrice stared at it blankly. Nothing could arouse her from her nightmare. The life was draining out of her.

Maria sat watching the sky lighten into a pale dawn as she listened to Beatrice's shallow breathing. Sylvia and Laura snored in their chairs. The previous day she'd ordered the blacksmith to make a thick door with a lock for the nuns' cemetery. She'd sent Laura to inform the mother superior that when fitted the door was to be kept locked. This didn't entirely satisfy Maria; she'd come to agree with what Federigo had once said, that the place should be burned to cinders. He'd once wanted to set it alight himself, but she'd forbidden him. Now his daughter was paying the price for her mother's fear of giving offence.

She'd been so shocked that Federigo, the nephew of a deceased pope, would suggest such a sacrilegious thing. Federigo had repeatedly shocked her in the first months of their marriage. She'd been so ridiculously naive that she'd thought the Clarisse nuns had chosen their way of life. She recalled Federigo's amazement, their conversation as they'd sat whispering in the castello's cathedral near the marble altar she'd sentimentally wished him to see, the altar where Ferrante Francesco d'Avalos had married Vittoria Colonna.

'Those women are aristocrats. Why would they choose such a cloistered, narrow life?' Federigo had asked.

'Out of virtue, to do God's work,' Maria had replied.

'My innocent darling, parroting your mother's pieties does not become your sensual nature. They do not choose it, I assure you. Shall I tell you how my cousin came to be here?' he asked, referring to Sister Aurelia, whom they'd just been speaking with.

Maria nodded, a little in awe of Federigo when he became serious like this and his grey eyes looked solemnly into hers.

'Aurelia is the firstborn in my uncle's family. Her real name, by the way, is Ginevra—she's had to give up her name as well as her life. My uncle's duchy and the rest of the inheritance is legally and rightfully hers. Except of course that my uncle wishes his estates to go to his eldest son, which, like everybody else, he considers only right and proper. So Aurelia has been shuttled off, out of the way. In becoming a nun she automatically relinquishes her inheritance to her brother.' He sighed. 'She was once a spirited, pretty girl and now her face is obscured by that ludicrous box-shaped wimple. They all look like deformed crows.'

'Federigo!'

'I feel for her, brought up in comfort and used to lying abed till noon like all of us, and now having to rise before dawn to say her damned prayers.'

'Federigo!'

'Ooh, I'm wicked, wicked, wicked,' he squealed, giving her neck gentle little bites.

'What if she'd refused?' asked Maria.

'Refused!' he boomed. 'Young ladies do not say no to their poppas. Let us say she would have been sternly encouraged to comply. I will spare you the stories of beatings and mishaps, one or two of them fatal, that have come to my ears in the course of my not practising at law.' Federigo had studied law, but did not practise it, saying that there were too many young men of his class doing so already. 'It's the case with all the Clarisse sisters. Ask them. They'll tell you they're the eldest children of noble families destined to eke out their lives as brides of Christ . . .'

'Federigo!'

'Come my darling, follow me,' he said, rising and taking her hand. 'I've something to show you.'

They'd been so young and insouciant, so in love, that they'd actually giggled as they ran toward the nuns' cemetery holding their noses at the nauseating stench. But their gaiety had soon evaporated. After only the briefest of glimpses, Maria had fled the crypt screaming in terror. Federigo had emerged a minute or two later and vomited spectacularly.

Afterwards they'd comforted each other, dwelling on their mortality for the first time, expressing the hope that they'd live long and die together. Then Federigo had become angry, muttering, 'Dignity is denied them even in death,' and it was then he'd resolved to set fire to the cemetery. And she'd tearfully begged him not to. 'Ischia belongs to my family. There'll be repercussions. You can't do this to me, Federigo.' And he'd reluctantly complied.

If only she'd let him set the wretched place alight.

On their return to Naples he'd written to Ferrante d'Avalos in Milan, requesting permission to destroy 'that loathsome pit, the disgraceful presence of which pollutes an enchanted place'. Ferrante's reply had been curt; he had intimated that it was no business of the Carafas, and besides it would require the permission of Pope Pius. Federigo had then written a formal request to the pope. The Vatican replied that His Eminence did not interfere in the affairs of the Clarisse nuns, nor indeed in the affairs of any of the orders of the sisters of God, which had set Federigo guffawing with scorn.

Maria stood up to look at Beatrice more closely. Her slippered foot brushed against something. Lifting the bedcovers, she spied the tip of an alabaster wing. The Victory had lain there forgotten for days. She retrieved it from under the bed and briefly examined it once again. Moving the statue of the Virgin, she put the Victory on the bedside table. She placed a lighted candle behind it and it sprang to life, glowing transparently with pale gold light.

Sylvia woke with a snort and Maria gestured to her to be quiet. 'Go to the kitchen and bring me a cup of your soup. Don't heat it. Quickly,' she whispered.

She opened the cabinet where Costanza had kept precious objects and drew out a golden goblet. She wiped it out with a cloth. When Sylvia returned with the soup Maria poured it into the goblet and placed it behind the Victory. Sylvia glared at the pagan statue with disapproval, noting that the Virgin had been relegated to the background. Maria gave her a stern look and waved her back into her chair. Then she sat by the bed and waited for Beatrice to awaken.

Half an hour later her daughter stirred and the eyes in her ashen little face opened. Maria gently took her hand.

'You have a very special visitor,' she whispered, and pointed. 'Look.'

Beatrice's eyes listlessly followed her mother's finger. The Victory's wonderful outspread wings seemed gently to beat to the rhythm of the flickering flame.

'Who is it?' asked Beatrice wanly.

A question at last, a flicker of interest in the world beyond the nightmare. Maria all but wept with relief.

'The angel of life,' she replied, barely knowing what she was saying. 'She's lifting your spirit out of Hell. See how her wings are beating. She's bringing you back up into the light.'

Beatrice appeared to consider this. 'What's that?' she asked, looking at the chalice gleaming in the candlelight.

'It's something she's brought you. She wants you to drink it so that you'll be better again.'

'Is it food?'

'No, darling.'

'Is it from Heaven?'

'Yes.'

'Does my father drink it?'

'Yes.'

'In Heaven?'

'Yes.'

A faint glimmer of interest shone in Beatrice's eyes. 'I'd like the angel to give it to me,' she whispered hoarsely.

'She doesn't perform earthly tasks. She only acts invisibly. She will allow me to give it to you.'

'What does it taste like?'

'Springtime. Would you like to try some?'

Dreading a refusal Maria put her arm around Beatrice's thin shoulders, lifted her and held the goblet to her lips, praying that the consommé of fowl, vegetables and herbs would indeed taste like springtime. To her surprise, Beatrice gulped it all down. She then sank back onto the pillows, exhausted with the effort, her gaze fixed on the palely glowing Victory as she drifted back into sleep.

In the ensuing days the Victory remained by the bed, Maria diligently replacing the candle each time it burned down, so that its luminous presence greeted Beatrice whenever she awoke. She regularly accepted the soup in the golden goblet and began slowly to regain trength, although Maria was still worried about her psychic health.

For days a letter had sat on the table unopened. Beatrice's crisis now over, Maria turned her attention to it. She broke open the seal, hoping it contained good news. She did not think her nerves would stand it if it carried bad news.

January 4, 1586

My sweetest angel
Do you see now which is the condition of people in love? When you were in Messina, it seemed to me that you were far away; now that you are in Ischia it seems to me that you are even further away. Every short delay appears to be long. Delicacy and enjoyment increase with the perfection of the same love.

But if love has wings, why don't I fly and come to you, my sweetest niece, my lady? Because this same love clips wings and stops me, and my lady, you know the reasons for this. Then is Love duelling with Love? Yes, of course.

Which one of these two combatants will win? LOVE. And therefore long live Love and may Love triumph; from it I acknowledge victory and loss, pleasure and sorrow.

Please love me, my lady, love me, because all my wishes are aiming at this and because this is the end of my wishes and, please, feed this very troublesome fast with some of your orders, because I assure you, if I can render you a service, it will seem to me that you are here, present, and it will seem to me that I am enjoying your nearness, and I wish this to happen soon, not in a dream, but with the vision of you.

Goodbye my sweetest niece: I kiss and embrace you with all my soul, you who are one of the dearest things I have in this world.
Antonia di Lannoy,
Princess of Sulmona

Maria smiled fondly at her aunt's wit, playing a game with the Petrarchan conceits of love poetry to convey her guilt at not having visited Maria on dreary Ischia. The protestations of love were in a sense genuine. Pleasure-loving Antonia was childless, a wealthy prince's widow who had lavished her affections on Maria when she was growing up. She had always been Maria's dearest friend, the relative closest to her in spirit and temperament. There was evidently a delay of some sort in the marriage negotiations. Maria wished her aunt had been more specific.

'Mama.'

'Yes, Beatrice,' said Maria, moving to the bed.

'When are we leaving here?'

'When we hear from Grandpapa, which will be very soon. We can't go until you're better, though.'

'I'm better now.'

'Beatrice. Look into my eyes. It will calm you.' Maria had been told so often that her eyes were mesmerising, she had almost come to believe in their power.

'You're very brave, Beatrice,' she said softly, stroking the little face.

'I'm glad you think so, Mama,' said Beatrice. 'That's why I went down there, to test how brave I could be.' She thought for a minute or two. 'What do the nuns do with the horrible stuff in the urns?'

Maria, relieved that Beatrice's insatiable curiosity was beginning to dispel her nightmarish experience, replied, 'I've no idea.' Here was an opportunity to begin to make light of the whole thing. She moved her lips close to Beatrice's ear and whispered conspiratorially, 'They probably fertilise the garden with it.'

Beatrice looked at her in disbelief. 'Ew,' she shrieked with disgust.

'Ew,' echoed Maria, artfully feigning laughter, bent on gently encouraging Beatrice back to a normal frame of mind.

It was midafternoon and unusually warm. Maria was alone, sitting at the edge of the hidden garden. An albatross appeared out of the sky. It glided to the island, wheeled, and hovered above her, airborne in the still blue afternoon. Then it dropped gracefully onto the terrace and settled its wings, eyeing her. The splendid creature began to preen, spreading first one enormous wing, then the other, its head disappearing into warm downy underwings as it combed and nibbled at its feathers. Maria watched it, intrigued and a little disturbed. Such a companionable creature, yet it was said to be a harbinger of ill fortune.

'My lady, my lady, where are you?' shouted Laura.

'In here, Laura. Wait. I'll come out.'

'This just arrived, my lady. It was rowed over especially.' Laura, breathless from running, held out a letter.

Maria noted the d'Avalos seal and broke it open impatiently. It was from her father. Pope Pius had granted the dispensation for the Prince of Venosa's heir to marry the recently widowed Marchioness of Giulianova.

Three

THE PHLEGRAEAN FIELDS

Maria's carriage laboured up the hill in the drizzling rain, passed through the elaborate entrance gates and arched carriageway into the courtyard of Palazzo d'Avalos, and pulled up near the main portal. A few servants ran out with head coverings and greetings, telling Maria that the prince and princesses awaited her in the family salon.

Beatrice looked up at Mount Vomero, which descended in stepped terraces to the Bay of Naples and formed a dramatic rocky backdrop to the palace. The d'Avalos family had built their new home in Chiaia in the mid-sixteenth century to escape the dark, crowded centre of Naples and live surrounded by wondrous natural beauty. For much of the year airy Chiaia was all sunlight, filling the interior of the palace with light. But today the stairwell was gloomy as Maria made her way up the wide marble steps to the third floor. Beatrice skipped ahead, then waited for her mother on the second-floor landing. Maria stumbled on the top step and gripped the banister to steady herself.

'The way these stairs go around and around is making you giddy,' observed Beatrice. 'Oh, poor Mama, have you hurt yourself?'

Maria shook her head and leaned her back against the wall of the landing.

'Why are you crying then?' asked the child, slipping her hand into Maria's.

'It's been six years, darling. I'm a little nervous,' she whispered. 'It feels strange to be seeing our family again after so long. It saddens me to think they'll look older, and I wonder how I'll appear to them. Wait a moment. I don't want them to see me like this.' She dabbed at her eyes with a handkerchief. 'Promise me you'll be on your best behaviour, Beatrice. I want them to love you as much as I do.'

'They should love me in any case. They're my *grandparents.*'

'Beatrice!'

'Yes, yes. I promise,' said Beatrice, excitedly taking off up the stairs again.

Maria heard a door open above them and the stairwell echoed with the clear tones of a familiar mellifluous voice.

'Who is this angel? Where have you come from, my sweetness? Has Heaven sent you?'

'I'm Beatrice.'

'What a charming curtsey. Let me hug you. I'm your Aunt Antonia.'

Beatrice felt her face pressed to a velvet bodice that smelled of roses. She looked up and smiled into the shrewd eyes of her aunt's small heart-shaped face. 'And here's your darling mother. I've done nothing but pray you'd both arrive safely, and here you are. What joy! Go and greet you grandparents, Beatrice darling, while I hug your mother.' She held out her arms to Maria's ascending figure. 'Home at last, Maria. We must never allow ourselves to be parted for so long again. Never.'

Maria's father, Prince Gaetano, embraced them warmly and with a large gesture swept them into the salon. With characteristic reserve Maria's mother, Princess Sveva, remained seated. She pressed her daughter's two hands in hers for a moment before making the sign of the cross over her. Maria impulsively kissed her mother on both cheeks; the princess was taken aback: she had never shown Maria much affection and had consequently received little in return.

They all sat down and, smiling and exclaiming, examined each other's faces. It had been such a long time. Prince Gaetano was unusually misty-eyed and he began to fuss over Beatrice. He'd grown paunchy, but his leonine head with its wavy grey hair and fine, straight nose no doubt remained irresistible to the women who sought his advice on connoisseurship, the prettiest of whom, to his wife's chagrin, he felt obliged to take under his wing. Gaetano was Prince of Montesarchio, an extensive fiefdom north of Naples with a splendid medieval hilltop fortress, but he went there rarely, relying on stewards to oversee the cultivation of his lands. Life in the capital was more diverting.

Princess Sveva sat quietly, dour and buttoned-up as always—she gave this impression even though she wore a fashionably low-cut dress. Maria felt a rush of sympathy for her, realising that her mother's coldness was attributable to more than her own nature. Princess Sveva had always carried her head high, as if her husband's indiscretions were beneath her notice, but now lines of disappointment had formed around her mouth. Her proud face under the coiled crown of black plaits, with its high-bridged nose and heavy-lidded eyes, had formed itself into a permanent expression of disapproval. She made Beatrice turn around in front of her, looking her up and down. The quick-witted little girl, feeling mildly humiliated by such an inspection, spun round and round and turned it into a kind of dance.

'That will do,' said Princess Sveva. 'You are very like your father.'

'I know,' said Beatrice, allowing herself to be taken onto Prince Gaetano's lap.

'Maria, you are a miracle,' purred Antonia, who had been unusually quiet while doing some appraising of her own. 'To think that you are still so beautiful at twenty-five, when age has crept into the faces of other women your age like a crawling spider. And after all you've been through! Is she not the very phoenix of beauty, Gaetano?'

Her brother had been silently thinking the same thing, but had held back from saying so in front of Sveva. The gossip surrounding his amorous adventures over the years had taught him not to discuss beauty and women in the one breath in the presence of his wife. It resulted in her making even more frequent visits to the palace chapel and maintaining a lofty silence for days on end.

'Why, your complexion is as radiant as it was six years ago and your chin as proud,' continued Antonia. 'Only your eyes have changed, my darling, but this only makes you even more beautiful as now their green glitter has deepened from mermaid innocence to the emeralds of wisdom. Carlo Gesualdo will be thrilled to have you as his bride for he adores beauty. I've been conferring with him regarding some of the preparations for your wedding and he has the most exquisite taste of any man I've ever known.'

'What is Carlo like these days, in himself, I mean?' asked Maria, her anxiety about Carlo falling into relief now that the date of their wedding had been set for five weeks hence. She hoped to gain a sense of who and what he had grown into, this young man whose character and destiny were now inexorably tied to hers.

'As erratic as ever, though even more passionate about music. He's quite taken over his father's *camerata*,' replied Antonia, referring to Prince Francesco Gesualdo and the company of musicians he kept at his court.

'My nephew attends assiduously to his religious duties,' interrupted Princess Sveva, speaking over the top of Antonia. 'His greatest ambition is to be a good Catholic. He worships his uncle, Cardinal Borromeo, and was deeply affected by his death last year. Carlo tells me there is talk of his uncle being made a saint.'

'Indeed? I heard that Borromeo was very unpopular when he was Cardinal of Milan. He took on the Spanish military with his own army and even tried to excommunicate the Spanish governor. One year he *did* excommunicate everybody who took part in Milan's carnival festivities, so that the pope himself had to remind him of how great human frailty was. Still, if it's true he's going to be made a saint, then it will be another coup for the Gesualdos,' Antonia said tactlessly, for Sveva was a Gesualdo, the sister of Prince Francesco. 'Not only have they married into the family of the pope, but now a saint as well.' Antonia was referring to the crucial connection between the Catholic Church and personal advancement, and its direct impact on Sveva's family. When her brother had married Geronima Borromeo—the niece of Pope Pius IV—King Philip of Spain had granted him the principality of Venosa.

'I think it more likely to be a coup, as you put it, for Carlo's mother's family, the Borromeos,' said Princess Sveva icily.

'Either way, it is a wonderful enhancement to Carlo,' Antonia responded breezily. She delighted in repartee and never allowed herself to become rankled by its occasional stings. 'The young unmarried women of Naples, and their mothers, will be even more envious of you, Maria.'

'What do you think, Father? How does Carlo strike you?' asked Maria, disappointed with the women's answers. What she had learned so far she'd known or half known already. She'd hoped for something more personal, something she could muse upon and turn to her advantage. No man would ever again control her as Alfonso had. Perhaps her father, as a man, would be more forthcoming.

Prince Gaetano lifted his chin and ran his fingers over it, staring at Maria's shiny hair thoughtfully. 'I believe young Carlo might not have married if he hadn't suddenly found himself Francesco's heir. He lives too much in a world of his own devising to devote himself to a family.'

'Gaetano! It's not wise to speak of this to Maria,' interjected Princess Sveva.

Prince Gaetano ignored her and went on. 'Yet his enthusiasm for his forthcoming marriage to you, Maria, surprises me. He has engaged an excellent master of festivities, whom he has brought from Florence. It seems your wedding is to be a splendid affair. The Holy Father's dispensation for you marriage was difficult to obtain. He granted it only because he is Carlo's great-uncle. Geronima Gesualdo herself went to Rome to plead your cause in a private audience with her uncle, and Carlo went with her.'

'And she told me Carlo spoke beautifully,' said Princess Sveva. 'He can be most eloquent.'

'Yes, when he chooses to be,' said Prince Gaetano. 'When he chooses to speak at all, that is. Often he chooses not to. I have never known anyone so temperamental.'

Antonia nodded agreement. 'He can be appallingly rude. So rude at times, I secretly find it amusing. He simply cuts one off with a dark look. And now that he's become the heir, well, one might say he's made an art of his mannerisms. It's not through arrogance, though. It's due to his impatience with routine formalities and conversation that does not interest him. And he never flatters, not unless something genuinely moves or strikes him. Allow me to say this, Maria. Unpredictable as Carlo may be, his saving grace is sincerity. And you will manage him, my dear. Your beauty will beguile him and your sweet nature soften him. What's more important, your experience of two marriages has armed you well to please him in the bedroom, and there is no better place for a wife to rule her husband than from there.'

Princess Sveva closed her eyes in silent sufferance at this remark, and then reopened them to bestow upon Antonia a withering look.

'Remember this, Maria,' said her father. 'The Gesualdos want you above all others for Carlo's wife. Naturally, the moment we heard of your poor husband's death, your mother informed her brother of it. But it was Prince Francesco himself who suggested the marriage. And it's not only because you're a d'Avalos; you happen to be his favourite niece. He couldn't be more delighted at the prospect of having you in his household.'

'Who is that?' asked Beatrice, pointing to a splendid painting she'd been studying for some time that took up a great deal of the opposite wall. 'She looks like Mama.'

'That is two very special women all at once,' answered the prince. 'First of all, it's Venus, the goddess of love and beauty. Isn't she beautiful?' Prince Gaetano's love of art came second only to his love of women. He was a connoisseur of both. Like his father, who had been one of the most cultivated men of his time, Gaetano was an enthusiastic patron of painters.

Beatrice studied the sensuous blonde woman with the pearl-entwined plaits who held a glass sphere in her lap. She took in the beautiful heavy-lidded green eyes, the delicate straight nose and rosebud mouth. 'Yes,' Beatrice concluded. 'She's just like Mama.'

'Do you know why that is?' asked the prince.

'No.'

'It's because she's my mother, Maria d'Aragona. She looks like your mother because she's her grandmother. Your mother's royal Spanish blondeness comes from her, for she was the niece of King Ferdinand. And you, Beatrice, are her great-granddaughter.'

'Why is she Venus as well?'

'Because she was painted by a master called Titian, and that is how he sometimes painted very beautiful women. It's called an allegory.'

'Why does she look so sad?'

'Ah, that's a very complicated story,' laughed the prince. Princess Sveva frowned at him, but he went on. 'Do you see that brave commander over there?' He pointed to another Titian painting, a magnificent one of an heroic general against an apocalyptic sky, addressing his troops with arm rhetorically raised. Even in the salon's dull light, the general's armour in the painting gleamed, his billowing cape glowed blood red. 'That's my father, Alfonso d'Avalos.' The prince loved the roll of his father's titles on his tongue, so he proceeded to enumerate them: 'Governor of Milan, Commander-General of the Holy Roman Emperor's imperial forces, Marquis of Pescara, Marquis of Vasto, Prince of Francavilla, Prince of Montesarchio, Count of Monteodorisio.' He stopped—Beatrice was losing interest—and continued with the story. 'He was the greatest military leader of his time and a learned man as well, a poet and patron of the arts. As a result, many ladies fell in love with him, and this sometimes caused my mother unhappiness.' He was careful not to look at Princess Sveva as he said this, quickly adding, 'So, my little one, do you see what a brave and special family you belong to?'

'Yes. I already know about Great-Aunt Costanza. Mama told me. The Carafas are also a very brave and important family.'

'Indeed they are,' the prince acknowledged. 'I know this very well for your Carafa grandfather, Luigi, sits in the parliament of Naples with me. So, my child, you're doubly blessed with good blood. Your Carafa relatives are most happy at the prospect of seeing you after all this time, but we've agreed it's best to wait until your mother's wedding celebrations. Our duty is now to the Gesualdo family and we must honour them first.'

Maria strolled through the darkened rooms of the second floor, where she'd spent most of her time while growing up. During her childhood the gaiety of the balls and entertainments arranged by her father at Palazzo d'Avalos had been more than balanced by religious devotions. Princess Sveva, like her brother Francesco—Carlo's father—had always been devout and had thoroughly schooled Maria in the ways of virtuousness.

As a child she'd often been in two minds about how she should act, what she should feel. Prince Gaetano's paternal pride in Maria's startling beauty had led her to believe it so beguiled others that she could have whatever she pleased, certainly happiness. Sveva, on the other hand, had instilled in her that beauty was a gift from God and that she must fiercely guard it with her virtue. With her father Maria was the adored child encouraged to exhibit and utilise her charms; with her mother she was the dutiful daughter who hid those charms under a veil of modesty. Growing up, she'd wavered uncertainly between these two polarities.

When she was a child Prince Gaetano had seemed to her expansive, representing light-heartedness, amusement and joy, while her mother had been a constrictive figure, representing duty and virtue. Even now that he was middle-aged Gaetano seemed buoyant, while Sveva appeared even more weighed down by the ballast of the pieties and religious observances she lived by. How strange, she thought, that she felt so close to her father in spirit, yet for the past six years she'd lived what she thought of as her mother's kind of life, one that revolved around duty and virtue. (Her losses and grief were another matter all together.) Maria the creature of joy and pleasure, rendered shameful by Alfonso's jealousy, had become a hidden, secret self. She longed to share this hidden part of herself with another as she had shared it with Federigo, so that she would once again experience joy. This was what she hoped to find above all in her marriage to Carlo. Though he was difficult, it was possible; wasn't music, after all, an expression of life's joys?

Maria glanced into the old schoolroom. Like her brothers, she'd been instructed by an army of private tutors. She'd outshone the boys in Ancient Greek and Latin, but what she'd enjoyed most of all was translating the poetry of those languages into Italian. It had awakened her interest in writing her own poetry. She'd learned to play one or two instruments only with enough skill to accompany herself when she felt like singing one of her verses. What she'd really excelled at was drawing. The prince and princess, in agreement for once, had been delighted with their daughter's gifts. With her beauty and her illustrious name, she had always been expected to marry into the highest echelon of Neapolitan society, and the entertainments of such noble houses required their mistresses to be cultivated.

She wandered through the rooms of her older brothers, unoccupied now, their shutters closed. Regularly aired and cleaned, they remained as Ferdinando and Alfonso had left them. Ferdinando, Princess Sveva's adored Ferdinando, the only child she'd ever shown herself capable of expressing affection to, lived in Rome with their Uncle Inigo where for the past ten years he'd been learning, then practising, the ways of the world and the Church. Alfonso had married the heiress cousin of Alfonso Gioeni and still lived in Messina. Though they'd been close as children,

Maria had seen little of him there. Alfonso's passion for restoring churches had bored him and his behaviour toward Maria disgusted him, so he'd rarely visited them.

How many hundreds of times had Maria and Alfonso run gleefully along this wide marble hall, two or three times accidentally breaking precious objects sitting on the consoles, bent on playing some childish prank on their older, more serious brother, interrupting his studies, hiding his spectacles, testing his forbearance, a little jealous that their mother doted on him. Ferdinando, who took a scholarly interest in the teachings of the Church, had thrived on solitude. Alfonso, by contrast, was fun-loving and gregarious, and as he grew older, he often brought fellow students home. Princess Sveva had forbidden Maria to go to Alfonso's room when there were young men there, but this was blithely ignored whenever possible.

There was a day when Maria was thirteen that she skipped to Alfonso's room and found only one other young man there. He was sprawled in the chair Maria now sat in, arguing good-naturedly with her brother about some philosophical matter. When Maria entered he rose and smiled at her warmly, his eyes never leaving her face as Alfonso introduced her, but he did not take her hand and kiss it as other young men did. He was a striking, dashing young man, unusually handsome and seemingly at ease in the world, and at a time when most men wore their hair long, he wore his cropped close to his head, Roman style. His appearance immediately reminded Maria of the guileful, fearless young warriors in legends and poems.

'It's my pleasure to introduce—' began Alfonso.

'No!' exclaimed the young man, holding his hand aloft to silence Alfonso. 'I will make my own introduction. Be so kind, my good Alfonso, to pay a call on your brother for a few minutes.'

At such an impropriety Maria glanced nervously at her brother who, to her surprise, rose and left the room, saying, 'It's all right, Maria, don't be afraid.'

The young man, who had not taken his eyes from Maria's, moved closer to her so that they almost touched.

'Do you know who I am?' he asked gently.

Maria gazed up at him wide-eyed and shook her head.

'I am your betrothed,' he said.

Maria stood lost in his eyes, amazed, astonished, yet knowing it was true from the way he looked at her and the way he'd said it, even though her parents had not yet told her of her betrothal, and it was then that he took her hands, both of hers in both of his, and smiled into her eyes and with infinite tenderness leaned down and kissed her forehead and both of her eyes. The exquisite sensation that flashed like lightning through her body at the touch of his lips made her feel as if they'd stepped into an invisible carriage and were rushing together toward some miraculous destination.

'And what do men call you?' she finally whispered.

'Federigo Carafa,' he replied.

She sat at the window of her old room, looking down at the sweeping palm-lined curve of the Bay of Naples. She was struck by some of the similarities between her circumstances now and those of ten years ago when she'd married Federigo. Her marriage to Carlo would again take her to Piazza San Domenico Maggiore and the chaotic centre of Naples, just as her first marriage had. The Carafas and Gesualdos were among the elite of Naples' old baronial families, as hers was, and both were noted patrons of the arts, especially music. Why, many times during her first marriage she'd accompanied the Carafa family to concerts at nearby Palazzo San Severo where they'd watched Carlo perform with members of his father's *camerata*. Though only a boy of ten or twelve, he was already a virtuoso lutenist. That she would one day marry that sensitive, highly strung child, become the Princess of Venosa and live in that very palace, would then have been unimaginable to her. Both families had the highest Vatican connections. Pope Paul was Carlo's great-uncle, just as Pope Pius IV had been Federigo's. Yes, there were all these similarities, but oh, how differently she felt. Then she'd been a young girl deliriously happy at the prospect of marrying a dashing cavalier, a young man so sunny-natured and beautiful he was referred to as 'the angel from Heaven'. She recalled sitting at this very window all those years ago thinking she was soon to be made whole by a sacred union with her perfect complement. On that bright day the waters of the bay had sparkled in the sun. Today the prospect was bleak, the grey sea dully reflecting the overcast sky, drizzling rain misting the view.

That was just how she felt about Carlo Gesualdo. It was as if she could not really see him. Who was Carlo? Was he tender or cruel, craven or brave, cold or warm, happy or melancholy, sociable or reclusive, good or evil? It seemed to her that Carlo as an adolescent had been all of those things; well, not evil perhaps, but evil-tempered.

Maria winced as she recalled an episode from when she was about fourteen years old. Carlo would have been only eight. She'd gone with her mother and her two brothers on a visit to the Gesualdo estate in Venosa. Growing bored with her mother and uncle's family gossip, Maria had wandered outside and meandered along the paths of the cool garden. She'd come across Carlo and her brother Alfonso crouching over a rectangle of bricks. Carlo was busy propping up another brick on a piece of branch that crossed the small opening hemmed in by the bricks. As he stood up and threw something into the opening, he caught sight of Maria.

'Come and watch this,' he said, beckoning her to follow him into some nearby shrubbery. 'Come on, Alfonso.'

They followed him and squatted there, concealed.

'What are you doing?' Maria asked.

'Sh. You have to be very quiet,' he whispered. 'Just wait a little while and you'll see.'

It was pleasant in the shrubbery, shaded from the hot afternoon sun. Maria lay on her back, hands cupped behind her head, and closed her eyes, breathing in the citrus perfume of the ripe oranges and mandarins dangling from the surrounding trees. Alfonso rose and walked over to them.

'Stop moving,' commanded Carlo.

Good-natured Alfonso, amused at one so young giving him orders, turned and smiled briefly before he reached up and plucked three mandarins. He returned, throwing one to Carlo, placing another in Maria's lap and peeling the third for himself as he flopped down beside them. Maria closed her eyes again and dozed to the drone of the bees.

She had no idea how much time had passed before she heard a thud followed by the frenzied flutter of small wings. Carlo jumped up shouting excitedly and sped off. Alfonso ambled off behind him, not before warning Maria, who had bolted upright into a sitting position, 'Stay there.'

She stood, hesitating for just a moment, then fled after them.

Under the collapsed brick, Maria caught glimpses of the tiny trapped bird's silvery body, the bright blue tips of its agitated wings. 'You see,' Carlo was explaining to Alfonso. 'It hopped onto the branch to get at the wheat inside and its weight made the brick fall and close the gap.' He beamed, delighted with his childish feat of engineering.

A cold feeling of rage swept over Maria. She bent over to lift the brick and free the little bluebird but Carlo, quick as a flash, grabbed her wrist. 'It's all right. It's all right, I'll let it out,' he said, crouching. He carefully removed the brick and then cupped his two small hands around the bird and lifted it. 'You see, it's free now. Come and look at how pretty it is,' he said to Maria. The three of them stood looking down at the fragile handful, its tiny chest rising and falling in terror, its black eyes fixed on its captor.

'You can feel its heartbeat,' said Carlo, gently stroking its neck with his thumb. 'Here, feel.'

'Let it go,' hissed Maria, grabbing at his arm. 'Alfonso, make him let it go.'

'It's all right. It's all right,' shouted Carlo, leaping out of her reach. 'I'm going to let it go now. Watch.' With a movement so slight as to be imperceptible, the childish thumb pressed upwards on the tiny tube of throat. The beating little body went limp. Carlo opened his arms in a theatrical gesture of freedom and the pathetic corpse dropped to the ground.

'For the love of Christ, Carlo,' muttered Alfonso, crossing himself.

Maria stood stock-still, aghast, unable to believe what had happened before her very eyes. The cry that escaped her alarmed even Carlo. He watched, mesmerised, as she half turned and delivered him a mighty blow across the face. It sent him reeling. The way he'd looked at her then with his deep dark eyes she would never forget. The meaning of that look mystified her still, for it was a curious combination of shock, triumph and—here was the crux of it—excitement.

Yet within two or three years that same Carlo had made music like an angel. Maria hated cruelty, hated the way men tormented and killed innocent creatures, and such extremes of cruelty and sensitivity in the one person baffled her. She meditated on him, trying to extract some essence of Carlo. What was his chief attribute? His eyes, those dark intelligent eyes. Yes, that was it: intelligence. There was no one Maria knew who matched Carlo for quick, penetrating intelligence.

The date for the wedding was set for February 26, five weeks away. Much of the intervening time would be taken up with the design and fittings for Maria's dresses, as well as pleasing her mother by frequently accompanying her to the palace chapel.

Antonia was managing the d'Avalos preparations and had already devoted the weeks Maria had been on Ischia to them, conferring with Carlo Gesualdo and the master of festivities, researching the latest fashions and hairstyles in Florence and Rome, sending off for sumptuous fabrics and accoutrements, and overseeing the progress of the frescoes in the dining hall, which she'd insisted on having redecorated for the occasion. 'Too heavy and Spanish,' she'd decided about the sombre murals that had been there since the palace was built. 'We must introduce some lightness, a touch of frivolity even, for the guests must experience the wedding as a happy occasion.' The prince gave his sister free rein. Princess Sveva was not especially interested in such matters, though she approved on learning that the subject of the new frescoes was the marriage of the Virgin.

While Sveva d'Avalos was in the palace's chapel, lighting candles to the Virgin Mary and praying that this third marriage of her only daughter's would be a lasting one and that she would bear sons who would go on living, Antonia went on attending to the practicalities of the wedding. She'd chosen Parisian, Venetian and the best of Neapolitan fabrics and jewelled adornments for Maria's gowns. Now it was time to oversee the making of these gorgeous creations.

Maria and Laura had set up a large makeshift fitting room near the bedchamber to which they'd brought long tables and additional mirrors and lighting. On the overcast morning Antonia arrived at Palazzo d'Avalos, the dressmakers were already with Maria. The room, with its long mirrors, yellow blaze of candles and rolls of fabric, resembled a couturier's establishment.

Maria stood in a linen sample gown that was modelled on the latest Florentine fashions; it had been especially prepared for her. She moved close to one of the mirrors and examined the neckline. This aspect of the dress she was well pleased with. It was flatteringly low and square-necked, showing her white throat and the sensuous swell of her bosom to advantage. As Antonia entered, Maria was turning so as to catch reflections of herself at different angles in the long mirrors placed around her. In the last year, the overall shape of fashionable gowns had increased in mass and bulk, with puffed and padded sleeves and thick folds of skirt at the hips. This made tall women look majestic. Maria, however, was short, barely five feet.

Maria greeted Antonia, returned to her reflection in the mirror and gave a despairing little sigh. 'Let's be honest, Aunt, this may be the very latest thing in the courts of Florence and Venice, but the shape makes me appear squat. I look nearly as wide as my height.'

Antonia stood back, studying Maria from head to foot, and was forced to nod agreement. 'But what can we do, my darling? We can't have you making your appearance in a narrower skirt that suits you better. That line is so outdated now it will be immediately assumed that your years in Messina have made you unsophisticated.'

'Would you prefer I appear rotund?'

'Of course not, but think of the embarrassment to Carlo.'

'I was thinking of the embarrassment to myself. We must find a solution. There must be some way of altering the shape so that it flatters my form and yet at the same time retains its fashionable look.'

'The fabrics I've found you are so marvellous the guests will be dazzled by them and not notice the shape. You must make your selection so we can have them delivered tomorrow. Naturally you'll want the blues or greens that set off your colouring.'

'For some, yes, but for others I have something more daring in mind, particularly the betrothal gown. My concern is not the fabrics, but the shape. It must be rectified immediately.'

'We have no time to achieve the impossible . . .' began Antonia.

'Sh, Aunt, let me think.'

Maria called Rosa, the head dressmaker, to her, and together they studied her reflection in the mirror for several minutes, Maria murmuring every now and again. 'The neckline is superb,' she declared finally. 'We will leave it as it is, with variations from gown to gown which I will draw for you . . . We will retain the bulky sleeves . . . The stays built into the bodice must be even stiffer. My waist must be drawn right in and my bosom all but spill from the neckline. I trust you to ensure there will be no unhappy accidents in this department . . . The bodice will of course be highly ornamented. With pearls mostly, I imagine. Now Rosa, pay close attention, for here is where I want a change in the shape. This area here, from the bosom to the hemline, I want you to introduce a straight central panel running through here. This will give an illusion of lengthening, don't you agree? Pass me that drawing paper and crayon over there. Laura, bring me a table and put it right under the chandelier, over there. The hip folds must be flatter too, and more flowing. Why not go the whole way and make them gracefully Grecian? But though you are making these alterations to the shape, and I wish you to follow the lines I draw exactly, the gown must be ruched and ornamented is such a way that it retains the overall look of the new Florentine fashions. Do you understand, Rosa? Can you have this new sample made up within three days, by Thursday? Yes? Excellent.'

So in this way Maria took a hand in designing her dresses herself. The seamstresses silently cursed her, for the infinite amount of fine hidden stitching needed to achieve this illusion of lengthening, with the thick silks, velvets and embossed fabrics Antonia had had sent from Cordoba and Venice, would have tried the patience of a saint. But the effect was achieved, and Maria rewarded the women with gifts of chocolate and perfumes. This, then, was the basic shape of all her gowns. The women of Naples were later to copy it and it became a distinctly Neapolitan fashion.

The day of the next full moon was, mercifully, clear-skied and dry. Maria quit Palazzo d'Avalos after lunch. Knowing her mother would be horrified at her destination, she told her only that she planned to spend that day and part of the next with Antonia. She rode along the coast to her aunt's palace at Mergellina. With two armed men and two attendant ladies, one of whom was built like an Amazon, they then set off on a long carriage ride to the Phlegraean Fields.

This wide arc around the Bay of Pozzuoli was referred to as the 'flaming fields' because it was a landscape of volcanic upheaval: steamy, sulphurous and tumultuous, shifting constantly over the centuries, volcanic craters becoming lakes, and eruptions creating mountains and burying cities and palaces under the sea. The most recent eruption in 1538 had reduced the size of the area, but the Phlegraean Lakes remained a fashionable pleasure ground for Neapolitan aristocrats, particularly women, as its boiling, bubbling nature was associated with female fertility.

Maria had been coming to the lakes with Antonia since adolescence, and they'd made special trips before each of her marriages. Antonia considered it her duty to bring her favourite niece to these ancient Roman spa towns, with their crumbling temples of Diana and baths of Mercury. It was fashionable, yes, with overtones of forbidden pleasure. But they held a darker, deeper appeal. Campi Flaegri, as it was also called, was steeped in ancient myth. In spite of Naples' heavy Catholicism, folklore remained a powerful psychological force in southern Italy. The memory of old gods endured. Campi Fleagri's pagan associations and the prevalence of witches there caused Princess Sveva to regard the site with horror, which was why Maria didn't inform her mother of her visits there. Antonia, on the contrary, believed that the old goddesses who still lurked in the substrata of Catholicism possessed powers well beyond those of a holy virgin.

Maria stared out of the window as the carriage travelled through Pozzuoli and Torre del Greco, once sacred to the Ancient Greeks and Romans. She felt a deep affection for this ancient landscape, tamed centuries ago but grown wild again. As the carriage slowly meandered its way along the rutted tracks, she glimpsed marble ruins and palms on the sides of the gentle green hills that surrounded steaming lakes. It seemed to her that spirits inhabited the massive, gnarled trunks of the overhanging trees. She found the mystery of the place soothing, its strangeness poetic. They passed through Cumae, the home of the sibyl who showed Aeneas the entrance to the Underworld.

'You're looking pensive, Maria. What are you thinking about?' asked Antonia.

'Of the sibyl's grotto being associated with the Underworld, and the fact that it resembles an enormous vulva and vagina. I'm wondering if there's a connection between the two.'

'It's men. They associate our genitalia with the infernal regions,' retorted Antonia.

Maria laughed. 'Perhaps. But it seems to me more profound than that. I was thinking more along the lines of the cycle of nature: born of the womb and returning to the womb.'

'Your explanation is similar to mine. It's merely more poetic.'

At Baia, they drove beneath the palms and sweet-smelling myrtle of paradise itself, the low green hills of the Elysian Fields. Further on they encountered the river that souls less pure journeyed along, the Styx. They meandered along its banks to Lake Averno, a place of ominous beauty whose name meant 'without birds'. Long ago, this silent and vaporous lake had been considered the entrance to Hell.

The carriage drew up on reaching *Stufe di Nerone*, Nero's ovens. This steamy hot cave and cluster of thermal pools had in Roman times been called *Terme Silvanae* and dedicated to Rea Sylvia, the goddess of fecundity, and its promise of fertility had survived the centuries.

Maria, clad in a white tunic with her hair braided in coils around her head, sat hunched over in the stiflingly hot, steamy, low-ceilinged cave, dripping sweat, forcing herself to remain there for as long she could bear it. Antonia, whose regular visits appeared to have inured her to the heat, rubbed more of the concoction she swore by into Maria's skin. Its ingredients included mercury, camphor, royal jelly and almond oil, and Antonia believed that its absorption by the heat prevented wrinkles from forming on the face. Now that it was inches from hers, Maria examined her aunt's face. It had few wrinkles. Astonishing. Antonia was nearly forty. Maria's red-hot face absorbed the thick white cream almost immediately. The heat was searing into her flesh; she could barely breathe.

She ran from the cave beetroot-faced, gasping. The Amazon ran to her with towels and cool water and rubbed her while she breathed in the cold fresh air. She then immersed herself in a large, very warm, greenish pool. She felt the heat relaxing her muscles and closed her eyes, breathing in the fragrance of the rosemary oil Antonia had rubbed on her body.

When she'd first soaked in this pool, she'd thought only of marriage, sex and devastatingly handsome Federigo Carafa. She was thirteen and had just been betrothed to him. She'd worn her beads and murmured her rosary, praying that she would bear sons, invoking the power of the waters. Now she invoked their power once again. Let me bear one more son, to Carlo. Let me do my duty by him and then let me rest.

She stepped out of the pool and plunged into a much larger, deeper one in the fragrant garden and began to swim, her hair loosening from the braids and streaming behind her, greenish under the water like a mermaid's.

At twilight they returned to Baia, to an ancient temple of Diana hidden in a thick wood near Lake Averno. Over the centuries Diana, goddess of the moon and the hunt, had fused with Herodias and transmuted into the queen of the witches. The Roman Diana and the witch-queen of Italian folklore were both associated with fertility and easy childbirth—and prophesy. The witches' powers were said to increase fivefold on the night of a full moon, which was why Antonia had chosen to consult them on this night.

Their carriage drove through the wood and pulled up before a grove of tall cypresses so old that each trunk almost touched its neighbour's. Men were forbidden to enter, so the men-at-arms remained with the carriage.

Two of the older witches escorted Maria and Antonia along the dark path of the grove. Antonia's maids followed, although it had been hardly necessary to bring the Amazonian—who, Antonia claimed, could fight like a man—because the atmosphere was profoundly calm here, even mystical. Myrtle and pine perfumed the air. Maria heard the sound of tambourines. She could see the marble ruins of Diana's temple gleaming supernaturally in the moonlight as she followed the two witches, who walked as tall and proud as the ancient priestesses of Diana. She liked these dignified elders of the group, their graceful bodies draped with indigo cloth in the classical manner, and their well-combed, grey-streaked hair flowing long and free. She secretly preferred them to the sisters of God, for they smiled more easily and exuded bodily fulfilment.

Maria and her party emerged from the grove into the full moonlight. The temple stood on a gentle rise in the centre of a large open space. The young witches began putting on a show for their visitors' benefit. To the right, one was seated on a rock playing a mandolin, while a circle of seven others spun first clockwise and then anti-clockwise as they shook their tambourines and clicked their castanets. Their eyes were drunken, the dance with its turns and tricks increasingly frenetic, until they seemed to Maria a whirring blur. They were performing a tarantella, the dance of female sexual desire sacred to the witch-queen. They made Maria a little nervous, these young ones with their sheer manic energy and the fluid, earthy sensuality of their movements.

The layout of the sacred garden that had once surrounded the temple was still visible; herbs and medicinal plants grown by the witches traced its centuries-old pattern. Stretched out on the grass or sitting atop broken pillars were numerous cats. A white one and its kitten followed Maria as she was led up the path to the interior of the roofless temple.

The witch Parthenope received only one person at a time and Antonia would have her turn after her niece. Maria had previously consulted witches at Baia but not Parthenope, a young witch who was said to be unusually gifted at seeing time: past, present and future.

Parthenope was beautiful. She sat against the far wall on a raised platform where the statue of Diana had once been, her enormous bare breasts gleaming in the moonlight, her penetrating eyes and long hair black as night. Her very full, pouting lips gave her a sulky look. As Maria drew closer to her she saw that she was not so young: thirty-five perhaps—young for a witch. She wore no adornments. The smell of orange flowers that permeated the temple seemed to emanate from her. Maria sat on a bench before this goddess of womanliness and was stared into by those knowing eyes. Two women on either side of the prophetess incanted spells and rhyming charms.

Parthenope dismissed the women. 'My people thank your two families, Maria d'Avalos. They saved us from flames and persecution,' she said in a perfectly normal voice; witches often spoke in an exaggeratedly high or low voice in order to appear otherworldly.

'I, too, am thankful to them, for here I am now, with you,' responded Maria, who'd known immediately what Parthenope was referring to. In the 1530s Spain has wished to establish a court of the Inquisition in Naples, as it had in many other European cities. The old Neapolitan barons opposed the Inquisition because it gave the already corrupt Spanish viceroys ample opportunity for more sinister kinds of corruption, including the seizing of property. This placed the great aristocratic families at risk of being accused of heresy or witchcraft. So Alfonso d'Avalos and Luigi Carafa had led the people of Naples in two surprisingly successful uprisings against Spain. Though a few burnings had occurred—like the one in Piazza Mercato in March 1564 when two noblemen, humanists, had, to the horror of the populace, been burned as heretics—the uprisings had ensured that no court of the Inquisition had ever been established in Naples. So while the Inquisition raged in other parts of Europe and hundreds of thousands of learned women were incinerated for their ancient knowledge of healing and prophesy, of pregnancy and childbirth, the witches of Naples had survived and their ancient culture endured.

'The past circles through your future, bringing deathly winters and one last glorious summer. Have no fear, your next infant will thrive. The dark one has rare gifts and you should fear your own nature more than you fear him, for you will never rise above your desire for love. One darker than he in appearance is more dangerous. On the tenth night that the man you love becomes a woman, you will die.'

'What do you mean, Parthenope? How is that possible?'

'I cannot tell you. To explain the future is to seek to change destiny and I cannot be the agent of that. Only you can change your destiny, but your insight is blinded by emotion. Remember my words, for they are a warning. Take this,' she said, holding out an iridescent moonstone. 'It has curative powers but must only be used in moments of extreme danger or its power will wane. Goodbye, Maria d'Avalos. You will live on in Naples.'

Four

FOUR CARNIVAL DAYS

Maria awoke late; the winter dawn was already filtering through the shutters. Sylvia had been waiting anxiously, for she was under instructions from Antonia not to awaken her mistress, who must look fresh and well rested on this important day.

Maria had, to her surprise, slept soundly, though she'd gone to bed feeling at the mercy of conflicting emotions: excitement about her betrothal banquet—her first public appearance in Naples since her six-year absence—and anxiety abut her first meeting with the adult Carlo.

She turned over, curled up on her side and closed her eyes again. Now that the day of both these momentous events had arrived, her excitement and anxiety had intensified. I must order my thoughts, she told herself. On today of all days I must be in command of myself.

She heard Laura and Sylvia in the next room excitedly laying out her clothes. 'My lady must be ready by eleven and here it is, already eight o'clock, and she's not awake yet,' fretted Sylvia.

'It will take but two hours to dress her,' Laura assured her. 'Fetch me that casket of pearls if you would.'

'Two hours! More like three. The poultice must go on now. Tell the kitchen girls to prepare it and have them make my lady's chocolate while you're down there.'

'I can't. I must steam her gown to raise the pile. Run your hand over this velvet, Sylvia. It's like silken fur.'

A loud bang of the dressing-room door indicated that Sylvia had herself gone down to the kitchens in a huff.

Maria felt in need of a confidant, a confessor. Too late to call for a priest now. Her mother? Her father? They would both in their different ways merely emphasise the importance of her impending marriage and she did not feel sufficiently close to either to embark on a discussion of her private feelings with them. Aunt Antonia? Perhaps.

Half an hour later Maria sat up in bed, occasionally patting the poultice of chalk, lemon juice and egg white that covered her face, neck and shoulders. Only her cupid mouth and large green eyes were visible. The purpose of the poultice was to give an even paler luminosity and dewy freshness to her skin—another treatment Antonia, who was living proof of its efficacy, swore by. There were even little packs strapped to the backs of Maria's hands.

She sipped the steaming chocolate Sylvia had brought her, thinking on her initial meetings with her previous husbands. When Federigo had introduced himself into her life, he had instantly provided her with an innocent foretaste of the heady sensations of passionate love. By contrast, Alfonso Gioeni had come to Naples and claimed her like a prized possession, his outward demeanour solicitous and paternal, his eyes avid with lust. At the first touch of his hand, she'd winced. Though she'd been told he was past fifty, and had been widowed the previous year, she'd not expected to have to stifle feelings of repugnance at his hanging jowls, his narrow watchful eyes. Thus had begun all those years of stifling her feelings. Her grief at losing Federigo had made her so careless of all else that she'd offered up no initial resistance to Alfonso's tyranny and had allowed him to instil into her habits of fearfulness. She worried that these had become second nature. If she'd stood on her dignity with Alfonso from the beginning, given voice to her dismay, her outrage, he'd have had to temper his behaviour toward her and would consequently have been less fearsome. Only now had she come to realise this.

How crucial first impressions were. So much was revealed in them. Those early experiences with her departed husbands had been preludes indicating the exact nature of those two vastly different marriages. Hence her anxiety about this morning's introduction to Carlo. And it was this very anxiety that she now must stifle, for Carlo would likewise be measuring his first impressions of her. She wished to command this meeting. She had determined that it should be so. Confident that she would at least impress him, she hoped in her secret heart to enchant him. And if this difficult young man admired beauty to the extent that Antonia claimed, then Maria would indeed have the power over him she desired.

'What jewellery is my lady to wear? She must appear before her betrothed as a queen,' pronounced Sylvia from the next room.

Hearing this, Maria smiled.

'The pink pearls. Look how their colour exactly matches those of the gown,' exclaimed Laura happily.

'Her bath is growing cold,' said Sylvia.

'Then have the kitchen girls bring up extra hot water. This gown could do with more steaming.'

'Oh, now there's a knock on the door. Who could that be?'

'I'll send for the kitchen girls myself.'

'No. You open the door and I'll go down.'

'Would it not be easier for you to do both, Sylvia?'

'Answer the door, Laura! It might be the prince or princess waiting out there.'

Antonia was suddenly in Maria's bedchamber. 'Don't bother answering the door,' she said loudly. 'My impatience has itself miraculously turned the handle. Good morning, my darling, you look well rested. Isn't it time to rise? Sylvia! Laura! Come in here at once and remove these poultices.'

Sylvia muttered something about hot water and banged the dressing-room door shut again.

Maria offered up her face and hands to Laura, saying, 'Let us all be calm, Aunt. I'm rather nervous and I wish to go downstairs feeling serene.'

'Nervous!' scoffed Antonia. 'This is one of the great days of your life.'

'I will shortly meet the adult Carlo for the first time, and he me, and I ask you to bear that in mind, Aunt,' responded Maria crossly.

'Be a little haughty with him, that's the secret with men,' advised Antonia breezily. 'If you start out with your heart set on pleasing them, you never do. Never. But if you hold yourself aloof and affect a dissatisfied air, then *they* fall over themselves trying to please *you*. Carlo is in any case passionate about this marriage. Simply *passionate*. And he's an artist. An absolute *artist*. What taste! What a sense of theatre! Never have I known a man to take such an interest in the details of his own wedding. The music, the entertainments, the food, the clothes, the wedding procession, the decorations, the animals, the guests. Simply everything!'

Maria sighed. Outward show was at the moment far more important to her aunt than Maria's private feelings, so it was pointless to try to discuss them with her.

'Ah!' Antonia exclaimed, closely watching the results of Laura's handiwork. 'Your complexion will be the envy of sixteen year olds. Your re-entry into Neapolitan society will be a triumph. Think on that in your bath.'

Maria did not soak in the wooden tub for long. When she returned to her bedchamber Laura began to dress her.

'I know how these women think. I am after all of their circle, although I'd hate to think of myself as one of them,' said Antonia, picking up from where she'd left off and making one of the fine distinctions only she herself understood. 'Gossip and speculation are among the chief pastimes of their idle days. The ones who have nubile daughters of thirteen or fourteen consider them a far better prospect for the Prince of Venosa than you, my darling. Their gossip reduces you to a twice-widowed woman of twenty-five, the brink of middle age according to them, although one would never know it to look at you. I'm determined you will disarm these viragos by appearing before them as a vision, an absolute *vision* of breathtaking beauty.'

Bathed and oiled and sitting in her petticoats, Maria stared into the looking glass as Laura artfully arranged her hair, plaiting the golden strands and then entwining the looped braids with pearls. In the reflection in the glass, she could see her aunt perched on the edge of a cream and gold chair on the other side of the wide room, her amethyst-ringed fingers smoothing her violet gown, a frown troubling her petite triangular face as she moaned, 'I am trembling, simply trembling, at the thought of what the *ruinous* colour combination of that dress will do to your complexion, and who but *puttani* wear red in the middle of the day?'

'Why don't you close your eyes, Aunt, and wait to see the finished effect?' suggested Maria. She and Antonia had had a spirited disagreement about the colour of the dress she was to wear today and the topic had become tiresome to her.

'If you wish. Sylvia, pass me that sleeping mask.'

The mask had the unexpected effect of silencing Antonia, so that when Beatrice rushed into the room a few minutes later she had her mother's full attention.

'Beatrice, how lovely you look,' exclaimed Maria on seeing her daughter's grey eyes offset by a pale blue dress with fine lace edging.

'Mama, Mama,' exclaimed Beatrice excitedly, her face appearing level with her mother's shoulder in the mirror.

'What is it, Beatrice?'

'Grandmama Sveva just told me that my Carafa grandmama will be at the party. She said I could sit with her if I wished. May I? Please?'

'You may, darling,' answered Maria, disconcerted at the thought of Federigo's mother being present at her betrothal to Carlo, but happy for Beatrice nevertheless.

'Why is my Carafa grandmama coming to the party?' asked the child, echoing her mother's thoughts.

'Because, my angel, the Carafas are the richest family in Naples and one must invite them to everything of importance,' explained Antonia from behind her mask.

'Why are you wearing that mask?' asked Beatrice.

'Because your mama and I are playing a game. When she's finished dressing you must tell me how she looks. I've noticed you always speak the truth, Beatrice, so I'm depending on you for an unbiased opinion. Are you excited at the prospect of your mama's marriage?'

'I don't know, Aunt. I'll tell you when I've met him.'

'Met whom?' inquired Antonia.

'Him.'

'Not *him*, Beatrice. Your cousin Carlo.'

'Our cousin Carlo. Mama is already looking very nice. Her hair is all twirled and pearled like a queen's.'

Beatrice watched with interest as Laura dressed her mother in the elaborate gown. Maria's interpretation of the newest Florentine fashion was a success: the proportions of her figure were retained in its softer lines and less exaggerated bulkiness. Laura arranged the skirt of the gown into graceful folds while Beatrice stood in silent admiration. It was a rich, deep vermillion velvet, offset with a green silk the colour of Maria's eyes in the fine ruching around the neckline and the inserts of the slashed sleeves. This was the colour combination that Antonia, on hearing of it, had declared was ruinous.

'You may look now, Aunt,' said Maria smilingly, her nervousness momentarily evaporating at the sight of herself in the long glass. This was indeed a dress in which she might enchant her betrothed.

'What's your opinion, Beatrice?' asked Antonia without taking off the mask.

Beatrice thought very carefully. The Fairy Queen. No. Though Beatrice did not think in such terms, the gown was far too seductive for a fairy queen. 'The Fairy Queen's older, more beautiful, married sister,' she finally announced.

To amuse the child, Antonia gasped dramatically and removed the mask. This sophisticated woman had seen hundreds of ravishing gowns, owned several herself, and not one of them could compare with the one in front of her now. Who would have thought it, but Maria had been right about the colours after all. The touches of green emphasised the unusual colour of her eyes, while the vermillion red—well, the *vermillion*, what *didn't* it do: it complemented the red tints in Maria's golden hair; its contrast with her paleness made her skin glow like mother-of-pearl; it accentuated her voluptuousness and yet at the same time endowed her presence with a regality, a roseate radiance. It was drama, high drama, so arresting as to be almost shocking.

'My darling,' breathed Antonia, 'I'm ashamed to say I had no idea how clever you are. It's a miracle of a dress.'

Laura draped the long strand of pinkish pearls that matched the pearl-encrusted bodice of the dress around Maria's neck, careful not to disturb her mistress's artfully arranged hair. She added matching earrings and Maria's toilette was complete.

Antonia stood back appraisingly, her kind eyes growing a little misty. Her favourite niece was still the most beautiful woman in Naples, indisputably so.

'Now I must leave you to go and meet *him*,' whispered Maria to Beatrice.

As they made their way down the stairs to the main salon, Antonia took Maria's hand in hers, saying, 'You can with all confidence be at your ease, my darling. Look at you! Prize enough for a king, never mind a prince. As for Carlo, he's no longer the boy you once knew. I confess, I previously found him to be of little interest when he wasn't plucking at a lute. But he's redeemed himself in my eyes.' They reached the landing just above the ground floor and Maria hesitated. 'Now let us see how you find him. Remember, be a little haughty.'

'Sh, Aunt. Allow me a moment's tranquillity,' said Maria, extracting her hand from her aunt's. A shaft of pale sunlight illuminated the landing. It seemed to Maria mystical, a sign perhaps, and she stepped into its centre, offering up a silent prayer to the Virgin.

A door opened and closed below and she heard brisk footsteps coming along the hall. Antonia, propelled by curiosity, continued down the stairs.

The footsteps slowed, the walker came into view, and Maria had an instant's impression of a dark widow's peak and pointed beard framing a pale angular face, a high, pleated ruffed collar of the purest white above a dense black velvet jerkin and doublet.

'Carlo!' Antonia exclaimed. 'Surely we are not so late that you have given up waiting for us.'

Maria remained on the landing. The thought flashed through her mind that she could not have chosen a more perfect moment for Carlo to first set eyes on her. She felt supremely calm.

'Ah, Donna Antonia, you must forgive me,' Carlo was saying with a bow. 'I'm expecting my valet and left the salon only for a moment to see what's detaining him, but I see I chose the wrong moment.' He paused and looked up at Maria, a vision indeed, illuminated by the shaft of light in the dim stairwell. She stared down at him silently. A knowing smile appeared behind his expressive eyes and hovered around his mouth. 'But perhaps it was the right moment, after all. I see you have a fine sense of drama, Cousin Maria.'

He climbed a few steps and offered up his arm to her. She gave him her hand and descended, taking in the arched eyebrows above his eyes, thinking they were still the most intelligent eyes she had ever seen, and saying, 'You've become rather Spanish-looking, Carlo. Your clothes suit you well,' as he was dressed in the Spanish style worn by the nobility on formal occasions.

'And I compliment you on your gown, Cousin,' he said, elegantly kissing her hand. His lips were firm and cool. 'Your aunt told me you designed it yourself and I'm pleased at your talent.'

'Thank you, Cousin. You don't think it too bold?'

'It *is* bold, but artful as well. That's the cunning secret of its charm.'

A bird-like man with greying hair came hurrying toward them from the other end of the hall, carrying a large casket.

'Here's your man, Carlo,' said Antonia. 'I'll go in and join Gaetano and Sveva.'

'Maria and I will be but a minute. Pietro, what have you been doing?' Carlo asked his valet.

'Helping Salvatore check the axle, Prince Carlo. He said one of the carriage wheels—'

'Yes, yes, never mind,' said Carlo, flicking his hand in the air dismissively, a gesture Maria was soon to become familiar with. 'Follow us,' he added, offering Maria his arm.

As they walked along the hall, Carlo, to Maria's astonishment, put his lips close to her ear and whispered familiarly, 'Slapped any faces of late, Cousin?'

'It may please you to learn I've had my own slapped,' she retorted, looking straight ahead. 'And what do you think befell the perpetrator?'

'Your vengeance?' he asked, amused.

'Not mine. God's. The man was dead within minutes.'

To her even greater astonishment, Carlo roared with laughter, a high-pitched, thigh-slapping kind of laugh that echoed down the hallway and propelled them into the salon.

'Maria, how splendid you look. I see you and Carlo are getting along very well,' said Prince Gaetano, rising and indicating that they sit on the pair of stiff-backed panel chairs opposite those he and Princess Sveva sat on.

'Will you share the joke with us?' smiled Antonia from her chair by the fire.

'We will not. It's of a private nature,' responded Carlo tersely, his mirth all of a sudden evaporating. 'Pietro, put the casket there.'

The valet, placing it on the table next to Maria, permitted himself the briefest glance at the exquisite golden lady who glowed like warmth itself in a room that was all dark furniture and cold colours. Then he bowed and departed, thinking, So that's the young prince's bride! No wonder there's been nothing but fuss and to-do at Palazzo San Severo these past thirty days.

Prince Gaetano, connoisseur of women, was proud and excited by Maria resplendent in red. Princess Sveva, though she whiffed of disapproval as always, could hardly take her eyes off her daughter. Looking at her parents sitting together in complementary colours, he in cinnamon velvet and she in amber—a welcome relief from her habitual greys—Maria felt a rush of affection for them.

'Carlo and Maria, your union cements an alliance between kindred already close,' began Prince Gaetano.

'It is not necessary to deliver the betrothal speech now,' interrupted Princess Sveva. 'We have but an hour—'

'Between them, the d'Avalos and Gesualdo families are related to all of the noblest families in the Kingdom of Naples,' he continued, ignoring her, 'from the northern border with the Papal States to the southern tip of Sicily . . .' To the princess's exasperation he went on in this vein for two or three minutes. Carlo's eyes roved around the room and over the smooth pale skin of Maria's neck and bosom.

'Gaetano, you can show Carlo which door to enter through in a few minutes,' began Princess Sveva, and she then went on to explain the formal procedure for the betrothal banquet that was shortly to take place. Carlo crossed his legs and angled himself more comfortably in his chair, listening intently to what the princess had to say.

Maria studied the Gesualdo coat of arms, which was intricately worked in semiprecious stones on the lid of the casket: a rampant lion encircled by fleur-de-lys on a silver field, surmounted by a red crown. This ancient Norman emblem was now hers, or soon would be. She longed to lift the lid and see the contents of the casket, but Carlo would no doubt reveal them soon enough.

'Are you listening to this, Maria?' Carlo suddenly asked, turning to look at her.

'I don't need to. I know the procedure,' she replied, returning his gaze and noting that his eyes were slightly almond-shaped. Now that he was sitting in the light and she could see their colour clearly, she remembered that this was one of the things she'd found strange about him as a child; at a casual glance his eyes looked dark, but they were actually a light brown with dark flecks.

'And what is your opinion of it?'

'My opinion? I don't have one. It's something that one simply does,' she said with a little frown. What was he playing at?

'Do you not think there might be a more suitable way of us making our entrance?' he asked.

'Do you have one in mind?'

'Carlo!' interjected Princess Sveva angrily. 'This is not an occasion for the exercise of your whims. There is a protocol, and as members of two noble families celebrating your betrothal, you will follow it.'

'Why?' he asked.

'What do you mean 'why'? I've no patience with this nonsense,' snapped Princess Sveva, holding her chin even higher and looking across at Carlo with her great hooded eyes half closed with scorn.

'Let us not squabble over a mere detail relating to such a happy occasion,' said Antonia soothingly. 'Maria enters the room from one side, and you, Carlo, enter it from the opposite, and you meet in the centre of the main table. That's all there is to it.'

'Why do you feel it necessary to reiterate what Aunt Sveva has but two minutes ago clearly described to me? Do you think me dull-witted?' said Carlo irritably.

'To the contrary. I wished only to emphasise that your formal entrance is symbolic of your impending union,' insisted Antonia.

Had such a dispute arisen prior to the formalities of her first betrothal or her second, Maria would have been content to be silent and allow the others to reach a decision. She would not do so now. How she did or did not enter the room was neither here nor there to her. There was something else at stake here, she wasn't sure what, but her instincts told her how to behave and whose to side to take.

'It is symbolic, Donna Antonia,' Carlo was saying, 'of a tired convention desperately in need of restyling so that it may once again have meaning.'

Maria rose, so that they all looked up at her.

'This is becoming upsetting,' she said, lifting her small white hand and placing it across her brow as if she might be getting a headache. 'Mother. Father. Aunt Antonia. Can we not at least hear what Carlo has in mind?' Her plea was so affecting and unexpected that they all concurred. 'Tell us, Carlo,' she said, smiling down at him.

And so, Carlo had his way.

'Wilful, typically wilful of that nephew of mine,' muttered Princess Sveva to her husband as they and Antonia quit the room so that the betrothed couple might have a few minutes alone.

'Do you not think this would better suit your dress?' asked Carlo, draping a necklace over his hand and holding it up for Maria's approval. He'd opened the casket, which to Maria's delight contained some of the finest pieces of the Gesualdo family jewels. She'd been running her eyes over emerald and ruby necklaces, bracelets and earrings, and a stunning diamond and Neapolitan sapphire *pièce de résistance* that Antonia had mentioned to her. She fingered an exquisite cameo framed with yellow diamonds, then her eyes moved to the strand of fine pearls Carlo was holding up. Unusually, it featured rubies at well-spaced intervals. She considered it for a moment. The subdued lustre of the pearls calmed the fiery stones of the rubies, so that their redness would not be too much with her dress.

Carlo held the necklace against her throat, his eyes appraising its affect. He seemed intensely interested in her appearance, or had he wished to touch her skin? In any event, the necklace he'd chosen indicated that Antonia had been right about him. Maria found it erotic, this young man of exquisite taste bringing jewels to her, selecting what she should wear.

'You're right. Its delicacy is a far better complement to the dress's richness. These pearls are crude in comparison,' she said, touching the large pearls that hung to below her breasts. Their pinkish sheen now seemed vulgar to her as well.

'Sit down,' ordered Carlo. With his nimble fingers he removed the long loop of pearls, tossed it onto a table, and fastened the shorter, more elegant necklace with the rubies. He worked quickly and efficiently; the touch of his fingers was light and cool.

'I will leave the casket of jewels with you so that you may select from it as you wish in the coming days,' he said as he drew her back to her feet. 'I would like you to wear the diamond and Neapolitan sapphire necklace for our wedding, if it matches your dress, that is. The emeralds would suit you very well, too.' He took a key on a golden chain from his pocket, locked the casket and gave her the key.

'Thank you, Cousin, it's very generous of you.' She rang a little bell to fetch a servant to take the casket to her room.

'It's my pleasure. You will soon in any case be their custodian.'

As they stood outside the banquet room, Maria appraised her reflection in one of the mirrors that hung on either side of the double doors. Carlo studied her closely as he took her arm in his, and it seemed to Maria at that moment that it was her appearance he was interested in, not her flesh.

'How do I appear to you?' she asked him.

He shrugged. 'Elegant, gorgeously attired, all the things you planned to be,' he said off-handedly, disappointing her for a brief moment until he added, 'But you have a luminosity that no artificer can invent. You are a natural beauty at ease with herself.'

Which was how she felt as she walked into the banquet room on his arm and they stood together, surveying the freshly decorated room with its elegantly attired guests grouped at their tables, the betrothal table on its dais at the back of the room. The guests looked back at them in surprise: who would have thought the betrothed couple would enter through this door, already arm in arm before the betrothal ritual had taken place? Though Maria was clearly older than Carlo, a sophisticated beauty with long experience in dazzling, they made a handsome couple, she resplendent in her extraordinary red, he princely with his proud bearing and deep black velvet with the snowy pleated ruff. Her smile at their little joke of simply walking through the door together like this, rather than making a formal entrance to fanfare, was a little self-conscious, but endearingly so. It encouraged the guests, too, to smile at the informality of their entrance. A few of them rose and applauded and others followed suit. It was exciting for everyone present, for they'd not seen Maria for six years; as for Carlo, restyling a tired convention and making an entrance with this charismatic woman who was soon to be his wife appealed tremendously to his sense of theatre.

A trio of musicians played as he and Maria made their way between the ten circular tables, greeting and being greeted. Though not showy, the music was superb as Carlo had selected the finest lutenists and violists from his own *camerata*. This was a banquet for the ladies. Eighty of Naples' reigning matriarchs and their daughters had been invited, many of whom were cousins or relatives by marriage of them both. How splendidly they were dressed. It was like walking through a sea of colour. Smiles of warmth from familiar faces greeted Maria, and it seemed to her that, though they were impressed by the splendour of her appearance, the majority of these noblewomen were genuinely pleased to see her again. There was Maddelena Carafa, Beatrice by her side and clearly at ease with her grandmother already. Maria felt a pang to see that Maddelena's hair had turned entirely grey, though her strong-boned face and frank hazel eyes had a youthful look still. She was dressed in black velvet. She'd worn nothing but black since Federigo's death. It suited her. Maria spontaneously touched her arm; had it not been inappropriate on this occasion she would have embraced this handsome woman who had once been her mother-in-law. Maddelena responded with a firm pressure of her own hand and a warm smile. 'We both loved Federigo so there will always love between us no matter what else may happen,' her eyes seemed to say. The pleasure on Antonia's face as she passed told Maria her entrance was everything her aunt had hoped for. How foolish she'd been to feel anxious, she thought as she sat down with Carlo in the centre of the betrothal table on its dais at the far end of the room.

The formal arrangement of the six people at this table was symbolic, and a hush fell over the room, the musicians resting their instruments, as the guests looked toward the betrothed couple and their parents. Princess Sveva and Prince Gaetano sat facing each other at the ends of the table, while its other four occupants looked out into the room.

A young servant girl brought in an egg in an ornate silver cup and placed it before Princess Sveva. At the same time a young male servant placed a plate containing a *panesperma* in front of Prince Gaetano, who took a bite of this phallic-shaped mixture of flour and fish and passed it on to Carlo's father, Prince Francesco. Princess Sveva cut the top off the egg and spooned some into her mouth. Carlo was gazing at her long pointed sleeves, which trailed over the edge of the table. She lifted her hooded eyes and stared back at her nephew as if to say, 'This is one betrothal ritual you won't be interfering with,' and passed the silver cup to Carlo's mother. Princess Geronima Gesualdo was a thin, hollow-cheeked woman with large, lugubrious eyes whose magenta gown suggested she'd resolved to brighten herself up and forego mourning garb for this occasion. With regard to the overall effect of the table it was a happy choice; the three women in their rich colours, Carlo in the centre in his stark black and white, and the aging princes on the other side of him in cinnamon and deep brown, provided a spectacle of royal richness. Prince Francesco, whose balding head bore remnants of a widow's peak like Carlo's, broke off a piece of the *panesperma* and popped it into his mouth. Princess Geronima turned to Maria and smiled soulfully as she partook of the egg and passed it to her just as Prince Francesco placed the silver platter containing the rest of the *panesperma* in front of his son. Carlo leaned back in his chair, listless and uninterested for a moment, but at Maria's sigh of impatience as she held the spoon with the remains of the egg in it to her lips, he put the ritual bread into his mouth and they swallowed together as custom demanded.

The ornate procedure over with, a servant brought in a fine, succulent ham and placed it in the middle of their table, indicating that the banquet could now begin. The music struck up once again and numerous servants wearing festive red kerchiefs for the occasion appeared carrying trays of sparkling drinks and platters of food. Within minutes the room was abuzz with chatter and laughter as the guests began chewing their way through twenty-three rich and elaborate dishes. Sweeping her eyes around the ten circular tables of familiar animated faces, hearing snatches of their convivial talk and returning their smiles, Maria felt an overwhelming sense of having come home.

Antonia had made splendid choices in her redecoration scheme. The heavy Spanish ancestral furniture had given way to delicate rosewood pieces. The airy frescoes depicting the marriage of the Virgin were all blue skies and billowing draperies, with playful *putti* sporting amidst pink clouds. Maria looked up, and the Virgin with her swirling blue mantle in the centre of the ceiling seemed to be reaching down and bestowing a blessing upon her. Though it would never be as blissful as her first, for a fleeting moment Maria felt a vague sense of excitement at the prospect of her forthcoming marriage.

Carlo ate little. The cuisine favoured by Prince Gaetano for festive occasions—fish and game in heavy sauces, rich meats in aspic—did not suit his delicate palate. So he talked. Never had Maria imagined that moody Carlo could be so loquacious. He talked of hunting, of the splendid breed of horses he kept at Gesualdo Castle—which he would soon have the pleasure of taking Maria to—and of music and his ambitions for his *camerata*.

'Ah, that's a particularly interesting passage, Carlo. Look, they've all got their ears cocked to it,' said Prince Francesco, indicating the circles of guests. The chatter in the room had indeed become subdued. Carlo had chosen a programme of songs or *canzone* with simple, original harmonies. But occasionally, as now, these were enlivened by more daring, expressive passages. Maria laughed at its concluding flourish, which managed to be both discordant and humorous. 'What a novelty,' she said. 'I've never heard anything like it. Did you write it yourself, Carlo?'

'No. I know one or two audacious composers. I hope to devote more time to my own compositions, though.'

'Surely much of your time will now be taken up with visiting your estates and learning your duties as Prince of Venosa,' said Princess Sveva.

'Naturally, Aunt, though surely such duties are not an entertaining topic of conversation at a banquet, nor at any other time I should think.'

Maria almost gasped. Never had her mother been so roundly and so publicly chastised. This was Maria's introduction to Carlo's brutal sincerity. Princess Sveva glared at her nephew as if she wanted to box his ears.

'Carlo has been a willing student in this regard. You must remember, Sveva, it is not yet half a year since our poor Luigi departed us,' Princess Geronima chimed in, referring to Carlo's older brother. Maria looked with interest at this woman who was soon to be her mother-in-law. She'd rarely seen her when she was growing up. Though thin to the point of being frail-looking, her voice was robust, her manner confident. Apart from the paleness of their skin, there was little resemblance between her and Carlo, particularly in matters of taste. The figured magenta velvet of Geronima's gown, while beautiful in itself, did little for her pasty complexion.

'Luigi's death was a shock to us all,' said Prince Francesco, glancing at Maria.

'He'd ridden to Venosa healthier than any of us. Who could have imagined he'd be struck down by marsh fever,' said Geronima sadly. 'There was no time even to send our doctor to him. On the Thursday we heard he was ill, and on the Friday . . .'

'Not now, Geronima, not now,' murmured Francesco. He turned to Maria again. 'Never had we imagined that Carlo would one day be my heir. As you know, Sveva, it is I who encouraged his devotion to music,' he added, his eyes moving pointedly to his sister, whose criticism of Carlo on the very day of his betrothal he found intensely irritating. Sveva could always be relied upon to find fault. 'I've managed to divide my time between caring for my estates and my subjects, and maintaining my group of musicians and poets. There's no reason why Carlo can't do the same.' He glanced back at Maria again and smiled at her encouragingly. 'What does the future Princess of Venosa have to say on the subject?' he asked.

'She agrees,' replied Maria. 'And she also considers that the present Prince of Venosa is gifted in the skills of diplomacy.'

The old prince beamed, and added mischievously, 'And does she also consider that the young Prince Carlo may have inherited such a gift?'

Maria looked at Carlo, who met her eyes challengingly. 'She thinks that the young prince's considerable gifts may lie elsewhere.'

Even Carlo laughed at this honest reply and the table recovered its festive mood.

The sweet-faced young servant girl who'd brought in the egg set down an enormous platter of gluttonous cakes and sweetmeats smothered in chocolate and crystallised fruit right in front of Carlo. He looked at it with disgust. 'Move it up there,' he whispered to her, indicating Gaetano and his expanding belly. Stifling her amusement, the girl did as she was bid.

During the dessert courses the formal seating arrangements relaxed and some of the guests moved to sit at other tables. Carlo and Prince Gaetano were locked in a conversation about the merits of arquebuses for hunting deer, and Maria asked Carlo if he would mind her joining the Carafas' table for a few minutes. 'Don't think you must ask my permission to speak to your friends,' he replied.

'Who do you think Beatrice most resembles?' Maria asked Maddelena Carafa after she'd embraced her and greeted a few other Carafa women sitting at her table.

'Federigo,' replied Maddelena. 'She's a female version of him at his age. Same eyes, same brow, same nose.'

'It's remarkable, isn't it?' said Maria.

'Yes, my dear. But she's far more serious that our angel Federigo ever was. She's a sensible child and you've brought her up well. She tells me she writes sonnets, just like her mother. If you ever grow tired of her she can come and live with her grandmother.'

'Would you like that?' Maria asked Beatrice, anticipating a childish 'no'.

But the child considered the question carefully. 'If Prince Carlo is nice to live with, I will stay with you. But if he doesn't like me, I will live with the Carafas.'

Though she laughed with the others at this sage reply, Maria felt hurt, a little desolate even, for she still thought of Beatrice as all she had. Then, to her delight, Beatrice added, 'But I would want you to come with me.'

'As much as I would like to,' said Maria, looking at Maddelena, 'I could never do that. I must always live with Prince Carlo.'

'What if he dies?' asked Beatrice.

'Sh. Sh. He won't die. I don't want him to. You must never talk of living people dying. It's very upsetting, Beatrice.'

'But they do. They die all the time,' insisted the solemn child. She began counting on her fingers. 'My father's dead. Poppa Alfonso's dead. My brothers and—'

'Enough!' Maria almost shouted, rising in alarm.

'What a gruesome little girl you are,' said Maddelena, cuddling her. 'People live all the time, too. Look at us. We're all alive. You can think sad things, Beatrice, but it's better not to say them,' she advised. 'You make people unhappy. Look at your poor mother's face. When people get married it's very special, so you must make sure your mother is happy during her wedding celebrations and not say bad things.'

'I'm sorry, Mama,' said Beatrice, shamefaced.

'I think you say such things because you like to hear yourself speak what you consider to be the truth,' responded Maria. 'I know you don't mean to be cruel, darling.'

'Is Carlo going to join his group and play for us?' asked Anna, Maddelena's sister.

'We should let him rest during his betrothal celebrations,' said Maddelena.

'But he loves to perform. I imagine he's itching for an invitation. Why don't you ask him, Maria?

'Perhaps Beatrice would like to ask him,' Maria responded, holding out her hand to the girl. What better way, she thought, for Carlo to become acquainted with her daughter.

Beatrice, who was looking charming in her pale blue dress, walked hand in hand with her mother to the bridal table. Her Grandfather d'Avalos drew her onto his lap, and she waited politely while present and future relatives made a fuss of her. She lowered her intelligent little heart-shaped face and examined her shiny brown curls, abashed for once. Usually it was her mother who was the centre of attention; Beatrice was unused to compliments on her looks. 'You'll be a beauty one day,' whispered Prince Gaetano. The child looked over at Maria and decided it unwise to say what she was thinking in front of all these people: that too many demands were made on women who were beautiful. She vowed that if she did indeed grow into a beauty, then she would dress her hair plainly and wear only the simplest of clothes. Her head to one side, she turned to Carlo. The two of them stared at each other as they might have studied exotic animals at a carnival. 'My aunt would like to hear you play some music, and she sent me to ask you if you would do so, please,' said Beatrice without shyness.

'Do you like music?' asked Carlo.

'I like to hear birds sing.'

'That is not music,' said Carlo.

'Yes it is.'

'I meant music played on a lute or some other instrument.'

'If you play for my aunt, I will tell you if I like it.'

'Do you that see that footman standing by the middle door? Ask him to fetch my lute.'

And off Beatrice went in the direction of the footman. Maria had no idea what to make of this oddly truncated conversation. Either Carlo and Beatrice silently understood one another, or there was no connection whatsoever between them.

Maria went to bed that night her body heavy with tiredness, but pleasantly and healthily so, and with a general sense of wellbeing at the events of the day. Carlo, however, mystified her still. Now that her anxiously anticipated meeting with him had taken place, the man she was shortly to marry seemed no less enigmatic. To her immense relief, she had found him attractive, and anticipated finding him more so as marriage brought them closer. He was not handsome, as Federigo had been, but proud and clever-looking with a princely bearing. And he'd been courteous, elegant—to her at least, if not always to others—and most certainly responsive to her. Yet Maria had sharp instincts where men were concerned. She could feel a man's desire like the sun on her face. No such invisible rays had emanated from Carlo. Perhaps he'd become adept at concealing his desires. Or perhaps he secretly loved another, whom he would be forced to renounce now that his marriage to her had been thrust upon him by convention. Then she thought of his rudeness to Aunt Antonia, his blithe disregard for her mother's love of ceremony. Though obviously well educated and well read, he seemed a self-centred man, aristocratic in his attitude but no less emotionally complicated than she'd remembered him. She wondered about his private life and heaved a little sigh. The disquieting child had grown into the disquieting man.

Their wedding took place a fortnight later. During four carnival days overseen by Carlo, the Neapolitan nobility enjoyed banquets, balls, tournaments, ballets, musical performances and other entertainments.

After the opening banquet at Palazzo d'Avalos on the first day, at three o'clock there was to be a display of jousting. This was to take place on the level ground between the palace and the Bay of Naples, a spectacular backdrop for the tournament. Workmen had spent days constructing the long line of tiered wooden stands that now faced the bay. Sand was laid over the grass to prevent the splendid horses from injuring themselves.

The *combatieri* had readied themselves while the guests were eating, and by the time they emerged from the palace, making their way down the slope like a rainbow flock of exotic birds, the display was ready to begin. Though it was cold and rather windy, only faint puffs of cloud appeared in the blue sky, so rain was not going to spoil their pleasure.

Maria had awoken that morning with an inclination to wear black. Although Laura had laid out an outfit of deep gold, and although she knew her family would make a fuss—which they did—Maria wore one of the mourning gowns made for her at Messina, its shape outdated but its figured velvet and contrast with her fairness magnificent. She wished to begin this first day of her marriage celebrations in mourning for her past; she would wear bright colours and look to the future tonight and thereafter. Carlo, a man of whimsy himself, merely smiled faintly and raised his eyebrows when he saw her.

Maria and her party of ladies were escorted to the middle of one of the upper tiers that provided the best view. At one end of the field were the three *mantenitore*, or masters of the joust, at the other were the *combatieri*.

Such tournaments had changed little since medieval times, and a few minutes elapsed to allow the audience sufficient time to admire the pageantry and knightly trappings: the jousters in their variously coloured combat suits reinforced with bolt-on protective steel, the matching body and head covers of the horses with their pinked edges, and the silken *contrade* flags with their bright heraldic designs in blues, yellows, reds and pinks flapping in the breeze.

The tournament began with the participants on foot, in what was essentially a piece of theatre. The ordinary combatants took on the most skilled and experienced players of all, the *mantenitore*, who were in fact the umpires. The most striking of the *mantenitore*, who had rich, longish black hair and an olive complexion, shouted in a deep, resonant voice, 'Let them go!'

The combatants, still on foot, ran at the *mantenitore*. Two of them managed to break their *picche* against the shields of two *mantenitore*. Not the dark one, though. He avoided their lance thrusts with such lightning ease he seemed barely to move. The crowd applauded him enthusiastically. Next, while the *mantenitore* looked on, the combatants came forward, fencing among themselves, dealing one another a considerable number of blows.

Then the real jousting began. The men mounted their horses and to Maria they looked splendid, the shapes of horse and rider outlined against the rolling waves of the bay and the blue horizon. As he mounted, the dark *mandatora* whispered something in the ear of his horse, a powerful dappled grey with a thick curling mane who affectionately nudged his master in response.

Maria was an adept horsewoman and she enjoyed this game of great skill, for it required perfect coordination between horse and rider, resulting in a safe but spectacular splintering of lances. The manipulation of a powerful horse and the long, heavy lance, complicated by the restricted vision of the visor, required enormous prowess and split-second timing. The *combatieri* took their stations and the one that was to tilt was brought forward. He spurred his mettlesome horse and galloped at full tilt toward his opponent, but the impact resulted in him striking his opponent's horse, which was forbidden. The creature whinnied and bucked, nearly throwing its rider.

A shouting match ensued, the combatant claiming that the restiveness of his horse had caused him to hold his lance too low. He demanded to be given another chance. The dark-haired *mandatora* rode up and summarily disqualified him.

'Who is that?' Maria asked Antonia, indicating the *mandatora*.

'They call him *Il Saraceno*, the Saracen, and not only because his hair's so black. He has a reputation as a fierce fighter. Some of the young women call him Mars. But really, darling, you know him, and you'll see him occasionally because he's a friend of Carlo's. He's a Carafa, the Duke of Andria, a nephew or cousin of Federigo's. He's—'

A deafening splintering rent the air as the next combatant's lance hit the boss of his opponent's shield. The crown rose and applauded.

An hour later the *combatieri* retired from these acts of gallantry to their respective ends of the field, hammering one another with *picedi*. The dark Duke of Andria announced the winner, and, when the young man rode up to him, presented him with the customary prize. The winner duly rode to the stand with this prize, a large golden ring, on the tip of his lance and gallantly presented it to Maria.

The ball that night was a blur for Maria: the white stucco and celestial blue of the ballroom airy as a blown kiss; the laughing women in their elaborate gowns and gleaming jewels; the dashing men in their ruffs and velvets; the hundreds of candles in shimmering chandeliers; and Carlo's delightful music. Maria had chosen to wear emerald green for this glittering occasion. 'Few shades, no matter how dramatic or daring, suit you better,' Carlo had said rather pompously as they'd begun the night dancing, which he loved to do. But he loved performing even more and it took little persuasion from the guests for him to take the stage and lead his musicians.

Amidst all of this, Maria's mix of emotions reached such a pitch that, as she smiled and conversed and danced the pavane, she had the strangest sensation, of déjà vu, as if caught in the confluence of past and present. This was her last night at Palazzo d'Avalos, just as it had been eleven years ago when she had married Federigo. Save for the vast differences in the man she had married and the one she soon would, the scenario was hauntingly similar.

Then, Federigo had barely left her side. When she thought back to the first time she'd danced with him it seemed their movements that night had set in train the perpetual motion of her incessant love for him. How strong and tall and agile he'd been; she glanced at Carlo and quickly looked away for he seemed puny in comparison. Federigo had had the chiselled features of a Roman soldier which became, when he spoke, surprisingly animated, but his energy had been of a far different order to Carlo's. There had been a moment on that night eleven years ago, after others had engaged each of them in separate conversations, when she'd looked across the room and caught a glimpse of the back of Federigo's head. Its manly shape was emphasised by his short hair, which tapered down into fine, softly curling tendrils where it met his neck, and this meeting of delicate hair and strong neck had struck her as so poignant, so moving, that it had seemed a very revelation of the meaning of the phrase 'to be in love with'. He'd turned and met her eyes and come to her, and those very thoughts of hers had been echoed in what he'd said: 'You have such eyes, Maria. Others remark on their colour, but shall I tell you what captivates me? They turn down slightly at the corners, ever so slightly, and this gives your expression a sadness, a vulnerability, that makes me want to protect you.' 'And shall you?' she'd asked, feeling her pleasure at his words rise up and colour her face. 'Yes,' he'd whispered, encircling her waist with his arm, pulling her to him and placing himself in front of her in the corner of the room, so that nobody could see their faces. 'Always. I'm smitten, done for, life-imprisoned.'

Now, as Maria stood barely listening to an elderly duke whose eyes feasted on her while he regaled her with an account of the draining of the malarial swamps on his vast estates, it struck her more than ever that her life had gone terribly awry. Federigo should never have died; he should be with her still. And so her mind began to float in an indeterminate realm, hovering between the losses of the past and anxiety about the future. The only real link between those two worlds was Beatrice. Protected no longer by Federigo, Maria must be the protector of all that was left to her of him, his daughter, whom Princess Sveva had expressly forbidden to attend the ball and who now stood in deep conversation with the relative of Federigo's they called *Il Saraceno*.

The determined child, no doubt in collusion with Sylvia, who adored her and denied her nothing, had had herself dressed in her favourite gold velvet frock and had simply appeared at the ball, heading straight for her more tolerant grandmother, Maddelena, who welcomed her rediscovered grandchild with open arms. Even Princess Sveva would not take on Maddelena Carafa, whose natural air of authority was reinforced by her powerful role as the matriarch of Naples' richest family. Beatrice seemed somehow to know this.

What would wilful Beatrice's life be like in the house of the equally wilful and temperamental Carlo Gesualdo? Their first encounter had not been auspicious. There was a strong possibility that he would despise her, and she loathe him. But then Beatrice had a talent for ingratiating herself with people who, in her curiously precocious little head, she judged could be of service to her. Even as an infant she'd won over Alfonso, who had initially regarded her as superfluous to his interests and ignored her. It occurred to Maria that Beatrice had a talent for managing people which she herself did not possess. Was that her Carafa blood? Or was it an old strain of the d'Avalos family that flowed back to Maria's Great-Aunt Costanza? Yes. If singularly Beatrice resembled anyone at all, it was the redoubtable Costanza d'Avalos.

And now, here was her recalcitrant daughter moving toward her, hand in hand with *Il Saraceno*. Why had Beatrice elected to befriend him? Had she simply gravitated to him because he was the most handsome man in the room, or because he, too, exuded a natural air of authority?

Maria excused herself from the elderly duke and stepped away, smiling a greeting at her daughter.

'This is my cousin, Fabrizio Carafa,' Beatrice announced. 'He knew you when you were married to my father, who was his uncle, and he wishes to meet you again. Do you remember him?'

Fabrizio Carafa bowed and kissed Maria's hand. He'd changed from his *mandatora* costume into a soft green jacket over a cream shirt with a loosely pleated collar and, in comparison with the other men in their stiff ruffs, looked relaxed and casually elegant.

'Yes, I remember him,' smiled Maria. Although she'd not recognised him on the jousting field, so much had he matured, she now recalled him as a laughing boy who'd liked to tease Federigo's younger sisters. Although Federigo was Fabrizio's uncle, he'd been only three or four years older than him. 'Federigo taught you how to fence, and the two of you would clash swords up and down the staircases and drive Mama Maddelena crazy.'

Fabrizio threw back his head and laughed, and in that moment Federigo's devil-may-care laugh echoed in her mind. 'That wasn't the only thing Federigo taught me,' he said. 'I remember you, too, Maria.' He smiled down at Beatrice. 'When I first saw your mother I thought an angel had descended from the skies. I was in raptures. I would follow her with my eyes as she glided about the palace without a sound, like a heavenly messenger with some divine purpose. She was always so silent. I used to pray to her at night.'

'Grandmama Sveva wouldn't like you saying that,' said Beatrice with a little frown.

He laughed again. 'What a quaint little girl you are, Beatrice. And you look so much like your father, don't you think, Maria?'

'Of course.'

'Everyone says that,' said Beatrice.

'Because it's true,' countered Fabrizio.

'What else did my father teach you?' asked Beatrice.

Fabrizio studied Maria's face as he considered his reply. 'Honour,' he replied, smiling down at Beatrice again. 'Not the kind of honour that everyone talks about, but having your own private sense of honour and being true to that.'

'Is that what he did?' asked Beatrice.

'Often he did, yes. He certainly tried to be like that all of the time, but it's not easy.' He looked meaningfully at Maria with his beautiful dark eyes. To look back at him was fascinating, like staring into the eyes of something dangerous. 'You must come and visit me soon and we'll talk about your father, but now I'm in the mood for dancing. Will you allow me to dance with your mother?'

Beatrice glanced around the room, on the lookout for Sveva who would have her taken back to her room if she discovered her unaccompanied. 'Only if you take me back to Grandmama Maddelena.'

'That's exactly what I was going to do. Come, let's—'

'No Fabrizio, please forgive me,' said Maria. 'I've danced enough tonight. I'm feeling quite tired.' Maria had initially thought to accept, but an instinct warned her that to do so would be somehow disloyal to Carlo. Fabrizio didn't resemble Federigo physically, but there was something in his laugh, his easy manner, the expression in his eyes, that reminded her of Federigo, and it made her uneasy.

'I think it's very rude of you not to dance with Fabrizio,' scolded Beatrice. 'He's our cousin.'

'He's *your* cousin. And I think it's very rude of you to behave as if you were an adult. It's time for you to go to bed. Come, I'll take you back to that scheming Sylvia. Excuse me, Fabrizio. It's been a pleasure to see you again.' Her hand rose for him to kiss it, which he did, a little too lingeringly she thought.

'Some day, Maria, you will dance with me.'

The next morning, after attending a mass with her family in the d'Avalos chapel, Maria was the central attraction in a dreamlike procession. The progress of carriages from Palazzo d'Avalos to the Church of San Domenico Maggiore in the centre of Naples was of royal magnificence. The master of festivities under the direction of Carlo had done himself proud. Being a native of Florence, where the art of princely festivities had become so exuberant it occasionally went a little mad, he had proven himself to be an artist of fantastic, if not feverish, imagination.

The horses drawing the numerous carriages were dressed with the fur and plumage of exotic animals, so they resembled a fabulous procession of lions, lynxes, tigers and leopards. Maria's carriage, the most wonderful of them all, was pulled by six white unicorns with silver horns and manes of silken curls. The gods of Olympus, come down to earth to honour the Venosa nuptials, lolled in four gilded carriages, and the host of young men and women who personified them were themselves gilded all over, their nakedness covered with classical draperies of cloth-of-gold. Winged Cupid trod underfoot three hideously ugly hags, and above his carriage was fixed a faux-antique tablet, which read, *LOVE*

VANQUISHES THE FATAL SISTERS. By this it was understood that the newly wedded couple would enjoy many long years of happiness by each other's side.

The procession, accompanied by pipe-playing minstrels, made its way at a stately pace along Via Toledo, a more populous part of the city with numerous palaces and administrative buildings covering the slopes of its steep, cathedral-topped hills. Along the route, aristocratic families had contributed to the festivities by draping precious tapestries and arrases from their balconies. People from all walks of life turned out to watch the spectacle: grandees and their ladies from high balconies; housewives at window ledges with their cats; kitchen maids giggling in entrance ways; shopkeepers leaning in their doorways; ruffians and wrinkled old women mingling on the sides of the road with students and young bravos; ragged, unhappy wretches begging for alms, scurrying for the few coins that were tossed to them, the nimble among them running along beside the procession; soldiers on horseback trailing behind. Here was an opportunity to look upon the woman reputed to be the most beautiful in all Naples, and they were not disappointed. Maria felt overwhelmed and profoundly unnerved by all this attention. To dazzle one person was enjoyable; a roomful gratifying, if often uncomfortable; but an entire city? Much as she loved Naples, no, no, no. The curious stares, the smiling waves, the leers, the cacophony of fanfare, music and cheering were punctuated by shouted jeers that caused her to wince. Many of the common people hated the old baronial class, she knew that, but to be the personal target of their insults and depraved cries was deeply shocking to her. She felt threatened, no, afraid, even though there was scant chance of harm befalling her in an arena so public, protected by she knew not how many of her father's and Carlo's guards. Thank God she was seated in a carriage, else she would have collapsed. She longed to pull the Spanish mantilla adorning her head down over her face and hide beneath it. But she gritted her teeth and bore it. It was expected of her.

The procession reached elegant Piazza San Domenico Maggiore, one of the main theatres of Neapolitan life. Maria's carriage drew up in front of the pale yellow Romanesque Church of San Domenico Maggiore, which presided over the square above a long, steep flight of steps, its crenulated top a reminder of its medieval origins as Naples' first university.

Many of the elite of Naples had lived in this district since the fourteenth century when they'd converted its medieval buildings into Renaissance palaces. The imposing, six-storey San Severo palace, where Maria was to live, faced the side of the church and its tall balconied windows looked down on the square.

Piazza San Domenico Maggiore was transformed, its motley, smelly crowds of thieves, prostitutes and pitiful beggars pressed into the darker labyrinths of Spaccanapoli by the Gesualdo men-at-arms. These men now guarded the piazza as Maria and her party entered the church. The walls of the piazza's buildings were draped with banners embroidered with the Gesualdo and d'Avalos coats of arms; doorways and windows were festooned with ribbons and garlands of fresh fruit and flowers.

In order to honour Carlo, Maria had promised herself not to think of Federigo Carafa on this day. But how could she not? San Domenico Maggiore was the very church in which she'd married him. This she may have been able to push to the edge of her thoughts, but as she entered the church, to her right was the richly decorated Carafa chapel. This was where Federigo and Ferrante, their infant son, were buried.

Not daring to look in that direction and terrified she would stumble, she fixed her eyes on Carlo waiting at the altar of the soaring gothic interior.

Hundreds of candles illuminated the altar, the sacred paintings and the gleaming jewels of the gorgeously attired aristocrats who turned to watch as Maria walked down the aisle, her face now obscured by the mantilla of finest Brussels lace. The rich blue of her sumptuous gown was set off by the stunning Neapolitan sapphire necklace Carlo had suggested she wear on this day, its midnight stones flashing in their intricate diamond settings.

The wedding ceremony was surprisingly brief in comparison with the paraphernalia and duration of the festivities. As soon as Maria had taken her position beside Carlo, his uncle, Cardinal Alfonso, intoned the Latin words of the ceremony, heard their vows, blessed them, and Maria and Carlo were married. Carlo's fingers looked twice as long as hers as she watched him slide on her wedding ring, a teardrop shaped ruby with a raised centre that looked enormous on her slender hand. That, in any event, was how she remembered things. If during those minutes Maria had noticed Carlo's expression or sensed what he was thinking, she had no recollection of it later.

While Carlo attended to the fine details for the banquet and ball that were to take place that night, Princess Geronima showed Maria through her new home.

The Gesualdos lived a different, far less intimate family life than the Carafas had, and this was reflected in the arrangement of the palace's apartments. Geronima and the prince lived on the third floor, Carlo on the fifth, and the women's apartment where Maria was to live was on the top floor.

The two women paused in the splendid music room on the second floor. It contained a stage at one end with a backdrop of an allegory of music in which swans and angels, draperies billowing, danced joyfully to rhythms heard only by them.

'The da Sangros had this painted decades ago,' said Geronima, 'but anyone who knows Carlo well would believe it was he who commissioned it. Look at this instrument here.' She pointed to a severed stag's head whose long antlers formed the shape of a lyre around lines of strings. 'This could be Carlo's personal symbol. As you will soon discover, his two great passions are music and hunting.'

The room opened into one almost as large but less richly decorated, where Carlo and his musicians worked and practised. Its walls were lined with neatly labelled cabinets containing scrolled manuscripts. Viols and gourd-shaped lutes rested on tables under windows. The centrepiece was an organ painted with scenes of nymphs disporting themselves in Arcadian fields. The ten musicians who lived permanently at the palace had their rooms on the floor below.

The two women eventually reached the women's apartment where, from today onwards, Maria would live with Beatrice and her servants. It offered her a novel situation: command of her own apartment. It was quiet up here on the sixth floor, pleasant and light-filled with the long windows of its rooms looking down on Piazza San Domenico Maggiore. The loveliest room was a spacious salon with light, feminine furniture, gilded and upholstered in pale blue silk. It led into a number of bedchambers and smaller rooms, some of which were empty.

Beatrice was already in her room arranging with Sylvia's help boxes of treasures she was so possessive about that not even Maria knew all their contents. Laura, surrounded by spilling trunks, was busy putting away Maria's clothes in the dressing room.

Geronima led Maria through to her new bedchamber. Maria stood in the doorway, wide-eyed. She took in the objects, their arrangement, the very ambience of the room. What was the meaning of this? What was Carlo playing at now? Geronima had crossed the room and she turned to smile at Maria, saying, 'Carlo has had all of this especially prepared for your wedding night tonight. He's taken such care with it.' And there was something in Geronima's smile and the way she'd said this which indicated to Maria that she regarded her son's careful preparations as an eccentricity it was her maternal duty to overlook.

'How thoughtful of him,' murmured Maria, at a loss as to what else to say.

Geronima opened a door on the other side, saying, 'This leads down to Carlo's apartment. Come, Maria.' As they descended the spiral staircase she confided, 'Carlo doesn't like people going into his private rooms, but I'm sure he'll forgive his mother and bride this once.'

The fantastically high room they descended into was richly ambient and strange. But for a large table and chair, it was empty. It was irregularly shaped, the lower regions sombre and darkly panelled, the upper flooded with light from a series of small circular windows near the coffered ceiling. The walls above the panelling were frescoed with trompe l'oeil architectural perspectives; theatrically outsized scroll and rocaille motifs surrounded the door and window frames.

'This is where Carlo draws and writes and composes his music,' said Geronima. 'It is the room of a recluse, is it not? He has always been rather reclusive and I don't know if marriage will change him. He became accustomed to being alone as a child. His father has two chief interests, his estates and music, and when he visited Venosa or Gesualdo, he naturally took Luigi with him, Luigi being his heir. As Carlo was gifted at music, he shared his father's musical life. Francesco was often away with Luigi, and I have my work, which I'm eager to tell you about, so Carlo grew up largely in a world of his own. Of course now he must visit the estates with his father, but when he's here at San Severo he practically lives in these rooms. He even takes his meals here.'

Maria was not as disappointed by these words as Geronima had feared she might be. For the first time in her life, it seemed that she, too, would be mistress of a world of her own.

The door to Carlo's bedroom was ajar and they entered it. Shelves of books lined the walls between tall cupboards with innumerable doors and drawers. Maria longed to open them and inspect their contents. The large uncurtained bed was covered with a thick bearskin rug. Maria ran her hands over the fur, soft as a kitten. Above the bed was a large wooden cross with a wonderfully expressive gilt figure of Christ. It was tortured, elongated, strange; the rippling muscles pronounced, the body savagely contorted, the Saviour's eyes ecstatically raised to heaven. Maria shuddered involuntarily, her eyes moving to the number of items on a large table next to the bed: a candelabrum with fresh candles, a neat stack of books, an open book, a glass goblet, a carafe of wine, a sword, a small arquebus, some sheets of paper, a quill pen, pots of ink, shells on a silver platter, a couple of pen drawings of a garden, one with a grotto, and a knife with a handle fashioned in the form of Mercury with his winged helmet. Maria lingered near this table, fascinated with its contents and the glimpse they offered into Carlo's mind. What was he reading? She turned over the open book to look at its cover—Vitruvius's *De architectura*—and then carefully left it as it had been.

'I see Carlo is interested in architecture,' she said to Geronima.

'Yes, he likes to find correspondences between architecture and music. And he's designing a garden at Gesualdo Castle. You'll see it soon.'

At the end of a long passage, they briefly explored another room stacked with paintings and objects. Carlo also liked to collect things. One door in this passage led down to the music rooms via steep stairs. Another opened onto the main staircase, and the one opposite it to a narrow back staircase. There was a fourth door. Maria turned the handle. It was locked. 'What's in here?' she asked.

'That was Carlo's schoolroom when he was a child.' Geronima shrugged. 'I've no idea what he uses it for now.'

'How mysterious,' said Maria. 'I wonder why he keeps it locked.'

'Oh, he probably keeps some of his instruments or equipment in there. Carlo's always liked his little secrets. I shouldn't bother about it if I were you. Shall we go back to your apartment and have a little talk? It'll be time for us to go downstairs soon.'

The two women sat in Maria's new salon. Geronima Gesualdo was not as Maria had expected. Though she had visited San Severo numerous times, both as a child and as Federigo's wife, she'd barely seen Geronima, so she'd imagined her to be aloof. She was, however, proving to be amiable. Geronima was related to the most powerful man in Rome: Pope Pius IV was her uncle. Cardinal Carlo Borromeo—whom many considered destined for sainthood—had been her brother. Maria had consequently presumed that Geronima would radiate piety and devoutness—she had in fact imagined her as a more ethereal version of her own mother—but this was not proving to be the case. Geronima was busy, not aloof, and her piety was expressed not by a devout demeanour, but in a more practical way by doing good works. She had founded, she was now telling Maria, a refuge for abandoned pregnant girls and babies. A friend, one of several she'd persuaded to become benefactors, had recently donated his rather shabby but serviceable villa in the Spanish quarter. She hoped Maria would become interested in this work. Not yet, of course, but when she had settled into marriage and begun to know Carlo better.

Whoever ate at Carlo Gesualdo's table judged the food exquisite. The fare at his wedding banquet was of a far different order to the rich dishes served at the d'Avalos household. Carlo's was simply cooked, and its succulence relied not on complex sauces, many ingredients and elaborate preparation, but on the freshest of ingredients. Though the servants had been preparing for the banquet for days, the seafood, game and various kinds of fowl had been delivered only that morning, the servants having arisen before dawn. The quantities of food kept them frantically busy until that evening, for there were five hundred guests to feed, and of oysters alone there were four thousand. The art of this banquet resided not in dishes intricately prepared, but in the drama of its presentation.

The baronial banquet hall had a cross-vaulted ceiling and a hooded fireplace at one end. On the walls were frescoes of dead game stretched out on tables amidst baskets of vegetables and fruit. Along these walls stretched real white damask-covered tables, laden with silver salvers and porcelain platters heaped with all manner of culinary delights: fish and shellfish from the Bay of Naples with parsley and slices of lemon; one hundred and twenty grilled baby goats, hundreds of stuffed quail on skewers, trussed fowls, mountains of veal steaks and processions of sliced cold meats.

The few cooked dishes included eels in tomato sauce, *parmigiana da melazane*, timbales, the garnished rice mould *Satu di Risu* and soft gorgonzola pastries. Pomegranates, grapes, fleshy figs and apricots were arranged with their branches and leaves. The centrepiece of the main table was a turkey pie presented in the scooped-out corpse of a turkey, artfully stuffed as if still alive, its feathers fanned and its beak delicately holding a rose. The frescoes and the laid tables set up a dynamic movement between depicted and real food; this was a spectacle to be contemplated as well as eaten.

It was growing dark outside and when the guests began arriving, the servants lit the candles so that in the warm half-light the glazes and various textures of the food, the chased and carved designs on glasses and platters, sprang into life. The bridal table, which formed a T at the far end of the room, was festooned with garlands of fresh flowers.

The musicians in the adjoining ballroom took up their instruments and the ceremony of the one hundred and twenty-five courses began. The guests, assisted by red-liveried servants, helped themselves from the tables. As the night wore on they spilled into the ballroom.

Carlo performed an odd little ritual as he ate. Maria had noticed this at their betrothal banquet, but today he did it more often as he was eating more. Whenever he was about to pick up his glass to sip wine, he placed a napkin over his plate, covering his food. She remarked on this, asking him why he did it. 'It's a Spanish custom,' he replied. 'My ancestors hated the Spanish but over time they developed a liking for certain of their habits.'

'And who taught you to cover your food?' she asked.

'I don't remember. My grandfather perhaps. I've always done it, and the reason I do it is because I like doing it. Rituals add dignity to life.'

'What other rituals do you engage in?' asked Maria. 'Will you require me to participate in any of them?'

'No. They're personal. I always practise music for at least an hour and a half each day. That, too, is a ritual, although it's also a necessary part of self-discipline.'

'I'd imagined playing music would always be pleasurable for you.'

'It is. Discipline is not always associated with an onerous sense of duty. It can also be what one most looks forward to each day.'

She studied his face, its skin so youthful, its expression much older. The shape of his lips was sensual but they were narrow, as if his sensual nature was something he also kept within disciplinary bounds. He was in a very different mood tonight to the loquacious Carlo of their betrothal banquet.

'You are quiet tonight,' she commented, wishing their conversation to take a more intimate turn.

He cast his eyes around the large room, crowded with hundreds of guests. 'I detest large gatherings. A thousand harsh noises come together in a cacophonous muffle and it grates on my senses.'

'What about your concerts? Don't you sometimes play to a large audience?'

'Yes, but anyone who comes to a San Severo concert knows he must be absolutely quiet when we play.'

'I remember coming here when you were a young boy.'

'I remember you, too.' he responded.

'How did I strike you then?' she asked.

'I'll tell you exactly.' He turned in his chair to meet her eyes directly. 'Your presence was as light as a feather as if your feet did not touch the ground. You were removed, utterly removed, from the day-to-day world, as if you saw only what you wished to see. You seemed so happy and so distant from the cares of the world that it seemed to me, even at the age of ten or eleven, that life held in store for you a terrible blow to force you back down to earth.'

'Oh, it did,' she murmured. 'And what of you? Has life dealt you any of its blows?'

'Yes. Luigi's death.'

'Were you close to your brother?'

'Not especially. Not in the sense that we spent a great deal of time together. But he was a vital part of the mechanism that allows the Gesualdo family to run so smoothly. I regarded him as a younger version of my father, whom he resembled. He was born to princely duties; I was not. His destiny as heir always seemed inevitable to me, and desirable, because it left me free to be as I am.'

Carlo turned his attention to a servant who'd come up behind him and Maria ran her eyes over the guests at their bridal table. Out of the corner of her eye, she had noticed Carlo's uncle, Don Giulio Gesualdo, who sat diagonally opposite her. His high forehead, dark-ringed eyes and overripe underlip gave him a saturnine look. His attention was so riveted on Maria he failed to notice that the food he shovelled through his fleshy lips occasionally dribbled down his front. Loath to endure this silent pantomime of gluttony and lust any longer, Maria addressed him, asking, 'Do you still have an interest in science, Don Giulio?'

Don Giulio's name would always be associated with one of the few attempts to set up a court of the Inquisition in Naples. In 1571 a terrifying trial had taken place, it being alleged that several noblemen were practitioners of witchcraft. In the course of the trial it was revealed that the central protaganist of these activities was Don Giulio. The accused were found guilty and sentenced to terrible punishments before being burned at the stake. No sentence, however, was pronounced against Don Giulio. He was not even interrogated. Many considered this was due to his family links with the Vatican.

'Not so much these days, my enchanting one, although I still have a fascination with the inner workings of the human body. As you may have heard,' he lowered his voice, 'those who pursue scientific knowledge are in danger of being associated with the magic arts. Let me tell you a dark secret.' He beckoned a servant and, to Maria's dismay, indicated that an additional chair was to be placed next to hers so that he could sit beside her.

He squeezed himself in between her and her father, sitting so close that she could smell his meaty breath. 'It's our esteemed Church fathers who established the association between science and witchcraft. Diabolically clever of them, because science challenges the authority of the Church and they know it.'

Maria drew back, offended by his speaking of the Devil and the Church fathers in one breath.

'Putting such fear into people inhibits the growth of knowledge,' he went on. 'I might have had an apt pupil in young Carlo for he is interested in all manner of things and has an excellent mind.'

'I fear you are boring my wife, Uncle,' said Carlo. 'What does a beautiful woman care for such things?'

'Even beautiful women are curious about the secrets of life, as all humanity is,' said Don Giulio, dabbing at his mouth with a serviette.

Carlo rapped his long fingers loudly on the table and said sternly, 'I am telling you, Uncle, that this topic of conversation is not welcome at my table.'

'Forgive me, Carlo. Your wife's beauty so dazzles me I've forgotten my manners.'

'You've forgotten more than your manners,' said Carlo darkly.

'Then allow me to compensate by inviting the two of you to San Regale. I have something very interesting to show you, Carlo.' He turned to Maria and touched her arm, which caused her to flinch. 'And you, my enchanting niece.'

'We are just married and the only journeys we will make in the next few months are to Venosa and Gesualdo,' said Carlo irritably.

'It's an open invitation,' said Don Giulio. 'Come when you please.'

Carlo sighed exasperatedly. 'I esteem your persistence in matters of science, Uncle, as it brings rewards. It is not so rewarding, nor is it appropriate, in social situations.' He made an impatient flicking gesture as if he was warding off a mosquito. 'You are looking flushed, Maria. It seems you need more space and air about you.'

Don Giulio returned to his side of the table, not before giving Maria a surreptitious little wink.

Maria had had to endure the idiocies of lustful men before, but she found this man markedly unpleasant and prayed she'd not have to endure much of his company in the future. Carlo, thank God, didn't seem particularly fond of him either.

The music coming from the ballroom was measured and courtly and several people went in there to dance a slow bassa dance while others went on eating. The ball did not officially begin until Maria and Carlo had danced the *lavolta*, a form of galliard for couples. This was a new dance, and considered rather scandalous because the man held the woman intimately and lifted her into the air as they made a three-quarter turn. It was an exuberant dance not unlike ballet, enjoyable to perform and enjoyable to watch and, while some members of the clergy condemned it as a cause of pregnancy and divorce, it was the perfect dance for a wedding couple. It was becoming quite a sport because watching the bride and groom perform it gave those wedding guests who were interested in such things, and most were, a very clear picture of the degree to which the new couple were—or were not—attracted to each other.

In Carlo's arms Maria felt weightless; his body moved as if tuned to the rhythms of the music. He led her with such grace and easy confidence that she gave herself over to his strong clasp like a feather to the breeze, and they moved as one, smiling with the joy of the music and the movement. Maria found it exhilirating. The impression the guests received of the feelings Maria and Carlo had for each other was therefore a false one, although for Maria it had indeed been a heady experience and one which only added to her uncertainty about the true nature of Carlo's feelings for her.

He stayed by her side for most of the evening, because, she suspected, he considered it the correct thing to do, and also because Maria was not overly given to making conversation. She'd noticed he abhorred women who talked for the sake of talking, rudely walking away or turning his back on them mid-sentence, or avoiding them altogether. Now that the grand gestures of the evening were over and had proved a success, Carlo had retreated back into his interior world, a little deflated, a little melancholy. So they sat in silent companionship listening to the music and watching the others dance. People left them alone because they thought they were in love, and so in a sense they protected each other, she him from unwanted intrusion, and he her from exhausting rounds of dancing and chatter.

Later in the evening Geronima drew Maria into conversation with people she thought it important for her to meet, people who might prove useful to her given that she'd been away from Naples for so long, particularly in developing an intimate social circle of her own, one perhaps, suggested Geronima, in keeping with Maria's literary interests. Though she did not wish to push Maria regarding the shelter for pregnant girls, there were two people she did want her to meet in this regard. The first was the benefactor who had donated the villa, a crotchety old fellow who was exceedingly hard of hearing.

'What a kind heart you have,' Maria practically shouted in his ear, and as this was such a flattering thing for so beautiful a bride to take the trouble to say to him, as well as being the first remark he'd been able to comprehend all evening, he thereafter regarded Maria as a living allegory of compassion.

'You have a natural gift for handling such people, who can be difficult to persuade to be kind, believe me,' whispered Geronima. 'The amount of good you could do is immeasurable.'

This remark had a whiff of something that left Maria feeling vaguely repulsed, although she felt guilty at being offended at the idea of helping the unfortunate.

'I now wish you to meet someone very special,' said Geronima enthusiastically. 'She works very closely with me. By a strange coincidence, my colleague has exactly the same name as you yourself once had. Maria Carafa! Ah, there she is.'

A thin dark woman in grey silk that did nothing for her sallow complexion walked toward them. Unlike Geronima, she had the look of women who press themselves into doing good works. She might have been beautiful, for her bone structure was good, but there was a sourness to her. When Geronima introduced her as the Duchess of Andria, what then flashed into Maria's mind—'This is Fabrizio Carafa's wife!'—remained there, uppermost, as she listened to her new mother-in-law's enumeration of the woman's sterling qualities. Throughout this, the duchess looked at Maria with a tight little smile and something like recognition in her eyes.

'Forgive me for telling our lovely bride what a treasure you are,' said Geronima. 'I'm hoping to interest Maria in our good works, after she's settled into her marriage, of course.'

'Such work involves getting your hands dirty,' said the duchess, her eyes glancing down pointedly at Maria's delicate white hands with their sparkling rings.

So this was how it was to be between her and the Duchess of Andria. Maria's hackles rose. She'd spent so much of her childhood in the company of Aunt Antonia and her glittering circle of idle chatterers that she was well schooled in the art of rebuffing remarks of this kind by meeting them head-on. She lifted one of her little hands and stared at it in mock appraisal.

'I take your meaning,' she said, 'but I don't think Princess Geronima intends me to scrub floors.'

'Perhaps you did not take my meaning for I was speaking metaphorically,' replied the duchess coolly. 'We do the work of Our Lord and deal with the fallen. The souls we try to save are wretched. The squalor of their upbringing and the sordidness of their minds would no doubt be a great shock to you. One must school oneself in methods of overcoming one's horror at such moral filth and degradation, and that requires great strength of character.'

'I pray that you have not yet judged me incapable of such strength for you have only just met me,' responded Maria calmly, all the while thinking, How dare this woman speak to me in this fashion, this daughter of minor southern nobility whom everybody knows was wed to a Carafa only because of her robber-baron father's immense wealth!

'Maria's wedding night is not the best time to discuss these matters,' said Princess Geronima tactfully. 'I've something quite particular in mind for my lovely daughter-in-law when she is ready, which I'll tell you about when we next meet. Only let me tell you, dear Maria, that she is quite brilliant at handling certain kinds of people. I witnessed this myself just half an hour ago.' Geronima leaned toward the duchess and added in a lowered voice, 'I see your husband is in the clutches of that bore Spinotti, so perhaps you ought to go and rescue him.'

Maria graciously held out her hand in farewell to the duchess. 'It's been most instructive to meet you,' she smiled.

'May God bless you with as many healthy sons as He has me,' responded the duchess with a firm grip of her dry hand, and departed in the direction of her husband.

'My poor Maria,' breathed Geronima when she was out of earshot. 'Allow me to apologise for the duchess's rudeness to you, and on your wedding night too. As much as I admire her, I confess she's charmless. I believe it is because she is unhappy, so I ask you to forgive her. That handsome husband of hers causes her a great deal of suffering, they say, but I refuse to take sides as he's a good friend of Carlo's. I must congratulate you, for you handled her very cleverly and prettily. Ah, what a wonderful asset you are going to be to our family. Your family now, my dear.'

'How does her husband cause her to suffer?' Maria could not resist asking.

'I don't like to gossip, Maria. I am very fond of Fabrizio Carafa as I find him utterly charming, but as you ask and you are now my daughter, and as you will no doubt hear it soon enough from other lips, I will tell you that he is constantly unfaithful to her. Women simply lose their heads over him. It's case after case of *innamorto cotto*, they say. May God forgive me, but I have asked myself once or twice, with a humourless wife like poor Maria, who can blame him?'

To her dismay, Maria felt the blood rushing to her face as Geronima imparted this information. 'Where is Carlo?' she asked, rising on tiptoes and looking distractedly about the room. 'Can you see him?'

'You're fond of Carlo, aren't you, Maria?' said Geronima a little uncertainly, taking Maria's hand and studying her with large soulful eyes that were suddenly a little moist.

'Yes, I find him fascinating,' answered Maria, recognising that this was so only as she said it.

Maria sat in her bridal chamber, mystified. After two long days of ceaseless festivities she was also exhausted, and the prospect of carnal delights with her new husband was far less appealing than crawling under the flounced covers of the elaborate bed and sinking into sleep. Laura had just finished dressing her in a silken nightdress embroidered with little red and gold crowns like the one on the Gesualdo coat of arms. Maria had told the girl to go to bed, wishing to be alone for a few minutes.

She dabbed her face and neck with orange-water, hoping its astringency would evaporate her sleepiness. Then she sat in a little red velvet chair and looked about the room, still puzzling the meaning of its decoration. Her mother had insisted that Carlo was devout. Until now Maria had seen no evidence of this. There was the possibility that his religion was to him a very private matter. Geronima had, afterall, said that he was secretive. Was this room then an expression of his private devotional life, and did he expect her, as his wife, to participate in it? There seemed to be no other explanation.

It resembled a church interior rather than a bridal chamber. An altar glittered in the light of large quantities of candles; there were red kneeling-cushions and numerous cream silk coverings and hangings with ecclesiastical motifs. An enormous painting of the Annunciation hung above the bed, flanked by two large gold and mother-of-pearl crosses. Incense burned in bowls decorated with rings of angels.

Finally succumbing to this ambience, Maria knelt on one of the cushions and begged the Virgin, who smiled beatifically down upon her, to bring grace to her first encounter with Carlo in their marriage bed. And pleasure, she added guiltily.

And this was how Carlo found her when he entered the room with a young priest. If she had been acquainted with the complexities of Carlo's mind, which at this stage she hadn't an inkling of, she could not have chosen a more appropriate posture for him to discover her in on their wedding night. The sight of her immediately transported him to that place he'd hoped to find himself in this night, but had had little confidence in reaching. He could now most definitely associate the matrimonial ritual he was required to perform with the idea of it being sacred. He, too, had been praying. He sank down on the cushion opposite hers. The young priest knelt between them, took their hands and joined them together and began intoning Latin phrases to the effect that fruit would soon spring forth from their holy union. Carlo's eyes looked not at Maria but at the delicate face of the priest. He was a handsome young man but there was something in his air that Maria found objectionable. His manner suggested a familiarity with Carlo. There seemed in fact to be some sort of silent communion between them. No doubt he was Carlo's confessor. She closed her eyes to shut out the sight of the man and concentrated on the warmth of Carlo's long fingers enclosing her small hand. Through the aroma of incense she detected another smell, a strangely pleasant one like dark crushed violets. The singsong intoning ceased and the young priest stood.

'You may go now,' said Carlo to him. 'Turn back the bed and snuff out the candles.'

The priest did so and quit the room. In a series of elegant movements that seemed dreamlike in the dark, Carlo lifted her and took her to their bed and it was there she discovered that the mysterious violet perfume, intoxicating as love, sensual as a caress, emanated from him, from his dark soft hair.

The next afternoon, the courtyard of Palazzo San Severo was transformed into an arena encircled by tiers of seated spectators. Some of the guests crowded at opened upper windows. The ladies had had their balls and tournaments; now it was time for some real sport.

A few years previously, Pope Pius V had outlawed animal baiting and introduced severe penalties for it, but it was so entrenched in Neapolitan society—and that of many other parts of Europe—that it continued nevertheless and was inevitably a feature of Maria and Carlo's wedding festivities.

Maria and Carlo made their way to seats in front of the stand. Carlo, in a relaxed, affable mood, made brief comments to guests as they passed. After they were seated, Maria expected some sign of warmth from him after their intimacy of the night before, a touch of the hand, a smile, but there was nothing. Folding his hands loosely in his lap, his eyes roved over the spectators, the animal-baiting ring and the noisy guests leaning out of the windows above. She put her hand gently over his and smiled at him. He looked down at her hand, removed his and scratched the bridge of his nose. So, she thought, hurt by his action, the hours we share in my bed are to be a world apart, with no continuance in our daily life beyond. The previous night, she'd sensed him striving to reach a transcendent state and, sensitive to this, she'd tried to guide him, but he'd quietened her movements and become engrossed in his own, determined that his sensations alone would lead him there. She'd relinquished her instinct to soar with him and settled back into passive enjoyment, albeit pleasurable enough in its way. There was time enough to school him.

'One of the most bizarre things I ever saw,' a man sitting above her was telling his lady companion, 'was an ape riding on a horse chased by dogs.'

'Really? What happened?' asked the lady.

'It was a very smart ape. It waited its advantage and leapt into a tree as the horse galloped underneath. Then it teased the dogs, and had a fine time leaping and swinging in the branches, shrieking and pulling faces at them. But it got too cocky and they got it in the end.'

A hush suddenly fell over the audience as a bear's cage was wheeled in and the end of the bear's chain looped over a tall iron stake. The cage door was opened and the keepers waited until the creature emerged and then fled, carrying the cage between them.

The bear padded forward as far as the chain would allow, then delighted the onlookers by standing on her hind legs and surveying the crowd. She was a tall and splendid bear, quite young and in good condition, with a pale, honey-coloured coat that made rippling motions above her darker under-fur as she moved.

Maria was fascinated. In the folktales she'd had read to her as a child, bears were hostile but gentle figures. And looking at this bear and the way she was taking measure of the situation she found herself in, Maria began to understand why humanoid qualities like bravery and endurance were attributed to bears, and why in heraldry they were associated with fierce protection of their kindred. But she failed to see why vanity and lust, even misanthropy and evil power, were also conferred upon them.

The bear dropped back on all fours and, jerking her neck and pulling on her chain, padded in a circle around the stake, searching for a way out.

The crowd watched in silence, captivated by both her creaturely nature and the humanness of her gestures. She began rattling the chain and tugging on it in frustration, and the audience laughed and jeered at the sight of this awesome creature reduced to an object of ridicule.

The yapping and baying started up before the dogs were led to the outside of the arena, for they could smell the bear. She tugged frantically on the chain, sniffing the air, and rose on her hind legs and roared. The arena vibrated with the wild sound and the crowd thrilled to it. The clamouring mastiffs strained on their leashes.

'I must confess, I don't like this,' said another woman at the back.

'Be grateful it's a bear and not a bull,' said her companion. 'Why, in Ferrara last year, a bull speared a dog with its horn and tossed it into the air, and the bleeding hound with its guts spilling out landed plumb in my friend Evangelina's lap. Her gown was quite ruined.'

Maria didn't like it either. How did these men of her circle—and they were mostly men who enjoyed these rude, cruel sports—reconcile their bloodlust with Saint Francis's teachings about the holiness of all God's creatures? She'd avoided animal baitings in the past, but she was compelled to watch this one. Oh that she could be like Beatrice and refuse to attend. 'You must prevent them killing the bear,' Beatrice had said to her that morning. 'It's your wedding, *you* are the queen of the day, so *you* are in command. You must not allow them to kill it,' she'd insisted, stamping her foot.

'They won't kill it. They'll tease it, and perhaps hurt it a little, but Carlo tells me this is a sport about the cunning and strength of the bear, and the perseverance and boldness of the dogs. The bear is far stronger than the dogs. And you must remember that this is Carlo's wedding, too. I can't anger him by interfering with his pleasures.'

A few moments ago, Beatrice had been at one of the windows: she had been unable to resist seeing the bear. But at the entrance of the dogs, she'd vanished.

Behind the barrier, a holder was having trouble restraining one of the dogs; its lustful gaze was riveted on the bear and it tugged and strained on its leash with all its might.

'That's Nero,' said Carlo proudly to Maria, pointing at the dog. 'He's my best hunting dog, a real strategist. He'll soon be in the ring and you'll see how intelligent he is.'

Maria began to feel nauseous at this piece of news.

Three of the dogs were released. They leapt over the barrier and circled the bear and crouched, eyeing her and eyeing each other. The bear swayed on her hind legs and let out a terrible roar, her pink eyes watching them. A young, inexperienced dog, trembling with excitement, bared its teeth in a growl and sprang at the bear. She saw it coming and with a mighty swipe sent it sailing in a yipping arc to the barrier fence. It landed with a crunching thud. The other two dogs leapt snarling and biting at the bear's stomach and brought her down, but she'd cleverly swivelled her body so that she fell on one of them, trapping it under her weight while she clawed and kicked at the other dog. The crowd roared with laughter at the trapped dog, its body splayed beneath the bear, its whimpering face appearing from under her. Its owner, one of Carlo's hunting companions, was mortified.

Three more dogs were released into the ring. They sprang on the bear with fur bristling and, as the flattened dog dragged itself out of reach, the four animals rolled in a furious ball. It seemed to Maria that the biting and clawing, the rattling of the chain, the roaring and snarling, tossing and tumbling, would never end. It went on and on, fur flying, the bear's pale coat turning pink with her own blood and the blood and slaver of the dogs. The dogs were all mouth and fangs, whereas the bear had razor claws as well, and the ability to kick, punch and swipe. She fought the four ferocious dogs valiantly and at last two were out of the fray. One had been punched senseless and another had lost an eye; blood streamed from the gaping hole in its head. The teeth of a third dog sunk into the bear's flank and locked there. The bear roared out with pain and distress. She managed to rise on her hind legs and endeavoured to free herself of the animal, twisting and punching at it while trying to keep the fourth one at bay. But the dog, which because she had risen was practically dangling in the air, had a vicelike grip on her. The bear shook her head and droplets of blood and sweat flew from her. Her pink eyes were beginning to glaze over with pain; she breathed in short huffs; she was growing exhausted. The silly young dog she had first felled had recovered itself and limped back. It crouched waiting like a jackal to pounce.

Carlo's dog was released and it flashed into the ring. The movement distracted the fourth dog and the bear lashed out and swiftly dealt with it. Now she could contend with this new dog. It slowly circled her with a slinking sideways motion, and then it crouched, silently, never taking its eyes off her.

Maria could feel Carlo next to her, so tense with expectation that he was almost rising out of his seat. Feeling sick to her stomach, and terrified she was going to retch, she stole a glance at him, but his expression was impenetrable as his eyes slid backwards and forwards from the bear to his favourite dog. The bear, forgetting the searing pain of the jaws that were still locked into her flank, drew on a hidden reserve of strength as she roared low at the newcomer. She seemed to sense that if she could fell this black devil of a dog she would be triumphant. All of a sudden she lunged at it in a surprise attack and would have been upon the black dog and perhaps triumphed had she not slipped in a pool of her own blood. Carlo's dog was at her throat before her head hit the ground. The crowd murmured and rose as one, eager to witness the spectacle of life giving way to death. This took some moments as the great bear clawed at the black dog, causing it to slacken its grip and bury its teeth in again, and again, so that by the time the bear's eyes finally stared at death the dog had made a feast of her throat.

This sickening display of wanton cruelty was intensified for Maria by her dread at having to tell Beatrice that the bear had been killed. Since her daughter's frightening illness at Ischia, Maria had watched her closely for signs of melancholy, but there had been no nightmares, no fits of despair or hysteria. Beatrice's mind was strong and it appeared she'd put the frightful episode behind her. Still, she was also sensitive to the sufferings of others, and she adored animals, so Maria was apprehensive of what the bear's death might trigger.

When Maria returned to her apartment later that afternoon her daughter was waiting for her, as she'd known she would be. At the sight of the distress on her mother's face, Beatrice's own serious little face crumpled and she fled the salon. Maria stood in the middle of the room as one stunned for several minutes, a tear spilling down her cheek as she listened to the sobs emanating from her daughter's room and Sylvia's clucking noises as she tried to comfort the child.

Five

MARRIAGE TO GESUALDO

In the following weeks, the pattern of their days was established. Geronima had been correct: marriage did not make Carlo less reclusive. Within the large palace he and Maria led virtually separate lives, he in his rooms or in the music room with his musicians, and she in the women's apartment reading or writing, and going out to attend church services or to visit her family, especially Antonia who often had a lively circle of friends at her palace.

Carlo's habits were eccentric. He did not rise until the afternoon, sometimes as late as four-thirty if he wasn't practising with his musicians. As Maria often retired as early as eight, whole days would pass in which they did not see each other. She sometimes wished for a greater intimacy with Carlo, her ideal being the model set by her first marriage where she and Federigo had been friends as well as husband and wife. Still, she welcomed the dramatic contrast with marriage to Alfonso. An absence of warmth and intimacy was far preferable to every minute of her day being supervised. At last she had the freedom of mind she'd craved, and she must soon, she told herself, devise ways of passing her time more fruitfully. She was sympathetic to Carlo centring his life around music, for his talent and scholarship were clearly exceptional and Maria admired gifted people. He could not pass an evening without it, and the faint strains of his lute or cembalo from the floor below gave her a vague sense of companionship. They even took their meals separately. Sometimes she welcomed being alone but there were evenings when she craved intelligent company. Carlo was unwilling to relinquish his long habit of eating his evening meal in bed, undressed, having himself served in a very grand way with little Spanish ceremonies—the lighted torch brought in before the cup, covering his plate while he drank—attended by a waiter, his valet Pietro, and the priest, Alessandro. This young man, with his overrefined features and haughty manner, was a special favourite of Carlo's, for as well as being his personal priest and confessor, he was a musician who played the viol de gamba well. Maria disliked him intensely, why exactly she couldn't say, other than the fact that his presence in her bedchamber on her wedding night had offended and mystified her. But these days she rarely saw him.

The only change to this daily pattern was when Carlo disappeared for days on end with his father to attend to business at his estates at Venosa or Gesualdo, or to go hunting with his companions at gli Astruni, fifty miles south of Naples.

Maria began to know her husband. Whatever Carlo was feeling was reflected in his eyes and Carlo felt things intensely. If he was happy, he was exuberant and his eyes shone with secret amusement. If he was angry, it was rage or cold fury. If it was scorn, it was biting, annihilating contempt. This intensity also took the form of a masklike demeanour when he chose to hide his emotions from others, and this was when people were most afraid of him.

Late one night, three weeks after their wedding, he came immediately to her bedchamber on his return from a hunting trip. He'd not changed his clothes or washed, which she considered indelicate of him. He was in a mood of quietly suppressed excitement, which in turn aroused her, so she determined to overlook the smell of his sweat, the bloodstain on the cuff of his shirt. Yet within moments she sensed that he sought sexual gratification not because he was aroused by the sight and nearness of her, but by something extraneous to her, something that had occurred before his appearance in her room. She had an unpleasant suspicion that it was the thrill of the hunt, the intensity of emotion he experienced when slaughtering animals, so she gave herself up to his caresses with a desire edged by a faint feeling of nausea.

He made a ritual of their coupling, before he touched her dabbing oil from a little phial onto her breasts, and she wondered if it was this smell of musk obtained from the horns of elks rather than the allure of her body that drew his lips to her flesh. Since their wedding night she'd allowed Carlo to guide their lovemaking, as he liked to command, and she'd taken only a passive pleasure in his movements. She'd lately come to realise, however, that things were as Antonia had once said they would be: that the only real power she would ever have over Carlo was in the bedroom. It was time to bring into play the accomplishments taught her by Federigo, unpractised during her marriage to Alfonso but by no means forgotten. Being a lover of refinements, Carlo smiled at her arts, responded to her deft caresses. She lulled him into the calm waters of sensations that were merely tinglingly pleasurable, lingering with him there, and then she began steering him toward passionate abandonment, believing she had beguiled him at last. Suddenly he stopped moving and unexpectedly withdrew. 'Are you attempting to suffocate me?' he asked coldly as he flopped onto his back beside her. She pummelled the pillow and wept in frustration, and he silently got up and left the room.

As the weeks passed, the infrequent nights on which Carlo mounted the spiral staircase to her room followed a similar pattern. Their encounters brought both of them a pleasure of sorts, but there was no real intimacy to them. There was between them no secret amorous world of the kind that lovers create for themselves, as she had hoped there might be. Just as it was in Carlo's nature to elevate the refinements of life to an art form in his household—food, music, the decoration of the rooms—so it was with his lovemaking. For him it was a kind of ballet, an elegant choreography of practised movements with exquisite passages, but which was at its heart mechanical. The pleasure he gave Maria left her craving for more, as it did not sate her: there was neither affection nor joy nor laughter. On the map of his relations with her so carefully charted by him, uncontrolled passion was a place that did not exist. He was never there the next morning, and so it became a secret longing of hers to lie with him in the fur-covered bed in his room below the spiral staircase. She was too proud to ask him to take her there, for she knew what the answer would be. In her secret heart she came to regard his unspoken insistence on controlling their sexual relations as a subtle form of tyranny.

Still, there were aspects of the marriage that pleased Maria, more so as time wore on. She experienced a new freedom. For the first time what she did with herself during the day was not circumscribed by the lives of others. At first it was both liberating and a little frightening that she could do as she pleased. Whole days yawned ahead of her. As the weeks passed she learned to fill them with personal interests and in so doing discovered parts of herself, latent until then, that began to grow. As Costanza d'Avalos had always interested her, she one day had a boat take her across to Ischia. There she gathered many of Costanza's things and began to amuse herself, desultorily at first, by beginning to chronicle her great-aunt's extraordinary life.

Maria was inevitably drawn into San Severo's world of music. This comforted her because it brought her closer to Carlo, although her participation in the meticulous preparations for concerts at the palace was instigated not by him but by his father, Prince Francesco. Princess Geronima, too, began taking an interest at last because she enjoyed Maria's company. Maria's happiest evenings were spent sitting with Carlo and his parents in their comfortable salon with the soft yellow walls and old Venetian mirrors, drawing up lists of who to invite, and discussing the programme, the guest performers, the refreshments, the flowers and myriad details. Unlike the ones that followed, however, the first such gathering was not a happy one.

Spring had arrived and the weather was warm but Geronima liked the crackling company of a fire in the evenings, so after a light fish supper, they sat around a square table at a distance from the flames and set to work.

'Look over this guest list, Carlo. There may be others you wish to invite,' said Prince Francesco, handing his son a thick sheet of paper covered with his spidery hand.

Carlo ran his eyes over the list and said, 'I hear Luciola Facetti from Parma is visiting Naples. He's the only one I wish to add. He's staying with the Colonnas so the invitation can be sent there.'

'Who's on the list?' asked Geronima. 'Let me look at it, Carlo.'

Carlo passed it to her and turned his attention to the programme he was preparing.

'Maria, you have a nice hand. Would you like to write the invitations and attend to sending them out?' asked Prince Francesco.

'Yes, I'd be happy to,' said Maria, pleased to be asked to do something useful.

'Do you use this list for every concert?' asked Geronima. 'It contains only the names of the people you always invite.'

'Yes, it's our master list,' replied Prince Francesco.

'Why ask the same old people?'

'Who else would we invite?' Prince Francesco lowered his spectacles and frowned at his wife over the top of them. 'They are the cream of Naples' music lovers and connoisseurs, and the patrons of our composers.'

'Why not introduce a few fresh faces?' suggested Geronima.

Prince Francesco's frown deepened. 'Who, for example?' he challenged.

Geronima made a show of considering this for a moment before cheerfully replying, 'I'm certain Princess Lucrezia Rosetti would enjoy the concert very much.'

Carlo, who'd been scribbling annotations on his programme, looked up at his mother sharply, while his father blinked at her as if she'd lost her wits. 'What are you suggesting?' he asked. 'The woman has no interest in music whatsoever. Her only passion is dining.'

'I assure you music does interest her. You don't know her as I do.'

'And I thank God for it. The sight of her gargantuan form and countless chins repels me.'

'A love of food does not discount a love of music. Princess Lucrezia is wealthy, so naturally she's devoted to all the finer things of life.'

'Oh yes, I can recall numerous elegant conversations with her,' sneered Francesco sarcastically.

'*You* recall a conversation! Huh!' scoffed Geronima. 'You never listen to a thing anyone says! I insist we invite her.'

'I'm hearing you now, believe me. I've never known you to have a sense of humour and it seems you're making a belated attempt to develop one. An inept one I might add, for your suggestion that we invite that bloated toad entertains none of us.'

The long-married couple relished hurling these insults at each other and Maria found it amusing. She noticed that Carlo, however, had begun drumming his fingers on the table irritably.

'An appreciation of music doesn't only exist in the rarefied musical Parnassus of your imagining,' sniggered Geronima.

'What do you know of Parnassus or music?' countered Francesco.

Carlo's right eyelid began to twitch. He seemed to Maria to be smouldering with anger. She watched his long fingers move to the stem of a glass goblet.

'The entire table for the evening will be crammed into that voracious mouth of hers,' continued Francesco. 'Your taste in guests is as delicate as her appetite.'

Carlo studied the wall behind his mother as he grasped the goblet's stem and thoughtfully caressed its bowl with his thumb.

'She'll be invited whether you like it or not,' shouted Geronima. 'There are other considerations in this world beside your unmanly obsession with delicacy. The purpose of refinement is only to—'

Maria watched in horror at Carlo picked up the goblet and hurled it at his mother. It sailed over her head and smashed against the Venetian mirror on the wall behind her, causing the mirror to crack. Maria realised that although Carlo had acted in rage, he'd calculated the result: he'd carefully aimed the goblet just above his mother's head. His parents, however, thought his intention had been to fling it directly into her face.

Tinkling reverberated in the shocked silence that ensued.

Geronima looked at him in horror, while the old prince covered his face with his hands and sighed deeply.

'Explain to me why you wish to invite that fat trollop to one of my concerts,' said Carlo, his voice dangerously calm.

'How dare you do such a thing to your mother!' breathed Geronima, shaken, her hands to her breast. 'Apologise or I—'

'If you can provide me with a sufficiently good reason as to why you wish to insult me, my father, our musicians and our guests with the presence of that sow, then I will apologise to you.'

Geronima stared back at him, speechless.

'I wish to know,' persisted Carlo. 'You never do anything without good reason and I can't even guess at the reason for your sudden affection for a woman who, strangely enough, happens to be one of the very few people I have ever heard you ridicule. So you must enlighten me.'

Silence. Geronima made to leave the table. The old prince put his hand on her arm, saying, 'I deplore our son's behaviour, Geronima, and am determined he will apologise to you, so please tell us your reasons. I, too, am curious to know.'

Carlo had a sudden flash of insight. 'Do you see her as being of benefit in some way?' he asked coldly.

Geronima reluctantly sat back down. 'Yes, I do,' she admitted. 'I know you think only of music and measure the success of our concerts solely in these terms.' She addressed her husband, her pride refusing to allow her to look at Carlo. ' But San Severo's concerts could also support me in doing God's work. I propose that now and again we invite one or two people who might be persuaded to contribute to my charity. Princess Lucrezia is immensely rich and her life is wasted in idleness. Where is the harm if our forthcoming concert provides an opportunity for asking her to see the wisdom in relieving the sufferings of others?'

Prince Francesco glanced at Carlo, glanced at Maria, and raised his eyes heavenward. Carlo calmed down and looked to be considering the matter. 'Very well, Mother, I apologise,' he said at last. 'The idea itself is not objectionable, although I tell you that the fat princess is. I will not subject our concerts to ridicule with her presence. Surely you can propose potential donors that would be acceptable to our guests as well as yourself.'

Things may eventually have settled down and they might have gone on with their planning had not Geronima unwisely added, 'What about Prince Colonna? I'm sure one little heartfelt plea from Maria, a mere sentence, would persuade him.'

'Whatever do you mean?' asked Carlo sharply.

Geronima then described the role she envisaged for Maria in all of this. Oh, dear God, no, pounded in Maria's head as she listened to her mother-in-law, whose judgement of people, she now realised, was beginning to be affected by her passion to do good. Maria had planned not to tell Carlo any of this, as it was unnecessary; had she agreed to assist Geronima in the future, she might have quietly done so without his ever knowing. She was annoyed at Geronima, for it seemed to Maria a betrayal of confidence, particularly as she was only considering the matter and had not agreed to it.

Carlo was staring at his mother in disbelief. He glanced at Maria and, barely perceptibly, raised his eyebrows inquiringly. She frowned and gave a little shrug. He looked back at his mother as if he might throw something else at her.

'So, Mother, you propose to prostitute my wife, to exploit her beauty and grace to obtain money and property for lowlifes. No. Never. Let me explain to you why. Your good work does you proud. Your asking men, and they are mostly men, for sponsorship involves no loss of your dignity, for people think of you as the niece of *Il Papa*. Besides, you are long past the age of being desired by men.' Carlo was growing pale as he spoke, his breathing becoming laboured. 'Maria is not, and her soliciting donations on your behalf would place her in . . .' He coughed and concentrated on breathing in short gasps, 'situations that threaten her dignity and her honour. I will not allow my wife to be so demeaned. Do you understand me, Mother?' He closed his eyes and gripped the edge of the table, wheezing, his chest rising and falling heavily.

'Yes, Carlo,' said Geronima, alarmed.

'The matter is closed. We'll speak no more about it,' said the old prince, rising. He rang a little bell and a servant appeared. 'Fetch Pietro. Tell him to bring his master's medicine, quickly. Send Anna in here. Run!' he ordered.

'What is it?' Maria cried, tears springing into her eyes. 'What's the matter with you, Carlo?'

Geronima gestured for her to be quiet.

Carlo, clutching his chest, looked at her. Perspiration beaded his face. 'Asthma,' he managed to say. In a desperate effort to breathe he stood up and his chair fell backwards.

'Be calm, Carlo,' said Geronima, moving around the table toward him and indicating that the prince and Maria should leave the room. 'Pietro will be here in a minute. You'll soon be able to breathe properly.' She took his arm and steered him toward a divan.

At the door, Maria almost collided with the servant girl, Anna. 'Fetch some boiling water and a bowl. Quickly,' ordered the prince.

Maria stood outside the door, wringing her hands helplessly. Francesco took her arm and led her into another room. 'Don't worry, Maria. Carlo will be himself tomorrow. These attacks come upon him out of the blue, sometimes when he's upset, sometimes when he's perfectly good humoured.' They sat down together. 'We've never been able to discover what causes them, but he always recovers so you mustn't lie awake all night worrying.'

Maria shivered. 'You're cold, Maria. Shall we go up to your apartment? They keep your fires going up there, don't they?'

She nodded, her teeth chattering. She heard one servant, then another, go into the salon where Carlo was.

'Let's wait a few minutes. I must know if he's regained his breath,' she whispered. Though she could not say as much to the old prince, it seemed that death once again hovered near someone close to her and it filled her with panic.

'We can't go back in there, Maria. Any unexpected movement or sound only aggravates his condition. Pietro and Geronima will be in there with him for hours. They stay with him even after he's fallen asleep when these attacks come on. You must be sensible and believe me when I tell you that he will be all right. We will go upstairs now.' He rose and offered her his arm.

Though the fire in Maria's salon was blazing, her teeth were still chattering after they'd been sitting in front of it for ten minutes. Hoping to warm her, and fearing she might be becoming ill, the prince had Sylvia send down for a steaming concoction of lemon, sugar and spirits.

Maria's hands were shaking and she was barely able to drink it through her chattering teeth, so Francesco spoon-fed it to her. Sylvia, hovering by solicitously, made as if to take over this task and the old prince shot her an irritable, dismissive look. For the first time, Maria saw Carlo in his father and it made her laugh. She went on laughing, her shoulders shaking, tears streaming down her face.

'You're becoming hysterical, Maria. Stop this shaking and laughing and carrying on. You're not a child. I thought you were more sensible. Drink this down now or I'll lose my temper with you. You're as bad as Carlo. You all drive me mad with your nerves and your tempers and your twitching.' He held the cup to her lips. 'Drink it. All of it,' he insisted.

Maria gulped it down, nearly choking.

The alcohol soon had its effect. She relaxed back in her chair and stared into the fire.

'Can't you please go down and see what's happening?' she asked, her green eyes pleading. 'You could open the door very softly and just peep in.'

The prince sighed, murmured something under his breath, and left the room.

He was gone a very long time. His apartment was right over on the far side of the palace, three floors down, and she calculated how long it should take him to go there and return by picturing in her mind his every step, allowing for time spent in the room where Carlo was. She imagined the scene there, the hushed conversation. She pictured Carlo's face as it had been when he'd clutched the edge of the table, gasping for breath. She imagined him lying on the couch gasping for breath. She pictured him throwing the glass, wondering, terrified, if he'd put a curse on himself by breaking the mirror. She imagined him stretched out on the sofa, dead, the figures of Geronima and the old prince bent over him in grief. What would she do if Carlo, too, died? No. No. It was unthinkable.

Then she began again, the steps there, and the steps back, counting far more slowly this time, although the prince, like Carlo, walked very quickly. It was almost impossible to keep up with Carlo when they walked anywhere together. She practically had to run. She pictured Carlo striding along the street in the long black overcoat he always wore when he went out, an eccentrically long coat that reached to his feet and which he always wore tightly buttoned up, as if to shield himself from something, God knows what. Sometimes he even wore it indoors. The inner door opened, and Maria started up. But it was only Sylvia.

'If you say anything, Sylvia, I'll throw this jug at you,' she said, reaching for it. Sylvia stepped back out and shut the door. Maria poured herself another cup of the lemon drink, tepid by now, and swallowed its contents. She began the count again and completed the imagined journey for the third time. The prince still had not returned. She rose, unable to bear the waiting any longer.

As she staggered down the stairs she encountered Francesco on his way up.

'Carlo's perfectly all right. I stood near the door where he couldn't see me and waited until he was breathing normally, so that I could reassure you that he's recovered and all is well. You've evidently had some more of that lemon drink. Good. You'll sleep well. Now I'll take you back upstairs,' he said, and firmly took her arm.

Maria certainly did not sleep well. She drifted in and out of consciousness as she tossed and turned, her mind filled with anxiety about Carlo; his stricken face and the sounds of his gasping, the thud of the overturned chair, all returning to her in unsettling dreams.

The next morning she awoke with a start and sat up in bed, straining her ears for reassuring sounds. She heard faint music, which indeed reassured her that all was well with Carlo. She relaxed back onto the pillows with a deep sigh of relief and lay there listening, puzzling over the same musical passage returning to her ears again and again.

The San Severo concerts were staged every one or two months. During the prior weeks, Carlo the perfectionist would make the musicians repeat difficult phrases or passages over and over, not only to perfect them but to facilitate the familiarity resulting in ease of execution, so that by the time the final week of rehearsals came around, the players focused not on the notes but on the expression of the music, its drama or intensity of feeling.

On this morning a particularly difficult passage involving the coordination of five instruments and four singers was being repeated. The repetition continued as Maria drank her chocolate and Laura dressed her. Though she could hear it only faintly from her rooms, the constant repetition was like a buzzing in her ear. On and on it went, to the point where Maria decided she must go out or go mad.

On the way downstairs, Beatrice suddenly skipped off in the direction of the music room, saying gleefully over her shoulder, 'I'll bet he's in a stinking mood.'

'No!' said Maria, running after her, ordering Laura and Sylvia to stay where they were.

She found Beatrice with her eye pressed to the large keyhole of the music-room door. Maria couldn't resist having a look herself. There was Carlo, clearly visible, slumped in a chair and holding his brow in his hands, the very picture of exasperation, muttering, 'Again.' He was wearing his long black coat. The passage was played for the thousandth time. The musicians must be in a delirium by now, thought Maria.

At the close of the passage, a silence followed. Beatrice pushed her mother's face aside to see what was happening. She immediately backed away from the door, which suddenly sprung open, and there was Carlo.

'Again,' he shouted over his shoulder, and closed the door behind him. 'What are you doing here?' he asked Maria with a puzzled frown.

Racking her brains for a suitable explanation, Maria instinctively looked toward Beatrice. 'We were just on our way out . . .' she began.

'Don't bother inventing some nonsense,' he said crossly. 'I want the real reason.' He stared down at Beatrice and folded his arms, waiting for an explanation.

'I was curious,' she said.

'About what?'

'You've been playing that same passage for hours and I wanted to see what you all looked like.'

'So you were spying through the keyhole?'

'Yes.'

'What did you see?'

'Not much.'

'Well come in and see a great deal more.' He grabbed Beatrice's hand, pulled her into the room and slammed the door. 'Again,' he thundered.

Maria stood there helplessly, not knowing what to do. She was loath to leave Beatrice in there, but at the same time she didn't wish to challenge Carlo's authority in front of her daughter. Besides, creating a scene in front of his musicians would enrage him. She decided to go out as she'd planned, telling Sylvia to wait upstairs for Beatrice. There was nothing else for it.

She returned two hours later, relieved to hear another passage being played as she mounted the stairs, although it too was being repeated.

She was deeply troubled to find that Beatrice had not returned. Though Sylvia was anxious, Maria refused to tell her what had happened because she felt ashamed of placing consideration of Carlo's feelings, and her own in not wishing to anger him, above Beatrice's. It would be torture for the poor little girl, sitting for so long in that room with Carlo in one of his tempers, her senses assaulted by that maddening repetition. Even Beatrice wouldn't know how to find her way out of a situation like this. The child's bravado and irrepressible curiosity was tinged with a fear of Carlo because of what had happened to the beautiful bear. She held him solely responsible: he had murdered the bear.

Another hour passed. Darkness fell. 'No, I'm not hungry,' Maria told Sylvia. She decided to go to the old prince and princess and ask them what to do. Surely, if she asked him, Prince Francesco would himself go and rescue Beatrice for her.

On the way down the stairs a sudden anger took hold of her. She headed for the music room, not knowing what she would do. If she had to create a scene with Carlo in front of his musicians, then so be it.

She thrust open the door and walked in. Carlo was now playing with the group, an entire piece, it seemed. He merely looked up at Maria and went on playing. Beatrice rose and walked to her mother with a surly face and protruding bottom lip, accusation in her eyes. They left the room without a word from Carlo.

When they reached the stairs, she broke down. 'How *could* you leave me there for so long,' she wailed, stamping her foot and tugging violently at Maria's arm in frustration. 'Even Prince Carlo forgot I was there. And it was so awful listening to that thing over and over, so boring, boring, boring.'

'Why didn't you sneak out?' asked Maria.

'Because even a *tiny mouse* couldn't sneak anywhere in a room with Prince Carlo,' she shrieked exasperatedly, stamping her foot again. 'He sees everything. He hears everything. You *know* that. How do you think he knew we were at the *door*? We made no noise, yet he *sensed* we were there. He knows *everything* that goes on around him. I thought you'd wait for a little while and then come for me. I expected you any minute. Why did you take so long? Why?'

Maria sighed and admitted shame-faced, 'Because I didn't want to have to fight with him.'

'You're my *mother*. You're supposed to look after me and not be afraid of people.'

'Listen, Beatrice. You spied on Prince Carlo. He didn't like it and you were punished. This will teach you to be more respectful of him in future.'

'You spied on him, too,' rebuked Beatrice. 'I hope he punishes you, too.'

'He has already, through you.'

'*You* didn't have to sit in that room for hours and listen to that *horrible noise*.'

How could Maria explain to Beatrice that her punishment had been to be made painfully aware of her own weakness in being more afraid of

Carlo's reactions than she need have been? She realised that the old habits of fearfulness instilled into her during the years with Alfonso lingered still. She would be more aware of this in future and combat them. Carlo didn't raise his hand to her and threaten physical violence as Alfonso had. It was more a game of minds, the strategies of which she must begin to school herself in. She, too, had learned her lesson.

The San Severo concerts had become thrilling events for the music lovers of Naples now that the programme was presided over by Carlo rather than his father. He eschewed the conventional florid, rhapsodical style of music and concentrated on the freer, more experimental compositions of younger composers. These often blended monody—the older form with a principal air supported by subsidiary instrumental accompaniment—with polyphony, the music of many voices balanced equally one against another. The madrigal form still predominated, but in the work of these new composers many of the singing parts were substituted by the lute, the Orpherian or the viol de gamba, which resulted in a complex interweaving of harmonies, the listener often surprised, his ear excited, by dissonances and digressions. And so the concerts attracted the musical elite: patrons and professors, and occasionally performers and composers from others cities as well as Neapolitans.

After the first concert since their marriage Maria looked forward to the second. Carlo was always in good humour in the days leading up to the performance. The palace came alive with the sounds of perfected music resonating through its rooms as Carlo led his musicians in rehearsal after rehearsal. He schooled her in how to oversee the preparations for the evening itself, the food, the flowers, the arrangement of furniture for the guests. They'd now been married for five months, and she'd become familiar with the layout of the palace, the chief servants and cooks and their skills, and the many details that were required to make the evening a success. She'd also accustomed herself to Carlo's eccentric habits and was more at ease with him. She'd learned to read the signs of his melancholy or anger or irritation and she avoided him at these times, but she also knew that the slightest thing might reverse his mood.

He was generous with her, and for this special evening encouraged her to select a sumptuous and expensive fabric for her gown. He had a cloth importer deliver lengths of exquisite fabrics to the palace, and they spent a happy afternoon in her salon deliberating. His mood was exuberant, his presence as light as the bright sunshine that streamed through the windows. He'd only just risen and was still in his long white nightshirt and black velvet dressing-gown. His dark hair, which usually clung to his head like a pointed skullcap, was uncombed and it fell boyishly over his face. He held up fabric after fabric against her to gauge the effect, saying 'Yes,' and placing it in a special pile, or 'No,' and flinging it on a chair.

They ended up with five selections, which he laid out side by side on the table. 'Which one will you choose?' he asked, smiling. This was a game, for she knew he'd already selected the one he liked best. He delighted in these games of taste. Her hair, too, was undressed and he amused himself by curling a golden tress around his finger as she looked at the five fabrics and considered. It was not only a matter of what she liked and what suited her best, but also of what would be complemented by the colours in the music room. It was summer, a particularly hot one, and all of these fabrics seemed too rich and heavy. She had a sudden inspiration.

'I don't like any of them,' she said 'They don't suit what I have in mind.'

He laughed at such fastidiousness. 'And what do you have in mind?'

'Something that suits the season, cools the eye.' She described her idea to him. Then she looked down and fiddled with the large ruby teardrop on her wedding finger, asking, 'How does that seem to you?'

'I like the idea and compliment you on its originality, but there's something wrong with it. It's too symmetrical.'

'Well, you think of something, Carlo, to give it movement.'

'Verve, not movement. And rosebuds, I think, are a little saccharine. How about another flower form? Let's draw it,' he said, leaping up and rummaging in her desk for paper and inks.

After a pleasant hour of drawing together, they had it.

On the evening, Carlo, elegant in midnight-blue velvet, sat in the little red velvet chair in Maria's bedchamber, watching silently as Laura dressed her mistress' hair. This took some time as Laura was used to working with pearls and, as she listened to Carlo's instructions, she was endeavouring to get the balance right. The finishing touches complete, Maria stood up and spontaneously swirled around and around before Carlo, feeling elated to be wearing such a highly individual gown that had been styled by the both of them.

'Does it suit me?' she asked.

He appraised her silently from head to foot, which gave her a moment's doubt. 'It more than suits you,' he said at last. 'It completes you. You are Flora come down from Olympus.'

They stood at the door of the music room, greeting their guests. Some complimented Maria effusively on the dress; others stared at her in astonishment. She noticed a few of them whispering behind her back. The dress was white, plain white silk with a lustrous sheen. Nobody wore white. It was considered tasteless. Adorning the low, square neck and strewn throughout the sleeve-slashings were tiny flowers in pale blue and mauve, all the stranger for being so perfectly made they looked almost alive, because their weird form had been invented by Carlo. Maria's hair, too, was adorned with these unearthly flowers. To the embroidered flowers at the V-shape of the waist were added delicate pale-green leaves that continued asymmetrically on five fine stems down the skirt of the dress and tapered away, another idea of Carlo's.

The guests stared at Maria so often it began to make her feel ill at ease. Quietly admiring looks she'd always enjoyed, but the unusual nature of the dress drew far too much attention of a more uncertain kind to her. The dress was clearly inviting gossip, and she detested being the subject of idle tongues. She'd wear more conventional gowns in future.

During the interval, the guests sat chatting and eating. Maria in her role as hostess moved from group to group, ensuring that all of those present were enjoying themselves. As she excused herself from one of Carlo's cousins to walk across and greet the visitor from Parma, a voice behind her whispered, 'Here's my angel.'

She turned to meet a face as seductive as hers and had a sudden impulse to smile. She suppressed it. 'Don't call me that, Fabrizio,' she said very quietly, looking around her.

'How can I not? I have never known a face as beautiful as yours and I have never seen such a heavenly dress. The combination overwhelms me.'

Her confidence in the dress was in that instant restored; in spite of that she whispered, 'I don't like such familiarity. You barely know me.'

'Forgive me, but I can't help feeling I've always known you,' he said gently.

'If you presume it follows that I have the same familiar feeling about you, then you are deluding yourself,' she replied and walked away from him. She was beginning to learn the advantages of Carlo's methods of dealing with people. Yet she felt a pang of guilt at behaving with Fabrizio Carafa in that way. He'd been kind, gentle, had complimented her. Why did she feel the need to defend herself in his presence? Doubtless because he was a notorious womaniser. Of course he'd behaved charmingly with her. What womaniser wouldn't? His manner with her was too familiar, and that was the truth.

She watched him that night from a safe distance, watched the grace and ease with which he moved about the room, laughing frequently and good-naturedly. She watched the faces of the women he spoke with as he stared into their eyes and listened to them so intently that they felt he was exclusively theirs. No wonder they lost their heads over him.

Her musing was interrupted by the last person in the room with whom she wished to speak: Don Giulio Gesualdo, who had been hovering near her all evening. Carlo's uncle had visited the palace several times since her marriage, bringing her gifts of antique glassware and little pieces of jewellery and assuring her that she could always think of him as her protector. At first his advances had merely embarrassed her, but tonight his presence was irksome beyond measure. His surreptitiousness disgusted her, for he always made sure that his unwelcome protestations of affection were heard by no one but her, and he had a habit of sliding his eyes about the room like an unpleasant amphibian before he addressed her.

'You take my breath away,' he now declared, fixing his eyes on a mauve silk flower at her breast.

'Then perhaps you should go outside and take the air,' she muttered, edging past so as to make no physical contact with him and making for the opposite side of the room, searching for a guest to strike up a conversation with in case he should follow and press himself upon her.

The Duchess of Andria sat alone, sipping a lemonade.

'How are you, Maria?' said Maria in greeting, and laughing as she sat down next to the duchess. 'I feel strange saying that as it's my name also.' Odious Uncle Giulio had indeed trailed after her, but now he'd stopped in his tracks and was ogling her.

'Yes, I know it is. I'm well, thank you, but rather tired.'

'So am I. My name was also once Maria Carafa. Did you know that?' asked Maria, obliged now to make conversation with this unpleasant woman and saying the first thing that popped into her head.

The duchess looked at her as if trying to place her. Why this pantomime? She suspected she knew very well who she'd once been. It made her determined to win her over.

'I seem to recall you were once married to a relative of my husband's,' said the duchess finally.

'Yes, Federigo Carafa, his uncle. He was very fond of your husband and taught him how to fence when he was a boy,' said Maria, feeling that she was babbling.

'Many people are very fond of my husband,' replied the duchess coolly.

What was that snide remark supposed to mean? Surely it wasn't directed at her. Though why say it if it wasn't? These thoughts raced through Maria's mind as she replied inanely, 'Yes, I know my husband is. They're quite good friends. I suppose you know that. Do you know Carlo?'

'I've met him, of course,' said the duchess flatly.

Maria, feeling the strain of this conversation, was searching her mind for a topic that didn't set up the unpleasant reverberations that had rung from anything she'd said so far. 'It's often impossible to discuss anything but music with Carlo. Do you like music? Are you enjoying the concert?' You are going to say that this kind of music is not to your taste, thought Maria.

'Very much. The tall singer with the long hair is my brother. Our mother had a marvellous voice, but unfortunately I haven't inherited any of her talent.'

'Your brother, is his name Massimo?' asked Maria in surprise.

'Yes.'

'Oh, he's Carlo's favourite singer. He has a wonderful voice.'

'Thank you. Yes, he does.'

'Do you always come to Carlo's concerts?'

'No. Only when the music of one of my husband's composers is being played. He's patron to four or five of them.'

'Which one is it tonight?'

'Pomponio Nenna.'

The duchess took a sip of her lemonade. The ungraciousness of the woman. Could she not at least have the courtesy to attempt to introduce a topic of conversation? How did Fabrizio endure being at the dinner table with her? Or was she only behaving like this with Maria? Any attractive woman probably. She no doubt imagined they were all in pursuit of her handsome husband. Still, after what Geronima had told Maria of his faithlessness, who could blame her? Maria searched her mind for something to say to fill the long silence. 'Do you prefer life at Andria or in Naples?' she asked pleasantly. Even as she said it she realised the question was ill considered, for it could be taken to mean that Maria was interested in her movements because she was interested in her husband.

The duchess looked at her sharply and replied, 'I am often in Naples.'

'Here's your husband come to join you,' said Maria with relief, rising as she saw Fabrizio approach. She bid the duchess a hasty farewell and departed.

Carlo was standing against the wall on the other side of the room, looking amused. Maria all but fled to his side.

'Congratulations,' he said. 'You've just survived ten minutes with the most boring woman in Naples. You were beginning to look desperate, so I sent Fabrizio across to rescue you.'

She laughed happily. 'A thousand thanks. What did you say to him?'

'I said, "Maria is stuck with your bore of a wife. Do something about it."'

'Really? Does he allow you to speak of her like that?'

'He's said as much often enough to me, so he can't pretend to be offended.'

'I hope you don't speak ill of me to him.'

'Why? Because you don't wish me to speak ill of you, or because you don't wish Fabrizio to hear you ill-spoken of?'

'You know the answer to that very well.'

'I wish to hear you tell me.'

'Because I don't wish you to speak ill of me. To anyone.'

'I would consider it beneath both of us to even discuss you with anyone.' He looked across the room. The singers and musicians were returning to their places. 'Now for Scamotti's sparkling new motet,' he said, and strode off.

Maria reignited her warm friendship with Maddelena and Anna Carafa. They made regular visits to San Severo, passing pleasant hours with Maria and Beatrice, and well understanding Maria's preference that they call on her rather than she on them. Though Beatrice begged to be taken there, Maria could not yet bring herself to visit Palazzo Carafa, where she had spent the happiest three years of her life followed by the most agonising one. Nor would she allow Beatrice to be taken there without her; she wished to be present when the child was shown the room she'd been born in, and learned the place and manner of her father's death. Maria anticipated the moment of walking inside the palace; memories would rush at her and she did not yet feel sufficiently Carlo's wife to withstand the power of them: Carlo did not love her as Federigo had. She could not defer the visit for much longer, however, for Beatrice pleaded with her daily and it was the child's birthright to be taken there, and to meet her Carafa cousins, who might perhaps bring some joy into her life.

Beatrice was not happy at San Severo. Carlo had made an attempt, not an entirely desultory one, to forge a bond with Maria's daughter. Under his guidance she had received lessons on the viol and the lute from two of the most gifted musicians in his *camerata*. Though Beatrice enjoyed being in the music room, it appeared, as her lute teacher told Carlo, that she paid more attention to the allegory of Music on the wall than to mastering the plucking and strumming of the instruments, at which she showed little talent. Carlo made one more effort, endeavouring to interest her in the organ, at which he sat with her himself, placing her little fingers on the keys and pointing out the correspondences between the notes on the sheet music and the notes on the keyboard. But this failed to excite or even interest her. Besides, she felt uncomfortable sitting so close to Carlo because she did not, as she told Maria, like the smell of him. It was soon clear to Maria, who *did* like Carlo's musky smell with its whiff of crushed violets, that Beatrice had no inclination for music. She was thus forced to concede that Carlo, being Carlo, had sufficient reason for relinquishing his interest in her daughter. Yet he did his duty by her, engaging the best tutors in the subjects Maria insisted she be schooled in—Latin, literature, Bible studies and drawing—but after the failure with the excursions into music, there was little personal engagement between Carlo and his stepdaughter.

Noticing the absence of joy in Beatrice's life, her grandmother Maddelena Carafa took the initiative. At the close of one her of visits, she insisted that Maria bring the child to Palazzo Carafa the very next day. 'I will send some of our men here tomorrow morning to escort you,' she said firmly. 'I will instruct them to wait in your courtyard. Come at whatever time it pleases you, Maria; they will wait. But it will be tomorrow, won't it, Beatrice?'

Six

SPACCANAPOLI

The Carafa palace was little more than a block from San Severo; it was but a matter of turning left from Piazza San Domenico Maggiore and following for a short distance the long, narrow street known as Spaccanapoli, and had it been any other city, Maria, Beatrice and their escort might have reached their destination in less than five minutes, but Spaccanapoli was the crowded heart of the most populous city on earth, so their journey was less a matter of walking in a straight line than one of negotiating a passage through a throng of biblical density. Naples' population had trebled in the past ten years. The majority of its two hundred thousand inhabitants lived on top of each other in the six and seven-storey buildings, the tallest in Europe, that hemmed in this sunless street which cut east–west through the city's ancient centre. In no other city was the contrast between opulence and squalor, magnificence and misery, more marked and jumbled together than in Naples and nowhere more so than Spaccanapoli. This was the quarter that had earned Naples its reputation as the world's richest and most vicious city.

For Maria Spaccanapoli was forever associated with violence, but not of the kind for which it was infamous—the knife fights and murderous brawls between the loafers, thugs, card players, pimps, thieves and other scoundrels that formed part of its picaresque street life. Violence could suddenly erupt at any moment. Even when there were no incidents and the Neapolitans who dwelt or loitered there were absorbed in their own affairs, eyes lowered as always, an atmosphere of latent menace hung about the place.

As Maria and her party set out, a crush of students and tutors blocked the entrance to Spaccanapoli. Naples University was nearby and the tutors were gathered in Piazza San Domenico Maggiore to advertise their intellectual merchandise to students dissatisfied with the university's Church-oriented teachings. Above the din, one long-haired tutor was shouting something about new sciences, brandishing a book in the air. Maria, noticing that he was armed, drew Beatrice close to her side. Some of the students, too, were armed. Encircling Maria and Beatrice, the three guards in their Carafa livery pushed through the crowd. Beatrice found it thrilling, protected by her father's family like this, as they slowly forged their way along Naples' longest and oldest street, a main thoroughfare of the Romans and, before them, the Greeks. Weed-topped ruins of ancient walls and gateways blurred by the dust of ages appeared between churches and palaces or down dark alleyways. The stink of sulphur mingled with the disgusting body odours of filthy beggars and cripples who slouched in entrance ways or sat slumped against the walls in the shadows. Maria handed Beatrice some coins to throw to them. Beatrice chose to give them only to the mothers holding babies in their arms. The faces of these unfortunates all looked the same to Maria: their eyes, their noses, the pasty colour of their grimy skin, all the same; a sisterhood of poverty. Though she felt sorry for them, their pitiful supplications and martyred expressions revolted her. Such women were the beneficiaries of Geronima's charity, and she silently thanked Carlo for forbidding her own association with them.

A young bravo in a short red cape doffed his plumed hat and bowed at Maria. The next moment a curly-haired ruffian cut rudely across their path and, loudly clearing his throat, spat on the boot of one of the guards before disappearing into the crowd. A wizened housewife in a headscarf gazing down on the street from a shadowy balcony showered down abuse on the guards while the daughter suckling a baby at her side made an obscene gesture. Occasional mutterings of 'Cafara thugs', 'Spanish bumboys', came from unidentifiable faces in the crowd. Beatrice, who had been captivated by the street life until now, looked at her mother in bewilderment at these signs of hatred. 'Why are they saying those things?' she asked.

'Because the Carafas protect themselves with guards whenever they go out, and the ordinary people dislike them for it.' This was a great oversimplification, but Maria thought that Beatrice would learn the truth soon enough—perhaps this very day from Maddelena. The insults and the memories they triggered made Maria feel sick to her stomach. Even so, compared to what had been hurled at the Carafas seven or eight years ago, today's sneers were half-hearted, more the habit of an old hatred than symptom of a fresh one. The next minute the isolated jeers were lost in a tumultuous roar of insult as a party of Spanish soldiers on horseback came into view ahead of them, knocking over street stalls as they arrogantly cut a swathe through the crowd. Maria's guards, stepping over an almost invisible beggar, steered her and Beatrice to the wall and stood protectively in front of them. A young servant woman in a low-necked shift, ripe with the overblown, fleeting beauty of the lower classes, cried out in revulsion as a grotesque old man with an enormous inflamed goitre on his neck backed out of the soldiers' way and into her. A grimy, barefoot child of no more than five, who looked as if he'd seen it all already, spotted his opportunity and with lightning swiftness snatched a round of cheese from her basket and vanished underfoot. Beatrice blinked. Had she really seen that? The servant woman hadn't even noticed. The soldiers had noisily clopped past and now a line of Dominican monks walked toward them on their way to San Domenico Maggiore, the two novitiates amused and lively, the older ones beady-eyed. Ignoring the produce of the fish and fruit sellers, Maria's eyes glanced over the ceramics and fabrics of the street stalls. She stopped to buy a polking-stick from a pedlar, to help stiffen the broad white ruffs Carlo wore for performances and visits.

An ostentatiously dressed couple emerged from a palace on the left, the woman dripping ermine and jewels and the man in a voluminous overcoat faced with sable. As they approached with their bodyguards, the woman stopped in her tracks, exclaiming excitedly, 'Maria! Maria d'Avalos! Is it really you? Of course it is. Look Lorenzo, it's your beautiful cousin with, who is this? Don't tell me it's Beatrice. Such a little lady already! You were hardly more than a baby when I last saw you.'

Maria happily exchanged greetings and embraces with this handsome, overweight couple, introducing them to Beatrice as her cousins, Lorenzo and Celestina Piccolomini, the Duke and Duchess of Malfi.

'Where are you and Beatrice on your way to, Maria?' asked Lorenzo, puzzled at the presence of the Carafa guards.

'To Palazzo Diomede Carafa,' answered Maria. 'It is time for Beatrice to see her birthplace.'

'Ah, yes,' murmured the Piccolominis, well aware of what had once occurred at the palace.

'We knew your father,' said Celestina, smiling down at Beatrice. 'Do you know what people in our circle referred to him as?'

'The angel from Heaven? Mama has told me that some people called him this,' said the child proudly.

'That is it precisely,' beamed Celestina. 'And do you know why?'

'Because he was a handsome and very good man?' asked Beatrice uncertainly.

The Piccolominis smiled at her indulgently. 'Yes, he was those things, dear,' replied Celestina. 'But the main reason was his sunny nature. He was always laughing and joking and was deliciously chivalrous to old married ladies like me.'

'I found him a perceptive young man,' said Lorenzo thoughtfully. 'He cut through all the claptrap and arrived at the essence of things.'

'He did,' said Maria sadly. 'And Beatrice is very like Federigo in that regard.'

'No doubt it was due to his schooling as a lawyer,' said Celestina, unintentionally sounding dismissive. 'I wanted so much to come to your recent wedding, Maria, but Lorenzo refuses to leave Amalfi these days. He's only dragged himself to Naples this week because there's a special sitting of parliament. What's it about again, darling? Oh, never mind, I won't remember and, in any case, what does Maria care? You must both come to Amalfi. It's been years since you've visited us. We'd love to see Antonia, too.'

'I'd very much like to visit you, Celestina, but at present my marriage occupies me.'

'And how is marriage to Carlo Gesualdo?' Celestina looked about her and lowered her voice to a whisper. 'I hope you're not finding it difficult.'

'Not nearly as difficult as you've evidently taken the liberty of imagining,' replied Maria tersely.

'Don't pry, Celestina. This is hardly the place to discuss such matters,' said Lorenzo with a frown. 'We must let Maria and Beatrice be on their way.' He kissed Maria's hand and then her daughter's.

'How charming it's been to see you both,' said Celestina, kissing their cheeks. 'You are welcome at Amalfi whenever it pleases you.'

Maria and her party eventually reached Palazzo Diomede Carafa, one of Naples' most ornamented and distinctive buildings, and the one for which Maria had the most affection. How beautiful it was. She'd once considered it the centre of her life, her real life, and although that was no longer so and had not been so for many years, now that she stood it front of it once again the feeling unaccountably welled up in her.

Beatrice's eyes roved over the façade. She was tense with excitement. 'I remember this, but I thought I'd seen it in a dream,' she exclaimed. Behind the delicate Catalan arches were spaced twelve niches containing marble portrait busts of members of the Carafa lineage. Maria waited while her daughter inspected these portraits of her ancestors; she pointed out the great humanist and art collector, Diomede Carafa, who had remodelled the palace in the previous century. In a marble portal festooned with sculpted laurel leaves they entered the palace through a large wooden door carved with the Carafa coat of arms.

Beatrice looked up and around her at the courtyard, its four walls a rhythm of arched, enclosed verandahs rising up six storeys. The lower floors were very old, built in the 1200s. They were darkly medieval, with seven-foot thick brick walls and small deep-set grilled windows. The servants and men-at-arms lived in these dark lower regions.

Maria and Beatrice climbed to the spacious, light-filled upper floors where the Carafas lived. These had been added by Diomede Carafa and were rich with brightly coloured frescoes. Maddelena was in the music room, having furniture moved around in preparation for a concert she was giving the following evening. 'Ah, Beatrice, Maria, here you are at last,' she said, embracing them warmly. 'We'll look at the rooms where you spent the first three years of your life, Beatrice, and then I'll introduce you to your cousins, but let us first go down and have some refreshment.'

Maddelena turned to Maria and, smiling, asked her, 'Would you like to see the old salon again?'

'Of course. I associate it with the warmth of family life here,' replied Maria. 'It won't have mixed memories, as some of the other rooms will.'

Maddelena placed her hand comfortingly on Maria's arm. 'I know what you are trying to say, Maria. And I also know how difficult this must be for you, believe me. Come, Beatrice, and see where your family takes its meals.'

This room was the heart of the house. Having grown up in a household where her mother, father and she and her brothers had often dined separately, on marrying Federigo, Maria had been immediately embraced into the warm circle of a large family that not only dined together, but conversed, laughed, argued, planned, prayed, ridiculed, gossiped and entertained together. The central figure of this family life was Maddelena Carafa and the day-to-day arena of it was the rectangular family salon in the old part of the palace. This salon had seemed very strange to Maria when she'd taken her first meals there as a new bride with Federigo and his numerous relatives. She had never seen a room like it. Situated in a part of the palace that dated back to medieval times, it was dark, with a low-beamed ceiling, and its walls were lined from floor to ceiling with Spanish majolica tiles that had perhaps been added later, nobody remembered. The tiles and the rudely adzed table that ran its length gave it a rustic feel. The windows facing the courtyard had been enlarged, so that in summer they looked out onto the sunlit grapevine that hung from the arched verandah.

Only the inner circle of the Carafa family ate in this room, so everybody was free to speak as they pleased. Much of what Federigo and his father and uncles had spoken of had been over Maria's head, but she listened. Later, after the tragedy that took Federigo's life and destroyed hers, she was to remember fragments of those conversations and they stayed with her still.

Maddelena now led them to this salon, and the moment Maria breathed in its lingering smell of bubbling sauces and roasting meats, a stomach-churning nostalgia gripped her: the joy of her first three years with the Carafas; the unspeakable grief of the final one.

As they ate figs and cheese, and the matriarch entertained her granddaughter with recollections of her infancy, vivid memories of Federigo during those three years came to Maria, he sitting opposite her, and she in the very chair she was sitting in now. Outside of her intimate life with him in their bedchamber, Maria had been at her happiest at this table. The angelically beautiful and sweet-natured wife of a favourite son, she'd been kissed, cuddled, fussed over and spoiled, as loved and pampered as Federigo's sisters Anna and Raimonda, who'd swiftly become her dearest friends. Small wonder that she'd felt so safe and in every way protected by the Carafas, for they lived cocooned in a world of opulence excessive even in Naples. How ironic it was that the changes in the kingdom beyond, which had in turn instigated changes in Federigo, were at their most visible and audible right beneath the Carafas' very windows in Spaccanapoli.

During the course of those three years these changes in Federigo had, to Maria, been imperceptible at first, but by the third year she'd been alarmed at many of the things he said. Sunny Federigo of the infectious laugh had become argumentative and disrupted the harmony of family meals. It was more than nine years ago, the night of the conversation she remembered most clearly. The spring rainfall had been the lowest in memory and it had been a summer of blighted crops, but what was any of this to Maria? What indeed. Winter arrived. The sky turned grey, the wind whipped up the long narrow thoroughfares, their darkness became ominous, and the Carafas remained indoors. Federigo's parents impressed on Maria that she must not under any circumstances go outside. She didn't ask why; she was an obedient daughter.

After silently picking at his food, Federigo pushed his plate away and turned to his father, Luigi Carafa, who sat on his left at the head of the table. 'How many different meats do we have at this table?' Federigo asked. 'Five? Six? How many dishes in rich sauces? Eight? Ten? How many fruits and confections? We'll eat less than a quarter of it and the rest will be thrown to the dogs. And yet we condemn the starving, whose unanswered cries of "Bread, bread," in the streets have inevitably resulted in them venting their wrath at the rise in bread prices, a rise so steep they can no longer afford to feed themselves or their children. And now we Carafas support the viceroy turning his Spanish soldiers on them and massacring them. Where is our conscience is all of this?'

'Whenever there is a poor harvest, grain prices rise. When the populace instigates rebellion, the city is obliged to crush it,' replied his father wearily.

'You know very well, Father, that the essence of this is not rebellion, but the viceroy profiting from the people's misery,' insisted Federigo. 'What scant grain there is, he's been selling to Spain. You told me this yourself. What do you expect me to do? Applaud? Spanish parasites suck at the very life blood of Naples, and we, Neapolitans ourselves, condone it. And when the viceroy slapped that tax on fruit, yet another tax nobly supported by the Carafas, it must have been clear to you all that in depriving the people of their one alternative to bread, you were condemning them to starvation. Or are such considerations beneath your notice?'

'I like it no more than you do, Federigo, but that is the way of the world. As to your uncle and I supporting the viceroy, I tell you it is essential to do so in order to retain our privileges and property. You will come to understand that one day.'

'I understand the price we pay for it well enough already,' retorted Federigo. 'The Carafas have become the most hated family in Naples. Are you aware of that?'

Maria pricked up her ears at this. Sheltered from the political realities of Neapolitan life, and loving the family as she did—basking in their warmth, affection and generosity—she'd assumed, childlike, that the Carafas were loved by all. But recently when she'd been out with various members of the family and their guards, there had been incidents in Spaccanapoli and other parts of the city that had alarmed her. Abuse had been shouted at them, things thrown from balconies, and people had developed a habit of muttering, 'The Carafas will pay for this.' She'd heard it several times over the past weeks and it frightened her. When she'd asked Federigo why they would say such a thing, he'd replied that it was because the Carafas supported the crippling tax increases the ordinary people were forced to pay.

'Of course we're aware of it,' frowned Luigi. 'How could we not be? It's no longer possible to go abroad without being shouted at or spat upon by rogues and idlers.'

Federigo looked across at Maria. 'Do you know why my mother began insisting two weeks ago that you not go outdoors, Maria?'

Maria shook her head in confusion.

'Because the poor are dying in the streets. The sight of their corpses piling up is unbearable. So is the stench.'

'If the sufferings of the poor so offend you,' said Maddelena, 'why do you not join the group of bravos who've set up that charity organisation. Some of them were once your fellow students.'

'Yes, and I commend them, for who else feeds the poor and helps the sick and the dying? But charity only diverts attention from the underlying problem. There would be far less need for it if justice were done and just a fraction of the wealth of Naples permitted to trickle down to its ordinary people. But no, those of us who have far more than enough are bent on lining our pockets further, and the—'

'Come Federigo, be honest,' interjected his uncle, Oliviero. 'Amusing yourself with those cavaliers you hang about with is far more attractive to you than soiling your hands in the service of the poor. You affect disgust at the means by which this family retains its wealth and privileges, yet it is that very wealth that enables you to lead the life of idle amusement that so pleases you.'

'You've never spoken truer words, Oliviero,' said Maddelena, nodding agreement. She looked warningly at her son. 'Now listen to me, Federigo, and mark me well. It suits your brothers and friends, that cavalier life of card playing and carousing because they're training for the military. But you've been schooled as a lawyer and to your shame you choose not to practise. You must begin to look about you, for you are expected to participate in the government of this kingdom, and your father and I will not have you shaming the Carafas. In spite of what may be said about us in the streets, in noble circles the Carafa is the most honoured of Neapolitan families still.'

'We were once an honourable family, but that was fifty years ago,' said Federigo quietly, glancing from his mother to his father. 'Compare our situation then with what we've allowed ourselves to become.'

'Spare us your lawyer's skills at argument,' said Maddelena dryly. 'We'll listen to what you have to say when you begin putting what you have learned to better purpose.'

'No, let him speak,' said his father. 'I'm most interested to hear what he has to say. Though he wastes his life in idleness, if he can still think, perhaps he's not lost to us.'

'Thinking is what I mostly do these days, Father. It's what I think that you may not like. This is the thing that irks me. Fifty years ago, your father—my grandfather—and Maria's grandfather took a stand against the Spanish. The popular uprising that occurred then was led by a Carafa and a d'Avalos. And they defeated Spain's plans to introduce the Spanish Inquisition in Naples. In those days, the Carafas were at one with the people of Naples. We were honoured by Neapolitans, not by Spanish profiteers and their hangers-on, and we were an honourable family indeed. Is not my marriage to Maria, after all, your way of cementing that old allegiance that prevented Spain exercising the full extent of its tyranny? Why cannot the Carafas take such a stance again?'

Maria stared at her husband in astonishment, her eyes like a wounded deer's. She'd known that their families were aligned, shared a history, but the casual way he'd just spoken of their marriage offended her innocent belief in their love. It caused her momentarily to doubt its purity and strength. Did he love her because she was a d'Avalos? If so, did he truly love her at all? Federigo caught her eye; his gaze as it caressed her troubled face assured her not to take what he'd said to heart, and immediately all was well with the world again.

'I won't have you speaking like that in this house!' exclaimed Maddelena. 'Not only is it dangerous, it betrays the full measure of your ignorance in matters of government.' She held up her hand for silence when Federigo opened his mouth to speak again. 'Quiet! You cannot imagine how it pains and angers me to hear my eldest son, your father's heir . . . You are the future Marquis of San Lucido!'

'Federigo is young and idealistic. I was once like that myself, if you remember, Maddelena,' said Luigi.

'Of course I remember. But you never once turned on your family, not at the dinner table or anywhere else.'

During her years at Messina, Maria had often thought about this family that was so dear to her. With the wisdom of hindsight and her own greater maturity she'd come to understand them. The Carafas were a mass of contradictions: avaricious and power hungry, yet immensely generous; capable of passionate loyalty to their own, yet contemptuous of those outside their circle; the young males sword-wielding cavaliers but cultivated patrons of the arts nevertheless; the women devout, the men politically ruthless. Federigo had broken this mould to some degree, although perhaps he, too, had been a contradiction. The family had been wealthy for generations but it was Federigo's great-uncle, Pope Paul IV, who'd made them immensely rich and powerful. As pope, he'd granted them favours and increased their influence by promoting three of his nephews to cardinals. But it was his scurrilous dealings prior to his papacy, as Archbishop of Naples, that had resulted in the Carafas' vast property holdings. Maria had come to understand Federigo's dismay at the family supporting the Spanish viceroy, for the Carafas had a history of hating the Spanish. The Carafa archbishop who later became pope was no exception. In 1555, determining to rid Naples of Spanish rule, he allied himself with the French and instigated what became known as the Carafa War. For two years he embroiled the population of Naples in battles with the Spanish-appointed king and viceroy. Carafa and the French were eventually defeated, but during those two years he seized estates belonging to the Spanish he so despised and passed them on to his relatives. Many of the numerous palaces in Naples owned by the Carafas had come to them in this way. Two they'd sold off to the Jesuits, but others—in true contradictory Carafa fashion—they'd donated to the Dominicans in expiation. In the second year of Maria's marriage, Maddelena had given to the Church of San Domenico Maggiore the magnificent five-storey Carafa palace that faced it. Federigo had been cynical about Maddelena's extraordinary act of generosity, saying, 'My mother thinks that by doing good works in this world she can be saved in the next.'

'What are you thinking of?' asked Maddelena, returning Maria to the present.

'Of Federigo.'

Maddelena reached across and took Maria's hand in hers. 'We must let him rest in peace, Maria.'

'Indeed,' said Maria sadly. ' But the memory of him haunts these rooms and I can't help but ask myself what kind of man he would have become. I recall something you once said to him: "Either you begin to assume your responsibilities as your father's heir or you continue on your present path and end up a wastrel." Do you remember?'

Maddelena closed her eyes and nodded.

'But there was a third possibility, was there not, Maddelena? I think in time Federigo might have followed his idealism and done some good in the world, struck out on a path of his own.'

Maddelena smiled ruefully. 'Now it is you who are being idealistic, Maria. Federigo was twenty-two when he departed us, and had such a path awaited him, surely he would have set out on it by then.'

'What, then, would he have become? You are his mother. You must know. The responsible heir or the wastrel?'

'As much as it me grieves me to say it, I'm afraid we will never know.'

'What should my father have done that he didn't?' asked Beatrice, who had been taking all this in.

'Many, many things. It's complicated,' replied Maddelena. 'He should have helped his father protect the interests of the Carafas.'

'And does my grandfather still do that all by himself?'

'No. We have our Fabrizio.'

'My cousin Fabrizio?'

'Yes.'

'Is he here?' asked Beatrice excitedly.

'Yes, but he's out on business all day. Fabrizio is the Carafa family's *consigliere*. Do you know what that is?'

'No,' replied Beatrice.

'It means he takes care of our business and legal matters. He holds the keys to all our properties and represents us in the Naples parliament. This is what your father would have done.'

'When will Fabrizio be back?' asked Beatrice.

'Not until very late tonight. Perhaps you can see him tomorrow if your mother allows you to return. Now, Beatrice, let us go and look at the room you were born in. You may remember it, as it's just as it was when you left.' Maddelena was referring to Maria and Federigo's bedchamber, part of an apartment they'd had on the fifth floor. This was the room where Maria had experienced the most blissful and the most terrible hours of her life.

With intense feelings of longing to see the room once again and dread at the thought of the old griefs it would stir up, Maria took her daughter's hand and they followed Maddelena up a flight of steep dark stairs and then two flights of broad marble ones.

It was a fine, light, beautiful room that stretched half the width of the palace. Its three long French windows had balconies that looked down on Spaccanapoli. It was well aired and scented but, as it was now unoccupied, the once-loved room had a faint smell of desolation. Beatrice chatted with her grandmother as she wandered about the room examining its contents.

'What's happened to my wedding portrait?' asked Maria, looking at the blank wall above a chest.

Maddelena tut-tutted irritably and called a servant. 'Have my son's wedding portrait brought from the duke's room immediately and hang it back here, where it belongs,' she ordered. 'And don't move it again. I am heartily tired of all this to-ing and fro-ing.'

Maria was looking at her with raised eyebrows.

'Fabrizio does as he pleases when he's here,' said Maddelena. 'He stays with us when he's in Naples and he likes to have the portrait in his room, so he has it moved in there. Then I have it put back, time and time again. I must impress upon him to not move it again. He knows very well I like things kept as they are in this room.' She looked down at Beatrice and smiled. 'Your father was a mentor to your cousin Fabrizio,' she explained. 'He adored him and I can understand him wanting to have his painting about him, but it's the best likeness we have of Federigo and the painting belongs in here. Fabrizio well knows that I like to come in here and look at my son—and at you too, dear Maria.'

Beatrice, on the verge of speaking, met Maria's eye. Maria put two fingers to her own lips to silence her daughter, whom she suspected had been about to say that Fabrizio perhaps also liked the painting for its likeness of Maria.

The three of them looked at the charming painting in silence as the men rehung it above the chest. Beatrice went to Maria and hung off her skirt, saying, 'Don't cry, Mama.'

'I won't, I promise.'

Beatrice moved to the painting and studied it closely. Her mother the bride, eyes demurely lowered, still a little chubby-cheeked at fifteen, and her father with his strong bone structure and grey eyes looking steadily out at the viewer, his hair cropped short. It was true that she closely resembled him, had his eyes, as so many people said. 'How many years after that was painted did my father die?' she asked.

'Three years,' said Maddelena. 'Come with me and I'll tell you all about it. You're old enough now to know. Yes Maria?'

Maria nodded, trusting Maddelena to soften the story.

'Let us leave Mama in peace for a while. I'll show you the little bedchamber where you used to sleep.'

Thin shafts of bright sunlight filtered through the half-closed shutters. Maria ran her hands over the green silk cover of her old bed. Here she and Federigo had soared together; whenever she thought of their lovemaking she pictured shimmering angels' wings beating upwards into a weightless, ethereal realm ablaze with golden rays. In the first weeks of their marriage she'd had a new bedhead fashioned as outspread angels' wings and now, wanting to remember Federigo in things she could touch, she traced with her fingers the gilt feathers of those wings. She'd decorated the room as a homage to their love: around the duck-egg blue walls ran a dado of painted garlands and swirling arabesques; between the tall windows were marble roundel reliefs of laughing cupids. The coffered ceiling was decorated with medallions fashioned as celestial and seasonal emblems. She sank into a gilt armchair next to the bed and stared at the wedding portrait again. The painter had captured Federigo's good looks but not his charisma. Still, that had largely been in his animated movements, in his sunny nature and infectious laugh. He'd been so young and exuberant, with a talent for seeing the comic side of things. In the early days of their marriage he'd spent nearly every minute of the day with her, and their private world in this room had been one of pleasure and joy and laughter. He'd delighted in expanding her limited understanding of things by teaching her the ways of the world, not in a patronising way by playing the tutor, but by entertaining her in his own inimical way. As well as being his wife and lover, Maria became the appreciative audience her young husband had craved. She saw the satirical and comic side of him that few others saw, certainly not his family. His opinion of his family oscillated between pride at being a Carafa and his irrepressible habit of poking fun at them.

The favourite butt of his humour was the most illustrious Carafa of them all: Pope Pius IV. Through family and friends in the Vatican he'd discovered a great deal about him, even though he'd died when Federigo was a child. This erstwhile pope epitomised the hypocrisy, love of dogma and abuse of power that Federigo despised, and he provided ample material for satire and gleeful irreverence. Federigo was in fact the only Carafa who openly acknowledged the truth about his uncle. Pope Paul had been one of history's most unpleasant popes, a rigid, authoritarian, anti-Semitic fanatic whose strengthening of the Inquisition in Rome had resulted in the imprisonment of cardinals he didn't like. Nobody had felt safe around him. He'd established Italy's first Jewish ghetto, in Rome, as part of a master plan to force Jews off the streets in all Italian cities.

One of Federigo's most memorable private performances for her was his pantomime of Pope Paul's reaction to the *Last Judgement* fresco in the Sistine Chapel the day Michelangelo had completed it. She'd nearly choked with laughter at Federigo's exaggerated gestures and expressions of outrage, while at the same time she'd been horrified—indeed frightened—that her husband could so sacrilegiously satirise the revered figure of *Il Papa*.

'Blot out that prick and balls that so offend my holy gaze,' thundered Federigo, referring to Pope Paul's tormenting of Michelangelo and his subsequent censorship campaign to have the fresco painted over. Federigo had told her that in Vatican circles this had become snidely referred to as 'the fig-leaf campaign'. 'I will not suffer the immorality and intolerable obscenity of this Michelangelo painting naked figures with genitals. It is offensive to me.' Then, as if an afterthought, looking heavenwards with an inanely beatific face: 'And to God.'

'Stop! Stop!' Maria had shouted, holding her hands over her ears and hiccuping with laughter.

'I am God's instrument,' shouted Federigo, grabbing his sword from the table and brandishing it. 'Hang on.' He scratched his head stupidly. 'It's the other way around. God is *my* instrument. In his name I will rid the streets of Rome of all heretics, Spaniards and Jews. An end to humanism in the Vatican!' he yelled, cutting at the air with his sword, then tracing a large cross with it as he intoned fanatically, 'Long live Thomas Aquinas and dogma.'

There was a loud knock on the door and Maddelena entered. 'What is happening here?' she asked sternly. 'What at you shouting at?'

Maria, red-faced and giggling, pulled the bedcovers over her head.

'I was telling Maria of my revered uncle's contribution to the spiritual advancement of mankind,' Federigo responded calmly.

'I trust you are not shaming our family, Federigo, by filling your wife's innocent head with your nonsense.'

'Mama,' gasped Federigo in mock horror. 'How could you allow yourself to describe the most illustrious of the Carafas as nonsense?'

The loud crack of Maddelena slapping Federigo's face Maria could hear still. She'd emerged from the covers, listening wide-eyed as Maddelena delivered her son a stern lecture on his responsibilities as a husband and as heir to the Marquis of San Lucido. 'You are soon to be a father yourself,' she'd continued, 'so it is high time that the child became the man.' Federigo had kissed her hand and apologised. After Maddelena had majestically left, he'd thrown himself on the bed in chagrin and rested his head on Maria's swollen stomach. She'd stroked his forehead, they'd caught each other's eye and exploded with laughter again.

Yes, they'd often behaved like children, but in spite of what Maddelena had said a few minutes ago in the family salon, Maria clung to her view that, had Federigo lived, he might have accomplished something of worth.

Shortly after the night he'd satirised the pope, Maria gave birth to a son. He was named Ferrante after his Carafa grandfather and Maria's great-uncle, hero of the Battle of Pavia and philandering husband of Vittoria Colonna. Not yet sixteen, Maria had fulfilled her mission to produce a Carafa heir and the family adored her for it. Beautiful Maria, living in the warmth and protection of the Carafas, married to the handsomest of them, and having produced a son and heir. That was her finest moment. She'd felt like a queen.

A few weeks later, little Ferrante died of a fever. The doctor was unclear about the exact cause, saying only that Naples was disease-ridden. From the peak of happiness Maria plunged into a pit of despair. She was inconsolable. At the age of fifteen, she'd experienced marriage, ecstasy, birth, and the death of her son—all in the space of less than a year. Ferrante had been with them only a few weeks, but oh, how they missed him. Federigo rocked Maria in his arms as she sobbed. She stroked his brow as he stared sorrowfully into space. Yet although they grieved together in this way and it seemed to them at the time that his death had made their love stronger and brought them even closer together—this, in any case, was what they whispered to each other—their infant son's death in fact caused an invisible rift in their marriage, one that neither of them were at first aware of. In the cruellest way it marked the end to the bliss of their first year together; their paradise lost was never to be regained.

Maria soon fell pregnant again. It was at around this time that Federigo began to express his disapproval of the Carafas' politics. He also began to return home late occasionally. By the time of Beatrice's birth in the following year, he was often out sporting with his friends until past midnight.

On the night of 15 October 1578—the date was forever imprinted on Maria's brain—she'd lain in this very bed waiting for him.

Laura sat keeping her company until he should return. The two women entertained themselves by discussing schemes for the partial redecoration of the bedchamber. Wishing to put their sorrow well behind them by filling the absence in their lives left by Ferrante's death, Maria had recently determined she would bear Federigo another son. She hoped to fall pregnant soon; she felt healthy and sufficiently rested as Beatrice was now eighteen months old. She considered that repainting the room in a fresh new colour would mark the beginning of the next stage of their lives, one she'd resolved would be as happy as the first.

'A warm, lively pink,' suggested Laura.

'A room this size could carry such deep tones,' agreed Maria. 'It might be too feminine for Federigo's taste, though. How does a creamy white sound to you?'

'It would go very well with the gilt.'

'Or even the blue of a summer sky to complement our angels. What time is it, Laura?'

As they moved from colours to the shapes of the panels to materials and textures Maria went on asking Laura the time and as the minutes ticked by and the night wore on she asked more and more frequently. By one o'clock all interest in decoration had evaporated. Her apprehension was such that she thought of waking the house, but was loath to do so because doubtless as soon as she did Federigo would appear on the scene. Truth to tell, she was superstitious that raising an alarm would cause bad fortune to befall Federigo.

'It's three of the morning, my lady,' said Laura sleepily.

'Open a window,' ordered Maria, sliding her feet into green velvet slippers as she stepped out of bed. She went out onto the balcony and looked down on Spaccanapoli, searching with her eyes the long ribbon of street from east to west. There was no sign of Federigo, no sign of movement of any kind. It was as silent as the night, eerily so. Looking up at the thin crescent moon, she waited impatiently while Laura helped her into her dressing-gown and headed off down the hallway before it was buttoned, Laura in pursuit.

Reaching Federigo's parents' apartments on the floor below, she rapped loudly on the door and entered, in tears as she flew through the salon and rapped again, on the door of the bedchamber this time. 'It's Federigo! Mama Maddelena! Poppa Luigi! It's Federigo! It's three of the morning and he's not returned,' she shouted, thumping on the door with all her might.

'Rouse the guards,' Luigi shouted to his valet a few minutes later as they all converged in the hallway in their nightclothes. Maria took off after the man. Not wishing her to be in the courtyard alone in the company of servants, Maddelena and Luigi followed.

Maria stood with Laura and her parents-in-law, shivering in the cold, crisp air. Laura ran back upstairs to fetch her mistress a mantle. 'Tell Rosa to bring one down for me as well,' called Maddelena after her. Luigi's valet went around with his flaming torch, and all of their faces became illuminated in the blackness as he ignited the other torches spaced around the courtyard in their sconces. Maria looked up at the sliver of crescent moon and watched as a dark cloud blotted it from sight.

The guards appeared within two or three minutes: Luigi had trained them to be alert for any contingency. As he ordered them where to go in search of Federigo, Maria went to Maddelena and dolefully rested her head against her shoulder, like a child. The taller woman patted her head affectionately, saying, 'He'll walk through that door at any minute and have a fine time laughing at us all.'

'Pray God that it be so,' murmured Maria.

One of the guards was referred to as Atlas because he was so large and strong. He'd unbolted the heavy wooden doors that sealed the entrance to the courtyard and was having trouble opening one of them. 'Something's obstructing this door,' he muttered, trying to force it.

Another guard opened the other door and stepped outside, followed by Atlas and Luigi's valet carrying his flaming torch. A silence ensued. Those in the courtyard looked with dread toward the open door.

'Oh, master,' came the deep voice of Atlas.

Although Maria remembered the events of that night vividly, the details of the ensuing moments were a blur. Only fragments remained: Maddelena's blood-curdling screams; her own terrible ones, which sounded unnatural to her ears even as they escaped her throat; and Luigi's strangled shouts of, 'Quick, after them, all of you. Hunt them down. Show no mercy. Keep one of them alive.'

What she would never forget was the sight of her beloved Federigo, cruelly murdered, expertly assassinated. He was sprawled in a dark pool of congealed blood, his legs splayed and his head slumped against the door as if he'd fallen down drunk. His handsome face was crisscrossed with spiteful cuts. He'd been stabbed right through the heart. His silent assailants must have known that he was the only Carafa who scorned being accompanied by an armed guard when he went out, and that he always came in the side entrance when he returned late at night. They'd evidently been waiting in the dark lane for his return for they'd knocked him out with a blow to the head before murdering him. Their work done, they'd swiftly disappeared back to their life in the shadows. They were never found. Nobody knew anything. A plot so secret, a killing so efficient, could only have been the people's retribution. 'The Carafas will pay for this.' And the Carafas did pay, with Federigo, the only Carafa who'd decried the family's politics and been sympathetic to the plight of the people.

Maria remained in the Carafa household throughout all of the following year. The blank horror that had seized hold of her when she'd first set eyes on the unendurable sight of Federigo murdered remained with her for all of that time and remained in the back of her mind still, and would cease only with her own death. At the sight of Federigo her mind had felt like the site of a gigantic explosion of two conflicting thoughts. The first was inevitability—she'd known, always known, that this or something like it would be visited upon Federigo. The second was impossibility—this thing hadn't really happened, it couldn't have, there had been a mistake; the clock would turn back, the night would begin again, and Federigo would return home just as he'd always been meant to. Maria's profound grief moved even her machinating relatives. They allowed a period of fourteen months to elapse before arranging another advantageous marriage.

During this time Maria wrote a poem that she'd kept with her ever since. She'd sung it to Beatrice then, and had gone on singing it to her during their first year in Messina when Alfonso was out of earshot. She recalled it now and could remember all of it, except strangely, for the first two lines and the last two.

They lived in a palace so golden and fine
And their blissful days were all strawberries and wine.

They had a sweet baby, an angel so fair
that Flora twined flowers all through his hair.
They called him Ferrante, and prayed he'd be blessed.
Never was a son so loved and caressed.

Early one morning just before dawn
a chariot appeared, drawn by a golden unicorn.
'I've instructions to fetch you,' the winged driver cried,
and Ferrante crawled in and they fled to the skies.

They had a sweet daughter, a girl so divine
that Beauty and Grace erected her a shrine.
Papa called her Beatrice because she was blessed.
Never was a daughter so loved and caressed.

Early one morning, just before dawn
a chariot appeared, drawn by a golden unicorn.
'I've instructions to fetch you,' the winged driver cried,
and Poppa stepped in and they fled to the skies.

Now Ferrante and Poppa watch over their girls,
And sometimes appear as beautiful birds.

What a terrible wrench she'd felt when she'd gone to live at Messina, on the eastern tip of Sicily, separated from the Italian mainland by the dangerous Strait of Messina, site of whirlpools and the devouring sea monsters Scylla and Charibdis who menaced Odysseus. What had Antonia said at their tearful parting? 'You'll be back, my darling. Messina is only ever a way station on the route to somewhere else.' How right she had been.

'Come, I must show you something before we leave,' said Maria. Beatrice followed her across the courtyard to a marvellous bronze horse's head mounted on the back wall. The sculptor had shown the wrinkled flesh of the horse's neck and depicted it with its mouth open baring all of its teeth, but the lines of the profile and the form of the eyes were so graceful that it managed to look the noblest of creatures nevertheless. Beatrice laughed in response to the horse showing its teeth in an equine smile.

'This horse was given to your grandfather Carafa by Lorenzo the Magnificent, one of the Medici,' said Maria. 'It's said to possess miraculous powers. When you were a little baby, people would bring their sick animals into its presence to be cured. On market days there was a constant stream of people with sheep and goats.'

'Why don't they still bring them?' asked Beatrice.

Maria hesitated. Putting her arm around Beatrice and leaning down, she drew the little face to hers. 'Did your grandmama Maddelena tell you how your father died?' she asked.

'Yes, but I think she left things out so as not to upset me,' said Beatrice frankly. 'She said some bad men killed him, but I don't understand why they did.'

'It was because they wanted to kill a Carafa, Beatrice, and in so doing they wanted to bring terrible suffering upon the whole family. Your father was the most precious of the Carafas. He was young and he was the heir. Therefore he was the one the family would most sorely miss. So it was him they chose.'

'Why did they want to kill a Carafa?'

'Your father used to say that the Carafas were too rich and that the ordinary people were too poor, and that the people hated and blamed the Carafas for this. It's far more complicated than this for it's to do with the politics of Naples and the Spanish and taxes . . . your father understood it all. Perhaps when you are older one of your cousins will explain it to you.'

'Cousin Fabrizio would know.'

'He would, but I was about to tell you why people don't bring their animals here any more.'

'Yes. Why?'

'Because after your father's murder the doors of Palazzo Carafa were never opened to the people again.'

Maria regretted not having gone to the palace sooner for Beatrice's sake. As they walked back to San Severo the little girl chatted excitedly about her cousins, how they had embraced her as one of their own, how they had invited her on their regular excursions to the bay, and how thirteen-year-old Marc Antonio Carafa had promised to teach her how to sail.

'Marc Antonio has his very own sailing ship,' Beatrice proudly informed her, continuing with the thrilling topic of her Carafa cousins even when she and her mother were back at San Severo, being fussed over by Sylvia in Maria's blue salon. 'It was crafted especially for him by the shipwrights who make the fishing boats.'

Carlo unexpectedly appeared in the salon, having entered by the spiral staircase via Maria's bedchamber. He looked untidy, one of the white shirts with billowing sleeves that he usually wore tucked into his trousers hanging loosely about him, only half buttoned. Beatrice stood and curtseyed to him with ironic politeness, a little habit she had developed of late.

Without greeting them, he sat on a sturdy panel-backed chair opposite them and fixed his eyes on Beatrice. 'Why this masquerade of curtseying whenever you encounter me, Beatrice?' he asked irritably.

'I'm being polite. I thought you would like it,' she answered, her happiness evaporated and now on her guard.

'If you were as clever as you like to think yourself, you would have observed by now that one of the very things I do *not* like is empty formality, particularly from a member of my own household.'

'I must take the blame, Carlo,' said Maria, noting he was in a strange mood and afraid that her daughter would be the target of it. 'Beatrice is merely following her instincts. She's not been schooled in how to behave properly with you.'

'That doesn't require an education,' he shouted. 'That is precisely my point. Let us cease this empty talk of manners and go swiftly to the heart of the matter. I suspect she makes these little curtsies as a way of annoying me. Or even of expressing a certain contempt for me.'

'No, Carlo!' exclaimed Maria.

'Is that not so, Beatrice?' he asked, tapping one of his feet in vexation.

The child reddened, one of the rare times Maria had seen her embarrassed, and looked from Carlo to Maria to Sylvia, unsure of how to respond. Sylvia hovered near the door, unconsciously wringing her hands.

'Answer me!' thundered Carlo.

Beatrice shot up out of her seat as if she must make ready to physically defend herself, flicking her hair back as defiantly as she dared. 'Yes,' she admitted. 'I sometimes curtsey to annoy you.'

'Beatrice,' sighed Maria, frowning at her daughter in consternation.

'And who else do you deliberately set out to annoy?' he asked coldly.

'For pity's sake, don't cross-question her like this, Carlo,' pleaded Maria. 'She's a child and sometimes acts thoughtlessly.'

Carlo ignored her and went on looking at Beatrice with a cold interrogative stare.

'Nobody else,' replied Beatrice, her face a study of willed calmness. She hated Prince Carlo when he was like this. Hated him.

'I am the only one who is so privileged?'

'Yes, Prince Carlo,' responded Beatrice quietly, at pains now to be genuinely polite. Maria's heart went out to her. It wasn't in the child's nature to dissimulate like this.

'Why am I so singled out?' he asked.

'Carlo, please!' begged Maria, rising.

'Sit down! Don't interfere,' he ordered, his eyes never leaving Beatrice's face. 'This is not the occasion for one of your heartfelt speeches. Answer me, Beatrice.'

The child considered for a moment. It was no use trying to pretend with Prince Carlo; he saw through even the mildest falsehood. Only the truth would do. 'I don't know exactly,' she began. 'I didn't plan on doing it. It just happened. It's a kind of game, a way of daring myself to be naughty to you. I only expected to annoy you a little, not make you really angry, and I thought you'd see it was a game and tolerate it from on high the way adults do. I thought that's what you *were* doing from the way you looked at me every time I curtseyed, as if you were saying, "Don't think I don't know what you're up to."'

Carlo stared hard at Beatrice. 'So I tolerate it from on high, do I?' He mused on this phrase as if it held a certain appeal for him.

Sylvia took advantage of the momentary lull in the impending storm to announce, 'It is time for my little lady to take her supper, Your Excellency.' She curtseyed, then, uncertain now if this was the correct thing to do, rose quickly, faltered, and half curtseyed again, provoking a laugh from Carlo that stopped as unexpectedly as it had begun. He waved them out of the room with his customary flicking gesture.

He then turned on Maria. 'Members of the Carafa guard spent the morning in the courtyard, disrupting the work of my men with their lounging about and idle conversation. Salvatore reported that they then escorted you and Beatrice somewhere. Pietro told me he saw you return with them but a short while ago. Would you be so good as to inform me of what is taking place in my household?'

Now it's my turn to be interrogated, thought Maria as she explained her visit to the Carafa palace.

'Why was it necessary for the Carafas to send a guard to protect you?' he asked angrily.

'Spaccanapoli is too dangerous for Beatrice and I to walk in unaccompanied. Surely you know that,' she replied, sensing that he would find fault with whatever answer she gave. Something had sparked this evil mood in him, and she racked her brains as to what it could have been.

He stood up and moved close, looming over her. 'Look at me, Maria, and take heed. Don't deflect my questions by stating the obvious while affecting an innocent air. As you pretend not to take my meaning, I'll ask you again. Why the *Carafa* escort?'

'Because Maddelena sent them,' she replied with a puzzled frown.

Carlo grasped his head with both his hands as if he was about to explode with exasperation. 'Your daughter gives more honest, intelligent replies than you, and she is but ten years old,' he shouted.

Maria sighed deeply, drawing her hand to her brow, closing her eyes and saying softly, 'Something has angered you, Carlo. I cannot guess what it is. You must tell me.'

'Not one thing. Several. Allow me to enumerate them for you. No, that's too tedious. Rather let me explain to you the appropriate behaviour required of you as the Princess of Venosa.' He thumped down in the chair next to hers, leaned close so that his face was inches from hers, and grasped her chin between his thumb and forefinger, pinching it so that it was ever so slightly painful. 'You do not go abroad with a *Carafa* escort,' he enunciated slowly and contemptuously. 'If you require an escort it will be a *Gesualdo* one. You do not disappear to entertain yourself with your first husband's family without informing me or one of the servants of your whereabouts. You do not permit Maddelena Carafa, who deludedly considers herself the matriarch of this city, to make arrangements that interfere with the efficient running of this household. And so on and so on. Are you getting my drift? In short, you behave as if the honour of the Gesualdo family was something that mattered to you.'

'It does, Carlo, it does, I assure you most sincerely. I will explain my behaviour, which I confess was careless, but first I ask you to let go of my chin. You're hurting me.'

He did so, turning the movement of his fingers into a strange, proprietary caress. She guessed his anger had spent itself for he was beginning to look weary and rather bored.

'I don't wish to anger you further, but I admit I didn't even consider the matter of my escort. My only concern was that Beatrice meet her cousins so that they can bring some joy into her life, which they have. I think now she will not need to play silly games offensive to you in order to keep herself amused . . .' She went on quietly speaking to him in this soothing fashion, knowing he was only half listening, but also knowing he liked the sound and rhythms of her voice, for he had only that last week told her so.

And so it seemed to Maria that she was gradually learning how to manage Carlo. Over the following weeks she spent pleasant summer days with Beatrice, watching her run wild on the shores of the bay with her cousins, scrambling over rocks or sailing along the shoreline in one of their graceful little sailing boats. Marc Antonio Carafa taught her how to man the sail alone and, standing next to him or mistress of her own ship, she skimmed across the sparkling sea with her hair blowing free like a little mermaid. These were the moments when Beatrice was most herself. Back at San Severo she took on a stoical air, attending to what was expected of her without much heart: taking her lessons, arranging her growing collection of treasures, sitting talking or reading with her mother, and keeping out of Carlo's way unless he happened to be in a good mood.

Although there had been all-too-fleeing moments of fulfilment, Maria had resigned herself to the fact that marriage to Carlo was the best that she could now expect from life, that she would never again experience happiness of the kind she'd known with Federigo. Joy was to be forever out of her reach.

In the new year a visit to a midwife confirmed that she was pregnant. She told no one of this. Carlo must be the first to know and she awaited her moment. The extent to which she dreaded living through another pregnancy she did not fully admit even to herself: it meant being racked with nausea for months, the agony and danger of childbirth, Carlo's disappointment if it was a girl—and only God knew how he would react to that—and the terrible fear that this child, too, would not survive. She'd had nearly three years' respite from pregnancies, but even so, she didn't yet feel up to the ordeal. Only one thing gave her hope: that it might forge a bond of intimacy between her and Carlo. This was the reason she awaited her moment.

Maria entered her blue salon followed by Laura, who bore a stack of books that Maria had selected from the downstairs library to read in the coming months.

'Arrange them there, in three neat stacks,' said Maria, indicating a square table in the middle of the room. She remained near the door, appraising her handiwork. She'd spent the day having the furniture in the room rearranged less formally and more to her taste. A pair of superb hand-painted cabinets had been placed together as a feature of the long wall opposite, at the far left of which were the double doors to the inner rooms of her apartment. The writing table was against the far wall in the full light of the tall windows, and now that winter had set in the larger chairs were grouped around the fireplace.

'Put that pair of painted candlesticks there, too, and fetch the majolica vase from my bedchamber. I want fresh flowers in here daily, Laura. Though it's past the season, tell the flower-seller to bring us whatever white and pale-pink blooms he can find.'

'Your Aunt Antonia has hers delivered directly from a hothouse. Shall I ask her maid . . .'

'All right. But try the flower-seller first and tell him we want hothouse flowers. They must arrive first thing each morning.'

Though the salon was arranged more comfortably, it still lacked intimacy. Carlo had selected the furniture and the decorative scheme before their marriage, and now that she'd been at San Severo for well over a year it was time to put her own stamp on her surroundings. She'd had no inclination to do this before her pregnancy; she'd been with child enough times to recognise that this urge to re-order her surroundings, and thereby claim them, was a nesting instinct. The room needed more personal touches, however.

Above the mantle hung a *capriccio* scene of an arcaded antique building, the figures standing on its steps casting long afternoon shadows. Its pervading yellow tonality had never appealed to Maria and she rang for a man to take it down. While he was doing so she had Laura search her three as yet unpacked trunks for the object she planned to replace the painting with.

Maria watched Laura place the retrieved Victory statuette she'd discovered at Ischia on the mantelpiece. Its pale alabaster, set off by the blue wall behind, was similar to the creamy marble of the mantel so that statue and fireplace formed a pleasing continuum.

Maria walked about the room making adjustments to the placement of objects, a little smile on her face, for the introduction of the Victory had indeed made the room feel her own. Something was still missing, though. What it was eluded her. Carlo would know. On the spur of the moment she called for Sylvia to have him sent for.

'I'm leaving for gli Astruni early in the morning,' he said as he strode in, then 'Ah' as he noted the changes to the room. He moved immediately toward the Victory and, taking it up and exploring it with his fingers, asked, 'Where did you find this? Is it a d'Avalos heirloom?'

'In a sense. I found it in my Aunt Costanza's chamber at Ischia. I suspect it's classical. What do you think?'

'Yes, it's Hellenistic. You can tell because of the extreme delicacy of the carving. The Romans were cruder.' He held it up to the light, inspecting its transparency. "It's exceptionally beautiful.'

'Its pagan nature doesn't offend you?' Maria asked.

'Should it?' There were bags under Carlo's eyes, as if he hadn't slept well.

'No. It's made me realise that beauty exists in a realm beyond faith.'

'You're philosophical this afternoon. Perhaps you should sit down and take up your pen. Did you wish to show me your rearranged salon or is there something else you require of me?'

'Yes, your advice. The room lacks something. The Victory has enlivened it, but . . .'

'It's in the wrong place. It must be placed in front of light.' He picked up the statue, crossed the room and placed it on her desk. 'Now it can watch over you while you write. The room does need something else but I've no time to think of it now. I'll be gone for three days and must make my preparations.' He made for the door.

'Carlo.'

'Yes, what is it?' He turned, his hand on the door handle.

'There is something I must tell you. Sit down for a moment.'

'Not now.'

'Yes, *now!*' she shouted, stamping her foot. 'It's important.'

He stared at her in astonishment before sitting on the edge of a stiff-backed chair next to the painted cabinets. 'All right, then. Quickly.'

She sank into a comfortable chair and spoke to him across the room. 'No, not quickly, Carlo. You'll soon see how important this is. Before I tell you though, there is something else I must say. Are you listening?' His eyes were fixed on the Victory.

'As my plans for the afternoon are being interrupted so that your priceless piece of information can be conveyed to me, yes, I am indeed listening.'

'What staggering intuition you have,' she said angrily. 'Priceless! Yes it is, this child of yours that I am carrying.' She paused, registering his surprise as he absorbed this piece of news. 'Now will you give me some time and listen to what I have to say?'

'I am pleased, Maria, I cannot tell you how pleased,' he said quietly and sincerely, his manner an abrupt about-face of what it had been but a minute ago. 'Is it really so? When did you learn of it? When might we expect the child?'

'In the autumn, late September perhaps. The midwife confirmed it a few days ago but I can in any case assure you it's so because the nausea that comes upon me in waves throughout the day can have no other cause.

Come and sit closer to me,' she said a little sadly, hurt that he'd not instinctively moved nearer to her, had not kissed or embraced her.

He sat down opposite her. 'What must I do?' he asked.

'You must be kinder to me,' she replied firmly. 'Often you are rude, cold and dismissive. I understand that this is a way of dealing with the world that you have long fallen into the habit of, and you may go on behaving with others as you please, but to me you must show more consideration. As I will often be feeling ill in the coming months, I ask you to be patient, gentle and kind. I know you to be capable of it from the tenderness with which you take up your lute. Do I ask too much?'

One of his sardonic smiles appeared. 'Are you using the occasion of your pregnancy to temper my behaviour?'

'Yes, I am, and with good reason. Wouldn't you say so?'

'I'm not sure. The role of lugubriously solicitous husband has never appealed to me.'

'You exaggerate what I ask of you and turn it into a nonsense! I'm not in the mood for such shallow repartee. I am pregnant with your child. Either you will behave kindly toward me and I will have a comfortable, healthy pregnancy, or you will not, in which case my burden will be all the heavier and the health of your child less certain. The responsibility is not mine alone, but yours equally. It's for you to choose. And now you must excuse me. I feel the need to vomit.'

When Maria returned to the salon after retching and lying on her bed for an hour, Carlo was still there. The room was noticeably changed, for Carlo had had another, far larger, painting brought up and now this joyous, Arcadian scene hung above the mantle. Beneath trees inhabited by bright songbirds, Orpheus played his viol surrounded by an audience of nymphs and delightful animals, a peacock arranging its gorgeous tail right across the bottom half of the picture.

'Does that add the required finishing touch to the princess's salon?' Carlo asked.

'Yes,' replied Maria flatly, the question of the room's decoration no longer important in the light of Carlo's response to the news of her pregnancy. The Orpheus painting was evidently his way of apologising, making amends, showing his interest, who knew what? she thought crossly.

If only he'd simply kissed her hand or smiled at her with pleasure. She rang for Sylvia.

'It's one of my favourite paintings,' prompted Carlo.

'Is it? Then perhaps you should have it in your room.'

'It was intended for the music room. I bought it only last week. Do you not like it? I can have others brought up.'

'No, this is the one I want. It's charming. Shouldn't you be preparing for your hunting trip?'

Sylvia appeared. Maria asked her to make the hot, sweet, herbal drink she had concocted especially for her mistress. ''Would you like some, too?' Maria asked Carlo.

'What's in it?' he asked.

'Honey, whey, nutmeg, and plants that grow only in Sicily which you would never have heard of, if you'll excuse me for saying so, your Excellency,' replied Sylvia.

'I'd be interested to try it.'

When Sylvia departed Carlo swept his eyes around the room and turned his attention back to Maria. 'Why don't we have your whole apartment redecorated?' he enthused. 'We must prepare two or three rooms for the child in any case.'

'Yes, of course, but not the whole apartment. There would be too much upheaval. I need to have peace around me.'

'I know a team of decorators who work very quickly. A mere three weeks and your rooms will be transformed into a paradisaical garden, Dido's Carthage, whatever you wish.'

Maria could not help but smile. It occurred to her that her news had indeed made Carlo happy, and his idea of redecorating her apartment was his way of expressing that happiness. 'Should we not tell your parents our news?' she suggested.

'I'll tell my father tonight.'

'I think the both of us should tell the two of them together. Let's take dinner with them.' The idea of a family meal suddenly appealed to Maria enormously. She realised with a pang that she missed the atmosphere of warmth and familiarity at such gatherings.

'No. Their constant bickering when they eat renders food indigestible. Besides, I like to eat alone, as you know. We'll go down after supper. Your favourite colour is green. Why not have the walls in here redone in the right shade of very pale green.'

'It's not necessary. Now that you have put the painting there I like things well enough as they are. In any case, it's better that I devote what energy I have to preparing the baby's rooms.'

'Do you have any ideas?'

'Vague ones. I'd like the nursery walls to be covered in fresco, something fantastical of the kind one imagines must appear in the dreams of happy children. An ancient lost city sunk beneath the sea. A magical forest inhabited by iridescent fairies and friendly, exotic creatures. I don't know.'

'A sapphire, starlit sky. Smiling angels floating on clouds,' suggested Carlo.

'No, not angels.'

'Why not?'

'I've seen too many rooms decorated with angels. I want something more unusual.' The real reason was that Maria associated angels with Federigo and their bedchamber at Palazzo Carafa, but she could not tell Carlo this. 'Why don't you ask one of your artist friends to sketch some ideas for us?'

'I was thinking along those lines, but my friends, no. They're not practised in scenes of fantasy. I'll find a painter who specialises in such things.'

'Good.' Maria stood up and rubbed the small of her back. 'I suppose he'll work with a team, but it'll still take weeks. And I can't bear the thought of remaining here amidst all the noise and the painters moving about. It'd be so disruptive. It looks as if Beatrice and I will have to move to an unoccupied part of the palace for a while.'

'Perhaps not,' said Carlo, thoughtfully running his fingers over his chin.

'What's the alternative?'

'For you and I to go on a journey.'

'You know I don't like leaving Naples.'

Sylvia returned and they watched as she set the tray on the table and poured their drinks.

'That didn't take you long,' observed Carlo.

'I keep a batch of it already made up, your Excellency. It's only a matter of adding the whey and heating it.'

She set up a little table between them and carried the drinks there, enjoying the rare sight of her mistress and young master sitting and taking refreshment together as other married people did. She could make neither head nor tail of their strange relationship, as she'd never struck anything like it in her life. It was a lonely sight, her mistress taking her meals by herself. Often in the evenings Maria ate early so as to have the company of Beatrice. Still, even Sylvia understood that Maria's enforced solitude in this marriage was far preferable to the relentless companionship of her husband in the previous one. Prince Carlo seemed to be enjoying the drink, and him so fastidious. She sent up a prayer of thanks. Perhaps the marriage was going to improve. They were discussing taking a journey together. Sylvia hoped with all her heart she'd be accompanying them, for as she left the room she heard Prince Carlo say they were going to a holy mountain.

Seven

GESUALDO CASTLE

Carlo had been to Gesualdo Castle three times since the wedding, but only now did Maria agree to accompany him there. She insisted that Beatrice go with them, though neither Carlo nor Beatrice herself wished for this. The castle was isolated in the foothills of the Apennine Mountains, remote from civilised society. Loneliness loomed and Maria wished for the comfort and amusement of her daughter's companionship. As she grew older Beatrice was developing a talent for astute observation, and her wry comments, the way in her innocence she cut through to the truth of things, gladdened Maria's heart.

Winter had settled over the landscape. Large patches of snow gleamed in the sun. As they drove south, the Apennines cutting across the horizon in the distance were the same steel blue as the sky, so that their snowy peaks seemed to levitate above low lines of rolling cloud.

Maria shivered. Carlo, rather tenderly, wrapped the bearskin rug more closely around her. Her pregnancy was now in its third month and was beginning to show in her thickening waistline and slight stomach bulge. Carlo wished for her and their expected child to be blessed by the Black Lady of Montevergine. The monastery that housed the famed icon was at Avelino, only a few miles distant from Gesualdo, and Carlo had consequently insisted on Maria accompanying him to the castle this time, before it became too late in the pregnancy for her to travel.

They stayed overnight at one of Carlo's country villas, continuing the journey early the next morning. By the afternoon the mighty sculpted forms of the Apennines surrounded them. Carlo had allowed plenty of time to reach the monastery before nightfall, but the steep, winding ascent was tortuous; the horses' hooves and carriage-wheels scrunched in the snow and Maria was terrified and nauseous. Twice the carriage stopped so that she could alight and retch convulsively, Beatrice clasping her hand and Carlo holding her from behind around the waist so she wouldn't slip in the snow. Even though it was growing darker—worryingly so—the snow's whiteness was blinding. Inside the carriage, Maria laid her aching head against Carlo's shoulder as he mopped her sweating brow. Alarmed at her paleness and the frailty of her body as he held her, he murmured, 'I shouldn't have brought you here.'

'No, you should not have,' echoed Beatrice.

Half an hour later they reached the monastery. Inside warm fires, wholesome food and clean beds awaited them. Maria could not even look at the food. She was soon fast asleep in the warm bed and did not awaken until eleven hours later.

She did so refreshed and eager to accompany Carlo and Beatrice to the chapel to be blessed by Our Lady of Montevergine. Carlo had told her that the ancient icon was the largest in the world—an astonishing eighteen feet high and almost ten feet wide.

Carlo went down on his knees in front of the image, his forehead touching the floor. Maria knelt as far as her growing belly would comfortably allow. Beatrice stood open-mouthed for a minute or two before following suit. This ancient, revered image of the Virgin was indeed awesome, only in part because of its commanding scale. It was not majestic. It was, strangely, the opposite. Its power resided not in the ethereal qualities of the Virgin, but rather in the southern Italian earthiness of her, for her ninth-century creator had depicted her as a black-haired, darkly olive-skinned young Neapolitan woman, hence her popular title, the Black Lady. Paradoxically, it was this very humanity that imbued her with a mysterious aura. She was of this earth and this region and Maria experienced her as a presence very near to her.

Carlo sat up and placed his hand on Maria's belly, murmuring in Latin a prayer that their child be a healthy son and that the Lady of Montevergine protect him now and always. With the warmth of his hand

Maria's nausea returned, and silently begging the Black Lady to come to her aid so that she would not vomit at this moment so sacred to Carlo, she held back the contents of her stomach with a mighty effort, surreptitiously dribbling what refused to stay down into her handkerchief.

Before they left the monastery, the abbot presented to Maria three earthenware jars containing herbal concoctions. He told her the monks had prepared them especially for the Princess of Venosa. Her husband the prince had last night told him the joyous news. Tied around the necks of the jars were instructions for use: one mixture to be taken during pregnancy, one to be taken after the birth by the mother, and the smallest trace of the third to be placed daily under the tongue of the wet-nurse. These potions would ensure the continuing strength of both mother and child.

'Don't regret having brought me here, Carlo,' said Maria as the horses carefully picked their way down the slippery mountain track. 'This holy place has dispelled my fears for our child.' And my darling Beatrice, she added silently to herself, for it had been her daughter in particular she'd prayed for. Carlo had a fiery energy that made her confident his child would thrive, and Maria, although he did not love her with the passion she would have liked, felt safe with him—at least in her role as mother of his child. It was Beatrice whose future was uncertain. Although Carlo did his duty by her daughter, it sometimes brought tears to Maria's eyes, when she contrasted the unbalanced nature of Beatrice's life at San Severo—often on her own, surrounded by women and rarely in the company of males—and what it would have been had Federigo lived and she'd been reared in the warmth of Palazzo Carafa. The Carafas would have planned a comfortable and, if possible, happy future for her. As it was, Maria felt powerless when she considered her daughter's fate.

They passed through Avelino, entering into a sublime ice blue and white landscape where nearby lines of mountains cut across distant ones that receded into infinity, powdered snow defining their muscular bulk. By early afternoon they reached the foothills. The carriage passed between rows of fir trees with wads of snow clinging to their branches. In the distance was a flat landscape stretching to the horizon, a great rock rising at its centre, on the top of which sat a stark stone castle with circular watchtowers at its four corners. This was Gesualdo Castle and its surrounding fiefdom.

As they drew closer the old castle became less forbidding: its upper tower windows were softened by arches; French doors and delicate iron balconies could be made out on the top storey. The thick fortified wall around the base of the castle disappeared into a forest of bare winter branches and patches of greenery.

Beatrice's face, pressed to the window, became alert with interest as the carriage approached the entrance. She gave a little cry of pleasure at the sight of a fantastic maze of topiaried trees, stone staircases and sculpted rock forms. A large area at the base of the rock on which Gesualdo Castle stood was being transformed into an oasis of artistic creation in this remote no-man's-land. Beatrice looked ready to leap out of the carriage and disappear into it.

'That is the garden I have been working on for the past two years,' said Carlo, and he looked at Beatrice long and hard. She knew the meaning of that look. It said, 'You can explore the garden tomorrow with your mother if she is feeling strong enough. For the moment you must behave properly and be introduced to the servants,' or something to that effect. Beatrice had learned to read Carlo's quietly threatening looks, for this was how he generally communicated with her. Once, only once, had he unleashed his cold anger on her and it had been so terrible that she had not told her mother, for it seemed to her that Maria was often miserable and she didn't wish to make her more so.

The incident had come about because one of her tutors had set her the rather silly exercise of writing a piece on Dante and his muse, Beatrice: what was the nature of Beatrice's influence on Dante's poetry? Beatrice had decided to write something more interesting than the standard story of Dante having glimpsed his Beatrice but once, fallen passionately in love, and conjured her up as his muse ever after. After having read Dante's own comments in the *Vita Nuova*, she'd written a short piece to the effect that Dante had come to regard Beatrice as the instrument of his spiritual salvation.

Beatrice had worked hard on her composition all morning and found she'd rather enjoyed it. She'd just completed it when Carlo came into the schoolroom to discuss her progress with her tutor. He did this once every week or two and usually, give or take a reprimand or exhortation or two, things went smoothly enough. This time, however, Carlo picked up her composition and read it. She was rather pleased, for she considered it well written and clever for someone of her age, so when Carlo glanced down at her upon reading it, she smiled up at him with confidence. His face impassive, he looked across at her tutor.

'Have you read this?' he asked him, ruffling it in the air.

'Not yet. I was about—'

'Then leave the room.' Carlo sat down opposite Beatrice, tossed the composition across to her and with narrowed eyes asked, 'Where have your ideas come from, for you to write such preposterous drivel?'

'From Dante himself,' she answered, stunned at this attack, trying to hide her disappointment that Carlo had not found it clever.

Carlo responded to this with the most horrible laugh, a hollow, sneering laugh that implied she was an imbecile. 'Dante attribute his salvation to a woman!' he sniggered. 'We are talking about a great poet's relationship with God.'

'He says as much himself in *Vita Nuova*,' she said quietly, although she wondered briefly whether she should have said anything at all. Her little composition had triggered one of Carlo's tempers, so be it, but if she contradicted him, perhaps his mood would take hold of him and worsen.

'Where? Show it to me.'

She showed him the passage. In spite of her instinct to leave well enough alone, she was not able to desist continuing to contradict Carlo when he insisted that her interpretation of the passage was wrong, that Dante had meant something else entirely. She became increasingly upset as their unpleasant debate headed the way of personal insult; to her mortification she came close to tears. It was not only Carlo's coldness and shouting that had upset her, it was a new element in his relations with her—injustice. He was denying the truth of what was before his very eyes in black and white. Beatrice suspected that Carlo had never before read this passage of Dante, and because he didn't like what he'd read, was pretending that Dante was saying something else entirely. What he did next was even worse: he tried to manipulate Beatrice into denying her own intelligence by insisting she agree with him in this. He did this by implying that Beatrice was stupid, stupid beyond endurance. There was malice as well as cruelty in this, for Carlo knew that Beatrice considered herself clever—hadn't Maria always told her so?—and that this was very important to her. Beatrice had determined there and then that she would never again present Carlo with an opportunity to speak to her in that way.

Now Beatrice returned Carlo's look with one of her own: a tight, ironic little smile followed by a slow blink. This was how she responded to his silent threats. It irritated him, she knew, but not enough to make him lose his temper.

The carriage passed under a broad arch and drew up in the central courtyard. The prince and his family alighted. Maria shivered as she looked about her at the walls with their arches punctuated by flat pilasters, above them a balcony extending around the four sides onto which the upper rooms led. She found it elegant but bleak. Beatrice walked with Laura, behind Carlo and Maria, nodding to the numerous servants who had gathered to welcome them. Maria noticed that they were all men, and that they greeted their prince with warmth in their eyes, a manner respectful but betraying a genuine affection that she had rarely seen anyone express toward her husband. This then, she thought to herself, was Carlo's kingdom.

His other fiefdom at Venosa, to which Maria had accompanied him shortly after their wedding, was far, far larger than this, but Carlo had a greater affection for Gesualdo, and now she understood why.

Gesualdo was his ancient family seat. Venosa, although it was a wealthier fiefdom—and carried with it the title 'prince', as well as having been a gift from King Phillip of Spain—had been in the family only since Francesco Gesualdo's marriage to Geronima: that is, less than thirty years. Their ownership of the Gesualdo lands went back centuries, to Norman times, and this accounted for Carlo's preference.

In the coming days it also became clear to Maria that Gesualdo Castle was where the prince's considerable creative energy was expended. Not only was there the extraordinary garden—which few palaces in Naples could match for beauty and invention—but considerable work had been and was still being carried out on refurbishing the interior, for the castle was over a century old.

The next day, Maria was well rested—she had again slept for almost twelve hours. Sleep was the only thing that kept continuous nausea at bay during her pregnancies; it was good to feel sufficiently relaxed to sleep for such long periods; it augured well for the child.

Carlo showed Maria through room after well-proportioned room on each of the castle's three floors. Tall inset windows framed panoramic views of the prince's snow-covered dominion: the tiled roofs of the surrounding township, the flat fields and distant mountains.

'I will bring you here next in the summer, after our child is born,' said Carlo. 'Then all of this snow will be field after field of corn and other crops that stretch as far as the mountains.'

Carlo was justifiably proud of the Gesualdo grain fields. Before her marriage, Prince d'Avalos had taken the trouble to explain to Maria why he considered Carlo such a good prospect for marriage. Contrary to the general state of the Neapolitan nobility, the Prince of Venosa's finances were healthy. The Kingdom of Naples was going through one of the worst periods of economic crisis in its history and the fortunes of many of its old baronial families were dwindling. Naples' wealth was tied up with the exporting of grain; yields had been so low of late that there had been a dramatic decrease in exports. Maria's father did not say that this was in part because the barons had neglected their estates and allowed them to fall into ruin, as he had his. As a result there was now a return to feudalism, to the old ways of making money. Prince Francesco Gesualdo seemed to have anticipated this, having years ago stepped up rather than neglected his responsibilities as a feudal lord. Carlo, schooled by his father, was also attending to moneymaking by adhering to the old feudal ways. The labour of the Gesualdo's subjects on the Gesualdo's lands guaranteed an income for generations. The Gesualdo's crops brought in a prosperous annual income of more than 40 000 ducats. Carlo could thus well afford to engage the best artisans to decorate and re-create areas of Gesualdo Castle in a style more to his taste.

One of these artisans was Massimo Redi, a master of the new style and one of the most fashionable garden designers in southern Italy. Redi ignored all the rules of classical design. Only he had the talent and daring to realise Carlo's vision of a garden of dreams around the sloping base of the great rock on which the castle stood. Although there were small areas of ground for growing fruit trees, vegetables and herbs within the castle walls, there was insufficient room to lay out a garden in the traditional manner, so the unusual choice of site was governed as much by necessity as whim. Carlo worked with Redi on the designs. This was the first and only time Redi had allowed such artistic interference, and he did so because he found the Prince of Venosa not only sympathetic but inspirational: it was a case of the patron being more eccentric than the artist, and Redi found this liberating. The garden was scattered over a wide area, amidst the sloping woods of recently planted trees. The idea was that the walker would suddenly encounter a surprising world of grotesquery and phantasmagorical plant forms, as if he had strayed off the path of reality into a daydream. The master designer had brought with him a team of workmen and his best rock sculptors, who were in the process of transforming outcrops of rock into grottos, fountains and mythological beings. Some of the ornamented stone staircases were carved out of the rock face itself; this was the most arduous and time-consuming part of the work.

Still, after two years, large areas of the garden were nearing completion. Work had ceased over winter. Redi and his workmen would return in the spring. The design was one of technical as well as artistic genius, for Redi had engineered hidden machinery and water catchments that trapped the melting snow, which was used as a source of water for the fountains, grottos and ornamental pools.

Beatrice ran up a curved flight of steps and disappeared into the enormous gaping mouth of goggle-eyed Orcus, the god of the Underworld. Inside, the cavernous, darkly dripping grotto of tufa stalactites was like nothing she had ever seen. It was nightmarish. Cold and sinister like Carlo in one of his tempers. She fled back outside, into the light. Further up, she encountered a statue of Ceres, the corn goddess, crowned with a breadbasket. The child sat on a stone bench beside this friendlier form and waited for her mother. It was silent up here and the air was cold. She pulled her fur-lined mantle tightly about her and looked around at the trees, manicured into fantastic shapes. Their dark alien forms seemed to threaten her. She imagined them moving, coming toward her. This place was Carlo's idea of a garden of delights, not hers. She hated it, hated its weirdness and loneliness and secrecy and monsters.

Laura appeared, panting up the path. 'Beatrice! There you are. Don't run ahead like that. You could get lost in here.'

Beatrice took the young maid's hand, asking, 'Where's Mama?'

'She's in a pavilion, resting. She's tired from all the climbing. She's going back soon, but said for me to stay with you if you want to go on exploring.' Laura crouched down next to Beatrice, gave her a little hug and kissed her cheek. The child responded with a wet little kiss of her own and Laura whispered smilingly, 'Shall we go exploring together?'

'Don't you think it would be nicer inside, by the fire?' asked Beatrice.

'I do, but you'll be bored after only a few minutes.'

'Let's go back anyway.'

Laura laughed and they walked back down the path hand in hand.

'Do you like this place?' asked Beatrice.

'I think it will be much nicer in the summer. It's too cold to be walking in gardens at this time of year.'

'Yes, I know. But do you like it? The monsters and the frightening trees?'

'I don't know. It's interesting, but I prefer gardens with roses and pretty coloured summer flowers that give out a beautiful perfume, like the one your Aunt Antonia has in Naples.'

'So do I,' agreed Beatrice. 'And Aunt Antonia always smells like she's just been in her garden.'

'Yes, she does. But your mother says that this garden is very fashionable, and she knows a great deal about what is fashionable.'

'This castle isn't,' scoffed Beatrice. 'It's too old even if Prince Carlo is trying to make it look new again by painting new colours and patterns on the walls and planting this garden.'

'You don't like it, do you, Beatrice?'

'No. It's like a nightmare.'

'Please try to keep this to yourself, or you'll offend Prince Carlo and upset your mother.'

'Mama won't be upset if she knows I don't like it.'

'Perhaps not, but she *will* be upset if you annoy the prince. Try to be tactful, Beatrice.'

'I'm too young to be tactful.'

'No Beatrice, you're not too young. You're too stubborn.'

'I heard dogs howling last night,' said Beatrice, deflecting Laura's accurate assessment of her character. Laura was surprisingly observant at times. 'Did you hear them?'

'Yes. They weren't dogs, they were wolves. Were you frightened?'

'Only a little bit,' replied Beatrice. 'Were you?'

Laura hesitated before replying, 'Yes, I was. It was such a lonely, mournful sound.' The young maid looked around her at the thick clumps of snow weighing down the branches of the trees, at the castle looming above them on its rock, at the icicle-encrusted mouth of a dark gargoyle on the fountain ahead of them. She looked down at Beatrice and their eyes met. 'It's so silent here, it makes me shiver,' she said.

The next day Carlo went hunting with a band of cavaliers that lived permanently at the castle. Maria heard an old servant remark to his master that they'd be lucky to find any game, as the animals would be hibernating in their sleeping hollows. Carlo replied that there were bound to be wolves or elk in the mountains.

He didn't return that night. Nor the next.

Another day and another night passed.

Maria spent her days by the fire with Laura. They found little to gossip about in this remote place. Reading now held no pleasure as Maria had found it difficult to concentrate since her pregnancy. Beatrice, too, was growing restless. With Carlo absent, Maria and Laura's insistence that she occupy herself with drawing or studies was fruitless. The child trailed through the rooms of the castle, striking up conversations with the servants, seeking out one who might show or tell her something of interest.

Carlo had had the rooms decorated with a masculine, rustic simplicity that held little appeal for Maria. She particularly disliked the lunettes above the doors, still lifes of massacred animals. He had reserved the large room on the top floor as her bedchamber and it was, she was forced to admit, quite beautiful, more like two rooms divided by a graceful central archway. It was painted a soft blue-green and was otherwise undecorated. There were, thankfully, no dead animals up here.

On the third day, out of sheer boredom, Maria had paper and inks brought to her and began sketching designs for small areas of fresco decoration to enliven the room. She drew several designs, working on them until it began to grow dark. One of them she liked, a column with an ionic capital and rocaille shell motifs. She intensified the colours, choosing a surprising indigo blue to delineate the columns. She went up to the room and had Laura hold the design against the wall while she stood back to see the effect. In the candlelight it looked quite marvellous. She went to bed wondering what Carlo would think of it.

She awoke an hour later. She didn't like Carlo's male servants coming into her bedchamber when he wasn't there and the fire had died down early that night. She lay beneath the covers, shivering with cold, feeling abandoned and desolate. Though she was used to sleeping alone, at San Severo there was the comfort of knowing Carlo was close by. And the bleakness of Gesualdo Castle made her long for human warmth and intimacy. Where was Carlo? How could he bring himself to sleep outside during these freezing nights? Perhaps he had little huts or hunting lodges dotted throughout the foothills and mountains. But why would he prefer sleeping in those to being in the castle? Men were different to women, she supposed. They enjoyed the rough outdoor life.

The men returned the next afternoon with a bloodied stag draped over one of the horses, its noble, antlered head with dead, staring eyes bobbing lifelessly.

Beatrice was hanging about in the courtyard and with a supreme effort buttoned her mouth. Maria had extracted a promise from her before leaving for the castle: she was not to comment on anything connected with Carlo's hunting, either in his presence or his men's, as it enraged him.

'Just a moment,' said Beatrice as the men were about to haul the stag's carcass off the horse. Carlo smiled sardonically as he dismounted, amused at the child giving his men orders. She walked to the creature and gently stroked its face and made the sign of the cross over it. Then she closed her eyes, placed her hands together and murmured a prayer. The men watched this ritual, flabbergasted.

'You have a vocation, Beatrice,' said Carlo. 'When you're older you can found a Franciscan sisterhood.'

'And you, Prince Carlo, can be its principal donor to pay for your sins against God's creatures,' she retorted and flounced off, her eyes brimming with tears at the fate of the innocent stag.

Carlo roared with laughter and bounded up the stairs, in an excellent humour after his hunting trip.

Maria had heard them arrive. Dismissing Laura, she sat in a chair near the fire, wondering how long it would take before Carlo came to her.

Hours perhaps. He would go straight to his room and play one of his instruments, for he missed his music when he went away hunting.

He entered her room only a few minutes later, inquiring after her health and sitting in the opposite chair. He'd obviously had a quick wash and hurriedly taken off his hunting clothes, for his hair was wet and slicked back and he wore a clean white shirt, which hung loosely over an old pair of scarlet breeches. He'd brought his lute with him and some roughly notated pages of music.

'You look well rested but bored, Maria,' he said. 'Perhaps some music will cheer you. I composed a little melody on our journey here. I don't know yet how I'll develop it, but perhaps you'd like to hear it.'

'Yes, Carlo. Very much,' she responded.

The tune was haunting, slow and rather stately. He was smiling, pleased with himself. He was always at his most attractive when playing. The hunting trip had done him good, ruddied his sallow cheeks and brightened his eyes. He stopped from time to time, trying different note formations in certain phrases and marking the changes on the manuscript.

'Yes, that's much more affecting,' she commented at one point.

'It is, isn't it?' he said. 'Now listen to this.'

He played a few bars as he'd written them, a conventional dying-away at the end of a cadence. Then he changed it, reversed it, so that rather than dying away it went up the scale, then down, then up, soaring and falling like a leaf caught in the wind.

He began it again, quickening the rhythms, feeling too energised for such a solemn pace. He was rapt. She almost loved him at these moments; that is, she had a fleeting impression of a passion for him that might have existed had he always been so engaging. He increased the tempo, and then finished the piece with a conventional little flourish, laughing, for this was one of his musical jokes, to revert to tradition at an unexpected moment. The music hung in the air, energising the room. She, too, felt energised and laughed as she complimented him.

'Let's have some chocolate,' he said, ringing the bell.

He moved to the back of her chair and lifted her heavy golden hair. He kissed the back of her neck. Maria hadn't had her hair dressed today. Laura had washed it that morning in rosewater. Carlo sniffed it, breathing in its fragrance and nuzzling the back of her head. She closed her eyes, smiling at the feel of his warm breath and the sensation of pleasure it gave her.

'That smells better that horse sweat,' he said. 'What's this? he asked, moving to a table near the window.

'I was going to show you those later, Carlo. What do you think? Do you like them?'

He studied the drawings, holding them out at arm's length. 'Did you do these?' he asked.

'Yes,' she said quietly, suddenly losing confidence. The drawings were perhaps not so good after all. She'd been carried away in the moment of creating them, imagining them elegant.

'What made you use the indigo blue?'

She shrugged. 'It seemed daring. I suppose the idea might have come from your music. I had thought to do something unexpected. My first instinct was to put a soft blue there, as it would have harmonised. But I liked the lines so well, at the time anyway, that I thought to emphasise them with a discordant colour, well not entirely discordant, but surprising.'

'They are exceptional,' he said, putting one down and picking up another, studying them closely.

'So you like them?' she asked, her heart lifting.

'I do. Very much. Alfredo himself couldn't match these for elegance and invention.' Alfredo was the architect overseeing the castle's renovations. 'We must do something with them.'

'I thought to have them adapted as a decorative border for this room, if you liked them, that is,' she said shyly.

'Yes! Perfect. You are gifted, Maria. You surprise me. Although perhaps I shouldn't be surprised, remembering your talent for designing your gowns. Yet you have done nothing since. Never mind, now we have these beautiful patterns.'

There was a knock on the door and old Lorenzo, the cook, brought their chocolate into the room and carried it to the table.

'Careful,' said Carlo, moving the drawings away. 'Lorenzo, tell Alfredo to come up here immediately.'

'He's not here, Prince.'

'Where is he?'

'I don't know, Prince.'

'Send the men off to find him. I want him here before nightfall.' He strummed his fingers on the table impatiently. 'No. I want him here within the hour. He will eat with us this evening. Set things up in the dining room. What are you cooking tonight?'

'*Zuppa francese*, Prince. Will that do?'

'Excellent. And a meat dish as well. Is there some of that boar left?'

'Yes, Prince.'

'Are you sure it's still fresh?'

'Yes, Prince. It's been outside, thickly covered with snow.'

'Good. Don't roast it again. It'll be too dry. Simmer it in a tomato sauce with plenty of herbs and a little nutmeg. And make some pastries, with preserves. Some of those bitter little ones you do with lemon as well.'

'Yes, Prince.'

'And send all of the men out to find Alfredo. Alessandro as well.'

'Yes, Prince.'

Carlo took a few sips of chocolate and played through the piece again, making little adjustments here and there. If only all of my days were like this, Maria was thinking as he played. She couldn't remember when she'd last felt so happy.

Carlo put down the lute, took a few more sips of chocolate and began pacing about the room, looking out of the window from time to time. 'Where could Alfredo have got to at this time of the day?' he asked impatiently. 'He knows very well he must be on hand at all times.'

Carlo had in fact not conferred with Alfredo since he'd arrived, and the man had probably thought he wasn't required for the discussion of any new plans, as he was still busy completing the modifications to the downstairs rooms. Carlo went on pacing, a tight ball of energy that seemed to Maria to be becoming alarmingly tighter. She knew him well enough now to read his moods and was alert to any danger signs.

'He will come, Carlo. We must give the men just a little time to find him. He can't have gone far. It has made me so happy that you like my designs. Do you think they should stretch right around the room in one continuous frieze or be repeated at intervals?' she asked to distract him.

He held up one of the drawings and his eyes swept around the room.

'I know,' he said sitting down again. 'Tell me what you think.' He enjoyed aesthetic games of this nature.

She already knew but pretended to think in order to eke out the time as they waited for Alfredo. She rose, picked up two of the drawings and placed them on the wall next to each other, then apart.

'At intervals,' she said.

'You knew that already,' he said looking at her with narrowed eyes.

'That's true, but I wished to test my judgement.'

'You would already have tested their effect on the wall.'

'Only in candlelight,' she said quickly. 'Not in this light.' He was beginning to make her nervous. His cross-questioning her like this was usually the sign of a shift into a darker mood. His dissatisfaction with her answers—and he was at these times inevitably dissatisfied with any answer she might give—would provide him with a means to become angry.

'Sit down,' he said.

Here it came. She sat down and looked calmly into his eyes. He rose and threw another log on the fire, then knelt in front of it, stirring the embers to make flames, staring distractedly into the glowing coals. She wanted to touch him, soothe him, but she didn't dare. He didn't like to be touched unexpectedly.

He turned and buried his face in her swelling stomach. Now she could touch him. She ran her fingers lightly through his hair. She put the fingers of her other hand against his throat to feel his pulse. It was racing. Usually when he returned from hunting and his nerves were wound up like this, he would make love to her, but he'd forsworn lovemaking since she'd become pregnant, believing it might harm the baby.

Later that night, Maria entered Carlo's bedchamber to tell him that Alfredo had finally been located and would present himself first thing in the morning. Carlo was sitting up in his bed, his clothes loosened and his head covered with a cloth. She stood at the end of his bed, horrified at the sound of his rasping and gurgling as he tried desperately to recover his breath. She took from her neck the moonstone Parthenope had given her, which she wore always now to protect her baby. Old Lorenzo was holding a steaming bowl of a peppermint-smelling mixture under his master's nose, but Carlo could not manage an intake of breath sufficient to inhale it. To her alarm, Lorenzo looked panic-stricken. What she could see of Carlo's face under the cloth was dark crimson and he began to thrash his arms about as his throat constricted. She thought he was choking. She had no idea what to do but she acted instinctively, going to him in a kind of trance and placing her hand gently on his head.

'Sh, Carlo, sh. Calm,' she chanted softly. 'Be calm and your breath will come. Hold this. It will help you.' She placed the moonstone in his hand. 'Be calm. You are becoming calmer. You have an obstruction in your chest and I'm going to release it, then your breath will come.' She ran her hand very gently backwards and forwards over his chest, praying to God for a sudden miraculous power to heal, just this once, please, God, please, praying with all her strength, picturing God's light entering her hand and its healing radiance entering Carlo's chest and opening his air passages, please God, just this once, send me Your light and let it penetrate Carlo's chest. 'There, it's releasing now.' She stilled her hand and kept it lightly on his chest. 'Calm. Calm. Now you can breathe. Breathe, Carlo, and inhale. Calmly. Breathe and inhale.' She went on chanting this, for the trancelike state she'd induced in herself had taken hold of her, and it seemed wonderful but not surprising to her that Carlo was indeed managing to take short gasps and inhale the mixture. She went on chanting for several minutes, Lorenzo holding the steaming mixture and looking at her with awe.

At last Carlo lay back on the pillow, breathing shallowly but normally, his face now deathly white. Lorenzo removed the cloth from his master's head. Carlo took Maria's hand in his and lay there, spent, his eyes closed and his face shining with perspiration. He opened his eyes and looked at her with amazement. It was impossible to say who was the more amazed, Carlo or Maria.

'Where did you learn to have such healing powers?' he asked weakly.

'The Clarisse nuns taught me,' she lied. 'What do you think brings on these attacks, Carlo?'

'I've had them since childhood, but I can't recall an attack as ferocious as this.'

'You must sleep now,' she said, giving his forehead a couple of light strokes. 'When you awake in the morning you will feel much better.'

He smiled at her wanly. 'Usually I have an attack when I'm feeling guilty about something.'

'And what were you felling guilty about this time?' she asked gently.

He closed his eyes and opened them again. 'About leaving you alone for so long,' he said, kissing her hand.

Maria had presumed that the attack had been brought on by Carlo's anger at Alfredo's absence, but she welcomed the idea that his feelings for her may have triggered it, and welcomed even more the new intimacy it had established between them.

Eight

A STILETTO, A SECRET

The child Maria bore in the autumn of 1587 was a boy. Carlo had his heir. Love shone in her husband's eyes at last. As soon as she'd seen the joy on Carlo's face, the pride, when he'd first cupped his tiny son in his large hands and lifted him to his face to breathe in the smell of him she'd known that it was safe to give the baby over to Carlo's care. Emmanuele, as they christened him, was the eighth child Maria had borne in twelve years. The labour, mercifully, was shorter than many she'd endured, a mere nine hours, but the birth itself had been excruciatingly painful and her bleeding stung its wounds still. Intensely relieved that the infant was both a boy and healthy, she'd sunk into grey exhaustion. She had no desire for anything, only to sleep and sleep, and though she didn't understand her state and had not even the strength to wonder at it, the thought that her old griefs and losses had come back to haunt her drifted foggily in and out of her mind. She remained in bed in this state for several weeks.

Sylvia took charge. She engaged a wet-nurse and set up her bed in the baby's room, next to Maria's. Sylvia's role in the Gesualdo household was defined at last. She was Emmanuele's fierce protector. The wet-nurse was summarily dismissed by her within a week and a younger one with bigger breasts and a more copious flow of milk engaged.

With the presence of this tiny helpless baby in its crib, it seemed to Beatrice that something in the palace—the focus of its occupants, their movements, the very air she breathed—had imperceptibly but irrevocably shifted. San Severo had a new heart beating at its centre. Prince Carlo had his son. Maria was that son's mother and therefore, so it seemed, less Beatrice's mother somehow. Beatrice would go into her mother's room and sit by her bed, chattering or offering to read to her. Maria would lie there staring blankly, with a weak, wan smile: distant from her. What Beatrice did not realise was that Maria was distant from everything, Emmanuele included, locked in the floating semiconsciousness of physical and spiritual depletion.

Prince Carlo, too, was distant, which was strange because he was kinder to Beatrice now in a vague, distracted way. He no longer checked with her tutors about her lessons, so she paid less attention to her studies. She rather missed his menacing glances. Laura spent her time fetching doctors and potions, carrying trays and bowls to and from Maria's room, and reporting back to Carlo. And now Emmanuele, not Beatrice, was the great love of Sylvia's life. Beatrice began to feel more and more as if she had no place at San Severo. She was superfluous to its daily comings and goings. She wondered if anyone would notice if she simply vanished. And she began to do just that. Taking off for hours at a time, walking out of the palace entrance by herself, turning the corner, hurrying along busy Spaccanapoli, and entering the Palazzo Carafa to be with those who did notice her. Laura was the only one at San Severo who noted and chided her for this, threatening to tell Prince Carlo that she dared walk out alone in dangerous Piazza San Domenico Maggiore. The third time Beatrice received a dressing-down from Laura she lost patience.

'You needn't fear for me,' she responded. 'I look about me and carry a stiletto hidden in the fold of my skirt. I always have its handle in my grasp, ready to defend myself.'

And it was true. She did. She took out the dagger with its coiled snake handle and unsheathed its lethal point with such lightning quickness that the maid didn't even see where she'd drawn it from.

Laura was dumbfounded. She didn't dare tell Prince Carlo. Neither could she bring herself to tell the Lady Maria. Where did the child get such ideas? From those Carafa boys, no doubt.

Shortly before Beatrice's twelfth birthday, Maddelena Carafa called on Maria. She was surprised to find her still in bed at one o'clock in the afternoon, and to see the exquisitely beautiful angel who had once been her daughter-in-law looking so grey, so thin, so unconnected to life. Maria had never been one of those beauties who charmed with vivacity and constant talk, she was on occasion rather quiet, but she'd had an inner radiance that glowed like a source of energy. That radiance was now dimmed. Maria's state explained much that Maddelena had come to discuss.

'We must do something about Beatrice,' she began.

Maria looked at her with a confused frown, trying to absorb the significance of this. 'What do you mean?' she asked slowly.

Her mind's not working, thought Maddelena, secretly praying that she was not going mad. 'Beatrice will be a young woman soon. We must ensure that her chances of making a good marriage are not impaired.'

'How could they be?' Maria asked. 'She is the stepdaughter of the Prince of Venosa.'

'Exactly. The stepdaughter. Beatrice is a Carafa, Maria. She belongs with the Carafas. As her grandmother, I cannot allow her reputation to be in any way tarnished. And she is not happy in this house . . .'

'How could her reputation be tarnished?' asked Maria, sitting up in alarm.

'By association.' Maddelena hesitated. 'I did not wish to tell you this, Maria, but there are whisperings about Carlo. They come from the servants so they are not reliable, but nevertheless they persist and I wish to remove Beatrice from this house.'

'What whisperings? What is being said about Carlo?'

'I cannot tell you. I would never utter such things. But I insist, Maria, that you make a serious endeavour to get back your strength and look about you. You must put your house in order. You are sinking, my dear.'

Tears began to stream down Maria's face.

'Here, my poor Maria,' said Maddelena, holding out her hand. 'Grasp my hand. Take my strength. You will recover. And you must begin now, or you will be lost to us.'

Maria clung to Maddelena's hand and drew it to her face and kissed it, one of her tears trickling over it.

'Here is what we will do,' said Maddelena. 'Come, wipe away your tears.' She took a napkin from a tray of uneaten food on a little table by the bed and handed it to Maria. 'This is not the Maria I know.'

'I am still Maria. I'm simply very tired and wish to remain in bed. Let life go on without me. I've had enough of it.' She sighed deeply.

'How can you say such a thing! You have everything to live for. You are a young woman still, with a healthy baby son. And you have Beatrice's life to consider,' rebuked Maddelena sternly.

'You don't understand,' said Maria, beginning to sob again. 'I'm sick of endless births and deaths and births and deaths. I'm sick of husbands and loveless marriages and more births. Carlo has his son and now I have a right to be left in peace.'

Maddelena's hazel eyes stared at her solemnly and Maria read profound accusation in them. 'Left alone! For how long? Until the lives of those around you are reduced to misery? You must think of others, Maria.'

Maria had had enough. She flicked the air with her napkin as if to ward off the entire world. 'What do you think you are doing?' she shouted hysterically, swiping crazily at the air with her napkin. 'Coming in here with your—'

Maddelena gave her a stinging slap across the face. 'Enough! Let this weakness and simpering be over with. What do you think *you* are doing? How dare you? How dare you allow Federigo's child to wander about alone in the streets. She'll be raped, you fool.'

Maria stared at her agape, shocked at the slap and even more shocked at what Maddelena had just said. 'You're exaggerating,' she shouted.

Maria's blind incomprehension of the danger Beatrice placed herself in daily struck Maddelena as so irresponsibly stupid that she took a jug of water from the tray and threw its contents in Maria's face.

Sylvia flew into the room.

'Get out,' thundered Maddelena.

Sylvia vanished. Never had she obeyed an order so promptly.

Maddelena flung Maria another napkin. 'Here, wipe your face with this. Now, compose yourself and answer my questions. I want the truth. Have you lost your mind?'

'No,' said Maria sullenly, outraged at Maddelena treating her in this way.

'Good. You are angry. So there is still some life left in you. Do you love Beatrice?'

'Of course.'

'I don't know about "of course". If you love her, how could you allow her to go wandering out of the palace by herself to come to me? Do you know that that poor child carries a knife to protect herself?'

No,' breathed Maria, shocked. 'I didn't even know she went out into the streets alone. How could she? How could she get past the doormen?'

'What chance do you think doormen have against Beatrice's cleverness? Every day she dreams up some fresh outrageous tale to bamboozle them with. She thinks it's all a game. And you didn't know. And you are her mother. I could slap you again, Maria.'

'Don't do that, Maddelena. I won't bear it.'

'What will you do? Scream like the weakling you've become?'

'I'll slap you back, Maddelena.'

'Good. Now let us forswear slapping and make plans. You will spend the next fortnight regaining your strength. You will eat your meals and you will take walks with Laura and the coachman every day.'

Maria suddenly remembered the elixir. 'The Montevergine monks presented me with a herbal potion. They told me to take it every day. I . . . forgot about it.'

'Good. Take it for one week and see if it has a beneficial effect. If it doesn't, throw it away.'

'Do you think it may not be beneficial?' asked Maria, worried. 'Carlo instructed Sylvia to make sure the wet-nurse took it every day so it would flow through to her milk, as the monks told us to do.'

'They tell me Emmanuele is thriving, is he not?'

'Yes. He's very strong, thanks to Our Lady.'

'In that case it will probably do you good, too. Take it and see. While you are recovering I will take care of Beatrice. She must come and live with me.'

'No Maddelena. That isn't possible. Carlo would never allow it.'

'Carlo! What has he to do with Beatrice? He has no interest in her. I should think it would be a relief for him if she came to me.'

'Quite the contrary. It's a matter of honour with him that she stay here under his roof. He is her protector.'

'Nonsense. Men and their ridiculous honour. Beatrice is my blood. What do I care for Carlo's honour?'

'He will not allow it, Maddelena. Believe me, I know how he thinks about such matters. Though he is absorbed in things that interest him, he takes his duties as a prince very seriously.'

'Does he indeed?' Maddelena said with a snigger.

'Don't think you can walk over him, Maddelena. He has powerful friends. These days, more powerful ones than the friends of the Carafas, if you'll forgive me for saying so. He will find a way to make you regret it, one that may be harmful to Beatrice. We must think of another solution. I must pay more attention to her and—'

'No Maria. The damage is done. She does not wish to remain here. She begs me to allow her to come to me. Let me think on it. Come to me in a fortnight when you are yourself again and I will have the solution.'

Three months later, in the spring of 1588, twelve-year-old Beatrice Carafa married her sixteen-year-old cousin Marc Antonio Carafa. Maria had reluctantly agreed to this only because it was the one course of action that was acceptable to her husband and pleased her daughter. Carlo's honour was intact and Beatrice herself was overjoyed. Her future as a member of the illustrious house to which she belonged by birthright and inclination was assured. Moreover, she was the wife of her favourite cousin, artful Marc Antonio who had taught her how to use a stiletto, so she was now twice a Carafa. Never again would she have to go to Gesualdo Castle. Never again would she have to steel herself against Prince Carlo's stings, and never again would she have to traipse through days of gloom and loneliness. She and Marc Antonio would build a brave ship and sail to Venice, to Constantinople, to the New World. Beatrice glowed. Watching her, Maria realised at last that her daughter's solemnity had been due not to precocious cleverness so much as unhappiness. Beatrice had never before felt secure and happy. Now she did. For his part, Marc Antonio revelled in the manly role of husband and chief protector of his amusing and adventurous little cousin. The pair reminded Maria of she and Federigo. Once they were married, her reservations dissipated and she acknowledged Maddelena's wisdom.

On reflection, she also came to understand that Beatrice had been the architect of her own happiness. She had single-mindedly pursued her wish to spend her days with those to whom she knew she belonged. Listening to her, smiling at this new wish to conquer the seas of the world, Maria was again reminded of Costanza d'Avalos. What Beatrice wished for now was a childish dream, but as she grew to maturity and her ambitions developed accordingly, perhaps she, too, would defy the limitations imposed on her sex and create for herself a world to her own liking, one in which she would shine. Relinquishing her old hopes of finding happiness for herself, Maria began for a time to live vicariously through Beatrice, visiting her often and drawing on her daughter's newfound energy to boost her own. Her recovery after Emmanuele's birth was slow, but Beatrice's enthusiasm brightened her days. Had she known that this was to be the most tumultuous year of her life, one in which she would sink into a far deeper pit of despair, only to be resurrected into new life, she might have taken to her bed again.

Maddelena's reference to rumours about Carlo played on her mind. Maria's pleas with her to at least indicate the nature of these insinuations proved fruitless. She tried to dismiss it from her mind but the thought that Carlo might be associated with something too terrible to speak of gave her no rest. She considered broaching the topic with Carlo himself but there was no tactful or cunning way of doing so. If Carlo wished an aspect of his life to remain hidden, he certainly would not reveal it to her. Her mere curiosity would invite his disdain, for he considered gossip and those who listened to it contemptible. Of late, Carlo treated Maria with a new deference that made her wonder if he did not perhaps care for her after all, and she didn't wish to destroy this. Though she'd barely noticed those around her during her illness, she'd sensed that Carlo had been afraid of losing her.

There was only one thing for it then. As the whisperings came from servants, it must be a servant who would set out to discover the nature of them. Sylvia sprang immediately to mind. Yet in spite of her protectiveness toward Maria, Sylvia's upbringing had trained her to show first allegiance to the man of the house. This had been more the case with Maria's second husband than with Carlo, but now Sylvia's adoration of Emmanuele had probably tipped the balance in favour of Carlo. Over the past months it must have seemed to Sylvia that Carlo loved Emmanuele far more than Maria did, for he'd paid infinitely more attention to the infant and his welfare than she had. Whatever Sylvia's loyalties, she could not be entirely trusted and whoever carried out this mission must be absolutely trustworthy.

Laura. There was only Laura. The young woman had been Maria's lady's maid since the early days of her marriage to Federigo. She would never betray her. Besides, Laura was liked by the male servants and perhaps they would confide in her; they might even enjoy telling her something salacious. But did Laura have the necessary wit and guile to carry it off so that Maria's involvement would remain unknown? Perhaps not. Maria shuddered, praying to God that whatever deeds Carlo might be involved in, please may they not be too dark and terrible.

She seemed to recall that Carlo's unpleasant Uncle Giulio had once mentioned alchemy. Though the Church regarded it as the Devils' work, Maria had heard of secret societies where intelligent men took a scientific interest in it. Perhaps Carlo belonged to one of them. Perhaps he conducted alchemical experiments in that mysterious locked room in his apartment. But Maddelena had hinted at something even darker.

Maria tormented herself several times a day with these thoughts. If she was to regain her health fully, her indecision could not go on. Maddelena had been right. She must look about her, put her house in order. Either Laura must be thoroughly schooled in matters of intrigue, or Maria must find another means of uncovering Carlo's secret.

During Maria's pregnancy and illness Carlo's uncle, Don Giulio, had kept his distance, and had faded from Maria's mind. However, now Maria was deemed well again, he began to insinuate himself once more. He called to pay his respects and to be taken to the nursery to meet his new great-nephew. Maria had sent a note to Carlo asking him to be present during this visit, but he'd declined. Since Emmanuele's birth Carlo had given himself up to a frenzy of composition. Only two days previously he'd decided to publish the resulting madrigals. As this would be his first published manuscript, he'd become swept up in the excitement of it.

In spite of Carlo's absence or, more accurately, because of it, Maria was careful to treat Don Giulio's visit as a family formality. She unsmilingly indicated to him that she found his presence acceptable; just that. He responded with effusive hand kissing and unwelcome assurances that he considered her more beautiful than ever. 'Your illness has made you less of this world! You are ethereal! Even more heavenly. Yesterday I merely loved you. Today I worship you.'

Taking a lead from that master of dismissive rudeness, her husband, Maria extracted her hand during the course of these protestations, rose and quit the room.

Undeterred, Don Giulio returned two days later. A similar scene ensued, though one with more ardour on his part and less rudeness on hers; she did not, that is, leave the room. For after he had dared to kiss the inside of her wrist and she'd jerked back her arm with an exclamation of repugnance, she'd had, as she walked toward the door, a flash of inspiration. It was time to put an end to these visits.

She turned back and with an irritable gesture indicated for him to sit back down. She stood beside his chair, looking down upon him with scorn, an intimidating trick she'd also learned from Carlo.

'Do you consider that you know your nephew well, Don Giulio?' she asked.

'Who knows Carlo well, my angel of beauty? I love him as one of my blood, naturally, though I cannot believe he makes you happy and I confess that is why I dare to hope that you will one day welcome my love or at least allow me to love you. I will—'

'If you persist in these declarations, Don Giulio, I will inform my husband that you are a plotter against my honesty,' said Maria, staring at him steadily.

Don Giulio was stupefied. 'My dear Maria, I . . .' Never had he expected to be so threateningly rebuffed by one so sweet-tempered. Maria was evidently as chaste and virtuous as many claimed.

'I can say in all honesty that I *do* know your nephew well,' Maria continued. 'Need I describe to you what Carlo would do should I repeat to him the words you have spoken to me tonight?'

Don Giulio looked uncertain. 'It would anger him,' he suggested lamely.

'Surely you know what is whispered about Carlo, Don Giulio?' said Maria darkly.

'Whispered?'

'Do me the courtesy of being honest and admitting you know. It is clear to me that you do. I for one am not afraid to have such things spoken of.'

Now that Maria had by accident stumbled upon a way of uncovering the nature of Carlo's secret, and simultaneously punishing this despicable roué, she would not desist until he was tricked into revealing either his knowledge or his ignorance of the subject.

'Pray torment me no more, Maria. Such declarations will never again be uttered by me. As to Carlo, his response to anything at all is as impossible to predict as the inner workings of Mount Vesuvius. So, if you will forgive me, I cannot answer your question.'

'But you're aware of what is said about him, are you not? By the servants, I mean.'

'I confess myself at a loss here, my virtuous niece. The only whispers that have come to me are those associated with his illness and his unusual method of . . .' Don Giulio broke off as if struck by a thunderbolt. 'Ah yes, I see. I understand. Yes, perhaps Carlo is capable of . . . but no! I am his uncle!'

Maria kept her voice calm. 'Capable of what? It is imperative that we understand each other, Don Giulio.'

He looked at her wide-eyed. 'Of having me flogged! Isn't that what you're referring to? You are suggesting that Carlo would have me whipped. I like to think he would not do such a thing to his old uncle. My brother the cardinal would certainly hear about it if he did. But even if he were capable of such an outrageous act, I assure you, my dear, that he will not have future cause to do so, for never again will I speak of my devotion to you, which from this moment onwards is of the most familial and sacred kind.'

Maria hardly listened to him. The phrase 'Carlo would have me flogged' made no sense to her. Whom did Carlo have flogged? Not the servants, surely. She would know of it. The servants were in any case fond of him. They respected rather than feared him. And Don Giulio had implied this flogging was connected with an illness. What had he said? 'His unusual method . . .' She couldn't remember the rest. Carlo's only illness was asthma. Since that terrible episode at Gesualdo Castle he'd become obsessed with keeping warm to ward off attacks. There could be no connection between asthma and flogging. It was all a mystery. Perhaps Don Giulio was mistaken. She looked down at him grovelling on his knees and felt disgust. 'You may go now,' she said.

The next morning Maria had Laura stay with her as she sat up in bed drinking her chocolate. 'A relative of Prince Carlo's said something very strange to me yesterday,' she began. 'You must help me unearth its meaning. You must tell no one of this. It is to be of the utmost secrecy, do you understand?'

'Yes, my lady.'

'Here is what you must do. Silvestro, the coachman, he's fond of you, isn't he?'

'He tells me I'm pretty, my lady, but I don't encourage him.'

'Perhaps you could for a while encourage him a little by speaking with him regularly. You can retain his respect, for I mean you to be friendly with him, not seductive. I wish you to discuss with him what the servants say about Prince Carlo. You understand, Laura, that you are the only person I can entrust with so delicate a mission and you must prove yourself to be as discreet and trustworthy, and as honourable, as I judge you to be. It pains me to say this to you, but should it ever be known by anyone other than you and I that I have entrusted you with this task, then I would have no alternative but to dismiss you, much as it would break my heart to do so. I love Prince Carlo and wish to hear no evil about him, but it has been brought to my attention that the servants have said worrying things about him and, whether these things are true or not, I must know what they are in order to protect the prince and our son.'

'I understand, my lady. I will speak of this to no one,' said Laura, kissing the image of the Virgin on the rosary she wore around her neck.

'Good. What I am about to tell you will sound very strange. I ask you to ignore what it might mean and concentrate on remembering it. Do not repeat it to Silvestro. Say very little to him, other than to express curiosity about Prince Carlo. Let him be the one to speak.' Maria drew a deep breath. She wondered for a moment if it was not better to drop the whole thing, but the reasons for taking this course were sound. 'It has been said that Prince Carlo has people flogged. I want to know if this is true, and if so, whom he has flogged. I am given to understand that this is in some way connected with an illness of the prince's. What illness? Discover anything you can. Anything the servants say about Prince Carlo. Begin today. Go now and strike up a conversation with Silvestro. I want to know as quickly as possible.'

Every chair in San Severo's splendid music room was occupied. The two hundred or so guests had come to hear the brilliant young composer, Pomponio Nenna, perform his own compositions with Carlo and the members of his *camerata*.

This was Maria's first public appearance since the birth of Emmanuele seven months earlier. Several of the guests, having heard of her illness, expressed pleasure at her recovery and complimented her on her still youthful looks, though two or three whispered to their companions that such thinness did not become her, and that the turquoise blue of her gown only emphasised her pallor.

Maria sat in the second row of chairs between Beatrice and Princess Geronima. The front row was reserved for important patrons of music and members of the Academy.

It was late afternoon. Spring sunlight broke in through the lace-curtained windows, making pools of light that shifted about the room as the gentle breeze lifted the curtains. After his introduction by Prince Francesco, Pomponio Nenna, a plump, balding man with an amused smile, took centre stage.

'Four years ago, the support of my noble patron, the Duke of Andria, was of such an unstinting nature that I dedicated my first book of madrigals to him,' he began, his smiling eyes roving over the guests and coming to rest on Fabrizio, who sat in front of Beatrice. 'Since that time his continuing generosity has enabled me to devote my life to composing music. Some of these pieces I have already had the privilege of performing at the Prince of Venosa's eagerly anticipated concerts. This afternoon, the prince has done me the honour of inviting me to do so again.' He turned and bowed to Carlo.

Beatrice tapped Fabrizio's back and, when he turned, she gave him a bright smile and waggled her fingers at him. He mouthed 'hello' and smiled at her warmly, and then he turned his eyes to Maria. Playing the serene hostess, she nodded graciously, noting that Fabrizio had had his hair cut shorter, which made him look fresh and young, and showed off his refined features to greater advantage.

'So I am doubly blessed,' continued Nenna. 'The duke provides me with the means to create music, and the prince provides his splendid company of musicians and this magnificent room in which to perform it. I take the liberty of hoping you will judge my humble efforts worthy of my noble patron.' He bowed deeply to Fabrizio. Nenna, Carlo and his players then took up their instruments, the singers moved forward, and they began to perform a *canzonette*.

The music was charming and unpretentious, as light as the sun that warmed the room, and the audience relaxed into good-humoured appreciation. Maria noted that Beatrice was smiling. Marriage suited her; her breasts were beginning to fill out and her sharp features had softened; she was becoming quite the young woman. Maria's gaze shifted to the back of Fabrizio Carafa's head. A circle of sunlight danced on his olive-skinned neck. She'd seen him several times since her marriage, at San Severo where he would come to discuss musical matters with Carlo, and at Palazzo Carafa when he stayed with his relatives. She was always coolly courteous, for she was wary of him.

She watched a little mesmerised by the circle of dancing light below the silky fall of blue-black hair at his nape, and imagined stretching out her arm and placing the backs of her fingers on his warm neck. Fabrizio turned his head and looked briefly at the man sitting next to him, in front of Maria, and then at the window beyond. Her eyes lifted to his dark lashes, his strong Roman nose, and the delicate sensuality of the line that followed his lips to the base of his throat. And then without warning he turned his head a little more and his fine dark eyes looked straight into hers. She dropped her gaze immediately, feeling the blood rush to her face.

The second half of the programme was devoted to an unknown composer, Gioseppe Pilonji. The audience was divided between those who were curious and rather excited to hear some fresh work, and those who considered that any newcomer could not possibly match the skill of more experienced composers and were impatient for these pieces to be over so they could discuss the popular Nenna's new work and congratulate him. Still, as they looked at their handwritten programme even the impatient ones were forced to concede that the range of this new composer was impressive: a motet, an aria and dialogue for three sopranos, and five madrigals.

Their ears pricked up as the first piece was performed. This was no callow amateur, but one who was well versed in the traditions of contrapuntal music. By the completion of the aria and dialogue several were convinced they were listening to the works of a master. The hallmarks were there: sureness of craft blended with novel and arresting personal traits. And then came the madrigals. These works for nine voices were the most popular musical form of the day; thousands of them were composed, but these by Gioseppe Pilonji were like no other. They were vivid and passionate, with complex passages involving surprising exchanges between bass and soprano, and a new use of the lower voice. Members of the audience strained forward in an effort to attune their ears to the novelty of the harmonies. Here was a composer of rare contrapuntal prowess. His complex pattern of notes had resulted in the creation of a chromatic inner voice and this had been achieved by something unprecedented: the use of double counterpoint. To those who were merely lovers of music, these were madrigals of intrinsic beauty that had an unusual power to move. Even Beatrice, who had little ear for music and was here only because Marc Antonio had deserted her to go hunting, which she despised, listened attentively.

At the end of the performance the audience rose and applauded as one. Who was this Gioseppe Pilonji? they asked each other as they helped themselves from tables of elegantly presented refreshments in the adjoining room. What style and individualism! What invention! Each sung word was invested with emotion.

Maria had drawn Carlo into a corner of the room. Fabrizio Carafa watched her smile warmly into her husband's eyes, take his hand in hers, stand on her tiptoes and whisper something passionately into his ear. He turned and walked the other way. He stumbled, causing Geronima to spill her drink, and apologised profusely.

'My dear Fabrizio. I assure you it's nothing to be so upset about,' she said, noting the distress in his eyes. 'It seems more of it has spilled on you than on me.'

Had Fabrizio known what Maria and Carlo were saying to each other, he would have been less distressed at the sight of such intimacy between them.

'It's you, isn't it?' she whispered to Carlo, her eyes beaming with admiration. 'I know it's you. Gioseppe Pilonji is the Prince of Venosa. You amaze me, Carlo. You're brilliant.' She squeezed his hand.

'Why do you think it is me?' he asked, hiding a smile.

'I've heard snatches of that music before. You know I have. Why are you playing this silly game with me?' She giggled, secretly delighted at this rare, light-hearted moment between the two of them. Besides, it was true: she was delighted and genuinely surprised at Carlo's mastery.

'Where had you heard them?' he asked.

'In my bed, when I was ill. You forget, although your room is a floor below mine, sometimes the sound carries when the stair door and mine are open. You began playing phrases of what we heard today on your lute and organ shortly after Emmanuele was born. They seemed elegant to me then, those individual harmonies, and calmed me when I was ill, but today, hearing them all put together—I can't describe how beautiful it was.'

He laughed with pleasure at being so praised. 'I was very happy when Emmanuele was born, happy in two or three different ways, and the best way to express it was in creating a new kind of music. Don't tell anyone. Let them puzzle over who Gioseppe Pilonji is.'

'Where did you find such a ridiculous name?'

'In my head of course. Such an idiotic name, yet people say it with such seriousness, as I anticipated. It secretly amuses me.'

'You are misanthropic sometimes, Carlo, but you are a great musician.'

'I am pleased to hear my wife thinks so. I had not thought she so appreciated music, nor indeed me.'

'Perhaps you should pay more attention to her.'

He looked at her silently. His expression was suddenly impenetrable. Then he kissed her hand and, bowing formally, quit her, saying he must attend to his guests.

But for his response to her final remark, the exchange between them had been an unusually happy one. Sharing his secret gave her a sense of privilege. She felt almost buoyant, so confident in herself that when handsome Fabrizio Carafa left toward evening she offered him her hand and accepted his reverent kiss with smiling grace.

Two days later, Maria's complicity in Carlo's secret identity brought her a profound sense of unease when Laura came to report what the coachman had confided to her. Maria told the girl to sit down and be silent for a while before she heard any of this. She was not sure if she wanted to know. She paced the blue salon, feeling that she was betraying Carlo, trespassing on the private world that was so vital to him. Laura followed her movements with puzzled eyes. Finally Maria sat down opposite the girl, saying, 'Very well, what did he say?' as if forcing herself to swallow a bitter medicine.

'I don't understand what it means, my lady,' began Laura, 'so I will tell you Silvestro's exact words so that you may interpret them.'

'Very good. Never mind that you don't understand. You are not required to.' Better that she didn't. 'First of all, where did the coachman say this information came from?'

'From one of the men-at-arms who attends closely to Prince Carlo, my lady. Silvestro says the others never speak of the prince. They are very devoted and loyal to him and keep silent. There is only this one who speaks with Silvestro because they grew up in the same village and are old friends. Silvestro would not tell me his friend's name because he was afraid it might bring trouble to him.'

'Never mind that. What did he say?'

'He says that Prince Carlo sometimes has himself flogged. He orders his men-at-arms to do this.' The girl hesitated, remembering what she had committed to memory. 'Sometimes the prince cannot go to stool unless he first suffers pain.'

'Is that all?' Maria asked, suddenly listless.

'No, my lady. Silvestro says the prince does not do this so often here, at the palace, as he does at Gesualdo Castle. And there, at the castle, he has developed another unusual habit.'

'What is it?' asked Maria with a sense of dread.

'It is connected with his asthma, my lady. It gets very cold there and the prince is afraid that the cold will bring on his asthma. So at night he has the priest Alessandro sleep in the same bed with him so he can hug the prince's back and keep him warm. However, they say it is not always winter when this happens. Alessandro sometimes sleeps with the prince in his bed in the warmer seasons. That is all, my lady.'

'Thank you, Laura. We will never speak of this again. And neither will you, to anyone. You understand the consequences if you do? Good. And no more conversations with Silvestro. Things will return to the way they were. You may go now.'

Maria sank to the nearest chair and closed her eyes. Though it was beyond her comprehension, she'd heard there were men who were secretly attracted to other men. There had been ugly rumours about a member of Naples' parliament. Though he'd been rich and powerful, other men, fearful of being associated with his crimes, had kept well away from him. But Carlo! Carlo one of these men? Her own husband; her son's father. She rose and began pacing about the room. It didn't seem possible. Carlo in his strange way was devout. He believed in the teachings of the Church. And this business of men being intimate with other men was a mortal sin, one so reviled that it was never spoken of. Had not Maddelena called it unspeakable? And what of this business of him having himself whipped? It was even more perverse, if that were possible. Though she was disgusted with herself for doing so, she could not help but imagine Carlo and that slinking Alessandro in that mysterious locked room together, or was that where Carlo had himself whipped? What was in there? Was it sensuously furnished, with another bearskin covered bed, or was it bleak and bare, empty but for a whipping post? The thought of Carlo and Alessandro being in the same bed, and Alessandro hugging Carlo's back, seemed preposterous to her. Yet it was Alessandro who'd presided as priest during the unusual nuptial coupling ceremony Carlo had arranged on their wedding night. And had there not been an unspoken communion between them? She felt a curious mix of revulsion and compassion. What strange agonies Carlo must endure to behave so oddly.

Though she could scarsely believe it was true, what Laura had told her explained things Maria had sensed about Carlo, things she could not put a name to that floated in the air about her like wisps of smoke. His bodily functions, the pains and punishments of his body, his desire for physical contact with the priest, it all came together and somehow complemented what she finally recognised as the amorphous thing she could never grasp in his sexual relations with her. Was it something to do with a disgust of the flesh? Her flesh perhaps?

These revelations altered her relationship with Carlo profoundly, in a way that she herself was not at first aware of. Only days ago it had seemed she was on the brink of sharing a new intimacy with him. Now the possibility of closeness had evaporated. Carlo had a secret world, one that she did not begin to understand, but her intuition told her this: the inexplicable bond he had with men, particularly his servants and men-at-arms, was far stronger than the bond he had with her. Maria's feelings toward him, always complex and uncertain, changed. Hope for their future together gave way to a tangle of feelings: pity, alienation, loneliness, despair, a touch of fear and a sense of desolation at the dissolution of her unspoken hopes.

She became stoical, endured it. She forced herself to devote more time to Emmanuele, taking him for daily walks with Sylvia or Laura, protected by a party of guards. They sometimes walked as far as Chiaia, where they'd call at Palazzo d'Avalos to see her parents. She returned to her old pastimes, reading and writing, becoming absorbed once again in her chronicle of Costanza d'Avalos.

She decided she would publish the book, have it handsomely produced with engravings by one of Carlo's artist friends, and she would dedicate it to Beatrice, whose personality was so like Costanza's. She would have fifty copies printed and give them to family members as gifts. Five of them she would consign to the royal archives of the Kingdom of Naples so that the remarkable Costanza d'Avalos would live on into the future.

She mentioned the project to Carlo. Relieved to see her occupied, he sent for his friend Silvestro Bruno so that he could begin work on the illustrations. Carlo would, he assured her, oversee Bruno's work so that Maria's book, when published, would be splendid.

A week after their first meeting, Bruno accompanied Maria on a trip to Ischia. He was an enthusiastic artist who delighted in the commission, even though it was only for illustrative drawings which would be translated by another hand into engravings. Carlo would never have said so to his friend, but he considered Bruno a conservative artist, which was why he had chosen him for this illustrative work. Bruno was a wiry, bald little man with an interest in the local landscape and Neapolitan history, which also made him ideal for the task. He made skilful drawings of Costanza's island, her castle, her library and the fort from which she had defeated the French ninety years previously. The return to Ischia with Bruno and the vivacity of his sketches inspired Maria and she began devoting whole days to the book.

After hours of writing she would look out of the window of her blue salon, down at Piazza San Domenico Maggiore, imagining the surprise and joy on Beatrice's face when she presented the book to her.

Maria planned to write of Costanza's visit to Leonardo da Vinci in Rome. For this it was imperative to have Leonardo's painting of Costanza so that Bruno could have a copy of it engraved for the book. What had happened to it? Where was it? She began to seek its whereabouts in earnest.

Bruno, through his contacts, learnt that Leonardo had kept the painting himself and taken it to France. The one that Maria remembered was evidently not the original, but a copy of it made by a Roman painter. This was the one that had once been at Palazzo d'Avalos.

Maria asked her father what had happened to the copy. She despaired when he replied that his brother Ferrante d'Avalos had taken it with him when he'd been appointed Governor of Milan. Perhaps Carlo could arrange for them to borrow the painting from her Uncle Ferrante. As soon as Carlo had agreed to do this, the dogged Silvestro Bruno unearthed yet another copy of the painting, one made by a Neapolitan artist, probably not from the original, Bruno surmised, but from the Roman copy. He knew the owner and had the painting brought to Maria the next day.

'I would love to see Leonardo's original,' said Carlo, looking at it after its arrival. 'It must be wonderful.'

'Yes,' agreed Bruno. 'They say the King of France himself now owns it.' Maria studied the Neapolitan copy. It was very like the one she remembered having seen as a child, but the smile was not nearly as enigmatic. Still, she determined not to worry that it was a copy of a copy: it was definitely Costanza. The precipitous rocks in its mysterious, strangely split background were definitely Ischia. It would do for the purposes of her book.

'Now you must draw a fourth copy of it,' she laughed to Bruno, 'only this time it must be much smaller than the original.'

Bruno returned to his studio and set about his task. He proposed to hand-colour each engraving of the Leonardo painting for each copy of the book. Now that things were moving so swiftly, Maria worked harder on what now amounted to Costanza's biography, planning to have it printed in time to present to Beatrice on her name day.

The week that Bruno began overseeing the engravings, Beatrice called at San Severo with Maddelena. The latter seemed glum, while Beatrice's mood was hard to decipher. She looked white and drawn. Something was evidently troubling them. After ringing for cakes and *limoncello*, Maria asked, 'Which of you is going to tell me what has happened?'

'I am sick all the time and yesterday the midwife Stefania told me I am with child,' Beatrice blurted out.

Maria frowned at Maddelena. They had discussed that she would make clear to Marc Antonio that Beatrice was not to be penetrated for at least another year. For him to impregnate her while she was still so young was dangerous, especially as Beatrice was unusually small for her age. Maddelena shook her head in despair and shrugged helplessly.

'You mustn't look at Grandmama like that,' said Beatrice to Maria. 'Marc Antonio told me she'd warned him to be careful with me. I've brought this upon myself. Nobody else is to blame. I was curious to see what it felt like. In any case, Marc Antonio and I are married. That is what husbands and wives do.'

'Beatrice! Where is your modesty? How can you talk in such a way about the sacred mysteries of marriage,' said Maddelena, shocked.

'Are you pleased at the results of your curiosity?' Maria asked quietly.

'No, I'm not. I'm ill all the time. I don't want any of that disgusting *limoncello*,' she said, waving Maria's hand away as she offered her a glass of the liqueur. 'And I know the poor little baby will die because I'm so small.'

Maria and Maddelena hastened to assure the unhappy child that this would not be so, but they, too, secretly suspected that the infant was doomed.

That night Maria lay awake thinking on her daughter's plight. The blame lay at her door, for if she had not neglected Beatrice and grown apart from her, the poor child would not have craved to live with the Carafas, and her marriage to Marc Antonio would never have taken place.

By dawn, Maria had made a resolution. Beatrice's little baby was going to live. Maria knew that her daughter always hid her deeper feelings: she would be devastated if the baby died. If it lived, Beatrice would return to happiness and normality within weeks. Maria determined to devote herself to ensuring that Beatrice remained in the best of health during her pregnancy and did not fall prey to anxiety and gloomy thoughts. If she stayed strong in body and spirit then there was every chance the baby would survive.

To this end, Maria spent hours of each day with Beatrice. She'd kept her work on Costanza d'Avalos a secret from her, hoping to surprise her on her name day, but now she shared her plans with her daughter. She let her read the completed chapters of the manuscript and showed her Silvestro Bruno's drawings of Ischia. Maria explained to Beatrice that the chief inspiration for the project had been Beatrice herself, the resemblances between her character and Costanza's. The pregnant twelve year old took great strength from this. What struck Beatrice was that this woman, who had defeated the French navy, governed a fiefdom and established a brilliant literary circle, had been single for most of her life. Though she had married at seventeen, her husband had died six years later and she had lived the remaining fifty-eight years of her life as a single woman. Yet Costanza had had many admirers, some of whom had become her lovers. This was the fact about her that most intrigued Beatrice. How had she managed to have several lovers and not fall pregnant? Perhaps she was barren, explained Maria. Beatrice was lucky to be fertile, healthy, she added, trying to encourage her to think of her pregnancy as a happy event, because Beatrice, now that she had the example of Costanza, was associating female fulfilment and longevity with childlessness. Ah, Beatrice and her gift of clear-sightedness. It was difficult to persuade one who was possessed of such lucidity to look at life through a rosy mist.

Maria continued to be riddled with guilt at having neglected Beatrice. She showered her with gifts, but racked her brains for a more meaningful way in which she might make amends, one that would truly benefit her daughter. What did Beatrice need above all else? To have her mind put at rest, to be confident that her pregnancy would have a happy outcome. Maria wished her daughter to feel blessed.

One afternoon in the nursery with its bright fresco of fabulous creatures, watching over healthy Emmanuele asleep in his crib, it came to her. Montevergine. She would take Beatrice there so that she, too, could be blessed by the Dark Lady.

Nine

MONTEVERGINE

It was late summer when they set out. The long journey was less arduous because the days were bright and warm. Carlo accompanied them, wishing to give thanks to the Dark Lady for the health of his son and wife. He'd written to the abbot, explaining the purpose of their visit, requesting that Maria and Beatrice be accommodated while he went on to Gesualdo Castle: he would return in a week to collect them. With his reply the abbot thoughtfully sent a sleeping draught, a herbal opiate, for Beatrice, so that she would sleep through the journey and not be wracked by nausea as Maria had been.

Beatrice lay asleep in Maria's arms, her body stretched the width of the carriage. Opposite, Carlo, a tray on legs across his knees, was writing music. From time to time he would stop to look out of the window, absorbed, not seeing the landscape, and then return to his rapid jottings, seemingly aided rather than impeded by the swaying and lurching of the carriage. In the carriage behind them were Laura and the men who would go to the castle with Carlo, among them the priest Alessandro. Maria had come to hate this aloof young man; he shared in the mystery that was Carlo. She almost blamed him for Carlo's evasion of love. Her hatred of Alessandro was not intense; it was a dull ache. Maria's concern for Beatrice was at the forefront of her mind.

As they rode on Maria studied Carlo's clever face. It was half in shadow. She mused that this was symbolic of the twin aspects of his personality—the exhibitionist and the secretive individualist. How admirably this was suited to his dual talents as a musician: the performer and the composer.

She looked down at Beatrice, sleeping, her dewy eyelids faintly bruised with exhaustion: she'd awakened three or four times each night for the past two months to vomit. Now she was sleeping peacefully. Maria's arm was tingling with pins and needles, and she carefully removed it from under Beatrice's head and placed a little cushion there. Carlo looked up distractedly as she rubbed her arm and flexed her fingers. 'You must not let your daughter exhaust you,' he said. 'I do not wish you to fall ill again.'

At the monastery Maria spent an hour each morning and evening in the chapel, praying to the Dark Lady to protect Beatrice and her baby. Beatrice would leave after fifteen minutes or so and return to her little room high up in one of the towers. There she would lie in bed, looking at the tops of the mountains and the floating fleecy clouds and fall asleep. She had developed a taste for the abbot's sleeping draught and Maria worried that she took too much of it. She considered asking the monks to give her no more, but Beatrice begged her not to, insisting it made her feel better. The herbal potions for the health of the baby made her feel ill, and it was surely far more beneficial for her to be sleeping than retching, she reasoned.

On the fourth day, Beatrice awoke at dawn, feeling wonderfully refreshed, better than she could ever remember feeling. Up in the still mountains the monastery was silent. The monks were at their early morning devotions. Her mother and Laura had not yet risen.

Beatrice went to the window and looked out at the peaks and plunging hillsides of the dawn-tinted landscape. She experienced a sense of transcendence, an elation of the kind she'd expected to find in contemplation of the Dark Lady but had not. She threw wide the windows and breathed in the sparkling air, opening her arms in a smiling embrace of the mountain vision. An urge took hold of her to be out of the monastery with its cunning-faced monks.

Dressing herself without waking Laura, wrapping a mantle about her, she crept down flight after flight of narrow then broader stairs and, once outside the entrance, the heavy doors of which had been almost impossible to open, she ran and skipped down a grassy mountain track, feeling miraculously like a child again, one, that is, who was not four months pregnant.

Beatrice stopped near a copse of fir trees to catch her breath. Looking up, on her right, she glimpsed a small rustic structure silhouetted against the splendid backdrop of the crystalline mountains. Curious, she climbed toward the structure, which looked like a memorial of some kind. She stopped now and then to catch her breath; the ascent seemed long and hard but in reality the climb took her only ten minutes.

She reached the memorial, a four-sided pillar with a peaked roof. On each of its four sides it had arched insets with religious paintings. Beatrice leaned against it, breathing heavily. A tree grew out of its base. She looked up. The distant mountain crowned the landscape like a cathedral of ice. Between Beatrice and this sublime peak yawned the steep sides of a chasm that disappeared into a black abyss. A little plaque on the memorial stated that it commemorated a goatherd who had once plummeted to his death. Beatrice looked up, above all this human catastrophe and plunging darkness, into the whiteness and purity of the cathedral in the sky.

She stayed on as the sun rose higher, enjoying the scene as it changed imperceptibly from shimmering, fantastic pink to icy white against a deepening blue sky. Elated by this sublime experience, her head full of a plan to bring Maria here at the same time the next morning, Beatrice ambled back down the mountain side, arms swinging, gathering pace as the stony path grew steeper. She slipped on some loose pebbles and, arms balanced trying to stop herself from falling, skidded down this precipitous section of the track, losing all control of her limbs for a hundred yards or so. She landed awkwardly with a thud against the massive trunk of a spruce tree. She lay there, stunned, wondering at the strange rushing noise in her ears.

The search party of monks discovered her an hour later. They gently turned her over, discreetly averting their eyes from the large sticky patch of blood on the front of her yellow dress. Wrapping her in a blanket, they carried her to the monastery infirmary.

Maria's failure to grasp the repercussions of her daughter's misadventure could only be attributed to shock. When the monks were out of earshot she remarked to Laura that it was a blessing in disguise that the Dark Lady of Montevergine had relieved Beatrice of her burden. It was sad for the poor little baby but Beatrice would soon be her old self. Maria said this while Beatrice lay groaning in agony. Laura looked at her mistress oddly, but she said nothing. Maria held her daughter's hot, limp hand as Laura dabbed at the girl's feverish brow with a damp cloth. It did not occur to Maria that Beatrice herself was in danger. Laura knew though, and it astonished her that her mistress did not seem to recognise this.

Carlo arrived at Montevergine four days later at noon. He planned to leave early that afternoon, which would enable them to reach his villa by nightfall and be back in Naples in the early afternoon of the next day. He'd worked well at the castle and was eager to hear the two madrigals he'd composed performed by his group of singers.

In a frenzy of impatience, he waved aside the old monk at the main door who attempted to intercept him and went straight to the chapel, where he spent the thirty minutes he'd allotted paying his respects to the Dark Lady. He then strode to the guest chamber where Maria slept and, without knocking, entered.

He found Maria sitting quietly by the bed. His first fleeting impression was that she'd fallen asleep in the chair. Then he saw that her eyes were open, fixed on some indefinite point in the middle of the room.

'Good-day, Maria. Here I am, come to fetch you. Have Laura pack your things. We must leave within the hour. I'll have the abbot prepare some food for us.'

Maria did not respond. She did not even look at him. It was as if he weren't even there. He crossed the room and took her hand.

'Maria. What's the matter with you?' She still did not respond. He wondered if she'd taken some of Beatrice's sleeping draught—too much of it perhaps—and had not awakened properly. He knocked on the door to the adjoining room where Laura slept, and entered. She wasn't there. Anger took hold of him.

He marched through the corridors on his way to the abbot's office, and ran into Laura as she was making her way back.

'Laura! Your mistress is in a strange state. What do you think you are doing, leaving her alone when she's like that? What's the matter with her?'

'Your Excellency, Please forgive me,' said the girl tearfully, curtseying. 'There is something the abbot must tell you.'

'Why must *he* tell me? You tell me. What is it?'

'I think, your Excellency, it is better—'

'Tell me!' Carlo thundered.

'The Lady Beatrice,' said Laura softly. 'She died last night.'

Carlo looked at Laura in disbelief for long moments. He rubbed his forehead, sighed, and crossed himself. 'How did she die?' he asked.

'As a result of a miscarriage brought about by a fall. She went for a walk in the mountains,' Laura began to sob, 'and the monks think she must have lost her footing and fallen.' She told him of the copious amount of blood Beatrice had lost, and how the dead foetus had slowly poisoned her body. Though Laura did not say as much to Carlo, Beatrice's last days had been an agony of fever and convulsive retching of vile black fluid. In her delirium she'd screamed of giving birth to a rotting corpse.

Carlo sighed deeply. 'What was she doing alone?'

'She went off by herself very early one morning. She had a habit of doing that.'

'Yes.' He closed his eyes and cupped his hands above them. He had in his remote way been fond of Beatrice, even though she'd sorely irritated him. He'd admired her courage and her odd angle on the world, which he'd found mildly interesting. 'And your mistress. How has she arrived at the insensible state she is in? What preceded it?'

'After Beatrice had received the last rites and the breath had left her body, my lady lay next to her. She would not be moved, though the abbot and monks were as kind and gentle as anyone could be. They sent for nuns and some other women from the village to support my lady in her affliction. She clung to Beatrice; all the persuasion in the world could not move her and all that could be done was to leave her there with her little daughter's poor cold body and cover her and see that she was kept warm. The nuns sat with them through the night. Then this morning when it came time to dress the body and prepare it for the journey back to Naples—for I took the liberty of assuming, your Excellency, that the family would want the Lady Beatrice to be put to rest in the Carafa family crypt—it became absolutely necessary to separate my lady from her poor child and when we did so she screamed and screamed so it lifted the hairs on the backs of our necks, and she kept up this screaming and wringing her hands and tearing at her clothes and the hair on her head for more than an hour, running about the room, and all our attempts to calm her were of no avail. She screamed until she could make no sound whatsoever. Then she was carried to her room and she would not lie on the bed but sat in the chair. I left her only for a few minutes when the nuns asked me to fetch items from Beatrice's chest to dress her little body.'

Back in Naples, Maria awakened from her catatonia only to attend to Beatrice's laying-out and funeral. She selected the softest velvet slippers and the finest gold-embroidered silk for her daughter's shroud. On the morning of the funeral, she steeled herself, went into Beatrice's room and opened the little casket of treasures that had been most precious to her daughter. Strangely, Beatrice had left this behind went she'd gone to live at Palazzo Carafa. Perhaps she'd felt she no longer needed to hang onto these things. Inside was a lock of Federigo's brown hair, a silver belt buckle of his, the blue and red feathers of her beloved South American parrot who'd died at Messina, a miniature of Maria as a girl, the perfect spiral of a pink mother-of-pearl shell and a little prayer book with a ruby cross inset into its ivory cover given to her on her eleventh birthday by her Grandmama Sveva. Maria dropped onto Beatrice's old bed, sobbing hot tears at the poignancy of these objects. She fingered them lovingly. Then she went to her own room and fetched a baroque pearl brooch in the shape of a heart that Beatrice had always loved, and placed it among the other things. She sank back onto the little bed and remained there, weeping uncontrollably. She drew the lock of Federigo's hair to her lips and kissed it. Now Beatrice, too, was lost to her. Flesh of Federigo's flesh, gone. With the loss of Beatrice she lost Federigo Carafa all over again. Nothing of her marriage to him remained.

She had no notion that an hour had passed, she'd lost all sense of time, when Laura came in and gently touched her arm. 'My dear lady, it is time to go to Palazzo Carafa.'

Accompanied by the Gesualdo guards Maria walked in a daze along Spaccanapoli, praying that some murderous villain would dart from the shadows, stab her in the heart and put an end to her suffering.

When she entered the darkened room where Beatrice was laid out, Maddelena was hugging Marc Antonio to her as they looked down into the coffin together in stricken silence. They rose and sorrowfully kissed Maria before leaving her alone with her daughter, but she hardly noticed. She placed the casket near Beatrice's heart. In the dim candlelight her daughter's light brown hair was shiny still. How waxen the little face. How unearthly cold to the touch. People spoke of the dead lying peacefully. What nonsense. Beatrice did not look peaceful. She looked dead dead dead. She'd gone, flown. Nothing was present but the casing of bone and flesh that had all too briefly harboured her bright spirit. Still, Maria spoke to the shrunken little form, whispering nonsense that seemed to her objective mind, even as she spoke, like the ravings of a madwoman. 'Open your grey eyes. Let me see them just one more time.' Somebody came softly into the room but she didn't hear them. She was going mad, was mad already. What did it matter? She had an impulse to scream and scream and scream and she gripped her head tightly in her hands to stop herself, and at that moment she felt her body enfolded in a darkness so comforting, so murmuringly tender, that she experienced a strange lightness, and she suddenly did not know whether the tears that gushed down her face were tears of sorrow or tears of joy, only that they were sweet release, and the gentle murmuring soothed her ears as the soft breath of the darkly cloaked form warmed her and she was lifted up off the ground, and only when was she gently placed on a long divan did she come to herself and see that the dark angel who now tenderly stroked her face was Fabrizio Carafa, but what did it matter if it was the Devil himself tempting her for all she wanted in this world was that his soothing caresses not stop. Then a longing for the touch of his lips against hers took hold of her and she sat up with a sharp cry of horror at what she was doing. And in the very room where Beatrice lay stretched out dead. She had indeed gone mad.

'Sh, my poor angel,' he soothed, gathering up the material of his voluminous white shirt sleeve and wiping the tears from her face with it. 'Sh.'

She wanted only to sink down into herself and allow him to minister to her grief but she could not allow it, and so she put all of her bodily strength into placing her feet on the ground and standing up, feeling as if she was going to faint, her head swimming. 'Let me be,' she breathed, lifting her arm and placing her outspread palm in front of his face, warding him off. 'Let me be.'

She hazily wondered if he'd deliberately caught her in this vulnerable moment. If he had, how despicable of him.

'You must stay seated, Maria,' he said softly. 'You were ready to faint just a moment ago.'

She sank into a chair. Fabrizio kept his distance, understanding she didn't wish him to touch her.

'I'd grown so fond of Beatrice,' he said. 'She was the most original of all my cousins. Your loss is my loss, too.'

'No it isn't. You cannot imagine the depth of my loss.'

'It's true, I can't,' he said gently, his dark limpid eyes shining with a sympathy that seemed to her almost reverential. 'There is something of Beatrice's I must give you.' His hand reached into his pocket. When it reappeared a metallic sound pinged and echoed twice, three times, as whatever he'd dropped bounced on the marble floor and came abruptly to rest. He went down on his knees and searched for the object under the furniture.

At that moment Carlo entered the room. His eyes glanced at Maria, swept across the figure of Fabrizio on the floor and came to rest on Beatrice in her coffin. He moved to the coffin and looked down at the corpse. Fabrizio retrieved the object and, returning it to his pocket, stood up.

'Carlo,' 'Fabrizio,' they said, bowing. Fabrizio make a deep bow to Maria and departed. She avoided looking him in the eye.

She watched Carlo as he stood looking down at Beatrice in her coffin. For several moments he remained standing there as if transfixed. His face was impassive. 'Say something,' her mind screamed. 'Say something or show some expression on your face that gives me a sense of what is passing through your mind. Show some pity, some regret, some sorrow.' Silence. She gave a great shuddering sigh.

Carlo looked across at her. 'They will come soon to close the coffin.' He walked across and offered her his arm. 'Come, say goodbye to your daughter.' She took his arm and he led her back to the coffin. She looked down at the pitiful little girl, the recent turmoil with Fabrizio forgotten as she thought that these were the last moments she would ever look upon Beatrice.

'Lean on me,' said Carlo, putting his arm about her and it seemed to her that his utterance was a formality: he was her husband and to be supportive of her at this moment was required of him.

She leaned her head against his shoulder in any case, and as they stood looking down at Beatrice together, he said the strangest thing. At the time she barely registered it and it was only later when she recalled this scene that she could not fathom whether he'd said it to comfort her or whether it had really struck him as so. 'The beauty of death,' he said.

'How so? Do you find her peaceful?' whispered Maria.

'No, not peaceful. She's beyond that. It's the stillness, the sublime stillness.' He turned to Maria and held her gaze with his flecked eyes. 'Death is very beautiful.' Then he turned his face back to Beatrice and made the sign of the cross over her silent form.

After the funeral, which she could barely recall, Maria sank back into her darkness.

Carlo allowed her to remain there for six weeks.

On the Monday of the seventh week, Laura came into Maria's room at noon and drew back the curtains, saying she must dress as Prince Carlo wished to speak with her in the main salon. The light hurt Maria's eyes. She kept them shut until Laura clothed her in her mourning gown, placed the black rolled velvet hat on her head and pulled its black silk veil over her face. Then Maria opened her eyes. She felt shielded under the veil, cocooned in the dimness.

She made a sorrowful contrast with the flamboyant pastel frescoes of the large salon. She dimly wondered why Carlo hadn't simply come to her chamber and spoken to her. All this unnecessary fuss, getting dressed and coming into this formal room as if she were a guest in her own house. She was too listless even to resent her husband for not showing more respect for her grief.

Carlo asked her to draw back her veil. She said the light hurt her eyes. He rose and himself drew the curtains, too impatient to call a servant to do so.

'Now draw back your veil. I wish to see your eyes as I speak, and I wish you to look at me.'

She drew back the veil listlessly. He frowned at her unhealthy pallor and the dark smudges under her eyes. 'You are becoming a ghost, Maria. I wish you to return among the living. You are the Princess of Venosa and the mother of my son, and you must now place your duties to the living before your sorrow over the dead.'

In truth, Carlo required her to do very little, although he liked her to be present at the concerts he gave at San Severo. He was rallying her because he feared she might be slipping into madness.

'From this day on, you will return to your old habits. You will rise in the morning at ten, you will have yourself dressed, you will breakfast and make and receive calls and attend mass, and occupy yourself with the pastimes that once interested you. I have instructed the servants accordingly, so you must tolerate them if they appear assiduous. I will keep a close watch on your progress. Next month, there is to be a concert here at which I wish you to be present. After that, Prince Carafa di Stigliano is giving his first ball of the season at La Sirena. Your uncle the viceroy and the aristocracy will be present and I am expected to attend. As this is two months away, you will be fully recovered. You will require suitable clothes for these two events. I have arranged for your dressmakers to come to you tomorrow afternoon at two. Your Aunt Antonia has suggested you accompany her to Rome next week as the finest black fabrics from all over the Continent are to be had there. As it will give me pleasure to pay a call on my uncle, Cardinal Alfonso, I will accompany the two of you. I have written to my uncle asking him to act as your confessor while we are there. Unburdening your heart to him will assist in your recovery.' He rose, taking Maria's hand and kissing it. 'I am paying more attention to you, Maria, as you once asked me to do.'

Though she'd removed her veil and exposed her face to her husband, his voice came to her from a great distance; she listened to his words but could not fully concentrate on them. She grasped the main thrust of them, however. She was to behave as if she felt alive.

Over the coming weeks she did so, though it exhausted her going through the motions of rising and eating and visiting Rome, of presenting a charming demeanour to the court musicians of Ferrara. He watched her, gratified at her efforts, wondering if the light would ever return to her eyes.

Ten

LA SIRENA

Maria and Carlo travelled in a carriage along the most beautiful stretch of the Neapolitan coast toward Posilipo. They were on their way to a ball at La Sirena, a villa on a jutting promontory surrounded by the sea on three sides. It was built of tufa, the dark volcanic stone of Mount Vesuvius.

Maria's rich velvet gown was as black as the night; against it her skin glowed moon pale. Her only adornments were a tufa pendant and black pearls in her hair. 'You look like the Queen of the Night,' said Carlo, who loved the dark drama of it. Maria's own interest in her appearance and its dramatic effect had all but evaporated; she simply went through the motions. Since the absence of Beatrice in her life, all that had once gladdened her days seemed like distant ghostly shapes in a pervading fog.

As they approached, the baroque outline of the black building on the sea was barely visible on this moonless night, and the lighted upstairs windows gave it a haunted look.

Jasmine and orange flowers perfumed the halls of the villa. The room leading into the ballroom was given over to elaborate meats and desserts. Maria touched none of it. She stayed beside Carlo as he walked through the festive rooms, barely acknowledging the other guests' greetings and expressions of condolence. Many of them had seen Maria in black ten years before, but now with her ripe, pale beauty and the richness of her gown, she resembled a tragic queen of old. Though they felt sympathy for her, they kept their distance. She had an air of not wishing to be engaged that struck them as a silent plea to be left to herself.

They sat with their host, Prince Carafa di Stigliano. He asked about the progress of Carlo's garden at Gesualdo Castle and the two men embarked on a conversation about the merits of commissioning Massimo Reni to design a garden for La Sirena.

As Maria sat there silently, the music, the buzz of conversation, the laughter and the festive and frivolous atmosphere began to grate on her nerves. She caught sight of Miranda, her great-aunt and the wife of the viceroy, entering the room with a group of friends. As they smiled and exclaimed their way across the room they made toward Maria and her party. Miranda was a loud, superficial woman. She would corner Maria, gaily endeavour to cheer her up with frivolous chatter, and Maria would be obliged to put on a public face and go through the motions of social intercourse with her.

Maria slipped out of the ballroom. She crept down the wide marble staircase to the villa's deserted lower floor, just above the sea, and stood in an arched alcove watching the tossing movements of the inky water. But for the lapping and faint sound of music many floors above, the villa was silent. She stood hidden under the arch, staring at the sea and losing herself in its hypnotic rhythm, taking pleasure in the silence and the sense of being suspended in a secret place, away from the company of others, where nobody would think to look for her. She might have stayed there for hours had she not heard voices coming from out on the water.

A boat was approaching.

'Perhaps there is a mermaid waiting for me here tonight,' said a young man, referring to name of the villa, La Sirena, The Mermaid.

'You think too much about women,' said a voice she recognised. She drew back from the opening of the arch into the shadows.

His companion laughed uproariously. '*You* say that to *me*. Come, cousin, I'm entitled to. I'm young and carefree, as you once were. You must confess that you are less and less good-humoured of late. I feel obliged to tell you that you are in danger of becoming permanently surly. I hope your mood improves; I propose to enjoy myself tonight.'

The boat was approaching the mooring. The light from the upstairs rooms fell on the men's faces. One of them was Fabrizio Carafa.

Maria moved into the darkness on the other side of the stairs. She waited so that they would be right below and not see her as she went back up. She'd last seen Fabrizio at Beatrice's funeral, after those tumultuous moments at her laying-out. Whenever she'd thought of that incident since, and it came unbidden into her mind many, many times, she was overcome by shame and confusion, and another emotion she dared not name. To her dismay Fabrizio had approached her at the funeral, his face sorrowful. She'd stared at him through her veil, incapable of speech, and he'd pressed something into her hand, bowed, and joined his wife and children. She'd opened her hand and looked at what he'd given her. It was a little ring, gold with an oval cameo depicting—what? She'd hardly looked at it as she'd put it into her pocket. It must still be there, in the pocket of her funeral dress.

She heard the two men mooring the boat and she made her way stealthily back up the stairs, keeping to the shadows, wondering at the motif and significance of the ring. She would retrieve it when she returned home.

Maria returned to the ballroom and sat in a corner with Carlo and the Prince di Stigliano. As she'd anticipated her Aunt Miranda, the viceroy's wife, had joined their party. Maria politely listened to their conversation, or seemed to. Whenever Fabrizio Carafa came into sight her eyes would follow him about the room, dropping quickly if there was a danger of them meeting his. She thought on it, this surreptitious gazing. It was shameful. Fabrizio's beauty and his Carafa blood beckoned her like the food and drink forever out of reach of parched, starving Tantalus in the Underworld. She felt drawn to him as a link to Beatrice, to Federigo, yet it was more than that too.

Outside, the inky water could be faintly heard lapping against the foundations of the black building.

Carlo detested social gatherings like these, but he was unusually animated tonight. He was discussing with Prince Carafa di Stigliano plans for a hanging garden on the lower floors of the villa, suggesting what a Babylon his friend Massimo Reni might create if commissioned for its design.

The prince rose to greet a party of newcomers and Miranda beckoned to Fabrizio to take the seat he'd vacated.

'Your nephew Fra Giulio's dislike of recitation has surprised us all, Fabrizio,' she said with barbed wit.

Fabrizio frowned as he sat down, glancing at Maria. 'I can't defend his action,' he said coolly.

'Whoever would have thought he was so impetuous?' Miranda continued, undeterred by Fabrizio's air of not wishing to discuss the matter.

'Who indeed,' muttered Fabrizio.

'As you're simply bursting for one of us to ask what you are both referring to, I will perform the courtesy of doing so,' said Carlo, looking at Miranda with a bored air.

'Have you not heard?' she asked excitedly. 'I must tell you.'

'It's clear that you must, whether we wish to hear it or not,' said Carlo, exchanging a looking of sufferance with Fabrizio.

'Yesterday Fra Giulio Carafa was standing in front of his house, enjoying the sunshine. The poet Giovanni Arcuccio passed by, reciting one of his verses at the top of his voice as he went along, in a state of lyrical exaltation. Fra Giulio requested him to lower his voice. A few heated words ensued. And then what do you think our gentle friar did?'

Maria watched Fabrizio put his hand to his forehead, close his eyes and sigh deeply. He was clearly upset. She felt for him. What a stupid woman her aunt was sometimes. Her love of gossip made her insensitive. Maria stared at Fabrizio's hand, not overly sensitive and elegant like Carlo's, strong and broader, but of a refined shape nevertheless.

'He raised aloft a stick he was carrying, smote our poet on the head, and killed him,' concluded Miranda.

'The particular poem he was reciting must have been a very bad one,' said Carlo.

A silence ensued.

When it was clear no one was going to comment any further, Miranda looked at those around her and, feigning a mischievous air, said, 'I hear the Duke of Andria has an interesting theory on the identity of the mysterious maestro.'

Fabrizio glanced at Maria.

'Yes Fabrizio, tell us what you know,' said Carlo playfully.

'I know very little. I've heard only rumours among the musicians themselves.'

'And what are these rumours?' asked Miranda.

'Just that. Speculation,' answered Fabrizio. 'Pomponio Nenna believes him to be a gifted amateur.'

'Not an amateur, surely,' prompted Miranda.

'An amateur in the sense that he is not a professional musician. A member of the aristocracy, perhaps.'

'An aristocrat! How intriguing. A Neapolitan aristocrat?'

'It is believed so, yes.'

'Ah! Let us see. Who among our aristocrats would have such a rare gift combined with such intensity of feeling? Might it be you yourself, Duke?'

'Regrettably no, my lady. I am merely a patron of musicians, not a practitioner.'

'The Princess of Venosa is acquainted with musicians of the highest calibre,' continued Miranda, looking at Maria. 'Perhaps she can enlighten us.'

'I'm afraid I cannot, Aunt,' said Maria uncomfortably.

'You cannot, my dear? Or you will not?'

'I will not, Aunt.'

'When we are all dying to know? I never thought you capable of such cruelty, Maria.'

'I know you mean that playfully, Aunt. But I assure you it is not cruelty in any sense. If a fine composer wishes to keep his identity a secret, it is not my place or anyone else's to divulge it.'

'On the contrary, Maria, it is possible that this genius wishes us to discover who he is. I believe he is playing a game with us, waiting for us to come to him and say, "We *know* it's you. It could only be you." After all, how many of our aristocrats are gifted musicians? Only a handful. We can arrive at the answer by a process of elimination.'

'Perhaps he's not an aristocrat,' said Carlo, who was finding the conversation tedious.

'Really, Carlo? Of everybody in this room, you would be the one to know, which is why I have reserved asking you until the last. Come, who is he?'

'Your husband's tailor,' said Carlo. 'And now I believe it is time to dance. Would you do me the honour, my lady?'

Miranda laughed. 'You are too wicked to be danced with. My husband's tailor indeed! But as you are the most divine dancer in Naples, I will accept your offer.'

They rose and she took Carlo's hand. Fabrizio rose also. 'Will you join the dance with me, Maria?'

'Thank you, no, Fabrizio. I'm in no mood for dancing.'

Carlo turned. 'As a favour to me, I ask you to accept Fabrizio's offer. Dancing will do you good.' He leaned close to her, cupped his hand over her ear and whispered, 'More good than staring at him, I think.' Then he returned to Miranda and led her onto the floor. Maria, shocked into momentary panic, despised Carlo in that instant. She hadn't once noticed him look at her, yet he'd clearly been watching her out of the corner of his eye. Oh, he enjoyed affecting this air of omnipotence, and it was as intrusive and nerve-wracking as Alfonso Gioeni's policing of her thoughts had been.

'Forgive me, Maria, I didn't mean to have you forced to dance with me,' said Fabrizio with embarrassment.

'It's not necessary for you to apologise for Carlo's bad manners. In any case, he's right.' She stood and held out her hand. He took it, but did not kiss it, as she'd half expected him to.

They danced the saraband, a rather old-fashioned court dance which involved the interweaving of couples in a graceful pattern and the regular changing of partners. Maria relaxed into its rhythms and began to enjoy it. Briefly coupled with the old Prince Carafa di Stigliano, he made her laugh by saying with mock trepidation, 'Though nobody in Naples has better taste than your husband, his ideas for my garden frighten me. It seems he wants to transform La Sirena into a Babylon, and we all know what happened there.'

'Calm yourself, Prince,' she replied. 'It's the hanging gardens he would have you emulate, not Babylon's tower.'

Her next partner was Carlo himself. 'This is the first time you've smiled for months, Maria. I myself am given to bouts of extreme melancholy, as you know, and I find giving myself up to the rhythms of music the best cure for it.'

'Why is it,' she asked sardonically, 'that you sound so pompous when you mean to be kind?'

To her surprise, he laughed. 'Welcome back to the land of the living.'

Two partners later, the dance ended.

Fabrizio came to escort her back to her seat. 'I spent part of my childhood in this villa,' he said. 'Come upstairs. I wish to show you something.'

She hesitated.

'You are nervous of me, Maria. I sense it. Please don't be. It grieves me. I would never do you harm. I am practically your relative, your cousin, and I would like you to think of me as such.'

'What a fine speech, Fabrizio,' she said coldly. They reached the door and stood there. 'What is it you wish to show me?'

'Now I've angered you.' He sighed and let go of her arm. 'I wish to show you a rare and beautiful artefact, a necklace they say once belonged to Cleopatra.'

The mention of jewellery caused her to remember the ring. Tears sprang into her eyes, and she turned her face from him, saying, 'Very well, let us go up.'

Fabrizio asked a footman to bring a lamp. She glanced back, looking for Carlo. He stood chatting with Miranda, his face in profile. Damn him. And damn whoever else noticed her leaving the room in the company of Fabrizio.

As she mounted the stairs, Maria told herself to be calm. Her nerves were raw: in the space of a mere two minutes she'd been angry, tearful and defiant.

'I wish to ask you something,' she said. 'The ring you gave me at Beatrice's funeral. Was it Beatrice's? I never saw it on her.'

'It was *to be* Beatrice's. I'd had it made as a gift for her.'

'Forgive me, but I hardly looked at it. It's in my pocket at home still. What is its design?'

'A bear, a sword and three stars: the Carafa coat of arms, as you know. Beatrice was so proud of being a Carafa, I thought she'd like it.'

'Yes, she would have. How kind of you,' she said, holding back tears, afraid that a fit of uncontrollable sobbing would come upon her, as it often did when she was alone.

'I was fond of Beatrice. She was the most endearing of my cousins. Even my wife liked her. She was planning to have her do good works.'

'I don't know if Beatrice would have been agreeable to that.'

'No. She was too truthful to be sanctimonious. She may have been charitable when she grew older but she would not have preached about it and . . . made it a way of life.'

'Is that what your wife does?'

'Yes,' he answered quietly.

They reached the top floor. Fabrizio led the way into a room on the left and placed the candelabra on a table. It was a large, uncurtained room, glass cabinets and old Venetian mirrors glowed softly in the warm light; paintings were stacked against the walls. 'This is where the prince keeps some of his family treasures,' said Fabrizio.

Maria went across to the wall of windows opposite the door and looked out. In the distance, the twin white peaks of Mount Vesuvius floated eerily in the blackness.

Fabrizio took a key out of a hidden compartment in a table and unlocked one of the cabinets.

'Will the prince mind us being here?' asked Maria.

'No. As well as being my uncle, we are good friends. He knows I have a particular fondness for this necklace,' he said, drawing it out of the cabinet. 'It is part of a bequest to me in his will.'

He placed the necklace on the table next to the candelabra and it sprang to life, a circlet with double rows of lozenge-shaped amethysts, turquoises and rubies, set within two thickly plaited, radiant yellow-gold bands. The cunning secret of its seductiveness was that it was barbaric in its boldness, yet a masterpiece of fine workmanship.

'How exquisite,' breathed Maria, touching it with her fingers, entranced by it.

'Yes, isn't it. It's Roman. It's said that Caesar had it made for Cleopatra when she was in Rome.'

'How does Prince di Stigliano come to have it?'

'It's come down through the centuries from the Carafa side of the family. An ancestor of ours was a member of Caesar's Praetorian Guard. Family legend says that he was stationed in Egypt at the time of Cleopatra's death.' Fabrizio ran his fingers over the necklace. The candlelight cast shadows of his black lashes onto his cheek. 'Members of the guard seized several portable items of hers as booty. They divided them up by lots and the necklace fell to my ancestor.' He shrugged. 'We don't know if this is true, but it's a wonderful story and I like to believe it.' He looked down and caressed her neck with his eyes. 'I like to picture Caesar placing it around Cleopatra's neck.'

He said this with such intimacy that Maria stepped back, although she longed to lean forward and rest her head on his shoulder. The sensation of being lifted by him, comforted and soothed by him, at Beatrice's laying-out flashed through her mind and she yearned for that heady experience again. 'It's true I was angry with you before,' she said. 'Do you know why?'

'No. Tell me.'

'It was because your words seemed insincere to me. I don't like conventional assurances of trustworthiness. I will be frank and tell you that I do not trust you. Although it may be true that you do not mean me harm, I don't for a moment believe that you think of me as a cousin. And there is always at the back of my mind your reputation with women.'

'Is that why you avoid me?'

'Yes. I have little regard for men of such dishonour.'

'It's true that I had several affairs early in my marriage. I don't deny it. There would be no point as the idle chatterers of Naples once took great delight in bruiting my conquests, as they called them. But that was long ago, Maria. For more than two years now I have loved only one woman and, as all the others are to me dull reflections of her radiance, I have no inclination to enjoy them.'

'And that woman is your wife?' What a stupid thing to say, she immediately thought.

'No, Maria. I believe you well know that I do no love my wife. Now it is you who are being insincere. You see? We make conversation and insincerity creeps in unnoticed by the speaker, detected only by the listener who draws it to our attention. Much of the time, we all speak with the forked tongue of conventional expression. But come, let us not bicker. I will offend your ears no longer with insincere assurances. Allow me instead to offer you a rare experience: to place about your throat the necklace of Cleopatra.'

He picked it up from the table and, placing it delicately across his fingers, held it out to her.

'You think no woman could refuse such an offer, don't you?'

'You may refuse if you wish.'

Maria looked long at the necklace. It spoke to her: for centuries I have not touched the skin of a beautiful woman. I am cold. Warm me, even if only for a moment.

Maria looked up at Fabrizio, who was watching her with a little smile, but it was the flicker of uncertainty behind his eyes that she liked.

She held out her hand. 'I will put it on. You may fasten it.'

The necklace felt very cold on her skin. She shivered as Fabrizio deftly fastened the clasp, and she could not help wondering how many other women he had led up here to try on this gift of Caesar to the legendary queen.

Fabrizio took up the candelabra and placed it on another table, before a large oval mirror. 'Come, look at yourself, Maria.'

She stood in front of the glass and saw a pale woman in black, brought to life by the rays of the golden disc that shimmered like the sun.

'The sun paying a visit to Diana,' said Fabrizio poetically. 'As the necklace speaks to you, why don't you ask it to answer to what is on your mind?'

'And what *is* on my mind?'

'You wish to know whether I have fastened it around the necks of other women.'

He moved close behind her so that the two of them were reflected in the mirror. Their eyes met in the glass. His face in the flickering amber candlelight was so beautiful as to be almost fragile, as if such beauty could not last the night. She dropped her gaze.

'Am I correct?' he asked.

She'd lost the train of their conversation.

'You know the answer,' he said. 'No other woman. Not even my wife.'

He waited until her eyes met his again in the mirror.

'It is you I love, Maria.'

She stood still, feeling the warmth emanate from him. He wasn't touching her, but she could feel his breath in her hair. She imagined leaning back into him, so that his lips touched her cheek. She touched the necklace.

'I pray that one day it will be yours,' he said.

They stood in silence, absorbed by each other's eyes in the mirror. One of the candles sputtered and went out.

'We must go,' she said, suddenly alarmed at the length of time they'd been away from the others. 'How long have we been here? Ten minutes? An hour? Unfasten the necklace, Fabrizio.'

He did. He held it to his cheek. 'Feel it,' he said, placing it against hers. She closed her eyes to shut out the closeness of his face. The necklace was suffused with warmth.

'We'll leave now, but I must tell you this,' he said quietly. 'For two years, knowing you are near me in this city has reduced everything else in my life to dullness. You are its only intensity. Only you make me feel alive. And I know it's the same for you. I know you love me, Maria.'

'What a vain creature you are. How could you know such a thing?'

'It's in your eyes. Even before tonight, it was in your very aloofness toward me. It pained me, your amiability to others, your coldness to me, but then it occurred to me to question why I was singled out. Why, I asked myself, did you so dislike me? Perhaps because you liked me too well. But I am not vain, as you say, for I was never certain, not until tonight. Since you're so fond of sincerity, I would like you to tell me what thoughts just passed through your mind.'

'I felt your breath in my hair and thought I might lean back into your arms and experience the pleasure of being enfolded in your warmth. But I chose not to succumb to such a temptation. I thought of Carlo, downstairs, and I chose virtue and my life with him, not the fleeting pleasures of desire with you.'

'The centre of Carlo's life is his music. The centre of my life is my love for you,' said Fabrizio ardently, an edge of urgency in his voice at her insistence on virtue. 'No matter what our faith would try to tell us, Maria, love is the highest of the virtues. When I look into your eyes I find there a mystery that echoes in my own soul. I know that mystery to be the love between us, for when you looked into me just now, I knew that you, too, recognised the same thing in my eyes. Carlo can never belong to you as I belong to you. Your heart knows this, does it not, Maria?'

'Don't touch me, Fabrizio, don't,' she said, panic in her voice now as he made to turn her to him. She stepped away and he dropped his hand in a gesture of embarrassment.

'Your choice is not between Carlo and me; it's between dragging out your days in a sorry imitation of life and condemning me to do the same. Our lives could be joyous. Only have the courage to love me.'

'You don't persuade me, Fabrizio. I've told you. I've made my choice. Come, let us go.'

He silently placed the necklace back in the cabinet, which he locked. His whole demeanour had changed. He looked defeated. She even noticed a slight stoop to his shoulders as he returned the key to its secret compartment, and took up the candelabra.

'Maria,' he said at the door. 'Just one word. Tell me what I must do.'

'Nothing,' she said. 'Nothing at all.'

He began to protest, but she placed her fingers on his lips, allowing herself at last the luxury of touching him. 'You know very well that anything else is impossible.'

Later that night she found the little ring in the pocket of the funeral gown. She held it to her lips and ran it over them, thinking of Fabrizio's face in the mirror. Then she put the ring on her little finger. It fitted. She wore it to bed, repeatedly touching it with her lips until she fell asleep.

Love is a madness. Resolving to cling to the role of virtuous wife in the days following the ball at La Sirena, Maria made a valiant attempt to introduce discipline into a life bereft of Beatrice and bereft of the warm companionship of Maddelena Carafa, for to be with her was to be reminded not only of Beatrice but, more dangerously, of Fabrizio. Determined to keep her mind occupied, she turned her attention once again to the story of Costanza d'Avalos. She was unable to concentrate on it. She attended mass daily, visited Antonia, called in the dressmakers, paid more attention to Emmanuele and threw herself into organising Carlo's next concert, for Carlo, she knew, was watching her—not from his usual ironic distance, but more closely, as if he was waiting for signs that would betray what preoccupied her. During all of these activities, not for one moment could she cast Fabrizio Carafa from her mind. Alone, she couldn't resist succumbing to the delicious pleasure of recalling his face and the words he's spoken to her at La Sirena—had it been only a week ago? She relived the sensations of his warm breath in her hair, the fleeting contact of his lips against her fingers; she recalled every word he'd spoken. Even when she didn't invoke his presence he was with her, the essence of him. Though she sternly admonished herself, these thoughts of him brought her nothing but joy, a feeling of such buoyancy that she could not help but smile.

She acknowledged it at last. She loved Fabrizio Carafa. And love was indeed a madness.

She sought out guilt. She knelt before her confessor, admitted her sinful love, and was warned of the terrors that awaited her if she did not cast such forbidden thoughts from her mind. All she could do was think perversely that God had been in error to create so beautiful a temptation as Fabrizio Carafa, because it was perhaps no longer in her nature to resist it. Not now that Beatrice was gone, not now that she knew Carlo sometimes shared his shadowy private world with another, or others—who knew what or whom his forbidden intimacies involved? Being unable to imagine or even begin to understand this aspect of Carlo's life, she couldn't bear to think about it, not consciously; she couldn't even give it a name; but it was always hovering in the back of her mind.

She spent the first week after La Sirena allowing herself to entertain these thoughts with no intention of acting upon them. Her visits to the nursery increased to twice daily. Emmanuele was eighteen months old now, a cherubic child with Carlo's quick, dark eyes and her fair hair. Though she loved him the least of all the children she'd borne—and loved him only in the sense that she hoped no harm would come to him—he was the one, the only one, she knew, who would survive into adulthood.

On the fifth day, Carlo came into the nursery in his long black dressing-gown, carrying his lute. Sylvia quit the room; Carlo liked to be alone with his son. Maria stayed to please Carlo. He often played and sang to the infant, looking forward to the time when he could teach him and they could play music together. Emmanuele was teething and was cranky and fretful, but as soon as Carlo began to play, he quietened.

After only one song, Carlo lay down his lute, pursed his lips, and looked at Maria silently.

'Why are you wearing the Carafa coat of arms?' he asked slowly.

'Because the ring was Beatrice's. I wear it in memory of her, to have her close to me.'

'You are my wife,' he shouted, suddenly enraged. 'If you wear a coat of arms it shall be the Gesualdo coat of arms. Who gave it to you?'

Emmanuele began wailing again.

'Fabrizio Carafa. He had it made for Beatrice.'

'Do not wear it in my presence, or when you go out. Has it not occurred to you, Maria, that your wearing the coat of arms of your first husband's family could make a laughing stock of me?'

'No, Carlo. Forgive me. It did not occur to me. I was thinking only of Beatrice.'

'I cannot believe you to be so dull-witted.'

'What *do* you believe, then? That I would deliberately set out to dishonour you?'

'I don't know what I believe. You baffle me.'

'And you me, Carlo'

'Because I ask you not to wear the Carafa coat of arms?'

'No. I understand that was wrong of me. I live in my own world sometimes. I meant generally, that you baffle me generally.'

'Well, allow me to illuminate you. Whatever you may imagine, you know me better than anyone. I have allowed you to come as close to me as it is possible for any human being to get. You know me better than my mother, my father, my brother, my sisters, better than anyone who comes to this house. You are the mother of my son.'

'But you do not love me, Carlo,' she said quietly.

He closed his eyes and sighed. 'Perhaps not in the way that you would like. And this is what baffles you?'

She thought on it. 'Perhaps that's it, after all. But no, it's more than that. There is at the heart of you a mystery, something that I can never know.'

'That is my soul, Maria. And my soul is the business only of God and myself.'

After that day, Maria kept the ring by her bedside and slipped it on before she went to sleep. The thought of Carlo and what he might do introduced a more sober cast to her free-ranging thoughts about Fabrizio.

She lived with the noble idea that she would allow this love only to warm her heart, brighten her days, lift up her spirit, and offer a heady possibility that would never be acted upon.

This, then, was Maria's state of mind in the first week. If she had meditated on the idea of love being a madness, she might have perceived that madness has a dynamic: it shifts and progresses over time, and like fire intensifies as it consumes. By the eighth day, her recollections of Fabrizio and the night at La Sirena were growing faded and she began to long for his presence. Now the torment began.

Eight days and not so much as a message, a note. Never mind that she'd made him swear to do nothing. Nine days. How was it possible, this silence of his? How could he love her as he said and yet keep away from her like this? Impossible. It could only mean that he did not love her. For the thousandth time she called to mind his fading image in the mirror, the love in his eyes. Of course he loved her. He was afraid for her, protecting her by doing as she'd asked. Ten days. Her joy had shrivelled. She began to hate him. He'd been toying with her. He'd deceived her. He'd regarded her only as another conquest and had cooled when he'd seen little hope of easily attaining her. He was dishonourable, a womaniser who spoke scornfully of his wife to other men. By the eleventh day her head was aching and she had lost any hope of his loving her.

Spring had arrived. Carlo had planned to go to Gesualdo Castle to continue work on his garden and confer with his steward about the planting of crops, but a fit of melancholy had fallen upon him. He hadn't stirred from his room for three days. But for the sounds from the street, the palace was silent. Not even a few bars of music, which was unusual. Never had Maria felt such loneliness. She couldn't even be bothered to take the trouble to dress. Her hair hung about her lankly.

Walking aimlessly about her bedchamber, she turned the handle of the door that led to the spiral staircase, which Carlo always kept locked. To her surprise, the door opened. Listening for sounds below, she stood at the top of the stairs, looking far down at the strange, irregularly shaped room and shielding her eyes from the pale afternoon sun that beamed through the high round windows. From this height, they were level with her face. She hadn't been in this part of the palace since Geronima had shown her through on her wedding day.

She crept halfway down the stairs. The silence here was palpable, for there were no street noises. On the large table was a single sheet of music in Carlo's hand. She turned to go back up, but then remembered what Beatrice had said about Carlo's uncanny ability to sense things. If he was conscious, he would know she was there.

The door to his bedroom was ajar. She continued down the stairs, her heart thudding. What she was afraid of, she didn't know. She hesitated at the doorway to his darkened room, then went in.

Carlo was sitting up in bed in his dressing-gown with the bearskin rug over him, staring into space. She moved to the end of his bed and stood there. Her eyes rose to the sculpted Christ above Carlo's head and it struck her that this tortured figure had a meaning for her husband beyond its religious significance, a meaning associated with his secret life.

Carlo eventually turned his eyes to her and they stared at each other in the silent half-darkness. She had never seen him like this; all the life seemed to have drained out of him. Even in the gloom the paleness of his face had a grey cast; his hair rose above his forehead in untidy clumps, and his quick eyes were dull. She felt a wave of sympathy for him. Something tormented him, his dark secret no doubt. Perhaps this moment offered an opportunity for her to make a deeper connection with him, to help him in some way, as she'd once helped him to regain his breath. And it would help her if Carlo came to need her in this way; it would give pause to her daydreams about Fabrizio, which in her rational moments she acknowledged were overlapping dangerously with the real world.

'Can I do anything for you?' she asked quietly.

'No,' he replied listlessly.

'When did you last eat?'

He shut his eyes and drew his hands over his ears as if the sight and sound of her assaulted his senses, and muttered almost inaudibly, 'I must be alone when I'm like this.'

She trod softly from the room and back up the spiral stairs to her bedchamber feeling wretched, utterly rejected. She slumped on her bed, overwhelmed by her sense of loneliness. It offered her a glimpse of what Carlo must endure when his blackness seized hold of him. It didn't resemble grief or a sense of loss; it was an all-pervading nothingness.

Carlo, however, would emerge from his agony in a day or two or three, whereas she, when or how was she to be delivered of her sense of emptiness? She lay on her bed for the rest of the day, experiencing the void within herself as a dark hollow in the pit of her stomach. Now that Beatrice was gone, who loved her in that vital, pulsing, blood-connected way that gave life its only real meaning? Not Carlo, certainly: he would always shut her out; he had just made that abundantly clear. Antonia? Yes indeed, but the love of an aunt was not the deep, energising love she craved. Fabrizio Carafa? She rolled over suddenly, burying her face in the pillow. She did feel connected to Fabrizio in that deep, familial way, through Beatrice, through Federigo, but amidst the many dangers lurking in the possibility of a disreputable liaison with him was the overwhelming question, did Fabrizio feel connected to her in this way? Or was his love merely carnal, and therefore ruinous? Besieged by these thoughts, she lay rigid with the frightening sense of inhabiting an emotional void, taking a tinge of comfort only from her awareness that two floors below, Carlo was doing the same.

The next morning a note arrived from Antonia. There was to be a reading of poems at the house of a friend in Chiaia on Friday evening. Maria must come because Antonia wished to show her his splendid garden. She'd collect her at eight.

The day after that, Carlo was himself again, although there was now a feverish intensity to his quick movements, to the alertness in his eyes. He came to her rooms to ask her if she wished to accompany him to Gesualdo Castle the next day. It was his habit to invite her, just as it was hers to decline, as she did today. He'd found her sitting in her blue salon, deliberating with Antonia over what they would wear to the poetry reading the following evening.

'You look an absolute fright,' he bent down and whispered in Maria's ear as Antonia prattled on. He always stood in Antonia's presence, ready to turn on his heel and escape at any minute in case she began digressing into some realm beyond the matter at hand. Carlo always went to the heart of things and expected those he conversed with to be direct and lucid in turn. Maria pushed back the hair that still hung about her shoulders lankly and whispered back, 'So do you.' His face was still pale and drawn and she could see beads of perspiration above his upper lip.

He sat down next to her, saying under his breath, 'You know my reason. What is yours?'

Antonia had stopped speaking and was looking quizzically at the two of them.

'I've been feeling lethargic these last few days,' said Maria aloud. 'But I'm now recovered.'

'Is your aunt the agent of your recovery?' Carlo asked, his eyes fixed on Antonia as if they would bore through her.

'Would you say so, Aunt?' smiled Maria.

'I would say it's the season,' chirped Antonia. 'How could one feel lethargic on such a day? Listen. One can hear the birds singing outside. You see, Carlo, I enjoy life, so people often feel more cheerful in my presence.'

'I'm not one of them,' he said rudely, rising again. He turned to go but swung back on his heel, walked over to Antonia and, standing over her, said, 'If I thought you to be trustworthy, I'd ask you to keep an eye on Maria while I'm away, but I don't consider you trustworthy. Not in the least.'

'Whether you consider me trustworthy or not is entirely beside the point,' responded Antonia in a high voice, flustered. 'There is no good reason for anyone to keep an eye on Maria.'

Carlo studied her face as she said this and then glanced across at Maria, whose only expression was one of discomfort on Antonia's behalf. He gave her a strange, sardonic smile, as if he knew something she did not, and left.

Eleven

THE GARDEN OF DON GARZIA DE TOLEDO

As it was a beautiful evening, unusually warm for early spring, Maria wore the white Grecian-style dress that she and Carlo had designed two years previously. The palace of Antonia's friend, Don Garzia de Toledo, stood high on the hill of Vomero and it had a wide arched terrace that looked down upon a sloping garden and the sea beyond.

Antonia was always late, just as she was this night in collecting Maria in her carriage, so that by the time they arrived at Don Garzia's, the assembled party was already seated and waiting impatiently for the readings to begin.

'We nearly began without you,' said Don Garzia, playfully slapping Antonia's hand after he'd kissed it, and looking at her with amorous eyes. He'd been in love with her for years.

'You should have,' retorted Antonia, turning her back on him, taking Maria's hand and walking into the music room. 'You waste half your life waiting for me.'

Don Garzia, bald and rotund, was elderly and his taste in both people and the arts was conservative; the majority of the guests were unknown to Maria as they did not move in Carlo's circle.

The poets, too, were middle-aged or older. Had Maria been listening to their Petrarchan-style verses as they read she would have found them elegant and measured but rather stale. Even in her cool dress her face burned. She had an urge to laugh out loud or burst into tears as her eyes moved restlessly about the room in a desperate effort not to look at the one thing that attracted them like a magnet. 'Look at me. Return my gaze,' compelled the face of Fabrizio Carafa, who sat by himself in a far corner of the room and had not taken his eyes off her since she'd entered. She forced herself to take deep breaths to still the fluttering in her throat.

'Stella, the only planet of my light/ Light of my life and life of my desire,' rang out the voice of a poet whose copious grey hair formed wings at the side of his temples. He was so transported by his own verses it seemed he might suddenly take off and soar through the ceiling.

Maria, briefly distracted, stifled a giggle and nervously bit her upper lip. Over there was the man who this past fortnight had made no effort to contact her and who now happened upon her by chance. Very well, she would glance at him, for she could no longer not do so, but she would meet his gaze coolly. She let her eyes travel very slowly toward his, stopping to appraise every other face on the way, though her mind registered none of them. When they finally met Fabrizio's, his face broke into a smile of such warmth she all but laughed out loud for joy.

'What oceans of delight in me doth flow,' enthused the wing-haired poet.

What a fool I am, she admonished herself, basking in Fabrizio's smile. I, too, have succumbed to this seducer. I think to bring damnation upon myself by giving myself over to a man who has not had one thought of me these past fourteen days. A man who smiles at me now as if I, and only I, light his days. A man who has smiled into the eyes of countless women this way. He's in love with me, it's plain, passionately in love. But how long will this love of his last? A year? Six months? One month? Fabrizio's affairs have all been notoriously brief. I will hold him only for as long as he believes there is yet more of me to conquer; the day he knows I'm his, he'll whirl away like a leaf in a breeze.

During the interval between readings when the others were served refreshments and began chattering and milling about, she went out onto the cool terrace and stood in the shadows, knowing Fabrizio would follow her there. The full moon cast a pale silvery light on the sloping garden and the sea beyond.

She considered the worst: what if it was to be only for a month, a mere month? Even so it would be four full weeks of summer days, enough to recall and savour for the rest of her life. In thinking this, she was reminded of the poet Vittoria Colonna. After Beatrice's death, when she had sufficiently recovered her mind to concentrate, Maria had read Vittoria's poems over and over again, seeking solace in their theme of irrevocable loss. She recalled some of these poems now, in particular one where Vittoria told that in her earliest sexual encounters with Ferrante d'Avalos she'd responded with such utter abandon to his lovemaking that she felt she could never lay with another man. Only a year after their marriage Ferrante had embarked on one of the many military campaigns that were to occupy him for the rest of his life, and Vittoria saw him only sporadically during the years leading up to his hero's death seven years later. Vittoria, though wealthy and still young, had never remarried. The sonnets she wrote during the remaining twenty-two years of her life were all to Ferrante d'Avalos, the most moving of which Maria knew by heart:

I live upon this fearful, lonely rock, like a sorrowing bird that shuns green branch and clear water; and I take myself away from those I love in this world and from my very self, so that my thoughts may go speedily to him, the sun I adore and worship.

She now wondered whether it was not those very feelings of longing and loss that had made such a great poet of Vittoria, and considered that this poet's life might offer a model for hers when Fabrizio abandoned her.

Maria went on romanticising what she might do with the bleak future she envisaged for herself as she stood in the moonlight watching the door. Then she imagined Fabrizio stealing up behind her, brushing her neck with his lips, sliding his hand beneath her bodice, biting her neck, turning her to him. She felt a strange compulsion to do physical battle with him, fight him off, hurt him, bite him, make him suffer, make him bleed. Because she could to longer resist him, she wanted to punish him. Fabrizio did not appear. The room beyond had grown silent again. Another poet began to recite his lines. She returned to the room and took her seat next to Antonia and only then looked across at Fabrizio. He was not there. He had left.

Antonia had been holding a glass of madeira for Maria and she handed it to her. Maria sat with the glass of red wine in her hand, not daring to take a sip in case she choked on it. She tried to focus her attention on the poetry, interminably dull stuff, all the while wanting to stand up and scream, wanting to throw her glass at the balding reciter who droned on about love as if it resembled a pair of sighing apes dancing the quadrille. Maria at last understood why Carlo threw things in a rage: it was a swift means of bringing intolerable stupidity to an end.

And what of Carlo in all of this? She'd asked herself so any times in the past fortnight, and had envisaged so any different scenarios, that, like a single word repeated over and over and over, the question had become drained of meaning. Suddenly the wineglass slipped out of her grasp and spilled its contents down the front of her white gown before landing with a dull thud on the thick rug. Antonia looked down at the long red stain with horror. She grabbed Maria's arm and pulled her from the room.

After a great deal of fuss on Antonia's behalf, and some expert rinsing and dabbing by two servants, Maria stood in front of the fire in Don Garzia's salon watching the stain dry to a barely perceptible parchment colour.

'Let us leave now,' said Maria.

'Just ten minutes, my darling. A mere ten minutes. It's unthinkable that you come here without taking the tiniest walk in Don Garzia's wonderful garden. He'd be mortified at such a lack of interest in one so beautiful and would inevitably imagine that you scorn his efforts, for I've told him you're an expert on such matters because of Carlo's interest in fashionable gardens, although I'm sure Don Garzia's is not so fashionable as the one at Gesualdo. After all it was begun fifty years ago, which means that the plants have had time to grow and flourish and reach startling heights. You couldn't do that to your aunt. It's unthinkable. Listen. They're finishing up now. Don Garzia with be with us at any moment and we'll go outside immediately. Of course you're upset because your beautiful gown is ruined. Why not have another made exactly the—'

'I'm not upset, Aunt. I merely wish to go home.'

'Well, you can't, and there's an end to it. Wait here. I'll be back in one minute.'

Twenty minutes later the three of them walked in Don Garzia's garden, one of the most admired in Naples. It was laid out formally in the old

Renaissance style. In the silvery light of the full moon the garden was indeed eerily beautiful with its pale marble statuary outlined against the black forms of tall cypresses. As they wandered along geometric paths bordered by parterres, the only sound was the plashing of fountains. They walked in the direction of the bay down a steep hill, where, at the end of a maze of paths, stood an octagonal summerhouse with a domed roof. Antonia was singing the praises of this new building, insisting they go inside and look at the dome.

Don Garzia opened the door, saying he would wait for them outside, and they walked into the large, open summer salon.

'We can light the candles if you like,' said Antonia, 'but it's hardly necessary.' Moonlight streamed in from above, through the lantern of the dome. 'Sit down, my darling, and look up at that dome. Isn't it marvellous? One would think one was in Heaven. Stay here for a while and rest. You seem a little strained. I was here for hours last week. I'm just going outside for a few minutes. Don Garzia has promised to arrange some cuttings of those old Roman roses to be delivered to my gardener. They have the most wonderful fragrance, rather like vanilla. Stay here and let your mind drift. The longer you look at the dome, the more marvels you will see.'

Antonia went outside, leaving Maria alone in the moonlight. She sat down on one of the large, comfortable divans and looked up at the dome. It was like a child's dream of the heavens, night and day fused, with stars and large planets revolving around the earth, and a golden-rayed sun surrounding the oculus. Maria studied it for a few minutes, but although it was lovely, the marvellous illusions Antonia had promised did not appear.

An owl hooted in the silence.

Maria suddenly had an uneasy feeling that Antonia and Don Garzia had deserted her. She rose from her seat, nervously turning the pointed ruby ring on her wedding finger, considering whether she should go out and look for them or return straight to the palace.

'Maria.'

Fabrizio Carafa's graceful form emerged from the darkness and he stood before her. He seemed absolutely calm, as if their meeting was taking place in a dream in which the logic of the waking world had no place. This effect was confirmed by what he softly said as he took her hand and, rather than kissing it, pressed it against his lips, savouring this first touch of her skin. 'I've dreamed of you so much, my arms have become used to embracing your shadow.'

She raised her other hand and delivered him a stinging blow across the cheek.

He gasped as if it thrilled him. 'Hit me all you like.'

Her ring, which she'd unthinkingly twisted so that the pointed stone was palm-wards, had cut the fine skin on his cheekbone. She stared at the wound, mesmerised by the dark blood trickling from it as they stood close without touching, breathing each other in. Then he bowed his head so that his forehead touched hers and a little sound between a sob and a laugh escaped her and she moved her lips to the wound on his cheek and sucked his Carafa blood.

Their rapture lasted all through the night. The dome's stars and planets circled above them but they didn't notice the passing of the hours. Just after dawn he carried her into the bedchamber he'd meant to take her to in the first place. On the second night, as he blew little gusts of cool breath on her eyelids, she fell at last into a deep sleep.

They stayed in the summerhouse for three nights and three days.

'Did my aunt conspire in this with you?' asked Maria on the second day.

'Yes, but unwillingly at first. I prevailed upon her by saying you might one day thank her for it.'

Maria laughed at the thought of Antonia, thrilled beyond measure no doubt at the intrigue of it all, allowing herself to be won over by Fabrizio's ardour. 'And I imagine she's arranged things so that there's no danger of us being disturbed,' she said.

'Yes. Though she refused to tell me the details, she assured me she'd arranged things so that nobody will come near here until we leave, and that there will never be talk of this from any quarter, nor talk of you not returning with her and Don Garzia to his palace after your walk in the garden last night. I trusted her completely for I know how precious you are to her. Was I right in this?'

'Yes,' answered Maria, who could well imagine the nature of the bargain Antonia would have struck with Don Garzia, something to the effect that he must do her bidding and ask no questions or he would see her no more. Until her aunt agreed to marry Don Garzia, as he dared to hope she one day would, his greatest pleasure in life was to be her humble servant.

Each afternoon Antonia left water and a basket of food at the door, but Maria and Fabrizio ate little of it. They remained in their rapture, whispering only of their love for each other, laughing and weeping for joy. She bit and slapped him, visiting upon her lover the griefs and frustrations of years, and he laughed, for though his lips bled, she could not hurt him.

'How long will this passion of ours last, do you think?' she asked him, playing the sophisticate, testing him. 'One month? Two?'

He turned his head and gave her such a look it made her ashamed of her flippant remark, ashamed of her lingering uncertainty about him that had provoked it. 'For as long as you want me near you. I found you again, my boyhood angel of love, watched while you married Carlo, and waited for you for almost three years. Now that I've won you at last, and I find you love me as I love you, what earthly reason would make me wish to relinquish you?'

On the third day, a great, expansive feeling of peace came over her, and she struck him no more. She lay beside him and stared at his profile, marvelling at the sensuality of the line that ran from the tip of his nose to the base of his throat, so refined as to be almost feminine. It was a Carafa characteristic, this nobility of profile; Federigo had had it and dear little Beatrice, too. Maria traced it with her fingers and Fabrizio closed his eyes and smiled.

She felt connected to life again, connected to joy and meaning and danger, and what was life if not dangerous? Yet she felt safe with Fabrizio as she'd never felt safe with anyone. Not even Federigo. Her first husband was the love of the springtime of her life. Fabrizio was her summer. Hot sun on the body, bursting fruits and warmth of the soul. Only from this perspective, lying beside Fabrizio, could she acknowledge that Federigo had clung to his boyhood, uncertain of how to complete the rite of passage into adulthood because of his equivocation about being a Carafa. There was nothing uncertain about Fabrizio. He'd attained manhood long ago.

She stretched languorously and he moved his legs—thick, heavy legs—and entwined them in hers.

He curled a tress of her hair around his fingers, musing before he said, 'I often think how strange it is that you and my wife are both named Maria, for you could not be more unlike. After the night of your wedding to Carlo, when I began once again to dream of you, I thought of her as Black Maria. You had always been, to me, the angel Maria, and that is how I still think of you both.'

'Did you ever love her?' asked Maria.

'I once respected her, but her sanctimony has made me despise her. It sometimes amazes me that she has borne me five children, for she regards the intimacy of love as a sin. The dogma of the Church suits well her own inclinations.' He raised himself up on one elbow, staring at a sunbeam that streamed in through a gap in the blind and slowly shaking his head. 'Whenever I went to her bed, ninety-nine times out of a hundred she would cite a reason for coupling on that night to be a sin. Even between man and wife. It was her menses. She was pregnant. It was Lent. It was Advent. It was Whitson week. It was Easter. It was Sunday, Saturday, or a feast day. It was daylight. Did I want another child? No? Then stop; it was a sin. My nakedness was a sin.' He turned to Maria, a little frown on his forehead. 'Do you know, Maria, she has never let me see her body. She goes to bed rigidly clothed.'

Maria stared up at Fabrizio. Since she'd seen him on the jousting field his charisma had drawn her like a magnet, but now that he lay beside her, that charisma had increased a hundredfold. How could any woman lie beside him and not want him?

'On our wedding night,' he continued, 'when she was a pretty girl of fourteen, not the sour woman she's become, I thought to introduce her to the delights of lovemaking and relax her body so that it would be less painful when I entered her, for there was no question that she was a virgin. I imagined she was enjoying my caresses, for her breast was heaving, but then a shriek escaped her and she began crossing herself. Anyone would have thought that the tongue between her legs belonged not to me but to the Devil. It was then I learned for the first time that the finer points of lovemaking were also regarded as a sin. "You have been with prostitutes to have learned such filthy things," she screamed at me, transforming what I'd intended to be joy into disgust. I think one of the reasons she is so devoted to the teachings of the Church is that they accord with her own feelings of revulsion for the flesh.'

This struck a chord with Maria. 'I think Carlo's attitude may be similar, but nowhere as extreme as your wife's. Tell me, Fabrizio,' she said, thoughtfully curling a strand of his silky hair around her fingers, 'had you been to prostitutes?'

'Of course. What young man with blood in his veins has not? My father and older brothers took me to the bordello by the bay they call Il Paradiso. I went back there numerous times, even after my marriage, for reasons I hope you are sympathetic to, but not once have I been there since your return to Naples. The thought of being with any woman but you disgusts me.'

That evening, as the time for them to leave approached, Maria awakened as from a dream and began to think how things would be when she returned to San Severo.

'What of Carlo?' she asked.

He looked at her, smiling, moving his eyes around her face, and then he broke into a laugh. He threw his head back on the pillow and laughed, stretching his body luxuriantly, laughing louder and louder. He laughed like the gods.

For the first time since Fabrizio had touched her, Maria frowned. 'What are you laughing at? Is Carlo so funny?'

'No, no, my angel. Carlo is not funny. I don't know why I'm laughing. It must be because I'm happy, so blissfully happy, to be in this heaven with you, my most beautiful angel. And not even the thought of Carlo can cloud my happiness with the faintest shadow. Your love makes me invincible.' He wiped a tear of laughter from the corner of his eye and gazed at her. 'What of Carlo? I have a strange feeling about him. When I tell you what it is you may think there is no logic to what I am saying, but I know Carlo. We've been friends for many years, not especially close ones, but we have interests in common, as you know. If you were not Carlo's wife, I'm certain he'd agree that it is me to whom you belong. He would concede it without question. But you *are* his wife, alas.

'Carlo has come to think of himself, above all, as a prince. In time he may think himself more a musician than a prince, for that is what he is, by gifts and temperament. But, for now, he is the prince. And as the wife of the prince, he is possessive of you. Very possessive. I have watched him with you. He loves your beauty, but he does not love your body and your soul, as I do. He holds himself aloof from you, doesn't he?'

'Yes.'

'I know because that's the way Carlo is. It's connected to what I said to you at La Sirena, that Carlo belongs only to Carlo. He is enclosed within himself. And there is something in his eyes sometimes, I don't know . . .' Fabrizio frowned as he rubbed his own eyes, thinking. 'It is as if he carries some secret about with him, something that torments him. Those foul moods he gets into, some unhappiness of his must be at the root of them. Who can know what it is.'

What insight Fabrizio had. It was tempting to tell him of Carlo's strange habits. Perhaps, as a man, he could shed some light on them. But no, as much as she loved Fabrizio, it would be ignoble to reveal Carlo's secrets to her lover. Her husband did not deserve such disloyalty. From the pinnacle of happiness on which she now stood, she began to pity Carlo.

'What are you thinking?' asked Fabrizio, running his fingers through her hair.

'That in embarking on the journey of you and I, I am beginning to know what you are really like, how perceptive you are. I've thought of you only as seductive, dangerous, handsome as a god, brave as Mars—for that is what they call you, as I'm sure you know—the man whom I must resist or be ruined. But now I'm beginning to see beyond this romance to the real man. Is that enough sincere flattery for you?'

He laughed, charmed.

'Finish what you were saying about Carlo,' she said.

'Here's the part you may think unreasoned. I think that if Carlo knew we were lovers, and we behaved with dignity and did not become a subject of gossip, he would in some way accept it, or, perhaps turn a blind eye to it. He would be angry and jealous, of course, but in time his anger would pass. Did you notice what he did last week, at La Sirena? Of course you did. He practically pushed you into my arms.'

'Surely that's an exaggeration, Fabrizio. He merely told me to dance with you.'

'Why did he do so? How many of his other friends has he asked you to dance with?'

'What are you suggesting? That Carlo *wants* us to be lovers? You would not have thought so if you'd witnessed his reaction to my wearing the ring you had made for Beatrice. He forbade me to wear it.'

'Because it's a Carafa ring, yes?'

'Where is this conversation leading, Fabrizio?'

'To an instinct I have, that Carlo would never harm you. You are the most exquisite pearl of his princely crown, an integral part of the aesthete's world he goes on creating for himself. If the princess behaves badly, she will be punished, but she will ultimately be forgiven. Don't misunderstand me, Maria. Don't for one moment think I'm suggesting that we must not be very careful and secretive, for I can't bear the thought of his punishing you. If he ever strikes you, I will kill him.'

'Don't talk of killing, Fabrizio. It pleases some women to think their lovers would kill for them. It does not please me. Even of it meant that you and I would spend all our days together, in love and harmony, I would not wish to see Carlo dead.'

Fabrizio's cheek flushed with jealousy. He cupped Maria's breast, to console himself, to claim her. 'I will ensure that our meetings are never discovered, not by anyone,' he said. 'The only person who knows we are here is Antonia and it will remain so. In finding places for us to be together I will be as guileful as Ulysses himself.'

Later, when Maria thought about what Fabrizio had said about Carlo, it seemed to her contradictory. On the one hand he'd said that Carlo might accept their love, and on the other he'd referred to him harming her. This indicated that even Fabrizio could not predict how Carlo would behave if he discovered they were lovers.

Later that night, they slipped out of the garden door into a waiting carriage, and Fabrizio took Maria to Antonia's palace at nearby Mergellina, where those who might have inquired about her whereabouts were told she had been for the past three days.

Antonia tried to exert discipline on these two adults who had reverted to a childlike state of happiness, but at their sorrow at their imminent parting she turned a blind eye and Fabrizio stayed with Maria that night, too.

Antonia knocked on Maria's door early the next morning. Silence. She opened the door slightly. 'I'm coming in,' she said, and entered. She sat at the end of the bed, charmed by the sight of them amidst the dishevelled bedsheets even as she admonished Fabrizio: 'You at least, a resolute and brave man by all accounts, must take some responsibility for the danger you are placing yourselves in. Carlo spoke to me in a very suspicious way just before he left and he may be thinking to take Maria by surprise with an early return. You *must* go now, Fabrizio. Laura is waiting to dress her mistress. And you, Maria, must think what you are going to say to the girl about where you have been. I will leave you and return in ten minutes. You must dress yourself and be ready to leave, Fabrizio.'

For hours that morning they had been awake, sorrowfully taking leave of each other, planning when they would next meet. Fabrizio kissed Maria one last time, and departed.

'Even queens would envy you your joys and your bed with that one,' said Antonia. 'Look at you! Such pleasures are a hundred times more beneficial than all the beauty poultices in the world. You have regained your youthful bloom and look ten years younger. Your hero has brought you back from the Underworld up into the sunlight. Would that a Fabrizio Carafa scheme a tryst with me in a summerhouse. I am not yet too old for such dalliances. You must tell Carlo that you have spent these last days with me receiving treatments for your complexion, or he will be set to wondering. That man is alert to everything about him; he notices even the flicker of an eyelid. I cannot tell you how I fear for you, my darling.'

Maria returned to San Severo a divided woman. The best part of her belonged with Fabrizio. The rest of her would protect that other self, which for now must remain secret. Her life would be snatches of joy followed by long days of duplicity, and those long nights when, alone, her grief at the loss of Beatrice would suddenly seize hold of her. She never knew when this would happen. Hours would pass in which she did not even think of her, and then the next instant, even during the day, the sense of irrevocable loss would well up in her and she'd bury her face in her hands and sob hot tears. Fabrizio had dulled the sharp edge of that grief, particularly as Beatrice herself had been so fond of him, but it would always be with her, always.

She longed to be with Fabrizio every moment of the day, but as this was not possible she'd vowed she would manage their affair like a woman who knew she was loved, not a silly love-struck girl, and find ways to let the joy of her love suffuse other aspects of her life.

Carlo returned the day after her night with Fabrizio at Antonia's. That night he came to Maria's bedchamber. She was sitting up in bed, annotating what she had written on Costanza d'Avalos, in another life, it seemed. Carlo hadn't been in her bed since Beatrice's death. She'd told him she hadn't wished to fall pregnant again, not yet, and he'd respected her wish, though he'd made it clear he wished for more children in the future. Now that she belonged to Fabrizio, she'd vaguely hoped that this state of affairs might go on indefinitely; indeed the thought of Carlo touching her distressed her. But tonight she sensed in him a devil of a black mood and she knew she dare not refuse him.

She put her manuscript on the table and drew back the covers on his side of the bed. 'Come, Carlo,' she said.

He sat on the edge of the bed. 'What are you writing?' he asked.

'I'm reading through my manuscript on Costanza, thinking I must finish it.'

'Show it to me,' he said.

She handed him the leather-bound folio. He leafed through it desultorily at first, and then to her surprise became absorbed in reading fragments of it.

'I had little idea you had such family pride, Maria,' he said, closing the manuscript and putting it back on the table. 'It is most interesting. You should finish it.'

'I intend to.' She leaned across and stroked his cheek, hoping to soothe him. 'Are you feeling unhappy, Carlo?'

He raised his hand and covered hers with it, pressing it to his cheek, moving his lips near it and holding them there. She marvelled at this tender moment between them. Loving Fabrizio had made her gentler and more confident.

'A fit of melancholy is upon me,' he said. Then, after a moment, 'No, not melancholy. A heaviness, a feeling of doom.'

'It will pass,' she said.

'No,' he frowned. He dropped her hand, rose from the bed and began pacing about the room, his hands pressed to his brow. 'Something is changing around me and I can't discern what it is.'

A feeling of panic fluttered in Maria's chest. 'It's me, Carlo,' she said, afraid of him suddenly, saying it before he did, because she'd sensed he'd been about to say, 'It's something to do with you.'

He dropped his hands to his side and stared at her intently. 'Is it? What has changed you?'

She had no idea of what she was going to say until the words came out of her mouth. 'I'm beginning to recover from Beatrice's death. I'm becoming accustomed to the fact that this world is an unhappy place, and that I must not look to find happiness in others, as I have always done, but rather try to find it within myself.'

He sat back down on the bed. 'That is only half the truth, Maria. Tell me the rest of it.'

'It's very difficult for me say such things. It embarrasses me.'

'Tell me,' he almost shouted.

'Very well. You said recently that perhaps you do not love me in the way that I would like. It's true, you don't. You belong only to yourself, as you implied to me. Once I wished to be . . . closer to you. Now I've accepted matters as they are.'

'Why?'

'Would you have me longing for your love for the rest of my life?'

'What has occurred to make you stop longing for it?'

'Time. The passing of time.'

He barely listened to her reply. His eyes slid in and out of contact with hers as they roved over her hair, her neck, the bed curtains, the red velvet chair. She sensed an excitement brewing in him. 'Perhaps you love another,' he said.

There was no turning back now. Any denial he would see through. It would enrage him. 'And if I do?'

His eyes went on moving about as he thought on it. They fell on Beatrice's ring, sitting on the table next to the bed. Her chest tightened. He stared at the ring as if he was considering picking it up and flinging it out of the window but then his eyes moved again. He fixed his concentrated gaze on her. 'If you do, I ask you to keep it to yourself for now. I will wait until I am feeling well enough to consider such a matter.'

'I will always be your wife, Carlo.'

'Not if you are another's whore.'

'I am no one's whore,' she shouted. 'How dare you say such a thing to me.'

'You have grown accustomed to thinking of yourself as virtuous. If you love another, and have acted upon it, you are virtuous no longer. Therefore, you no longer have the privilege of expressing virtuous outrage at my saying such a thing to you.'

'You sound like a priest, like that snivelling young priest you always have about you. You're a fine one to speak to me of virtue. Is he virtuous? Are you? Have you any idea what . . .'

He stared at her in astonishment. Something approaching fear crept into his eyes. Oh, now there was indeed no turning back. How could she have allowed herself to say such a thing?

'Have I any idea of what?' he asked menacingly.

She shook her head. A sob rose in her throat and tears spilled down her cheeks. She covered her face with her hands.

'You must tell me what you mean, Maria. I will not leave here until you do.'

'I don't know what I mean,' she sobbed. 'I don't understand it. I have heard that the priest sleeps in your bed sometimes. There is an inference that there is something unspeakable about it.'

Carlo sighed deeply, muttering under his breath. He pulled her hands from her face. 'Stop crying, Maria. I should not have called you a whore. It was said in anger and I am angry no longer, not at you. Who told you this salacious piece of scandal?'

'Oh no, don't make me tell you that, Carlo.'

'I must know. I must know who is saying such things about me.'

'It was said to me in confidence, not as gossip, but as a warning to me, one that concerned Beatrice. Have no fear that this person—'

'Then it was a Carafa, wasn't it?'

'Yes.' Maria hesitated, terrified he would suspect Fabrizio. 'It was Maddelena,' she said.

'Those damned Carafas!' he shouted. 'They buzz around us like hornets around a honey pot.'

'If they irritate you so much, why did you force me to dance with Fabrizio Carafa?' she shouted back.

'Because you could not take your eyes off him,' he said slowly, in a lower voice.

She frowned at him in puzzlement. 'If that was the case, shouldn't you then have behaved in the very opposite way? Shouldn't you have *not* wanted me to dance with him?'

Carlo looked down at the long fingers of one of his hands. 'For months you were a ghost. Do you I remember I told you so? Your eyes, it was as if they were sightless. Then beauty dazzled them and they sprang back into life. I know the power of beauty; it has healing properties. It soothes the soul, or excites it, depending on what the soul is in need of. I am not so stupidly jealous that I would deny you a moment's pleasure with a man whose beauty makes you feel that life is worth living. Not when you had been so ill. I'd thought myself condemned to spend the rest of my life with a phantom.'

'As you said to me before, Carlo, I believe that is only half the truth.'

'Then what the other half is, I don't know. I don't always understand why I do things. I am whimsical, as you know.'

'Perhaps you are also perverse.'

'That is possible.'

'I must tell you something, Carlo,' she said nervously.

'Yes? I await your revelation,' he responded with a strange little smile.

'That . . . gossip about you. I believe it came from one of our servants.'

'Indeed? Why do you say so?'

'Because Maddelena said it came from the servants.'

'Her servants?'

'She didn't specify whose servants. But what would her servants know about . . . your habits. If it did come from them, surely it was told to them in the first place by one of your servants.'

'You wish to protect Maddelena Carafa. Your allegiance to that family grieves me. It is traitorous to me and this house.'

'No, Carlo.'

'Yes.' He removed the manuscript from the bed, walked around to her side and put it on the table. Then he sat back down on the bed, very close to her. He was becoming more agitated but disguised it with an exaggerated calm. 'And now I have something I must tell you, Maria,' he said confidentially.

'Yes?' she said, the flutter of panic returning to her chest.

'I noticed that after you danced with Fabrizio Carafa, the two of you left the room for some time. It was for more than half an hour. Where did you go?'

Here it was. He was going to torment her. His purpose was clear: for the next hour or so, he'd question her until she'd be forced to confess her affair with Fabrizio. That had been his purpose in coming to her room tonight. The unexpected detour into his own secret life had deflected him only momentarily. When the truth was out, God knows what he would do. Violence was never far below the surface when he was in these moods. Thankfully, they were rare. When they'd come upon him in the past, he'd raged at her, terrorised her, but he had never struck her. She suspected, however, that that was how things would end tonight. He would strike her again and again, injure her perhaps.

'You toy with me, don't you, Carlo? Like a cat with a little bird. You let me flutter off a short way so I delude myself that I'm free, and then you pounce. I hope it does not disappoint you to learn that I have nothing to hide. Fabrizio took me upstairs to see the Prince Carafa di Stigliano's treasures. Nothing of a dishonourable nature passed between us.'

'I am not disappointed. What makes you think I would be? I am exceptionally pleased, indeed gratified, that my wife spent half an hour alone with a man whose beauty clearly dazzles her and nothing of an amorous nature passed between them. I take pride in your reputation for virtue, and now I learn it continues to be well deserved. What did you and he speak of?'

She sighed impatiently. He watched her, his smile sardonic, the cat with the bird. 'The objects in the room.'

'Of course!' he exclaimed sarcastically. 'The objects in the room! I know that room. The prince has taken me there several times to show me new acquisitions. He has some wonderful things. Which ones did you speak of?'

'Jewellery, mirrors, I don't remember all of them. I forbid you to go on interrogating me in this way, Carlo. I've committed no crime. It's demeaning.'

He grabbed her wrist tightly and held it. 'I have every right to interrogate you,' he said threateningly. 'If you have committed no crime, then you have nothing to fear.'

He let go of her wrist. She rubbed it, wincing.

He continued in a more pleasant tone. 'I recall that the prince has two or three antique objects of exceptional beauty and rarity. Did Carafa show you any of those?'

'Yes, a necklace they say belonged to Cleopatra, gold with precious stones. It's exquisite. Do you know it?'

'Indeed I do. Did you see how it shimmers? Did Carafa take it out of the cabinet?'

'Yes. It was dark, so he took it out and held it to the candlelight.'

'Did he place it around your neck?'

'I placed it there myself,' she replied, repelled by the implicit voyeurism of this question. Carlo seemed to be taking a perverse pleasure in his own anger, worse, a perverse pleasure in knowing the details of an intimate moment between her and Fabrizio.

'And did you see yourself in it?'

'Yes, I looked in the glass.'

'And how did you look?'

'It did not suit me. It made me look pale. It would look better on a woman of darker complexion.'

'Still, I would like to have seen you in it. How did it feel, to have about you the necklace of Cleopatra?'

Carlo was watching her face closely. To her dismay she inadvertently reddened. He wasn't talking about the necklace; he was speaking metaphorically of what had transpired between her and Fabrizio. Maria silently cursed the necklace. 'It was rather thrilling, to know that what had touched her skin was touching mine. It's natural that such a thought would pass through my mind. I don't know why you feel it necessary to ask me such a question.'

'I will tell you why. You put on the necklace of Cleopatra, a thrilling experience, as you say, one I would imagine to be unforgettable. And yet you did not tell me about it. In the carriage on the way home you were silent, especially so. A wife who has just put on the necklace of Cleopatra would surely tell her husband. I find it very strange that you did not.'

'I'd forgotten about it.'

'Forgotten about it!' He laughed, and his laugh had a shrill, sinister edge to it. Then he leaned forward and said, 'And don't tell me you had forgotten about it because your mind was on your grief at Beatrice's death. You have of late used that too much as a pretext. I am surprised that you so demean the memory of your daughter. Such duplicity does not become you. Your mind was certainly elsewhere but it was not on Beatrice.'

Maria stared at him aghast. 'You've said many cruel things to me, Carlo, but that is the cruellest. I wonder if you know what you're saying. When have I ever used Beatrice's death as a pretext?' Her voice rose. 'A pretext for what? I don't even mention her to you. I keep my sorrow to myself, as I know you've no patience with my tears. Tell me what you mean or apologise.'

He picked up the ring from the table and turned it around in his fingers. 'I wonder if you take this to your bed at night only because of Beatrice,' he said coolly. He put the ring back. 'Where *was* your mind that night?'

She wanted to scream at him to get out of the room, but knew this would achieve nothing. She must keep calm, otherwise his mood would spiral out of control. 'It's weeks ago. How can you expect me to remember?'

'Because I believe you do.'

'You are exhausting me, Carlo. If you have such a talent for knowing the contents of my mind, then remind me what I was thinking of.'

'Did Carafa tell you he loved you?'

There it was again, the voyeurism. 'Yes.'

'Perhaps your mind was on that.'

'No, it was not! I'd told him there could never be anything between us.'

'What did he reply?'

'He asked me what he should do, and I replied, "Nothing, nothing at all."'

'And then you came back downstairs?'

'Yes.'

'Did he touch you?'

'No.'

'Yes, it seems that's the way it was. Carafa looked quite distressed.'

Carlo rose. To her surprise, he took off his long black dressing-gown, snuffed out the candles and climbed into bed beside her. She felt dismay, a tinge of fear still, but, above all, relief that he had not harmed her and had not pursued the subject further. He put his arms around her. She would endure this. Give him pleasure, try even to take some for herself, for she must give no sign that she longed for another. For this night, she must banish Fabrizio from her thoughts, adjust her mind and body back to what they had been before she became his mistress.

Carlo caressed her body with his long fingers, lightly, tenderly. Rigid, she began to relax. 'Don't cry any more, Maria,' he whispered, brushing the tears from her face. 'It will make me think you do not want me.' He began to play her like an instrument, rhythmically, slow then fast, gentle then forceful. She relaxed into him and gave a shuddering little sigh. His body felt electric. She had never known him to be so aroused. She breathed in the dark violet smell of his hair, which she'd always loved. 'How may times have you seen Carafa since that night?' he whispered. 'Once,' she answered more or less truthfully. 'For how long?' 'A few hours,' she lied. She found it possible to lie to him in the dark. He could not see her face; she was not intimidated by the scrutiny of his gaze. 'Your body feels different,' he said.

'How?' she asked, dreading his words, praying for them to stop. 'It's softer, moister.' 'That is because,' she whispered in his ear, her heart pounding, 'you are caressing me tonight. Usually you do not do so.' 'Has Fabrizio Carafa told you again that he loves you?' he asked as he mounted her. She'd expected this question earlier, before he'd got into bed with her, and she'd prepared her answer. 'Yes,' she said. 'But he does not importune me as your disgraceful Uncle Giulio once did.' Her answer had the desired effect: it arrested Carlo's movements; his back stiffened. 'You must tell me of this tomorrow,' he said. 'But what did you reply to Carafa?' 'That I was your wife and I wish no harm to come to you.' She did think of Fabrizio during this after all, conjured up his face, the ecstasy of him, imagined it was him moving inside her. 'I do not believe you,' said Carlo. 'Sh, Carlo,' she said, biting his neck as she did Fabrizio's, giving herself up to rhythm and sensation.

Unusually, Carlo soon fell into a heavy asleep beside her. He did not return to his room that night.

When Maria heard him get out of bed the next morning, she kept her eyes shut, afraid of what his mood might be. His last words to her had been, 'I do not believe you.' What did he not believe? What she had said about his uncle, or the reply she said she'd made to Fabrizio? It was certain to be the latter. Perhaps it was both.

She opened her eyes. Better to face him now, rather than spend the entire day, and the next one perhaps, in trepidation.

'Carlo,' she said softly.

He was on his way out of the door. He returned and stood at the end of the bed, looking down at her.

'Tell me now that you are not a whore,' he said, and left.

Twelve

AMALFI

It was a scorchingly hot summer. Naples sank into a torpor of heat and stench. The foul miasmas from the urine-soaked, excrement- and rubbish-strewn alleyways rose as high as the upper floors of the six- and seven-storey buildings. Those who did venture outside held gauze handkerchiefs to their mouths and noses. The baked, silent piazzas were deserted even of beggars, who crowded along the shoreline of the bay and sat in the shallows to keep cool.

A rider galloped into Palazzo San Severo's courtyard and all but fell from his horse from heat exhaustion as he dismounted. He shouted hoarsely for His Excellency. A fire had broken out at Venosa and blazed uncontrollably through orchards and outbuildings. They'd managed to save the palace by pumping water in pipes from the river, but it had taken every soldier, servant, woman and child in the principality to so. The fire had wreaked havoc, incinerating horses, destroying tools and equipment, and causing the annual harvest to be brought to a standstill. Their Excellencies had best ride to Venosa today. The steward awaited their instructions.

Carlo ordered the servants to prepare for their immediate departure.

Maria was in the cool, spacious kitchen with the cook, going over the menu for the concert the following evening. Carlo strode in, visibly distressed. Maria saw that his hands were trembling. He told her what had happened. 'Cancel the concert for tomorrow evening,' he said. 'Can you manage it all?'

'Yes. I'll write notes with apologies and send the servants out with them,' she replied like a schoolgirl seeking the approval of her tutor. 'Shall we reschedule it for next week or some other future date?'

'No. I might be gone for weeks.' He nervously strummed two fingers on his chin, considering something. 'Go to Amalfi if you wish,' he said finally.

She raised her eyebrows. Last week Antonia had invited her to accompany her on a visit to their Piccolomini relatives at cooler Amalfi until the summer heat subsided. Carlo had stormed and raged, forbidding her to be so far away from him for so long. But now that disaster had struck at Venosa he was anxious that it would strike again closer to home.

'This kind of heat brings epidemics,' he continued. 'Leave Naples. Take Emmanuele with you. Stay there until I send word. I might come myself in two or three weeks.' He studied her face closely as he said this. Although she longed to dance for joy, her features remained impassive. After his devastatingly cruel remark as he'd quit her bedchamber that morning a month ago, there was no doubt in her mind that he knew of her affair with Fabrizio, yet he'd mentioned nothing of it since. Did he accept it? Did her affair, in his mind, somehow balance his own secret pursuits? Was it in some perverse way gratifying to him that she, too, was now a sinner? This was what she liked to think in her more optimistic moments, but she knew that even if it were so it could never be the whole truth. It was far more likely that Carlo was biding his time, awaiting his moment, and what he would do then she could not bear even to speculate about. Doubtless he did not yet know himself.

Amalfi was remote, a tortuous four-day carriage ride south along one of the most breathtakingly beautiful coastal regions of the Italian peninsula. Maria's party travelled in two carriages, each with a four-man guard of Carlo's mounted soldiers. Their first overnight stay was in a cramped inn at Torre del Greco and their second, far more comfortable one, at the Sorrento villa of friends of Antonia. Here it was considerably cooler and the entire party, Emmanuele included, began to feel energised. Emmanuele was almost two years old now, a happy even-tempered child because Sylvia was with him constantly and showered him with love. Carlo, too, was devoted to him. He'd been twice with his father to Gesualdo Castle and delighted in the rocking speed of long carriage rides.

From Sorrento to Amalfi they travelled along a hair-raising, twisting cliff-top road. While Antonia dozed, Maria looked out of the carriage window, exhilarated by the sheer drops of hundreds of feet to the crashing sea below. At the worst stretch near Positano the carriage teetered dangerously on a hairpin bend the driver had taken too fast. Antonia awoke with a shriek; Maria squealed with delight. Once this would have terrified her—the entire trip would have made her nauseous—but since Fabrizio had come into her life she feared nothing.

As soon as Carlo had left she'd entrusted Laura with a letter to Fabrizio. Free, glorious whole days and nights in Amalfi with her adored one. When and how he would get there and where he would stay, she left to him; Fabrizio was adept at finding secret ways to be with her. Since those three blissful days in Don Garzia's garden, however, they had contrived only to snatch a series of brief hours that flew by like minutes.

The last steep lap into Positano offered a spectacular view of the wild scenery below, edged by the twists and turns of the ribbon of road. Maria put her head out of the window, looking back to check the progress of the carriage bearing Emmanuele, Sylvia and Laura. It was out of sight. Maria was unperturbed. Before his departure Carlo had extracted a promise from the driver of that carriage to walk the horses around the dangerous bends to ensure the safety of its precious cargo. Maria had heard him say this out in the courtyard at San Severo, and it had struck her that he'd not extracted a similar promise from the driver of her carriage.

They made their last overnight stay at picturesque Positano, where houses tumbled down to the sea from its high cliff top. It was late afternoon, still very warm, and Maria ran along the shallows barefoot, with her skirts lifted like a girl. Tomorrow she would be with Fabrizio.

'You exhaust me,' said Antonia languidly, sitting on the beach, fanning herself under a large embroidered parasol. Winded and cooler now that the bottom half of her skirt was sopping wet, Maria joined her. She watched Emmanuele and Sylvia gathering little crabs on the sands and placing them into a bucket. The child was naked as a cherub and the breeze had matted his fair hair into spun gold. What a beautiful child he was. Perhaps she loved him after all. She called and waved to him. 'Emmanuele.' He looked up, briefly meeting her gaze with his serious dark eyes. Then he looked back at Sylvia who pulled a funny face that made him laugh, and went back to collecting his crabs. Maria felt a pang at this rejection from her son. She squinted in the direction of the sun and Amalfi, wondering if Fabrizio had arrived there yet.

The Duke and Duchess of Malfi, Lorenzo and Celestina Piccolomini, came out to greet them, welcoming them warmly as they walked up several steep flights of steps to their palace on the hill just beyond the sands. A marble plaque announced that these steps were called *Salite da Costanza d'Avalos*. Costanza had often stayed at Palazzo Piccolomini because her daughter, also Costanza, had married the previous Duke of Malfi, their son being the current duke. Lorenzo was thus the grandson of Costanza d'Avalos, and Maria's and Antonia's cousin.

'You've come to visit us at last,' said Celestina, putting her arm affectionately around Maria's waist. 'How charming you look and what an adorable cupid your son is. I won't mention your tragedy but to say this. Though we met Beatrice only once after her infancy, on that day when we encountered you both in Spaccanapoli, she looked such a remarkable young woman. Both Lorenzo and I remarked on it. All of us felt for you when we heard what had happened, even though we were far away. She is now one of Heaven's wise angels, my sweetest Maria, I have no doubt of it. She's up there with my two darlings, so let us be happy for her.'

Maria nodded, biting her lip, not wishing to speak of this lest she become tearful.

'As for the here and now,' continued Celestina, 'we've planned to make your stay with us a memorably delightful one. I'll take you up to your rooms right away so that you can rest before we have lunch. We've prepared one of my favourite apartments for you both. I hope you like it. Emmanuele I've put in the old nursery, which is on your floor. Antonia's bedchamber is right next door to yours. I know how you two love to gossip. I remember her bringing you here as a child. You'd sit for hours whispering away together. Do you remember?'

'Of course, Celestina. I loved coming here.' Maria didn't say that as much as she'd loved Amalfi and the cheerful Piccolominis, this was the very place where she'd learned to her dismay that beauty and happiness did not always go hand in hand. They reached the top of the steps and Maria looked back at Torre dello Ziro, a dark medieval watchtower that crowned Amalfi's highest cliff. The story Antonia had told her as a child about what had happened in that tower in 1512 had terrified her.

Maria's room was charming, with a large enclosed balcony spilling with bright summer flowers and looking down on the water's edge and far out across the turquoise sea.

'There's a letter there for you, Maria, and some cool lemonade to refresh you,' said Celestina, pointing to a table with a bright faïence jug, goblets, bowl of oranges and a silver salver on which the letter was placed. 'Pull the silver cord for a manservant and the gold for a maid. We'll see you at lunch in two hours. I'll send a maid up to show you the way. Rest well.'

Maria tore open the letter as soon as Celestina was gone.

My dearest Princess
A thousand kisses from a loving friend who, it seems, has not set eyes upon
you for many long years and longs to do so again. If you follow the steps
behind the duomo to the very top, turn left and walk a little way, you will
find a green door in a long white wall. It will be open. Come at any time
and let us renew our warm acquaintance. I await your visit.
Your devoted friend
Amarilla

Maria kissed the letter and went to the side window that looked down on the Amalfi township, searching for a long white wall near the top of the duomo steps. But the town was such a maze of buildings stacked one on top of the other up and up the steep hillside, she could not make it out. Her eyes wandered over the picturesque confusion of arches, lines of windows, statuary and domes; the meandering, steeply rising cobbled laneways and lines of steps. Beneath her window, the gentle waves of the sea rushed transparently over the yellow sand.

There was a tap on the door and Antonia entered. 'My dear, will you meet with the divine duke while you are here?' she whispered conspiratorially.

'Of course, Aunt. There's no need to whisper. Who can hear us?'

'I've made a discovery which may be of great interest to you.' She was still whispering. 'Come. I'll show you.'

She took Maria's hand and led her to her bedchamber, unlocked a door on the far wall and opened it, saying triumphantly, 'Look.'

It opened onto a flight of steps at the side of the palace that led to a private garden and joined the main steps further down.

'Are you suggesting that Fabrizio sneak up here at night? Surely it wouldn't be safe. Someone is bound to see him. And it would be a discourtesy to our hosts, don't you think?'

'Sh,' hissed Antonia. 'The Piccolominis are very sophisticated. Celestina has had more than her fair share of young lovers, I can tell you. And everybody knows the duke keeps a mistress in this very palace, in some secluded part at the back, although nobody ever sees her. Celestina puts up with it of course for it entitles her to do as she pleases, although she's getting rather too fat for it now, but she won't tolerate her being seen by the rest of the household, the mistress, I mean. For the love of Heaven that's why I brought you here, my dear, although I didn't tell you because Carlo seems to be able to read your mind. Mine, too, if it comes to that. Which is why I've kept away these last few—'

'If the Piccolominis are so sophisticated, why are you whispering?' asked Maria with an amused smile.

'I wouldn't want Celestina to hear me saying she's fat. She'd be most offended. The Piccolominis aren't gossipers. They've too many secrets of their own so they don't invite retribution by discussing those of others. In any case, they're terribly fond of you and they know how difficult Carlo is, the whole world knows *that*. But what's the sense in announcing our plan to the world by speaking it aloud? It's the servants I'm worried about. I don't know about yours, I suppose they're terrified of Carlo, but mine sneak about all day with their ears to keyholes. Why, only last Thursday I came across Anna reading a letter I'd screwed up and tossed on the carpet. God knows who taught her to read; some priest probably. Celestina and Lorenzo are so insouciant their servants practically rule the place and God knows what they stick their noses into and tell the servants of other houses. All servants are bored, poor creatures. We are their entertainment.'

'I don't know about Fabrizio coming here at night, Aunt. I'll discuss it with him. He's here. I'll go to him as soon as I can politely leave after lunch.'

'It's better that he comes here at night than you go sneaking off for hours during the day. Then they *will* be offended, if they see you only rarely. I suggest we change bedchambers. Celestina won't mind. I'll think up some good reason. In any case, why tell her? What does she care?'

'I believe you've cooked all this up simply so that you may have the bedchamber that overlooks the sea,' laughed Maria.

'Everything amuses you now, doesn't it? I sometimes think you were better natured to me when you were miserable.'

'What a cruel thing to say, Aunt.'

'And it's not cruel? What you just said to me?'

'It was, Aunt. I apologise. I didn't believe such selfishness of you for a minute. I was teasing you. You're right. Happiness is causing me to be flippant and careless of what I say. It's because I suddenly feel so free, being here, far away from Carlo and knowing that I'll see Fabrizio every day for weeks perhaps. You can't imagine how liberated I feel. Quite light-headed. Please forgive me for teasing you. Come, give me a kiss.'

'I'm all you have, you know. Your only true friend,' said Antonia kissing her sulkily.

'I know, Aunt.'

'You have Fabrizio of course, but lovers can never be friends, not true ones. Believe me, I know.'

Lunch was a leisurely affair. Maria was impatient to run off to Fabrizio, but she could not help enjoying the company of the light-hearted, lazy Piccolominis, who lived only for pleasure. Learning what she had from Antonia, she looked at Celestina with new interest, She'd grown stout, it was true, but her aristocratic insouciance and dancing, mischievous eyes made her still attractive at forty-two. She had an Egyptian maid who'd introduced her to henna and her hair was rather too red. Lorenzo's proud bearing allowed him to carry his fifty-three years and his portliness with majesty. He helped himself to titbits from every dish on the table, popping them straight into his mouth and waving away the hovering servant who offered to spoon them onto his plate. Occasionally he would offer one of these titbits to his daughter, Cosima, who sat next to him and was evidently not interested in eating. She would pucker her lips with distaste and he would pop the morsel into his own mouth. Occasionally she would deign to open her pursed red mouth with its pointy little teeth and be fed like a baby bird. Lorenzo was greatly devoted to Cosima, indulging her every whim and keeping her close by him. She was sixteen and not yet betrothed. Maria considered this accounted for her high-pitched giggle and air of distraction. Her youth gave her beauty: unfashionable, pale olive skin glowing with health, shining chestnut hair worn loose, and grey eyes so large and round they gave her a startled look. Maria envied her this youth. Before coming down she'd examined her own face in the looking glass and Amalfi's clear bright sunlight had revealed crow's feet at the corners of her eyes and fine lines around her mouth. The years were beginning to take their toll. She was twenty-eight; thirty was but sixteen months away.

The Piccolominis had arranged a musical performance after lunch. Maria listened to this with growing impatience, picturing Fabrizio waiting for her behind the green door in the white wall. Courtesy required her to sit through it, however, for Celestina, knowing Maria lived in a world of music, had arranged it especially for her. It was pleasant enough, but constant exposure to Carlo's superior playing and that of his musicians brought home to her just how exquisite was her husband's ear, how adventurous his taste. She missed the surprises of the San Severo *camerata*, especially now that the more alert of their guests had deduced the true identity of Gioseppe Pilonji. One never knew when Carlo would introduce an adventurous new piece, ascribing it to the mysterious Pilonji. The audience would laugh and clap appreciatively, Carlo enjoying sharing this little joke with them. He never publicly admitted he was Pilonji, though, and Maria was sufficiently familiar with the creative side of his nature to understand why he refused to do so. It allowed him complete creative freedom. Removed from the social pressure of questions like, 'What have you composed since we last heard you?' and 'Can we hear it?' he could compose when, where and what he pleased, at whim. This kind of freedom was essential for Carlo. It had been a week since he'd had rushed off and she wondered how things were going at dull Venosa.

When the concert finally came to an end, she complimented the musicians effusively, more from relief at their having finished than their talents. They were deeply gratified, for they knew whose wife she was.

She then took Celestina aside. 'It's a joy to be here with you, Celestina. I could have come to no better place to relax and regain my old enthusiasm for life. As you may imagine, my life in Naples is often rather frantic and I rarely have the space to think my own thoughts. Your soothing environment offers me the perfect opportunity to do so.' Celestina tut-tutted and took Maria's little hand in hers. 'I wonder if you would mind, dear Celestina, if I sometimes spend time alone, away from your delightful company. I thought I might take walks along the sands or explore the hills of this lovely place. Would you mind terribly much?'

'Of course not, my poor darling. Oh, let me hug you. Though you look as happy as a breeze and as flushed and pretty as a pink rosebud, your heart is a wounded bird and you must heal it. I've lost two darlings of my own and I well understand grief's craving for solitude. Do as you please, my flower. There will be food, drink and welcoming faces awaiting you whenever you choose to return here from your rambles. It's happiness enough for Lorenzo and I to know you are among us. I have Antonia to entertain me. I'm bursting to hear the gossip from Naples. Off you go now, to be alone with yourself and your thoughts.'

Maria went straight to Fabrizio, not before dabbing heliotrope oil on the secret parts of her body. The smell of it intoxicated him. She began at a leisurely pace but almost broke into a run when she was out of sight of the palace. The duomo steps, though, were heavy going and she was winded by the time she reached the top.

She found the green door and opened it and there was Fabrizio sitting in a little walled garden with a book on his lap and he stood up and laughed with joy, and the book dropped to the ground, and she laughed and ran to him and sank her teeth into his warm brown neck and their world could not have been a more blissful place.

Hours later Fabrizio told Maria that he had rented the villa under an assumed name for the remainder of the summer. Its owner was informed, Fabrizio told Maria with a mock-serious expression and deepened voice, that the scholar Massimo Millefiore was writing a treatise on the superlunary effects of the planet Venus and wished not to be disturbed. Only his close-mouthed valet, who had served him all his life, and two of his soldiers, attended Fabrizio. The lovers would be safe as nobody in

Amalfi knew Fabrizio by sight, except for the Piccolominis, and there they would have to be careful.

In the following days, when they were not cocooned in Fabrizio's villa, the pair spent hours walking the hills and beaches, sometimes going as far as Minori, a tiny fishing village beyond Amalfi. The wild, deserted landscape of sea and rock, of sheer cliffs, windblown trees and secret coves, complemented their passion and expanded their sense of liberation. After midnight, Fabrizio would come to the bedchamber Maria had exchanged with Antonia and leave at the first light of dawn. Maria would then sleep until the maid called her for the Piccolominis' extravagant lunches. During these idyllic two weeks she lived her dream of love and happiness.

There was only one blot on her horizon and it was literally so. From the windows of her bedchamber the ominous form of Torre dello Ziro loomed on its distant cliff top. When Fabrizio wasn't with her she was constantly aware of its presence and it began to haunt her dreams. She did not mention this to her lover, for she'd come to regard the dark watchtower as a symbol of the threat that hung over their lives, and she'd resolved that her hours with him were to be unmarred by anxiety about the future.

On most evenings after she returned from being with Fabrizio, Maria visited Emmanuele in the old nursery. He and Sylvia spent their days on the beach and the child was growing so brown and strong.

'We've been teaching ourselves to swim, haven't we, Emmanuele,' cooed Sylvia as the child sat on the floor and inspected some coloured shells Maria had brought him.

'Surely not, Sylvia. He's far too young for that,' frowned Maria.

'It's just in the shallows, and I hold his little body underneath, although it's hardly necessary now. He took to it like a sardine. Babies are natural swimmers.'

'All right, but be careful.'

'As if you need to tell me that,' snorted Sylvia. 'It's time for his feed. We'll call Teresa now, won't we, my darling.'

'Just a moment, Sylvia. I've been thinking for you to dismiss Teresa when we return. It's time Emmanuele was weaned.'

'No, my lady, it is not,' said Sylvia firmly. 'The longer they take the breast, the healthier they become.'

'And the more difficult it is to wean them. I'll allow it for a few more weeks, until his second birthday, and then Teresa must go. I know she's a good girl so I'll try to find another posting for her. And now if you'd leave us for a few minutes while I say goodnight to Emmanuele.'

Maria sat the infant on her lap and began singing him an amusing little song with squeaking and whistling noises that Carlo had composed for him. Emmanuele's face broke into a smile and he looked around him as if he expected his father to materialise. Maria exaggerated the silly sounds until the child was giggling with glee. Delighted, she picked him up and held him to her, breathing in his warm sweet smell.

At the sudden silence, Sylvia appeared in the room with the wet nurse. As soon as she sat down and loosened her bodice, Emmanuele made for her nipple with greedy little cries and Maria handed him over and made to leave the room. Emmanuele took a few sucks at the large brown nipple, then, looking about him, began to make fretful noises. Maria hesitated at the door and began the song again. Giggling at her silly braying sound, he took the nipple again, but with his eyes still on his mother, making it clear he wished her to stay with him. And so Maria sang to her child as he was fed, and it warmed her heart that this little cupid wanted her there. Almost every evening after that, after she had had her fill of Fabrizio, she came and sang to her son.

'I have a delightful surprise,' announced Celestina as they sat down to lunch. 'If I may compare our life here at Amalfi to a garden, let me say that it has some good old trees and flowers pretty enough, but there's a uniformity to it and one grows tired of the same old blooms. Don't protest, Antonia, for when I tell you of the exotic variety of wild rose I encountered this morning, you will agree nothing could do more to enliven our setting and refresh our eyes, not to say dazzle them.

'Excuse me, my dear,' she twinkled at Lorenzo. 'This is ladies' talk, but I know you, too, will be pleased. It is in any case all because of you that this has come about. My dreadful husband tells me I am becoming a little overblown and encourages me to take exercise, although he himself wouldn't dream of doing anything so tedious, would you? Always the obedient wife, and having before me no better proof of the benefits of beach walks than Maria's increasingly radiant bloom, I swore myself to follow her example with walks along the sands.

'This morning I walked as far as the convent on the promontory and, rounding the point, I saw a man in a modest boat rowing toward the shore with his back to me. I assumed him to be a mere fisherman and took no further notice of him. I sat on a rock to catch my breath before starting back and as I mused away to myself, the man stepped out and drew the boat to the shore. I couldn't see his face but his noble form and the manner of his dress attracted my curiosity. Though his clothes were simple, they were of the finest cut and cloth. It excited my imagination to think he might be a pirate or a smuggler. Perhaps he'd been shipwrecked, but I soon saw his air was too calm for that. As I stared at him he looked up and met my eyes and I can't say which of us was the more astonished.' Celestina slid an oyster into her mouth and beamed around the table. 'Who do you think it was?' she asked excitedly.

'Not a notion. You must tell us,' replied Lorenzo.

'The Duke of Andria! He has come here, he tells me, to withdraw from society for a time and to reinvigorate his mind with reading and solitude. That's all very well, I told him, but one cannot pass every single day as a hermit. One must fertilise one's mind with occasional company and conversation as well, so I insisted, absolutely insisted, that he join us for supper this very evening.'

Celestina looked around the table to gauge the effect of this amazing piece of news. Maria's stomach was by this stage in a knot. She imagined Fabrizio's horror when he'd looked up and seen Celestina, his valiant attempts to extricate himself from her invitation, which an insistent refusal would only have rendered highly suspicious, arousing greater curiosity on Celestina's part. What a disaster, having to sit through a supper with her lover and pretend to these people that he was nothing to her. It would be unendurable, not only for her, but for Fabrizio.

Antonia noticed that Maria's polite smile of interest was rather too tight, so, to distract attention from her niece, she responded with, 'What a happy encounter, Celestina. I see what you mean, an exotic flower indeed. I am very fond of the duke, what woman isn't, although I don't know him well.'

'Here is your opportunity,' chirruped Celestina. She leaned forward confidentially. 'It would not surprise me to learn he has a new mistress. Reading in solitude indeed!'

'They say he is very fond of scholarship,' said Antonia.

'He's fonder of women, from what I've heard.'

'I do know he's fond of music,' added Maria, afraid she would draw attention to herself if she remained silent. She had regained sufficient equanimity to speak calmly. 'He comes to my husband's concerts from time to time.'

'Then you know him better than any of us,' responded Celestina with interest.

'Perhaps. His wife tells me he is a generous patron to young musicians.'

'What more can you tell us of him?'

'Very little, I'm afraid, other than he's charming. My husband could tell you more. They're quite good friends, through music of course. They—'

'His wife is by all accounts devout,' interrupted Antonia, detecting a reddening of Maria's cheeks. Celestina was adept at picking up such telltale signs. Antonia was beginning to regret having brought Maria to Amalfi. What an unendurable situation! Antonia's wits were on pinpoints to deflect the table's attention from her niece and keep the conversation light.

'I've never met her. What is she like, Maria?' asked Celestina.

'We *have* met her,' interrupted Lorenzo. 'She's so dull you've forgotten. It was two years ago, at the Baldinis'.' He took a sip of wine and laughed. 'She was hoping to interest you in some charity for babies or orphans, trying to extract sponsorship from us if it comes down to it, and your eyes were quite glazed over. She reminds me of a crow, the way she sits with her head on one side and forages with her sharp black eyes.' Lorenzo held a piece of crabmeat in the air and dropped in into his mouth. 'Small wonder Carafa seeks his pleasures elsewhere. I like him. He's decisive. When I do drag myself along to one of those interminable parliamentary sessions with the viceroy, where they all sit about debating and deliberating and digressing into blind alleys, it's Carafa who moves things along.'

Lorenzo guffawed. 'He has a little habit that makes me chuckle to myself. I'll show you. When the members arrive at a stage of such feverish and irrelevant deliberation that all sane men have lost sight of the original question at hand, Carafa secretly looks at his watch.' Lorenzo surreptitiously drew his watch from the inside of his jacket and returned it there. 'He times them, and by my reckoning he gives them about ten or fifteen minutes. Then he grows alert, waiting for a remark that he can turn to the advantage of the way he wishes things to proceed.' Lorenzo darted his eyes around the table in a caricature of Fabrizio's mental processes. 'When he's seized on the remark he's been waiting for, he will say, "Exactly," or something to that effect. "That is exactly what we have been saying all along, that the so and so is such and such. Then, in spite of small differences which we acknowledge don't affect the larger question, we are all agreed, gentlemen." The older members are so befuddled by then they have no idea of what he's talking about, and the younger ones are in awe of Carafa's dialectic talents and nervous of contradicting him. So they all sit there, stunned into submission. Carafa then makes a meaningful gesture of pulling out his watch and looking at it, making us all aware it's time to bring things to a close.' Lorenzo again pulled out his watch, made an exaggerated play of looking at it meaningfully, and returned it to the inside of his jacket. 'Carafa then proceeds with, "Congratulations, gentlemen. Tonight we have reached a happy resolution. Write this down carefully, Alfredo. We will do such and such."' Lorenzo roared with laughter, slapping his thigh and looking at each of them for their reaction. 'There you are, Celestina,' he laughed. 'There you have the Duke of Andria.'

Maria had forgotten her discomfort. She'd listened with fascination to this glimpse of her lover's public life. This unknown side of Fabrizio thrilled her. She felt honoured to have such a man as her lover. It awakened a fierce protectiveness in her, of him and, for his sake alone, their secret. She felt energised in a new role as his guardian. There would be no blushes, no further trepidation and discomfort. She would meet the challenge unwittingly offered by the Piccolominis at supper tonight and triumph. They would never learn the truth of what had brought Fabrizio to Amalfi. She would speak with him about it later that afternoon. As Celestina suspected he was meeting a mistress here, it would be dangerous to deny it, for that would lead to even greater suspicion on her part. If the subject came up, as it no doubt would through Celestina's teasing and gentle prods, Fabrizio with his mastery of elegant conversation could imply it might be the case and perhaps drop hints as to the identity of a mythical mistress, one who had little resemblance to Maria. Though they might survive the supper with their secret intact, Celestina's chance encounter with Fabrizio had nevertheless brought misery into their lives: it would now be too great a risk for Fabrizio to come to Maria's rooms at night.

'Please don't worry so, Aunt,' said Maria after she and Antonia had returned to their rooms. 'It was inevitable that a situation such as this would arise at some time, in some place or other.'

'I'll tell you what truly worries me,' responded Antonia. 'Carlo suspects there is something between you and Fabrizio, I know it.'

Dear Aunt Antonia, so astute, so frivolous, so endearingly protective of Maria's interests. What a contradiction she was. Maria was glad to have her as a confidante; it made her feel more secure somehow, although she knew this was ludicrous. Maria hadn't told her of Carlo's visit to her bedchamber to repossess her, as it were. So now she took her aunt's hands in hers and said, 'He more than suspects it. He knows it.'

Antonia looked at her gravely. 'How does he know?'

'Was it not you who said only recently that he notices everything? He deduced certain things from my behaviour at La Sirena, subtle things.'

'And what was his reaction? Did he make you confess?'

'Carlo goes about things in a more roundabout way. He chose to torment me and titillate himself by making an excruciating game of it.'

'Titillate himself?'

'Something I don't care to go into, Aunt,' said Maria, waving it away with her hand.

'Have you told Fabrizio of this?'

'Of course not. He'd feel compelled to play the protector, and what can he in reality do that would not make matters far worse? No, Fabrizio must remain ignorant of Carlo's knowledge of us. I don't want him fretting about it. I want our times together to concern only the two of us. I want only happiness with him. As to your question about Carlo's reaction, I've no idea. It is not something I have any desire to press him about.'

'Perhaps he tolerates it as my husband did and many husbands do. But what Carlo will not tolerate is his wife becoming a subject of gossip. If his honour comes under threat, you are lost.'

'Why do you find it necessary to tell me something you know very well would already have occurred to me?' Maria looked at her aunt with irritation and noticed the hurt in her eyes. 'Oh forgive me, Aunt, I didn't mean to speak sharply to you,' she said, giving her a little kiss on the cheek. 'I sound like Carlo sometimes, I know. You may be right about him, but as you always say yourself, who can ever predict what Carlo will do? Have no fear, Aunt. Fabrizio and I will not become a subject of gossip. We will give no sign of what is between us. I could not have more confidence in this. You must cast your fears aside for they will give you an uneasy demeanour and it's crucial that you behave with Fabrizio as you behaved with him before we were together. Relax and enjoy his company. I know you secretly adore him.' Aunt and niece fell into each other's arms giggling.

'I knew Maria when I was a boy.' Fabrizio went on to entertain a charmed Celestina with his swashbuckling adventures with Federigo on the stairs of Palazzo Carafa. He did not mention he had prayed to Maria as an angel. Celestina had arranged a supper of delicious fresh fruits of the sea and the atmosphere at the table was jovial and relaxed. Cosima giggled at Fabrizio's every utterance; she could not take her eyes off him; so transported by his presence was she that she distractedly swallowed every morsel her father offered her.

'Tell us the real reason you have graced our simple life at Amalfi with your presence,' cajoled Celestina.

'Let our guest be,' said Lorenzo gruffly. 'He has told you why he is here and that is that. He deserves to have a holiday after that last parliamentary session, which was tedious beyond measure. All that talk of taxes and trying to guess what the pope's next move will be. If they think that bull they've been waiting for will—'

'I'll have no talk of politics tonight,' interrupted Celestina.

'Why does something so fascinating not interest you?' asked Fabrizio.

'Because it is neither fascinating nor even mildly interesting. It is in any case a topic I could discuss with Lorenzo at any time if I had a mind to, but his own irritation with it tells me that such conversations do nothing to gladden our precious hours on this earth. As we have the rare pleasure of your company tonight, it is you I wish to discuss. Tell me, my mysterious cavalier, how have you been spending your days here?'

'Just as you met me. Andria, as you know, is far from the ocean, and I have always loved being near the sea. You spend each day in its company, Celestina, so you are perhaps unaware of its powerful attraction to those who do not.'

'Surely you see enough of it in Naples.'

'The sea at Naples and the sea at Amalfi are two different things entirely. The first is all commerce and crowds, the second nature and contemplation.'

'And what do you contemplate, dear Duke?'

Fabrizio put his chin in his hand and leaned toward her, his eyes earnest. 'I confess I am at a turning point in my life. This is just between all of us, you understand,' he said confidentially.

'Of course.' Celestina's eyes sparkled at this promise of revelation. She fingered the cameo brooch at her bosom.

'My life at Andria has begun to irk me. I am thinking of setting up a residence elsewhere. My stewards manage my estates perfectly well and I'm not needed there to supervise them. The Kingdom of Naples is not engaged in warfare at present, and it is unlikely that it will be in the foreseeable future, so my army is not needed. I can in any case train new soldiers at any time if the necessity arises. The question is, where will I settle? Naples?' He shrugged. 'When I have business there I stay at Palazzo Carafa which suits me well and I see no reason to change this. I am therefore considering acquiring a villa in some quiet place near the sea.'

'Do you plan to reside in this new place with your wife?'

'My wife is very fond of Andria. This is another matter I must consider.'

'Surely she is also fond of you.'

'Forgive me, Celestina, I do not discuss my wife.'

'Are you considering settling in Amalfi,' she asked keenly.

'Perhaps. It is very beautiful. But I am also drawn to coastal regions in the north of the peninsula.'

'The *north*,' she said scornfully. 'For a Neapolitan to go north is a big step indeed. What draws you there?'

'That I can't say,' he replied mysteriously.

'A beautiful woman perhaps?'

'Celestina! That is enough,' growled Lorenzo.

'I myself enjoy Ferrara and Torino,' began Antonia, who went on to treat the company to a meandering discourse on the charms of these cities and their inhabitants.

As she spoke, Maria turned to Lorenzo. Bestowing a winning smile on him she asked, 'Do you not think it time Cosima was betrothed?'

'She may marry when she pleases,' he replied nonchalantly.

Cosima surprised them all by turning to Maria and saying loudly, 'Yes, I may marry when I please. But I may not marry *whom* I please,' and thumping the table. It was the first time she'd spoken all evening.

'Whom would it please you to marry?' asked Antonia tactlessly.

Cosima bit her lip and stared at her empty plate. To Lorenzo's irritation, Celestina said, 'Our daughter took a spring fancy, as young girls will, to a most inappropriate young man, a member of our household whom we were consequently compelled to dismiss. He filled her innocent head with all manner of romantic nonsense, had her believing that the two of them were Paolo and Francesca, if you please. Giovanna d'Aragona and Antonio da Bologna would be more to the point.' Maria and Antonia exchanged glances. 'Is it not true, Maria, that marrying beneath oneself results only in tragedy?'

'It certainly did for Giovanna d'Aragona,' replied Maria. 'Aunt Antonia told me about her when I came here as a child and it haunts me still.'

'Who is Giovanna d'Aragona?' asked Fabrizio.

'Do you not know her story?' asked Celestina. 'It is famous. I thought everybody knew it. Ah, it seems everything is forgotten with time. But it is not forgotten here in Amalfi. It has become a legend.'

'I'm sick to death of that story,' whined Cosima. 'In any case, I don't have a brother who's a cardinal so I don't see how it pertains to me.'

'You have a father, brother and cousins who value your honour highly and would not tolerate you marrying some upstart,' Lorenzo said to her gently. 'So you must take it as a moral lesson. Fabrizio wishes to hear the story, so I ask you to be polite to our guest and listen to it again.'

'And think on it again, if you have any sense,' added Celestina.

'Giovanna d'Aragona was my grandmother,' began Lorenzo, 'although I never knew her. She was auburn-haired, very beautiful. The d'Aragonas have paintings of her still. I believe she was related to your grandmother, Maria.'

'Yes, she was her first cousin,' said Antonia.

'You see, Fabrizio? The d'Avaloses and Piccolominis are doubly related. She married my grandfather, the then Duke of Malfi, at fourteen, bore a son and a daughter, and they were by all accounts happy until my grandfather's death when Giovanna was twenty. In time, her brother, Cardinal Luigi d'Aragona, engaged a young steward, Antonio da Bologna, to oversee her estates. She immediately fell in love with him and he became her lover. Regrettably for them both, this was no mere dalliance; it was passionate love on both sides. Giovanna was exceedingly devout, genuinely devout, not like her ambitious brother whose idea of Heaven was to rise higher and higher in the Vatican hierarchy. Giovanna had not committed adultery: neither she nor her lover were married. Nevertheless, in the eyes of the Church she was committing a mortal sin and this soon became unendurable for her. She and da Bologna secretly married and she bore him a son. The marriage was inevitably discovered. Cardinal Luigi was enraged, for the stain it placed on the d'Aragona name obstructed his advancement in the Vatican. He removed her elder son—my father—from her house and took him into his own care. The daughter, his niece, he left with Giovanna. Giovanna and da Bologna fled north, well knowing the cardinal would seek to have his revenge and remove the stain on the house of d'Aragona. Da Bologna went on ahead to arrange a safe house for his family. The cardinal's men ambushed and murdered him. The cardinal then seized Giovanna, her maid, her daughter and the infant son she'd borne to da Bologna. He brought them here, to remote Amalfi, and imprisoned them in Torre dello Ziro. Do you know it, Fabrizio? It's the ancient watchtower on the hill up there.'

'I've noticed it, yes. A very grim place.'

'Yes, it is. It was once part of a castle that crumbled away over the centuries. I can't look at it without thinking of my poor, lovely grandmother in that damp, lonely place. It would have been freezing during the winter. She was there for months.

'Back in Naples, nobody knew what had happened to her and the children. They had mysteriously disappeared. One night, the cardinal's henchmen appeared. They strangled Giovanna, her children and her maid. Their bodies were secretly buried somewhere in the wild woods behind the tower. Their bones would be there still. I sometimes wonder if someone will stumble across them one day.' He turned to his daughter, his eyebrows raised in gentle warning. 'So Cosima, you are again warned of what happens to those who think to place love above all else.'

'Yes, I am warned for the hundredth time. And for the hundredth time I say the circumstances do not apply to me,' she pouted.

Fabrizio's eyes had met Maria's and they did not smile. 'What happened to the cardinal?' he asked.

'The murders were never discovered, not officially, although Giovanna's fate was known within my family. The cardinal's career continued apace. He ended up advisor to the pope of that time, I forget who it was as it all happened sixty years ago. My father grew up to marry the daughter of the most famous woman of her time, the heroine Costanza d'Avalos. She, of course, is my other grandmother and her life could not have been more different to poor Giovanna's. I must tell you her story some other time.'

'It will be a pleasure to hear it, ' said Fabrizio, who already knew it very well from Maria.

'*She* did as she pleased,' pouted Cosima.

'She did as she pleased when she was more than thirty years old, and you are but sixteen,' chided Celestina. 'And she would not have been so foolish as to wish to marry a mere tutor. Not foolish like Giovanna,' she ended with emphasis.

'Giovanna was not foolish,' insisted Cosima. 'She was unlucky because she had a wicked brother.' She looked at Fabrizio, blushing as she asked, 'Do you believe she was foolish, Fabrizio?'

'I believe she was perhaps too noble for this world,' he answered.

'Too Catholic for her own good, I say,' snorted Antonia.

'What is your opinion of her, Maria?' asked Lorenzo.

'As a woman I can understand her. Why should she live as her brother wished merely to serve his advancement in the world? What of *her* life? She had her own standards of honour and she lived by them. She was extraordinarily brave, as brave as Costanza in her own way. It is foolish to judge her.' She looked across at Cosima and said gently, 'Which is not to say, Cosima, that you should have married your tutor. Your father loves you very much. He could not bear to see you live a miserable existence without the luxuries and privileges you take for granted. This means he would have had to provide for your husband. In time, you would have come to feel contempt for a man who was kept by your father, and nothing kills love like contempt.'

'There's the crux of it, Cosima,' exclaimed Lorenzo. 'Why didn't your mother or I think to explain that to you? You've grown wise, Maria.'

'Not in all things, I assure you,' she laughed.

'Do you speak from experience?' asked Celestina. 'I imagine the Prince of Venosa would not be an easy husband. Have you come to feel contempt for him?'

'Indeed not!' exclaimed Maria, offended at the rudeness of this question. Had Celestina drunk too much wine? 'On the contrary, I am fond of my husband. I admire his taste and talents. People who know Carlo only slightly see only the arrogant side of him, whereas I know myriad aspects of his nature. I saw his vulnerable side just before we came down here. He was greatly upset by the fire at Venosa. His elegant hands were trembling. He has several such vulnerable moments. Unlike many Neapolitans, he takes his responsibilities as a prince very seriously. And he is a devoted father to Emmanuele.'

Except for Cosima, everyone looked with surprise at Maria during this little speech. She was rather surprised herself, for as much as she loved Fabrizio, after the words tumbled out of her mouth she realised she'd meant what she said.

'I wonder if I might ask something of you all?' said Fabrizio shortly before he left.

'It will be our pleasure to do whatever you ask,' promised Celestina.

'You may think it a strange request. Except for Lorenzo, before tonight you have known me only as an acquaintance. But now, I hope, we are all friends.'

This was greeted by warm murmurs of concurrence as his eyes moved around the table and met all of theirs in turn. The effect of this was mesmerising. He continued to do this as he said with gentle urgency, 'For reasons I can't disclose it's imperative that my presence in Amalfi be known only to all of you, not only during my time here, but after I've left. I ask you never to speak of it to others. I do not exaggerate when

I say it's a matter of life and death.' He locked his beautiful dark eyes on Celestina, As she was the greatest threat, he paid her the compliment of addressing her first. 'Celestina?'

'A matter of life and death for whom?' she asked, thrilled by it all. 'For you, or another?'

'For me,' he breathed.

'My dear Fabrizio, you are a wild flower of rare beauty whom the winds of fortune have blown into our tame garden bed. I wouldn't harm a petal of your head.' She had positively had too much to drink. 'I swear with my hand on my heart to do as you ask. As concerns the wider world, we have not had the pleasure of your company. You have never been here.'

'Thank you,' he said firmly. 'Lorenzo?'

'The thought of those appalling parliamentary sittings without your presence brings me such grief I swear on the honour of the house of Malfi that no member of my family will dare betray your trust,' he boomed.

'Cosima? Can you keep my secret?'

The girl reddened from brow to bosom. She could barely speak. 'No, I wouldn't. I mean yes, yes, I promise,' she stammered. 'Of course I promise,' she added soulfully.

'How kind of you. Maria?'

'Be assured that you can trust me, Fabrizio,' she said with calm conviction. 'I will mention it to no one, not even Carlo.' She felt a terrible urge to laugh at the irony of this last remark. Fabrizio himself for a moment lost his equanimity and she detected a tremble in his voice as he said, 'I can't thank you enough.'

Had the others noticed? She looked around the table. No. They remained in his thrall. If this spellbinding self-assurance was the technique he used in parliament, which it doubtless was, small wonder he exerted such power over its members. Carlo, it now occurred to her, exercised his will through inspiring fear; Fabrizio exerted his just as effectively through sheer charisma.

'Antonia?'

'Nothing could distress me more than the thought of you lying dead, bleeding from some terrible wound,' she began, hands to her bosom. Please, please don't overdo it, prayed Maria. This much was effective: it reinforced the horror of what would result if one of them broke their promise. The faces around the table plainly shared Antonia's distress. 'It terrifies me that such power over one so gallant as you has been placed into our frail hands. If there is an ounce of love, honour or justice in this world, nobody here will speak of your presence in Amalfi, certainly not I. You have the word of a d'Avalos.'

What did it matter, Maria's uncertainty as to whether the word of a d'Avalos could ever be relied upon? It had the requisite dramatic effect.

The evening had so excited Celestina that, although it was after midnight when Fabrizio left, Maria and Antonia were compelled to sit up listening to her effusive praises of her memorable guest. Lorenzo said his goodnight and departed to the rooms of his mistress. Inevitably Celestina approached the topic Maria had prepared herself for and schooled Antonia in.

'He must have a mistress, don't you think?' They calmly concurred. It was the most obvious likelihood, although not the only possibility. Who might she be? A local woman? But they were all so unattractive. Perhaps she was someone beneath him. A fisherman's daughter, for instance. How truly romantic. What, after all, had he been doing in that boat? Enjoying the sea, as he'd said? Perhaps. No, he was too sophisticated to be attracted by an illiterate girl. It could only be a noblewoman, married of course. Perhaps it was a lady of the north. Why else would he consider settling in the north? Perhaps he didn't have a mistress at all. He might be involved in something illicit. Piracy. Smuggling. Treason. Perhaps he'd gone over to the French and was raising an army. He'd mentioned warfare. Imagine him on his horse, his black hair flying in the wind, brandishing a sword at the head of an army. She'd heard he was a fierce fighter. Mars, they'd once called him. The Carafas had rebelled against the Spanish in the past. Hadn't Paul IV, the Carafa pope, instigated a civil war in the Kingdom of Naples? But *Fabrizio* Carafa a traitor? No, no, it had to be a mistress.

And so it went on for more than two hours. Antonia rather enjoyed the sophisticated nonsense of pretending to guess at Fabrizio's motives, but Maria felt strained and duplicitous. This was her first experience of the social cost of a secret love affair: having to lie and feign no connection with Fabrizio. She climbed the stairs to her bedchamber beset by a swirl of emotions, not the least of which were fear at having unwittingly given something away and anguish at being unable to proclaim her love to the world. This is what in her heart she wanted to be able to say: 'Fabrizio Carafa loves me as he has never loved another and all of you women may look upon him and sigh, but he is mine, mine alone.' But as it was, in the eyes of the world Fabrizio was a free agent—apart from his wife whom everybody seemed to regard as superfluous to the man—and the fact that Maria could have no public claim on him carried with it the stings of jealousy and possessiveness at his being therefore regarded as available to other women. Worst of all, though, it brought a devastating sense of emptiness: the one thing that gave meaning to her life had no reality in the wider world. As Fabrizio's lover, she did not exist.

She then faced the anguish of her first night without Fabrizio for over a fortnight. She lay, sleepless, sending pleading messages through the ether for him to come to her, damn the risk.

Just before dawn she could bear it no longer. She quickly dressed herself in a simple blouse and shift, threw on a dark hooded mantle and crept down the side steps.

It was eerie walking in the deserted township in the darkness, silent but for the hypnotic rhythm of the waves. Torre dello Ziro loomed above her like a promise of doom. She felt frightened, imagining ne'er-do-wells lurking in the darkness, and began to run. Never before had she been abroad alone in the dead of night.

She approached the duomo steps, which rose above a nightmare maze of dark angles and deep hidden recesses, into which the thin sliver of moon cast not the faintest illumination. The ghostly white stone of the steps beckoned. She paused to catch her breath and thought of turning back, her eyes frantically searching the space between the steps and the base of the duomo where its structural supports formed a warren of angular niches frequented by beggars. The lure of Fabrizio so close, however, was irresistible. She imagined him sensing her danger, coming toward her from the other direction. At any minute he would appear at the top of the steps. Surely he must. Why didn't he? He loved her less than she did him or he would appear any minute. She ran on, the pounding in her ears drowning out the sound of the waves, the hood of her mantle falling back from her face to reveal her streaming hair.

To the obese halfwit lurking in his lair near the steps she appeared as a vision in a dream. He limped out of the darkness and grabbed at her as she flew past. Only to touch such a sight. Only to place his paw on her breast. He gurgled with joy. Horrified, Maria knew that she must not scream. She kicked his leg and he released her but proceeded to gallop up the steps on all fours after her. At the top she turned and almost screamed at the sight of this human spider within a few yards' reach of her. Gurgling and grunting he lurched after her along the lane to the green door, which was locked. She pounded on it desperately, eyes fixed on her approaching molester.

A window opened and the face of one of Fabrizio's soldiers looked down. He ran and opened the door just as the halfwit made another lunge at Maria.

'Begone or I'll kill you,' snarled the soldier, brandishing his sword. The idiot limped off despondently.

'Are you hurt, my lady?' the soldier asked as he opened the door.

'No, only shaken.'

Inside, Fabrizio was running down the stairs, sword in hand. 'Maria! What has happened?'

She shook her head, trembling and sobbing as he wrapped himself around her. 'How could you not come to me?' she sobbed.

'Sh, sh,' he whispered, briskly rubbing her back to calm her. 'It's what we agreed.' A moment later he laughed.

She swung back and delivered him the mightiest blow she was capable of. 'How could you laugh?' she shouted.

He frowned as his hand sprang to his cheek. 'I was laughing with happiness to think you can't be without me.' He gripped her arms and planted little kisses on her face. He stopped and stared at her earnestly. 'It was madness for you to come here alone at this time of night. What happened to you?'

Still trembling, she told him about the halfwit.

'Why didn't you bring Laura with you?' he asked.

'It would have increased the risk of being seen or heard. Surely you know that.'

'Maria,' he said exasperatedly. 'Coming alone increased the risk of your being raped or murdered or both. You must never take a risk like this again. We risk our lives as it is. You know I come to you whenever you wish. You mustn't increase the danger by reneging on our agreements and acting on whim. Swear to me you won't do anything like this again.'

She smiled, feeling calmer. Suddenly it mattered only that she was here, with him.

For the first time they did not immediately go to Fabrizio's bedchamber, but sat close on the divan, talking and laughing about the evening at the Piccolominis'. She confessed to him her dismay when he'd spoken of looking about for a place to settle. He'd never discussed such a plan with her. He told her it was a fiction, adding that, nonetheless, he often dreamed that one day they might have a house that was all their own. He confessed to her his jealousy when she'd praised Carlo so highly. 'I didn't praise him,' she responded. 'I defended him.'

As noon approached, Maria sat in front of a looking glass in Fabrizio's dressing-room as he brushed her hair and attempted to arrange it into some semblance of a style Laura might have dressed for her. It would look too curious if she was seen abroad with it streaming about her shoulders. They'd decided on simple plaits to be coiled around her head and fastened with a Spanish comb he'd found in the villa. She sat with her soft round breasts tumbling over her unbuttoned bodice, feeling like Venus at her toilette attended by Adonis. Fabrizio brushed away, happily distracted by the two inviting breasts rising between her long tresses and the two in the mirror, teasing their nipples from time to time, enjoying the feel of her luxuriant hair, bending down to inhale the perfume of it and nuzzling the back of her white neck, moving his lips around it and biting when she arched her back, and drawing her mouth into his when she threw back her head and opened her lips to him. He emerged from their kiss and smiled at their reflection in the mirror. Straightening his back he stared into the eyes of her reflection and his face became serious. 'These last weeks have been paradise,' he said. 'We have our lives ahead of us to find further occasions for such freedom. But now the snake in the form of Celestina has entered our Eden . . .'

'You're beginning to sound like her,' laughed Maria.

'Yes. I wasn't aware it was contagious, though this time the metaphor is apt. The danger we've always sensed around us has now taken a real form. Do you understand, my angel, that I can no longer come to your room after midnight?'

'Yes,' she sighed sorrowfully.

'And that you must never again come here at night?'

'Yes.'

'And that we can no more go out walking together?'

'Can we not make love one more time to the sound of the waves in the little cave on the beach near Minori?'

'No, my darling, no,' he murmured. 'It isn't wise for us to be together anywhere outdoors. I've become known by sight in the township. People are curious about me. Who knows who will turn up where? Celestina may suspect what she likes, but we mustn't afford her proof by being seen together. Do you agree?'

'Yes.'

'For the happy afternoons left to us in Amalfi, our world is these rooms, and it's world enough, for our love is endlessly inventive, is it not?'

'Yes,' she laughed.

To prolong their delight, they'd begun to play elaborate erotic games, lengthy tableaux involving narratives and costumes. They didn't always do this, only when they felt especially light-hearted and had hours before them. They'd begun by acting out Costanza d'Avalos's victorious battle with the French king as a sexual encounter, but they'd soon realised they could be any two people in the world, historical or imagined. Fabrizio's man always packed a sizeable wardrobe for him when he travelled and Maria delighted in dressing up in his clothes, pretending to be Julius Caesar or a verse-sprouting poet or an imperious sultan. They were the characters in their own plays. Fabrizio would often take the female lead, costumed in Maria's jewels, furs, lace-trimmed nightgowns or draped fabrics. In the beginning he'd suffered it, but he'd begun to enjoy this reversal of male and female, for it excited Maria to take the lead and it opened up for them an intoxicating world with strange and novel erotic delights. He had never known a woman like her, and she, for her part, had not even imagined a lover—certainly not one as manly as Fabrizio—who would allow himself to be her plaything.

Fabrizio suspected that this flouting of conventional behaviour between lovers had something to do with Carlo. Perhaps it was inspired by the more perverse aspects of his personality. Fabrizio never said as much to Maria, for he assumed she was unaware of it.

Fabrizio's gracefulness and longish hair lent itself well to feminising. To put a billowing nightgown on a lover noted for his manliness and thread pearls through his hair was to have a power over him that Maria could never have over Carlo, but this was only the simplest aspect of it. She had always craved a secret amorous world, and with this one she created something that was in its way as inventive and bizarre—and as pleasurable—as Carlo's more capricious musical compositions.

'Swear to me you will be content with these rooms,' said Fabrizio, fixing the comb in her hair and holding her eyes in the mirror with his own.

'There is no need to bewitch me with your gaze as you do Celestina,' she laughed. 'I swear, my darling Fabrizio,' she said more soberly.

Celestina had extracted from Fabrizio a promise to be their guest the following week. Each time he went she invited him again. Though Celestina's curiosity made him uneasy, he could not politely refuse such invitations. Maria came to be increasingly at ease with the situation and each time he was alone with her Fabrizio pleaded with her to be on her guard. Light-hearted Celestina may have been, but she was no fool. One evening she drew Fabrizio aside and asked, 'Do you think it is true that Maria is as devoted to Carlo as she claims? I've always found him to be unpleasant. He is certainly not attractive, and Maria is a strikingly beautiful woman, don't you agree?'

'No one could deny Maria is beautiful, but the more one knows Carlo, the more attractive he becomes,' he replied calmly. 'Dullness is something women can't abide, and Carlo is never dull. Will you permit me to tell you something in confidence?'

'Of course,' she breathed.

'I happened upon them together once, in a private moment at one of Carlo's musical gatherings. She was gazing at him with such warmth that her affection was clear.' Fabrizio secretly cursed the duplicity that hiding their love entailed, for he was referring to a moment that had been intensely painful for him.

'Really,' said Celestina. 'And did he respond with equal tenderness?'

'I believe so. I don't recall exactly. You women notice these things. We men are not so perceptive.'

'Yet you noticed the way she looked at him.'

'Yes, but only because I'd been crossing the room to speak with him and, seeing them in such intimate conversation, decided it was not the right moment.'

'What a gentleman you are, Fabrizio. We have all fallen under your spell, my daughter in particular. It seems she's quite forgotten that ridiculous tutor. Be kind to her, won't you?'

Though Naples still sweltered, the calendar indicated that summer's end was only two days hence. To mark its last day Celestina arranged a small outdoor banquet for her intimate party, as she'd come to refer to them, Fabrizio included.

A messenger had arrived with a letter from Carlo. Its tone was businesslike. The debris from the fire at Venosa had been cleared and rebuilding had commenced. Due to his fondness for Venosa his father would remain there indefinitely. Geronima was on her way to join her husband. Carlo would be back in Naples in a week's time and looked forward to seeing Maria there on his arrival. This meant that she must leave Amalfi within three days.

Maria enjoyed the banquet as a prisoner enjoys his last days of freedom before a life sentence. Only one more afternoon with Fabrizio, for she and Antonia were leaving the following day. Fabrizio was compelled to remain at Amalfi for at least another week, so as not to arouse the Piccolominis' suspicions. Carlo would want Maria close by him for a few days; doubtless he would wish her to reorganise the cancelled concert. It would be a fortnight, probably far longer, before she and Fabrizio could be together again. Social protocol required Fabrizio to attend Carlo's forthcoming concert and this only added to Maria's distress.

The late afternoon was pleasantly soporific, the lulling swoosh of the sea and the tinkling of the fishing boats the only sounds in the all-pervading calm. Even Antonia and Celestina were unusually silent. They all ate in a leisurely fashion, looking out to sea from the broad, open terrace, above them a festive silk baldachin that billowed in the soft breeze. Maria had grown fond of the Piccolominis. The thought of leaving them made her feel nostalgic and she told them so. They begged her and Antonia to return the following summer. Maria told them she hoped this would be possible, knowing that she would not do so, for Fabrizio could not return to Amalfi again, not if she was there.

Cosima had begun to irk her. She'd insisted upon being seated next to Fabrizio. She touched his arm, his hand, on the slightest pretext. She even dared to remove an imaginary speck from his hair, just to run her fingers through a few strands of it. Celestina indulged her in this. Fabrizio forbore it with kind smiles. Too kind, Maria thought. She wanted to shout at the girl, 'Don't touch him. He's mine.'

'Don't have more wine,' whispered Antonia to her.

Maria usually drank very little but on the few occasions when she drank more it made her reckless. In the bright sunlight Cosima's skin radiated youth. Her eyes sparkled with excitement at Fabrizio's every move, his every utterance. The wretched girl made Maria feel old: the sunlight magnified every tiny blemish, every line on her face, or so she thought. Maria took several sips of wine. Fabrizio was staying on for at least a week here, without her. Cosima's perky breasts sat upright beneath the low, square neckline of her dress, Maria's were beginning to droop; Cosima's hair gleamed, hers was growing dull; Cosima's pointy little teeth were far whiter than Maria's, her pouting lips far redder. Maria took another sip of wine and felt her face begin to flush. The Piccolominis should teach their daughter how to behave in the company of men. The girl had no idea. She felt a compulsion to say this out loud.

'Let's go for one last walk along the sands together,' said Antonia, painfully pinching her niece's arm.

'Very well. Just to the point and back.' Maria had no intention of leaving Cosima and Fabrizio out of her sight for longer than that.

When they reached the bottom of the steps Antonia turned to Maria and gently shook her. 'You can't go back so soon. If you do, all will be lost. Something is boiling inside you. You looked as if you were about to burst out with some idiotic remark. Look at you. You're quite red. It's the wine. Can't you see that that silly girl makes Fabrizio just as uncomfortable as she makes you? Let us for the moment put aside what is at stake; at least think not to demean yourself in Fabrizio's eyes by revealing your jealousy of Cosima. Has it not occurred to you that Celestina might be allowing that girl to paw Fabrizio in order to provoke you? I'm not saying that she knows anything, merely that she's alert to the possibility. You must not allow yourself to give her proof. I'm fond of Celestina, but she has little to occupy her sharp mind down here. It's you I'm surprised at, Maria. Think of who you are.'

'You sound like Carlo.' The sound of her husband's name rang like a bell in her wine-befuddled head. She'd wanted them to know, wanted to claim Fabrizio as hers, wanted to squash Cosima like a gnat.

'I sound like a woman who has successfully avoided all the snares of a society ravenous for titillation. They will make a meal of you if you do not school yourself in self-control. It's not enough to love Fabrizio; you must also consider his welfare. Carlo's, too, although I never thought I'd say it.'

Antonia was of course right, but there was a far more pressing matter at hand. 'Are you certain, Aunt, that Fabrizio has no interest in Cosima?'

'How can you ask me such a question? He is forced to endure her attentions because of you. He is here because of you. How could you even imagine that a worldly man like Fabrizio would have a grain of interest in that fawning snippet? Are you losing your mind?'

'I hope not.' What did it mean, to lose your mind? She'd felt close to it on two occasions, on the deaths of Federigo and Beatrice. It was a letting go, the obliteration of decorum. Everything in the outside world was swallowed up by a darkness thrumming inside one's head. Yes, she'd verged on that state, sitting there watching that girl nigh on half her age hungering for Fabrizio.

'The poor man is nearly paralysed with embarrassment. It's ludicrous that Lorenzo indulges Cosima to this extent. Keep walking. I'll not allow you to go back until your head is clear. Consider that it does you well to be gone for an hour or so. It will convey to Celestina that you have no special desire to be in Fabrizio's company.'

The party had gone inside when they returned. Fabrizio had been about to take his leave as Maria and Antonia began slowly mounting the long flight of steps. Antonia was becoming short of breath.

Maria walked ahead of Antonia as they went in the front door and passed through the foyer. As she turned into the long entrance hall Maria saw Fabrizio and Cosima at the end of it, her lover tenderly placing his fingers on Cosima's youthful lips. She drew back and, placing a finger on her own lips for Antonia to keep silent, leaned against the wall and closed her eyes. She'd been right, after all. She felt as if she was going to be violently sick.

'You must tell Fabrizio,' she whispered, 'that if he does not come to my room tonight I will commit some desperate act.' She took a few deep breaths. 'I'm going to the nursery to say goodnight to Emmanuele,' she said in a louder voice, which trembled, and she disappeared down the opposite hall that led to the children's rooms.

Maria's rage and panic were like nothing she had ever experienced. She wished to communicate them with nobody. Later, when Antonia knocked on the door, Laura told her Maria was about to go to bed, and went back to holding a damp cloth to her mistress's forehead and wiping her mouth after each time she heaved into a large basin. Maria's head was spinning. Every time she retched her head banged and she felt as if she was going to vomit her heart out.

The nausea eventually subsided. As Laura undressed her, Maria caught a glimpse of herself in the looking glass and almost gasped at the gaunt-eyed ghost of herself she saw reflected there.

Laura bathed her, dressed her in her favourite green silk nightdress and put her to bed. The devoted maid sat beside her mistress holding her hand, listening to a sobbing narration of what had transpired.

'Your duke is very gallant, my lady. Perhaps it didn't mean anything,' comforted the girl. 'You must not let him see you in this state. You must rest now so that you'll be feeling better when he comes.' Laura stroked Maria's troubled forehead.

'What if he doesn't come?' moaned Maria.

'He will come, my lady.'

Laura's soothing words and her gentle presence eventually calmed Maria and she sent the girl to bed. She lay for a long time in a cold rage, staring sightlessly at the gold fleur-de-lys pattern on the crimson silk wall-covering glinting in the candlelight.

Alert for any sound of her lover's arrival, she jolted upright at the faint clicking sound of the latch as he carefully, quietly opened the door.

She flew out of the bed like a harridan and slashed at him, ripping his cheek with her nails and sobbing, 'I saw you, I saw you touch Cosima's lips.'

Fabrizio was shocked by her onslaught into giving her face a little slap. 'It was to quieten her.'

'I saw you kiss her hand and bow so soulfully she all but swooned.' She slashed his other cheek.

He struck her again and this time it stung. 'You stupid, jealous fool. How could you imagine that pampered, hysterical virgin would interest me?' He pushed her onto the bed, gripped her wrists and pinned them above her head, straddling her to keep her writhing body still. 'Quieten down. Listen to me or I'll hurt you. Are you listening?'

She spat in his face.

He winced and closed his eyes, taking deep breaths to dispel his anger. 'Now you love me as much as I love you, don't you, Maria? Now at last you can imagine what I've suffered all these years. Let me tell you there was a moment once when I saw you look at Carlo with such sweetness I wanted to crawl off into a ditch and die.' He brought his face close, longing to kiss her.

'I wouldn't kiss me if I were you,' she hissed. 'My only desire is to tear at your lips with my teeth.'

He squeezed her wrists until she cried out with the pain. 'It's plain you didn't hear my conversation with that silly girl. You didn't, did you?'

'No,' Maria sobbed, tears spilling from her eyes.

'She bailed me up in the hallway, giggling and fiddling with my buttons and twittering away about the lack of manly cavaliers such as myself in the Piccolomini circle. I told her that, charming as she was—you know very well courtesy required me to say so—I was a married man with five children whose heart and soul had belonged to the one woman for nigh on all my life and that no other woman could ever hold any interest for me, be she Venus herself. She looked so forlorn I felt sorry for her. I assured her that she, too, would one day, I hoped, find such a love. She began twittering again and endeavoured to slip her hand into mine. I extracted it, and the reason that I then placed my fingers on her lips was to silence her for she would not be quiet. I feared the scene would end in hysterics. I wished to get away from her, so I kissed her hand and bowed as courtesy required.' He stared at Maria silently. 'Can I let you go now? Or are you going to scratch me again?'

'Tell me you don't desire her.'

'I don't desire her,' he said flatly.

'I don't believe you,' she sulked.

'What *do* you believe? That I propose to throw our love away on a fool who is not even beautiful?'

'I believe you are bored here and you look for distraction. I believe there is insufficient stimulation here to keep your mind fully occupied.'

'Perhaps it's you who are bored, Maria. Perhaps you miss the daily stimulation of Carlo's ever-shifting moods, the excitement of his unpredictable tantrums and flashes of good humour, the thrill of never knowing what he might do from one moment to the next, the undercurrent of menace and violence that he always carries about with him. Perhaps you have become addicted to this way of life. Perhaps I'm too even-tempered for you, too gentle. Perhaps *you* are finding *me* dull. Rather then simply asking me in a reasonable fashion why I touched that girl's lips and listening to my answer and weighing the merit of it, you've created this unnecessary scene, which I must tell you hurts me more than I can say.' He released Maria and sat on the bed with his head slumped, distractedly running his fingers through his hair.

Maria sat up beside him. He didn't look at her. The blood from her scratches had run down his cheek and congealed in thick lumps. There were spots of blood on his jacket. She didn't dare touch him. He was offended, she'd deflated him, and it suddenly frightened her.

'It occurs to me you've created this scene because you crave another kind of passion,' he continued. 'Conflict and uncertainty. Fear and doubt. Violence perhaps.' He sighed deeply and turned to look at her. 'I'll strike you no more, Maria, no matter how much you may anger me. I swear it. I have violence in me, terrible violence, which is appropriate for warfare but unsuited to my treatment of the woman I love.'

He stood and began pacing the room. 'I beat my wife, you know. After those first nights with you I began to hate her in earnest. When I returned to Andria she seemed to me ten times as coarse, ugly and stupid. When she said she could smell a whore on me I struck her a blow that sent her reeling across the room. I picked her up and struck her again. She endured it silently. Not a word. Not a sound. She rose to her knees and began to pray wordlessly to God with a sanctimonious expression on her face that would have tested the patience of all her bloodless heavenly angels. I kicked her. I wanted to beat her to death. I grabbed her by the throat, told her I'd been with the woman I'd loved for years, one that she was not fit to wipe the arse of, and extracted from her a promise that she would never, never refer to my private life again. The next day her eyes, cheek and neck were black with bruises. I've not been back to Andria since. So there, Maria, is your gentle Fabrizio.'

He put his hand to his cheek and stared at his bloodied fingers. 'Lock the door after me. I wish to be sure you're safe. I can't be with you tonight.' With that he departed, leaving Maria on the bed white-faced with stupefaction.

An overwhelming sense of desolation washed over her. She began to panic again. She'd lost him. Antonia had been right: her ridiculous jealousy had demeaned her in his eyes. Even Laura, a mere servant girl, had warned her not to let him see her in such a state. And now he believed there to be something destructive in her, that she had deliberately created a scene in order to destroy their happiness. Might it be true? Had her life with Carlo infected her with violent inclinations? She had, after all, picked up some of her husband's mannerisms, both deliberately when she wished to dismiss tiresome people from her company, and inadvertently when she was unthinkingly rude or hurtful. Had Carlo's perversity also insinuated itself into her? Must she, too, now have helpings of pain with her pleasure. No, no, that wasn't it at all. She wasn't perverse. She was afraid, afraid of losing Fabrizio as she'd lost all else she'd dearly loved.

Though her anguish allowed her no sleep, by the morning she'd regained her pride. If he did love her still, let him suffer as she suffered. She did not go to him on that last afternoon.

To keep occupied she went down to the beach with Emmanuele and Sylvia. There was one moment of pure joy when Emmanuale spontaneously placed a wet little kiss on the tip of her nose. But apart from that, though she was charmed by her son's acrobatics on the sand, the gnawing anxiety in the pit of her stomach allowed her to think of nothing but Fabrizio.

He came to her that night. She'd prayed in her secret heart that he would. She'd kept the candles burning so as to see his face when he came in the door and she saw exactly what she'd prayed to see. Fear. Fear that he'd lost her.

Thirteen

THE SECRET PALACE

The Duke of Andria sat in the large gloomy office of Juan de Zuniga, Naples' Spanish-appointed viceroy. Fabrizio had been called to Castel Capuano that morning to discuss an urgent matter. He wondered if this would take the form of a reprimand or an invitation to participate in some intrigue. More likely a pointless exercise in power—ever since the days of the ruthless viceroy Pedro de Toledo, who had all but forced the feudal aristocracy to move into the city within easy grasp of Spanish authority, the viceroys had liked to remind the Neapolitan barons on occasion that Spain was in charge.

The matter presently at hand was evidently a weighty one for Juan de Zuniga's large head, darkly silhouetted against the light of the paned window behind him, had been resting sideways on his bent arm for some moments. Outside a storm was brewing and Fabrizio glimpsed lightning flash across the sky. A gust of wind lifted the papers on the viceroy's desk. A large, full-bearded man, de Zuniga rose heavily and closed the window. Then he ambled to the front of his desk, sat on the edge of it, and began spinning a large globe on which Spain's numerous territories were marked in green. Fabrizio waited. The viceroy's silence was no doubt meant to intimidate him, but he felt only impatience. What a ponderous manner the man had, although his eyes were wily.

'The matter I must discuss with you is a delicate one,' began the viceroy, thoughtfully studying the globe as he spun it around. 'My instructions come from above, so I ask you not to take what I have to say as a personal judgement of you.'

Fabrizio raised his eyebrows. He had learned to read the man and what this probably meant was that the matter, whatever it might be, had been stewing in no other mind than that of this shrewd politician himself, not in the minds of those on high as he claimed, and that he would brook no argument.

'From far on high,' emphasised Juan de Zuniga, suddenly looking Fabrizio directly in the eye. The emphasis made Fabrizio uneasy: perhaps the matter had indeed been discussed in the higher echelons. Lightning crackled, an ear-splitting clap of thunder rent the air, and Juan de Zuniga returned to his chair.

He positioned himself squarely at his desk, arms placed before him in an attitude of authority. It was time to get down to business. He cleared his throat. 'Don Fabrizio, your amorous affair has of late come to the attention of the Vatican. It has most grievously wounded the one who is most dear to us all, so much so that he has been moved to consult with His Spanish Majesty. They have arrived at a resolution.'

'With respect, Don Juan, my private life is my own affair. It is no duty of mine to take instruction in this regard,' said Fabrizio tersely.

'Is it not indeed?' responded the viceroy. He rubbed the chin under his copious beard and leaned forward. 'Let me for a moment be personal, Don Fabrizio, and advise you as I would my own son. All of Naples is buzzing with knowledge of your affair with the Princess of Venosa. You must put—'

'That is impossible!' exclaimed Fabrizio, taken aback.

'Is it? You don't deny the affair then?'

Fabrizio stared at him silently, his features impassive as he debated whether or not to simply get up and leave the room. How dare this man presume to interfere in his private life! But then how was it that Naples was buzzing with the affair? He and Maria had been so cautious. The only unforeseen event had been Celestina's coming across him at Amalfi, but he had left there a week after Maria confident in the knowledge that the Piccolominis suspected nothing. Better to hear the man out, have himself fully informed of how matters stood so as to devise the best means of confronting them. 'I don't discuss my private life in the public domain,' he said curtly.

'None of us like to. Few of us are compelled to,' said the viceroy, playing at being agreeable for a moment before he changed his tone to one of stern admonition. 'Your situation, however, is of a different order. A far different order. Your private life has spilled over into the public domain. It is an embarrassment to us all. A threat to us all,' he boomed.

The next minute he said almost jocularly, 'Let me be frank, Fabrizio. When I was first appointed viceroy three years ago your reputation for romantic gallantry with the ladies found its way to my ears. In the ensuing months and years I anticipated receiving news of fresh liaisons, but to my agreeable surprise none came. I surmised that the heat of youth had given way to the more considered behaviour of maturity. But now what do I hear?' His voice rose again. 'Not the mere dalliances of old, but a ruinous affair, *ruinous*, one not only reckless and prolonged, but one in which your partner in adultery is none other than the wife of a beloved nephew of His Eminence himself!' Don Juan raised his fist and thumped it on the table. 'Your amorous intrigues have been overlooked in the past, but your attachment to the Princess of Venosa is different. It is excessive. Spain will not tolerate it.'

He leaned forward confidentially. 'Our emperor has of late enjoyed the most amicable accord with the Vatican after having sought its allegiance against France for many decades. You know this very well. And yet you put that accord at risk. I cannot imagine that you wish to take upon yourself the onerous burden of inciting the Holy Church's disapprobation of Spain's government of this kingdom. Surely I do not need to spell it out more clearly than that for a man of your subtlety.'

The viceroy let the unmistakable meaning of this sonorous statement ring in the air before he softened his voice and said, 'I admire you, Fabrizio. It would be a cause of personal injury to me if calamity were to fall upon your head. Allow me give you a warning. You are standing in its shadow. In calamity's shadow. Right at this moment.'

'A calamity of what nature?' asked Fabrizio flatly.

'A calamity commensurate with your crime against the Holy Catholic Church! Do you yourself feel no compunction at your sin?' Receiving no answer, he continued, 'As you at present participate in the government of this kingdom, you are compelled to abide by its laws and by the emperor's wishes. You must put an end to you affair with the Princess of Venosa. Immediately.' He stared hard at Fabrizio before arranging his face into the semblance of a warm, encouraging smile. 'I'll be generous. I'll allow you three days. I expect you this Thursday morning with the news that you will see her no more. I will then pass your wise resolve on to those who await it.'

Fabrizio had access to an abandoned palace in the Spanish quarter owned by the Carafas. He and Maria had been secretly meeting there for months, ever since their return from Amalfi. In the centre of the third floor, Fabrizio had sparely furnished a large room. He had chosen it because it resembled an island, surrounded as it was by echoing, empty, once-grand rooms. It had no windows, only muted light from the windows of the rooms it opened into, and on the nights when Carlo was away and Maria stayed there, the candlelight could not be seen from outside. Fabrizio had also chosen the room for its fading frescoes of Olympian erotic exploits: Leda and the Swan, and Zeus manifesting as a shower of gold raining down on Danae in her bed. When Fabrizio and Maria lay in their bed looking up at the ceiling, they saw smiling Venus, just risen from the foam of the sea, about to step onto her scallop shell.

Maria's journey to their secret palace on this day followed the routine of months. She and Laura walked from San Severo through the labyrinthine alleys of old Naples in the vague direction of the Spanish quarter. They always took a different route. Reaching a dim, deserted lane they stepped into a doorway and drew up the hoods of their mantles. They then crossed wide Via Foria and proceeded to the Church of Santa Maria Assumpta. On entering the church Maria lit a candle and prayed to the Blessed Virgin to watch over her and Fabrizio. When it was safe they slipped out of a small door next to a side chapel, crossed a narrow lane, and entered the secret palace by a side door, which Maria opened with a key given to her by Fabrizio. Once inside Maria sighed with relief and laughed, as she usually did. They then made their way up the dusty, silent staircase to the third floor. Nobody but the three of them knew of this place. Even the furniture had been purchased by Fabrizio under an assumed name in Rome and delivered by strangers in the dead of night. They felt completely safe there.

Only one small incident had marred their sense of security, one they'd soon forgotten about. Having crossed Via Foria early one morning and entering Via Duomo, Maria had encountered Carlo's lustful uncle, Don Giulio Gesualdo. She'd tried to hide her face from him and sidle past but, too late, he'd recognised her. 'Good morning to you, Don Giulio,' she'd said too quickly and too pleasantly, endeavouring to hide her alarm. 'I see you, too, are taking the air.' He'd returned her greeting with what seemed to her an unpleasant, knowing look. For a few days after that she'd had the sense of being followed, but each time she turned to look, there was nobody there. On discussing this with Fabrizio they'd decided her suspicions could only be the result of fear and they'd cast it from their minds.

Fabrizio sat in an armchair, his right foot resting on his left thigh, his head on his hand, thinking what to do, what to say to Maria. He'd been sitting there like that ever since his return from Castel Capuano. The danger he'd done everything in his power to keep at bay was now upon him. For the hundredth time he mulled over the viceroy's exact words and how the calamity he'd referred to was to be interpreted. What was at stake: his position in Naples' parliament, or his life? For the hundredth time he concluded it was most likely to be the latter. He'd become an embarrassment, not to say politically dangerous. His life would be snuffed out in some dark alleyway by anonymous assassins, just as Federigo's had been. He wondered at the meddling of the pope, wondered if Carlo had played a role in any of this. Who else's prompting would make the pope feel grievously wounded, as the viceroy had so euphemistically put it? He longed to discuss this aspect of things with Maria, but would not. Her life with Carlo was fraught enough.

Could he endure life without Maria? He had his public life, his private interests, his illustrious name, his children. But Maria had only him. His love for her had not diminished; he loved her still, but the thought of dying ignominiously was unbearable to him.

He lifted his head and rubbed his arm. It had gone numb. He looked around the room and could not but smile affectionately at its chaos. Garments of all descriptions spilled from three chests. The long table was covered with dirty glasses and empty carafes. The bed with its smiling gilt cherubs was a muss of linen under its crumpled fur rug. It had irked him when Maria had insisted he find a great bearskin rug, for he knew Carlo had one just like it. Still, it was warm. They couldn't even light a fire in the palace for danger of the smoke being seen. He must ask Laura to tidy the room today.

He threw back his head and sighed. Streaming-haired Venus stepping onto her shell seemed to be laughing at him. He felt weary and cold. He went across and lay down on the bed and pulled the rug over himself. Breathing in the heliotrope perfume of the sheets, he fell asleep.

Maria found him like this. She stood looking down at the delicate line of his profile, his thick black hair across the white pillow, his eyelids faintly bruised, his mouth a little open, the scar on his cheek from her scratches marring his beauty. She thought it made him more beautiful. She never tired of gazing at him. How vulnerable he looked in sleep. The only sound in the room was his deep breathing.

'Tidy the room, quickly,' she whispered to Laura. 'Take the things on the table into the next room to wash.'

Maria sat in a chair looking at Fabrizio from time to time as Laura performed these tasks. Fabrizio would wake to a clean room, a pleasant surprise for he disliked untidiness. It was difficult to maintain order in their secret palace with only one servant. When Laura had finished, Maria asked her to go down and fetch some water from the well. 'Close the door after you,' she added.

She lay down next to Fabrizio and kissed the scar on his cheek. He smiled without opening his eyes. 'I was dreaming of you,' he murmured.

Later, as they sat up in bed, he told her of his meeting with the viceroy.

'Tell him it's over between you and I,' Maria said with a shrug. 'Nobody knows of this place. Things can go on as they are.'

'No Maria. To lie is impossible. We cannot say we are ending things and not end them.'

She stared at him aghast. 'Why not?'

'Because it will fool no one. How is it that Naples is buzzing with the knowledge of us, as he said? Who was the original source of this gossip? The Piccolominis? Don Giulio Gesualdo? We don't know. It may have been someone who has not occurred to us. Perhaps Antonia unthinkingly made some careless remark. No! Don't be angry. She'd never hurt us, I know. But she chatters on and there are times when she's not aware of the implications of what she's said, or indeed what she has in fact said. There are several possibilities. There are my valet and my soldiers, whom I perhaps trusted too much.' He sighed. 'There is that dark servant-woman of yours.'

'Sylvia?' Maria laughed. 'Remember that first time you came to me at San Severo, when Carlo had gone off to Gesualdo?'

'When you were forced to tell her of me?'

'Yes. She swore herself to secrecy on a Sicilian oath that she would never dare break. If you knew Sylvia as I do, you'd know that superstition is her real religion. In any case, she's rather morose and knows nobody outside the household, so who would she tell? No, it would definitely not have been Sylvia.'

'There is Laura,' said Frabrizio. 'Yes, I know. There's no need for you to protest in her defence. What I mean is, secrets, no matter how closely guarded, inevitably come to light. Who knows by what means.'

Maria stared blankly into the distance and asked tonelessly, 'Are you trying to say that we must truly end our life together?'

He stroked her cheek. 'Do you wish me to die?' he asked softly.

'You are afraid,' she cried, withdrawing from his touch. 'If your heart is capable of such fear, I best have a lackey for my lover. Has nature created you with the heart of a woman? And me with the heart of a soldier?'

'This is not play-acting, Maria.'

'I'm not play-acting. I mean it sincerely. I'm not afraid. And it's not worthy of you to be afraid. The fear in your heart chases out your love for me. If you continue to harbour this fear, then I will see you no more.' Her face was white with anger. Or was that her own fear he saw in her eyes? Yes, fear of what she next said. 'The moments you are away from me are more deadly to me than a thousand deaths. If you leave me, I shall not continue alive.'

'This is the fear that makes a coward of me. I have no heart for this. I have the strength to meet my own death, but I doubt if I have the fortitude to suffer yours. You wish me to die? Then I'll die.'

'Then I will die in any case,' she responded flatly. She turned to him and said quietly, 'Here is the true essence of what you must resolve, Fabrizio: to show yourself disloyal by going away from me, or to show yourself faithful by never abandoning me. Your argument about secrets always being uncovered, you should have given consideration to before, and not now that danger has found us at last. You should not have loved me, nor I you, if such fears were to present themselves.'

'I won't abandon you,' he assured her. 'Even before I spoke with you of my meeting with the viceroy, I knew in my heart that things could resolve themselves in no other way but this.'

He took her hand and kissed it and they looked at each other solemnly. And at that moment the lines of an English poet Fabrizio had read only the previous week came into his mind to haunt him: 'A man has three loves in his life. The first is calf love. The second is the woman he marries. The third is his death-bed bride.' He could not bear to tell Maria of this.

'I ask only one more thing of you, Fabrizio. Don't set your mind on doom, for that will bring an evil destiny to us. Have faith in our love. Even though you scoff at such things, I pray to the Virgin for us twice a day. Already we have been together more than a year. We have withstood Carlo's knowledge of us. Why then can we not withstand idle gossipers and the viceroy? I swear to you that Laura could not be more faithful. It was your own family, the Carafas, who engaged her for me. She has been my companion for fourteen years and my chief solace, sometimes my only one, through everything I have suffered. Why would she endanger her happy life with me by endangering my life? What would happen to her if I died? Carlo would throw her out and she'd be adrift. She will never reveal our secret. We will continue to meet here safely.

'You are too noble, Fabrizio. You do not like to tell lies, but now you must lie with conviction. Don't allow yourself to be intimidated by the viceroy's threats. Men, being men, always take the official voice of authority so seriously. But women who have their wits about them secretly scoff at such bombast, for that's all it is. I beg you to be strong for us. I have faced Carlo for you; now you must face the viceroy for me. Tell him our affair is at an end, and mean it. Look at Venus up there smiling down upon us. Our love is blameless. Who do we hurt by it? Only Carlo perhaps, and he has the dignity to allow me the liberties he allows himself.

You once said to me that love was the highest virtue. You cannot allow yourself to think and act in accordance with those benighted men who claim our love is a crime.'

Fabrizio reported to the viceroy the following Thursday morning that Church and State were more important to him than Maria and that he had, as a consequence, ended the affair. He was believed. And so their love continued happy in the secret palace until the autumn of the following year.

Fourteen

THE NIGHT OF THE HUNTER

Maria sat in the library reading Boccaccio's *Il Filocolo*, caught up in the adventures of the Princess Blancheflour who'd just been imprisoned in a seraglio. Now that it was late autumn she enjoyed escaping the day-to-day familiarity of her own apartment and coming to the library to read. It was a sombre, comfortable room, cosily lined with dark shelves of leather-bound books.

A log in the fireplace dropped onto the coals with a hissing noise and she looked up to find Carlo staring at her intently. He'd been sitting opposite her for an hour or so, desultorily annotating the sheets of music spread out around him, and had been so silent his presence had slipped her mind.

'The sun has blessed you with a halo,' he said pleasantly, referring to the effect of the early afternoon light on her hair.

'Does this please you, Carlo?'

'Yes. It's made me think we should leave Naples immediately and live permanently at Gesualdo.'

Maria let the book drop into her lap. 'Why would we do such a thing?'

'It would save us all,' he replied solemnly, staring into her eyes as if trying to hypnotise her with his will. He did this rarely, only when he'd made a prior determination to have her agreement on some matter. Usually she acquiesced, but the thought of leaving Naples and eking out her days in his isolated castle sent a little shiver of panic up her spine. It would be worse than Messina. Never show fear: she repeated the mantra inside her head, willing herself to be calm. Carlo could smell fear. Perhaps, in any case, he was only toying with her. The way she'd learned to deal with him at these moments was to affect polite disinterest.

'That's too cryptic even for me, Carlo. You'll have to explain what you mean.'

'We cannot go on living here. Until now our life has been the subject only of fools' gossip. Of late, it's become of concern to people worthy of respect.'

'Oh, that,' she said with a sigh, relieved. Carlo no more listened to wagging tongues than she did. He was above such things. So he was toying with her after all.

'Yes, that. It's reached quite a crescendo. It's thumping in my ears. It's passed the point of no return. There's going to have to be a finale of some sort.'

'And you're suggesting that we run off to Gesualdo like those fleeing animals you hunt down? Isn't that rather an ignominious and dull finale?'

'Would you prefer something more exciting?'

'I'd prefer something more dignified.'

'*Dignified.*' He emphasised the word with narrowed eyes, his gaze fixed on some point above her head. Then he closed his eyes and laughed sardonically.

'Perhaps you think I've cast my dignity to the winds, Carlo, but I assure you—'

'You have, dear Cousin, you have. Yours and now mine,' he said, gathering up the papers on his lap and thumping them down on the table next to him. 'These past days I've been receiving letters from innocent parties whom your actions have grievously wounded and I've been required to attend tiresome tête-à-têtes. It has been made clear that it is incumbent upon me to restore honour to my house.'

'What letters? Tête-à-têtes with whom?' asked Maria, alarmed now.

'To tell you would only increase their unhappiness, for I know your gallant knight would immediately set out to redress such *a stain on his mistress's honour* and I am not such a fool as to think you would not immediately impart such information to him.'

Maria met his eyes silently, her mouth a little agape at the way he had just spoken so blatantly of what had been unspoken between them for nearly two years. She waited for what she dreaded would come next.

'Poor Maria,' he said gently, leaning forward in his chair. 'You have gone quite pale.'

She rose, her book thudding to the floor. 'Don't toy with me, Carlo. I tell you, I won't bear it.'

'There is much, dear Cousin and Wife, that we are all past bearing. And I tell *you* that the pleasures of Naples are at an end. Our life here has run its course. We leave for Gesualdo next week. I will instruct the servants to pack our clothes and the rest can follow.'

'No!'

'Sit down!' Carlo bellowed. 'Please remember that you are the Princess of Venosa,' he said coldly.

She looked at his proud face and felt a pang of regret for the absence of love between them. Tears welled up behind her eyes and she willed them to dry up, for after Beatrice's death she'd sworn that she would never again allow herself to weep in Carlo's presence. Tears made her contemptible in his eyes.

'I will not go to Gesualdo, Carlo. I will never agree to live there. Doubtless you think this is because I can't bear to be parted from Fabrizio. But there's another reason. Naples is the centre of my life. Anywhere else, I feel bereft. When I returned from Messina I promised myself that I would never again live anywhere but Naples for any length of time, and I won't, not ever. Perhaps you think you can force me to go to Gesualdo. You probably can, but I promise you I will find a means to return here, over and over again if necessary.' She was about to add that he would then have even more gossip to contend with, but stopped herself: it would seem like a threat and anger him more.

Carlo picked up a little bell on the console and rang it loudly. A servant opened the door. 'Tell Laura to come here,' he said.

Maria's outward demeanour remained calm but her mind was in turmoil. What could he want with Laura? Only one thing. He was going to order her to pack Maria's clothes.

The young woman knocked, entered the room, and curtseyed to Carlo.

'Undress your mistress's hair,' he ordered.

Laura looked at Maria, and then back at her master, bewildered.

'Do as I say,' he said impatiently.

Laura walked across to Maria and nervously began removing the pins from her looped plaits and loosening the long string of pearls entwined throughout. Maria sat as still as a statue. If Carlo was trying to shame her by having Laura perform an intimate routine of her toilette under his gaze in this public domain, then he was going to have to endure Maria's eyes never leaving his. She would not be shamed and would not look down.

Laura dropped the pearls and stammered apologetically as she stooped red-faced to retrieve them. The poor girl was mortified on Maria's behalf. When the plaits were undone, not having a comb, Laura gently ran her fingers through the long, silky golden hair and arranged it around Maria's shoulders and breast.

'Now go,' said Carlo. Laura curtseyed and left the room, looking back in consternation at Maria when she reached the door.

Carlo walked to Maria, took an end of one of her thick tresses, and began looping it around his left hand. She thought he'd left his right hand free in order to strike her, and she rose to face him. He went on winding the hair until his hand was level with her chin, tugging it so that it hurt, drawing her face close to his. His eyes bored into hers, and each time he spoke he gave her hair a painful tug.

'Will you go to Gesualdo?'

'No.'

'Do you understand that you bring dishonour to this house?'

'Yes.'

'What would you have me do?'

'Exercise your princely disdain for idle chatter, just as you always have. Burn the letters you receive. Refuse to discuss the matter. Retreat into the private world that pleases you so well.'

'Do you really believe I can do that after what I have just told you?'

'Perhaps not,' she whispered sadly, wincing in spite of herself at the pain of his pulling her hair so hard. 'I'm surprised you haven't asked me to put an end to my meetings with Fabrizio.'

'That is because I know you would not do so. Even with the best intentions, a week would pass, or a month, and you would contrive to be with him again, just as he would contrive to be with you—as he did in the beginning. I know you well, Cousin, and I admire you. You would not throw away your virtue and your good name lightly, so I have concluded that you love Carafa, just as you are in love with that entire wretched family. Therefore such a promise from you would offer no lasting solution. Can you think what else you would have me do?'

'No, Carlo. I can't. We've been happy enough until now, and the happiness of us both resides in allowing things to go on as they are. Please let go of my hair. You're hurting me.'

'Not my happiness. Not any more.' he muttered, tugging harder, so hard her eyes began to smart. 'And not the happiness of those whom your actions have driven to despair, so that they look to me to relieve their sufferings.' He clasped the hair on the other side of her head in a kind of caress, pulling her face even closer to his so that their lips were almost touching. Her head throbbed with the pain. 'Maria, consider this carefully before you answer me, and think of our son. For the last time, will you come to Gesualdo?'

Maria imagined herself marooned in Gesualdo Castle, longing for Fabrizio, her lonely days bereft of love, of passion, of laughter, of friendship, of life itself. Could she be like Vittoria Colonna and devote herself to poetry? No. In any event, there was no Michelangelo Buonarotti at Gesualdo. There was no cultivated society at all; there were only those uncouth or dull men whose allegiance was to Carlo. Could she devote herself to the upbringing and education of Emmanuele? No. This was the job of servants and tutors and what was left to her would only be sorry remnants. She would become one of those embarrassing women who filled their empty lives with an obsessive interest in their sons and ended up by being ridiculed by their daughters-in-law. She thought of Proserpine, whose winters were spent confined in the gloomy Underworld with the dark god Hades, yearning for the spring when she was permitted to journey upwards into the light of the sweet green earth. This ancient myth of the seasons symbolised for Maria the contrast between what her life would be at Gesualdo and what it was in Naples.

Carlo had slowly unwound her hair from his long fingers. The aesthete in him who had once loved touching it now took equal enjoyment in using it like a weapon. 'Well?'

'No, Carlo. I won't live at Gesualdo.'

'Then you are condemning us both to Hell!' he shouted, violently pushing her to the floor. He stood over her and stared down hard into her face as if she might still change her mind. He raised his hand and she flinched, but then he thought better of it and strode from the room.

Carlo retreated to his apartment for the next two days. Though he had not struck her, he had never been so physically violent with her before, not so as to cause such pain. And he'd wanted to strike her; she could see that. He'd stopped himself. Why? Her head ached. As Sylvia gently massaged a balsam into her sore scalp Maria contemplated what Carlo might do. It didn't bear thinking on. She felt afraid of him now, truly afraid, not merely tremulous as she'd been in the past. Nevertheless it was possible that the scene in the library was Carlo merely acting out his anger, creating a scene and instilling fear into her in order to dramatise his chagrin at being called upon to defend his family honour. It was his habit to become obsessed for days on end with an idea, a performer, a painting, a piece of music, and then the obsession would evaporate, only to be replaced by another. She prayed that this current preoccupation of his would soon be eclipsed by another. She felt safe only in the knowledge that Fabrizio was her fierce protector as well as her lover.

Toward the end of the second day she heard faint music emanating from Carlo's apartment. The strains were not familiar. He was composing again. Thank the heavens. Relief washed over her as she sat down and listened to make sure it was not simply an old piece that he was rearranging. No, it was quite new, its melancholy lilts rising and falling, crescendo-ing into a violent chromatic flurry of piercingly discordant tones.

As soon as Carlo emerged from his rooms on the third day he went out. Maria, chatting with Laura on a balcony, glimpsed him crossing the square. Although he looked withdrawn and preoccupied, his step was quick and purposeful.

A half-hour or so later she saw him return with a workman. She wondered vaguely why he hadn't sent one of the servants to fetch the man.

A few minutes later Sylvia appeared to tell Maria that repairs were being done in some of the rooms, and Prince Carlo, not wishing her to be disturbed by the noise, thought it best that she and Laura went out for a drive. The carriage was waiting. This boded well. If Carlo was making repairs to rooms in San Severo, it could only mean he proposed to go on living there.

On her return in the late afternoon, Maria was greeted with the news that Prince Carlo had gone hunting at gli Astruni and would not return for two days. This confirmed that the storm about Gesualdo family honour had blown over and that life at San Severo would settle back into its customary pattern. Now she was truly relieved. Her sense of danger all but abated, she turned once again to reckless thoughts of happiness and sent Laura out with a note for Fabrizio.

She didn't feel inclined to leave the comforts of her apartment so late in the day for the haven of the secret palace, increasingly chilly now that winter was approaching, so she'd invited her lover to come to her at San Severo. There was no danger of Carlo returning before the following evening. His parents were still at Venosa, where they appeared to have settled permanently—Carlo had snidely remarked that the fire at Venosa had caused enough suffering to keep Geronima happily occupied for years. So, this evening, San Severo was hers to do with as she pleased. The rare sense of liberation in her own home was such that she began to sing to herself.

That night Maria ate a solitary light dinner. She looked in on Emmanuele to see that he was sleeping soundly. She was still in high spirits at Carlo's unexpected departure, chatting with Sylvia about what clothes she should wear the following day as Laura undressed her. She bade Laura goodnight. Though it was only seven o'clock she had Sylvia undress her and she climbed into bed, telling the woman to leave the bed curtains open.

It was the night of the full moon. Maria lay in the silvery silence, wide awake, wondering if Fabrizio had received her note. Laura had reported he'd not been at Palazzo Carafa when she'd delivered it. She strained her ears for sounds from the street but all she could hear were the faint noises in the adjoining room of Sylvia cleaning and preparing her clothes for the morning. Fabrizio must come tonight; it was nine days since she'd last been with him. She ached for him as she did every night, but on this night her mind refused to be soothed by her conjuring the taste of him, his warm, wild strength. She lay on her back, her mind zigzagging feverishly between voluptuous thoughts of Fabrizio and the question that for the past two days had left her little peace. Who had written to Carlo? With whom had he had the tête-à-tête he'd found so tiresome? Were they the same, or was more than one party bent on destroying her and Fabrizio by tormenting Carlo? Was it done out of malice? Idleness? Jealousy? The letters would at this very moment be in Carlo's rooms, secreted in a drawer, but Maria didn't dare go down there in search if them. He would know, either through Pietro or his own sharp instincts, and would never forgive such an invasion of his private domain.

'Sylvia,' called Maria. 'Bring some clothes to me. I wish to dress.'

'Whatever for?' asked Sylvia, appearing in the doorway. 'You undressed not an hour ago.'

'The duke's here. I just heard him whistle from the street. Hurry. A petticoat and shawl will do.'

So dressed, Maria went to the window and opened it. Sylvia stood beside her and looked down, and there was the duke smiling up at Maria for any passer-by to see, although there were likely to be few at this hour of the night. Maria stepped out onto the balcony. 'Go and check the staircase,' she ordered Sylvia. 'Warn me if you see anyone stirring in the palace or the courtyard.'

Sylvia moved across the bedchamber, stopping at the door to make a sign of the cross in the direction of her mistress. She then crossed herself.

All was silent. Sylvia waited a few moments and went back upstairs to report it was safe for Fabrizio to come up.

'Close the window and undress me.'

When Maria was in bed she called to Sylvia again. 'This nightdress is wet with perspiration. Bring me another, the green one with the black silk cuffs and collar.'

Sylvia brought it to the bed. 'Let me take that one off you and I'll have it washed, my lady.'

'No, no. Leave it on the bed.'

Sylvia tut-tutted, lit a candle and placed it on the chair near the bed.

'Goodnight, Sylvia. Shut the door without turning the handle and don't come in unless I call you.'

Sylvia lay down on her bed fully clothed in case Maria called her. She fell asleep reading a book.

Maria and Fabrizio lay sprawled across her bed, sated. The green nightgown was now also soaked with sweat, the delicious salt of Fabrizio's sweat. She breathed him in as she straightened the nightgown on his body; it had become twisted during their contortions. And now to quietly feast on the sight of Fabrizio's manly form in her nightgown, to caress his strong limbs beneath the silk. He watched her with a glint in his eye, knowing what she was thinking. She dropped her head back onto the pillow and smiled. She would never tire of Fabrizio nor he of her. Never. It had been more than eighteen months, and as soon as he entered her presence all her senses still sprang immediately into life as they had on that first night in Don Garcia's summer pavilion. Fabrizio was her life energy. She dropped her hand onto his neck, savouring the throb of his strong pulse against her fingers.

After a moment a frown appeared on her face and she sat up, leaning her head on her hand as she turned to her lover. 'I've something to tell you. Someone has written letters to Carlo about us. And he's met with him to discuss them. It worries me terribly because it's changed Carlo. He's been brooding about it and even insisted that we leave Naples and live at Gesualdo. He became most dramatic and said we were condemned to Hell. Though he says such things when he's in one of his tempers, this time he was cold and rational and it frightened me.'

Fabrizio ran the back of his hand over her face soothingly. 'He'd never dare harm you, Maria, so don't be afraid. He knows you belong to me.'

'I'm not so certain of that,' responded Maria, thinking of Carlo's reminder that she was the Princess of Venosa. 'Who could have written such a letter? It'd be no mere gossipmonger. Carlo would trouble himself to visit only someone of importance. Think with me. Who could it be?'

'What precisely did he say?'

'When I asked him who it was, he replied that he wouldn't tell me because I would of course tell you, and that you'd seek to avenge my honour.' She thought back to her conversation with Carlo. 'And that this would cause the person more suffering. Who suffers because of us, Fabrizio?'

'Carlo himself, perhaps.'

'Really Fabrizio, even if that were true, Carlo would not write letters to himself. Nor would he pretend to have received a letter from a person who doesn't exist. Carlo has no patience with such subterfuge. In any case, it was clear to me that someone had been whispering in his ear because he had that air of quiet, angry determination that comes upon him only when an offensive thought has been implanted in his mind and he's impatient to rid himself of it.'

'It seems likeliest that one of his relatives in the Church has been tormenting him about our mortal sin, as those dogma-ridden interferers in lives happier than their own choose to call it. It might be his uncle, Cardinal Alfonso. He's obsessed with the honour of the Gesualdos. He's an ambitious man. It seems we are perceived as a stain on their honour. Damn their honour, I say.'

'Don't talk of cardinals and honour, Fabrizio. Do you recall what happened to Giovanna d'Aragona and her lover?'

'Of course, but remember you once expressed contempt for my fear. Are you afraid yourself now?'

'Yes, I confess I am, but only of the thought that one of us will be killed and not the other, or that we'll be far apart from each other when we die. I can think of no more fortunate end to our lives on this earth than we die together. If that must happen soon, so be it.'

'Look at the moon,' said Fabrizio, turning her face toward the window. 'Its fullness is making you have melancholy thoughts. Now look at me and forget tomorrow.'

Sylvia had been sleeping soundly for hours. The lamp in her room was dying out. She was dreaming of unfamiliar noises outside her room. She sat up to listen more intently. Then she knew she was dreaming for when she opened her eyes she was still lying on the bed. She closed her eyes again, foggily recognising that her opening them had been part of this strange, indefinite dream of muffed footsteps and whisperings. It was oppressive and she wished she would awaken and be rid of it.

Her door opened silently and three strange men entered the room. They made their way through it and opened the door of Donna Maria's room. Sylvia, half awake, attempted to rise from her bed, but discovered she was paralysed by fear. She was still uncertain if she was awake or dreaming. She saw that the last of the men was carrying a halberd. She realised she was having one of those nightmares where dream closely resembles reality but, though you cannot escape it, at the back of your mind you know you are dreaming. She was certain of this for she had herself locked both of those doors and checked them before retiring. So the three men who had passed so easily through them could only be phantoms.

On one side of the Church of San Domenico Maggiore was a boxed-in balcony that faced the second storey of the San Severo palace. It was large enough for two or three men to secrete themselves and commanded an unhindered view of the street below. Two hours previously, Carlo had been on this balcony, awaiting with the infinite patience and suppressed excitement of a hunter the appearance of his unsuspecting quarry.

Before that, when Maria had thought him on his way to gli Astruni, he had been in his rooms following his customary evening routine. He had dined at seven, in bed and undressed, served by a waiter, his valet and Alessandro. After he had eaten, the waiter and the priest had left. Pietro had locked the door, arranged the bedclothes around his master and had then gone to bed himself.

At nine, Pietro heard his master call for a glass of water. He went down to the courtyard to draw the water from the well and noticed that the palace's street door was open, which was unusual at that hour. Returning with the water, he found his master dressed in coat and trousers. Carlo bade Pietro fetch him his long cloak.

'Where are you going at such an hour, Prince Carlo?' asked Pietro.

'I am going hunting,' was the answer.

'Pietro looked at him in perplexity. 'It's not the time to go hunting.'

'You will see what kind of hunting I am going to do,' Carlo responded tersely.

Pietro helped him on with the cloak.

'Light two torches,' said Carlo. He reached beneath his bed and pulled out a sword, a stiletto, a dirk and a small arquebus and put them on the table. 'Keep the torches alight. I will return later,' he said. Then he departed.

By prearrangement, a monk had let him into the Church of San Domenico Maggiore and guided him to the balcony. He'd been waiting there for nearly an hour, darkly cloaked and hooded so that he blended with the night. Apart from a pair of loitering young men and a beggar woman cradling a baby in a ragged bundle in the doorway of a neighbouring palace, the piazza was deserted. Carlo's nerves were tingling with irritated frustration at the possibility that his meticulously executed plan, centred on this night, might at this crucial point go awry.

Minutes later he heard footsteps and, hugging the wall so as not to be seen, looked down and saw Fabrizio Carafa, his sword at his side, turn into the piazza from Spaccanapoli. He walked to San Severo and stopped below Maria's window. Fabrizio looked up, emitted three shrill, one-note whistles and stood there waiting. A few minutes later Maria appeared on her balcony, which was diagonally opposite and above the one where Carlo hid himself. In the moonlight he saw her look down with a joyful smile, her dainty little hand fluttering a welcoming wave. At the sight of the lovers enacting before him the secret signs of their trysts, a cold rage overcame him. There had been moments, long ones, during his recent days of planning, when the thought of what he would do gave him pause, tormented him even, but now, whatever qualms he'd had evaporated and his mind raced forward in anticipation of the final act of the drama he was orchestrating. He watched Fabrizio enter the palace through the open street door, and minutes later he, too, passed through the portal and disappeared into the darkness.

Reaching the second floor, he re-entered his apartment via its private entrance and waited there until midnight, when he became alert for the sounds that would signal the denouement of what he had almost come to regard as a work of art.

Miles away, at Andria, the Duchess Maria Carafa had prostrated herself in front of a painting of the Holy Virgin and made her devotions before retiring to a tormented sleep. She awoke fitfully, again and again, besieged by recollections of the events of the past week. Her exhausted spirit was torn between gloating triumph and terrified remorse at the knowledge of what she had irrevocably set in train. Evil, it was evil, what she had done. She felt her face. It was hot, burning with the memory that she had called upon the Devil himself, summoned the Dark One, to assist in delivering her from a misery that was past endurance. Her once-devout soul recognised that it was hatred that had driven her to it, filthy hatred of that strumpet Maria d'Avalos who presented to all the world the visage of an angel, knowing all the while that she had stolen the very soul of the duchess's husband. Though she had been a faithful and fertile wife to him, that adulterous whore had led Fabrizio to despise her. The Prince of Venosa during their recent interview had despised Maria Carafa no less, it seemed, even though he'd acknowledged that the insults to her virtue and his honour by her criminal husband and his own criminal wife could be tolerated no longer.

The tormented woman rose from her bed and fumbled for a candle. Unable to locate one in the dark, she stumbled toward the window to draw back the curtain and tripped on her long, pure white nightgown. Her knees hit the floor painfully and she lay there with her cheek pressed against the prickly carpet, a sorry, sobbing, abandoned wretch, beseeching the Virgin to deliver her from her agony.

Prince Carlo appeared in Sylvia's room, and after him his valet Pietro with two lighted torches. At last Sylvia knew that she was really sitting up in her bed and not dreaming. Prince Carlo was carrying a halberd.

'Ah, traitress, you shall not escape me now,' he hissed at Sylvia. 'Don't allow her to leave,' he said to Pietro. 'Fix one of those torches near the door.' Then he strode into Donna Maria's room.

Sylvia sprang out of bed, pushed Pietro violently out of her path as he raised one of the torches, and fled into Emmanuele's room, screaming, 'For the love of God, do not harm the baby.' Trembling and crossing herself, she hid under the child's bed.

Awakened by a faint click of metal, Fabrizio sprang out of the bed, awakening Maria.

'There he is!' shouted one of the men.

Two shots exploded in the moonlight.

Maria's lips formed a scream, but nightmare terror robbed her of the ability to make a sound. She shrank back against the head of the bed, her eyes fixed on the horror of three shadowy forms plunging their swords again and again into Fabrizio.

The door to the private staircase was flung open and Carlo burst into the room. 'Kill that scoundrel along with this harlot,' he shouted. 'Shall a Gesualdo be made a cuckold?'

Maria, in a pitiful gesture, pulled the sheets over her head. She began reciting the *Salve Regina*. 'Hail our life, our sweetness and our hope. To you do we cry poor banished children of Eve. To you do we send up our sighs, mourning and weeping in this valley of tears.'

Carlo ripped the sheets away. In the instant that she saw her husband's form loom over her like a dark angel of death she understood he would not be merciful and she closed her eyes. 'Show us the fruit of your womb, Jesus. O clement, O loving, O sweet Virgin Mary,' she mouthed as his dagger sliced her nightgown open and she felt him violently push her legs apart. The last resolve of Maria d'Avalos on this earth was that she would not scream. She emitted only low animal groans as she felt the cold agony of steel plunge into her vagina. Fabrizio was dead. Fabrizio. Carlo pulled the dagger out and drove it again and again through the womb that had so offended him. Waves of blackness descended upon Maria and she welcomed them, signals of her passage to that unknowable realm where she would be reunited with her love.

Carlo dropped the bloodied dagger. The forgotten arquebus under his arm clattered to the floor. Maria was now silent. He drew out the dirk and slashed and thrust at her breasts and belly, his frenzy mounting as he released years of suppressed anger at this marriage he had never wanted, at this woman he had been compelled to share his life with, at her soft fleshy body with its stinking troublesome heat. His mind exploding with anguished rage at Maria's sightless eyes, he began slashing her face. His movements, quickening in tempo to the staccato rhythm pounding in his head, became random, the dirk stabbing at the arms, the shoulders, the legs, the flaccid flesh of her lifeless, bloody body. His three co-assassins, having by this stage pinioned Fabrizio's torso and thighs to the floorboards with their swords, stood transfixed at their master's convulsive jabbings.

Eventually Carlo stood back, drew the dirk in an arc through the air and, in one final, exquisite movement, slashed through Maria's neck.

He walked to Fabrizio's body and stood over it, looking down at the once beautiful face, ghastly in the moonlight, the right side blown away, the brain oozing.

'Remove those swords,' he commanded.

The three men retrieved their weapons and quit the room, followed by Carlo, his long fingers dripping blood. At the top of the spiral staircase he hesitated.

'I don't believe she's dead,' he muttered.

He turned on his heel and re-entered her bedchamber. 'I don't believe she's dead,' he chanted as he raised and plunged the dagger twenty-four more times into Maria's bloodied corpse.

He called for Pietro.

His valet, entering with his torch, saw Maria's bed a sea of blood and Fabrizio's body still in the position near the bed where it had been stuck.

'Don't let the women cry out. And lock that door,' Carlo ordered, indicating the cupboard where Maria kept her jewels. He then left and descended the spiral staircase to his rooms.

'He's gone,' Pietro informed the hidden occupant of the adjoining room. Sylvia emerged more dead than alive from under the bed.

'They are both dead,' he informed her, in shock himself.

Pietro devoted over an hour to undressing and bathing his master, making several trips to the well. It was necessary to wash his hair twice. The manservant dared not utter a word, for beneath Carlo's blank-eyed exhaustion he could detect a storm of emotions. He re-dressed him in fresh linens and sturdy clothes. He finally spoke only to bid him goodbye when Carlo quit the palace with his assassins. Pietro guessed that a considerable period would pass before he saw his master again. He had murdered a Carafa.

Though it was past midnight, Carlo went immediately to the house of the viceroy, Juan de Zuniga. He had him awakened. Carlo had indeed murdered a Carafa and the threat of a vendetta from that damned family and the d'Avaloses loomed over him. He asked the viceroy's advice on the best course of action, after which he set out with his men on the long ride to Gesualdo Castle.

Just before dawn, the Duchess of Andria's maid entered her bedchamber to awaken her at the customary time. Placing a lighted candelabrum on the table, she noted her pious mistress was already at her devotions and, not wishing to disturb her, made to leave the room. But the duchess, crossing herself, rose and told her to sit down. Having summoned her considerable powers of self-discipline, Maria Carafa had regained something of her equilibrium, but felt an urgent need to speak.

'I have had a vision this night,' she informed her startled maid, who, noting her mistress's dishevelled appearance and distracted air, could well believe it. 'My husband has met his death.'

The woman rose in alarm, but the duchess indicated for her to remain seated.

'I have prayed to the Holy Virgin to intervene on his behalf and my request has been miraculously granted,' she went on, a rapt expression on her pinched face. 'The grace of repentance for his sins has been received.'

Maria Carafa had almost persuaded herself of the truth of this, and finding that saying it to the woman made it somehow more true, she repeated it to other members of the household throughout the course of the morning, interpreting their dismayed stares as awe-struck regard for her as the saviour of Fabrizio's immortal soul. But few in fact believed her, not until news of the disgraceful murder reached Andria several hours later.

It was well after dawn before the head servants of San Severo felt sufficiently in command of themselves to summon the court officials.

When the three lords judiciary and the fiscal lord advocate entered Maria's bedchamber they found Fabrizio's blood-covered body stretched out near the bed. His only clothing was Maria's green nightdress with the black silk collar, ruffs and fringing. It was red with blood. They noted his two gaping arquebus wounds, his brain spilling from the one on the temple, and the numerous vicious sword thrusts to his face, head, chest, flanks, shoulders and arms. On a crimson velvet chair was his burnished iron glove and gauntlet, his green breeches and green silk hose, his yellow doublet, white pantaloons and cloth shoes. His shirt with its frilled, starched cuffs was across the end of the gilt bed that Maria lay in. The bed was filled with blood. The officials noted Maria's cut throat and the innumerable dagger thrusts to her temples, face, right hand and arm, breast, belly and those parts 'she could have kept honest'.

The men also noted the damaged locks to the doors, which closed but did not lock fast. They puzzled over this, not knowing that the workman Carlo had brought to the palace the previous day had been a master locksmith. He had tampered with the locks so that while the keys turned in them and they appeared to lock fast, all it took was a downward pressure on a fine sliver of metal, inserted between the door and the jamb, to release them.

The officials ordered two coffins to be brought to the room. A Jesuit father and two priests arrived to wash Fabrizio's body. Several more sword thrusts were discovered beneath the congealed blood, many of which had passed through his body from back to front. When they lifted the body the priests discovered the thrusts had penetrated deeply into the wooden floor. When all the blood had finally been washed away, Fabrizio was dressed in black silk breeches and a black velvet jerkin and placed in one of the coffins, which was driven by coach to Andria, to be received by the duchess and his grandmother, the Countess of Ruovo.

Laura had fled. Maria's body was washed by a disconsolate Sylvia and other servants of the house. Antonia, sobbing convulsively, dressed her niece in a black silk gown. On Maria's index finger was the Carafa ring Fabrizio had given her. Antonia slid it off and secretly placed it on her niece's wedding finger. Prince and Princess d'Avalos did not make an appearance.

It was the Carafas who claimed Maria's body. By order of Maddelena Carafa, her coffin was carried to the Church of San Domenico Maggiore. She was buried in the Carafa chapel with her first husband and first love, Federigo Carafa, together with their infant son and Beatrice. Fabrizio's coffin, too, was later brought to San Domenico Maggiore and it was placed next to his father's in the royal vestry that contains the coffins of Angevin kings.

Shortly after the murders, the Carafa family publicly demonstrated their loyalty to Maria by commissioning a painting which hangs in the Carafa chapel of San Domenico Maggiore to this day. The painting is a

Sacre Conversatione, and it depicts both the living and the dead. Fourteen Carafas making various supplicating gestures are grouped around the enthroned Virgin with the Christ child in her lap. Angels with billowing draperies levitate overhead. The Carafa Pope, Paul IV, stands on the Virgin's left, blessing the Child. Maddelena Carafa as the family matriarch commands the right foreground of the picture. Above her are Maria and handsome Federigo Carafa, with his strong bone structure and steady gaze, his hair cropped Roman-style close to his well-shaped head. Maria's face is angelic and the transparent veil she wears is Madonna-like. Her eyes are demurely lowered as she reads the prayer book she is holding. She is dressed in a simple olive-green tunic, caught at the waist with a red belt, over a lighter green blouse. Federigo is in the shadows behind her and casts a deeper shadow on the pillar behind them, which indicates his early death. The sleeping, cherubic infant above him, about to be raised up to Heaven by an angel, is Ferrante, their infant son. Beatrice kneels near Maddelena at the feet of the Virgin, her hands clasped in prayer. The painting conveys the warmth and intimacy of the family that embraced Maria as one of their own, one that she loved above all else.

Eight days after the murders the Grand Court of the Vicaria held an inquest. The evidence given by Sylvia Albana and Pietro Bardotti clearly established what had occurred on that Tuesday night of 27 October 1590. The inquiry was, however, discontinued at the command of the viceroy, who considered that Carlo Gesualdo had manifest justification for his acts.

The rest of Naples did not agree. There was widespread horror at the brutality of the murders, together with universal contempt for Gesualdo's cowardice in commissioning his thugs to slay Fabrizio. The Venetian ambassador gave a succinct account of the tragedy to his government, writing that the three princely families, Gesualdo, d'Avalos and Carafa, were connected and related to all the other nobles of the kingdom and that everyone seemed stunned by the horrendous event. Fabrizio, 'the handsomest and most accomplished nobleman of the city', was deeply mourned, while Maria was lauded as both virtuous and the most beautiful woman in Naples.

The poets of Naples, from the great Tasso down to the most obscure rhymester, burst into a simultaneous howl of anguish. One of them was Fra Giulio Carafa, that same nephew of Fabrizio's who had struck a murderous blow to the overloud poet. He evidently knew Carlo better than most, and his lines were in a sense prophetic:

> *Oh barbarous cruel and savage murderer*
> *To your own self minister of shame*
> *what need have you to fly away so far?*
> *Although the good Duke is dead, still thou fleest?*
> *What then is it you fear?*
> *Perchance his unconquered spirit causes you remorse,*
> *perchance reviles you.*
> *It might well be so, for the offence was too grave;*
> *seeing that when he was defenceless*
> *with many weapons you severed the thread of his life.*
> *How could you think that blood poured out*
> *by the hands of vile creatures*
> *could wash out your dishonour while you were straying*
> *and caring so little to keep your couch inviolate?*

Three poems by Torquato Tasso were the most moving of those concerning the lovers. These poems cost Tasso dearly, for Carlo was his friend and patron.

> *O souls, marvellously lovely and beautiful, who suffered in dying bitter torment, whether it was death, or love, or fortune, or Heaven that united you, nothing divides or uproots you any more.*
>
> *But like rays conjoined, or even torches of immortal splendour in the third circle, you already flame, and the serene stars shine more brightly because of your gentle desire.*
>
> *Nay, Heaven is even adorned by your sin (if ever there is sin between two courteous lovers), it is made more lovely by your amorous disgrace.*
>
> *Whoever blames you for straying among the sad sighs of love, let him accuse the sun which brought forth the day when the wandering stars so erred.*

Fifteen

THE PRINCE OF MUSIC

After the murders, Gesualdo behaved like someone out of *Macbeth*. The frenzy he'd whipped himself into in order to commit them did not subside. It intensified.

On reaching Gesualdo Castle he immediately called four of his men. They followed him down to a claustrophobic stone room in the lower regions of the castle. There he had them flog him. The men were accustomed to this. They summarily stripped him and gave him the ten lashes necessary for the level of pain that brought him relief. But he spurred them on, urging them to flog him until his back was cut and bloody. The pain seared through every fibre of his nerves, the blood pounded in his ears, but it brought no respite from the tempest raging in his head. The horror of what he had done. Damned. Eternally damned to the fires of Hell. 'Continue,' he ordered yet again, barely able to get the word out, his vision growing blurred, and it became clear to the men that their master was ordering them to flog him into unconsciousness, to death perhaps, so they ceased and, enduring his curses, faint and breathless as they were, carried him up to his room and gently set him down on his bed.

Old Lorenzo came in and applied dressings to his wounds. The old man then forced his master to drink some water. He hovered by his bedside, trembling, distraught at what the men who'd arrived with him had told him of the events of the previous night, barely able to take in the news that his master had murdered the gentle Lady Maria, yet knowing it must be true for who would else dare utter such an abomination.

'Go,' ordered Carlo hoarsely. 'No one is to come near me. Tell them.'

Night was falling. Carlo lay there in the half-dark, barely conscious of the agony of his wounds, his mind like a black storm. Lightning flashes of two rational thoughts crackled on its horizon: reprisals from the Carafa and d'Avalos families were inevitable; and as the Prince of Venosa he could not take his own life.

Unable to remain still, he rose, barely noticing his wince at the searing pain caused by his movements. He lit a lamp and staggered out of his room and along the corridor. He opened the door of Maria's room, hesitated, leaning down on the door handle for support, and entered.

Placing the lamp against the back wall, he slowly, agonisingly, lowered himself onto a backless stool. The twilight was cold and he was all but naked, yet perspiration from the heat of his punished body streamed from him. He sat in the semi-darkness, looking at the decorative patterns on the wall with their indigo highlights, illuminated from below by the light of the lamp and darkened in the centre by his eerily elongated shadow.

He sat meditating upon his wife's innocent, charming creations, and waited for remorse to sweep over him like a delicious tide and relieve him of his anguish. But it did not come. What came instead caused the storm in his head to rage more fiercely. Fury. Hatred. She had brought him to this, Maria and her mad attachment to those damned, damned Carafas. She'd damned them all. Women and their insane desire to love and be loved. Placing it above all else: home, family, honour, pride, life itself, as if the love between a man and a woman was all that gave meaning to life. What shallow creatures women were, their entire lives spent oscillating between hankering after love and mourning its loss. How brief in comparison the enjoyment of its pleasures, and yet it was these fleeting moments that had become Maria's sole purpose. Even her deepest maternal love she had lavished on a Carafa, not on Emmanuele.

When he'd been compelled to marry, his father's choice of Maria had brought him a sense of relief, not so much because she was his cousin, but rather because he'd then thought of her as a mature, sophisticated woman six years his senior with the experience of two marriages already behind her. Her hankering after love, which he considered girlish, had surprised him. He'd thought she'd be content with the comforts of her third marriage, and to enjoy the pleasures of Neapolitan society, bear him sons and sink into middle age. A fleeting, discreet affair he could have endured, *did* endure though it was neither fleeting nor discreet, but her *passion* for Carafa had been a contagion, infecting first Carafa, then Carafa's wife, and through her, Carlo, destroying all of their lives. At the thought of that poisonous harpy, Maria Carafa, a blinding flash of intolerable loathing fuelled his torment. The artist in him felt a perverse admiration for his victims, a kind of twisted love for Maria and Fabrizio and the pure white flame of their passion, but the passion that had driven that woman to seek him out as the agent of their destruction was a sordid thing that had thrived not on intolerable dishonour, as she had pretended, but on her hag's envy of Maria's beauty and its power over her husband. In his mind Carlo began to strangle her by pressing his thumbs down on her scrawny neck, but then he released her and let her drop before her life drained away, his imagination repulsed at the thought of touching her sour flesh.

He sat through the night, waiting for first light, the black storm raging in his head gathering momentum, his head banging with thoughts of further destruction. Toward dawn he noticed that he was shivering violently. He returned to his room and threw on some old clothes, gritting his teeth in an agonised grimace at the pressure of his shirt and jacket against the torn flesh of his back. On his way outside he passed Lorenzo, who was dozing by the fire in the kitchen. The old man rose and made to lift the kettle off the hook, pleading with his master to take a hot drink, but he was impatiently waved aside.

Gesualdo went to the room where the garden tools were kept and selected three of the strongest and sharpest axes.

He then went outside into the chill dawn. The caw of a raven sitting on a bare branch echoed ominously in the winter silence. Carlo set upon this tree first, hacking at its trunk until it was felled. Then he moved on to the next one. He attacked the trees in this way for the rest of the day, and the next, and the next, hacking in solitude until the days became weeks, and the weeks months, so that by the end of three months, all the forests and manicured shrubberies around Gesualdo Castle were cut down, the statuary and fountains defaced, and his marvellous garden destroyed.

Later, those who tried to make sense of his act claimed it was done through fear of revenge, saying that the forest would have obstructed the sight of hostile forces sent by the Carafa or d'Avalos families, but Carlo's rage was incandescent, artistic: like an artist who burns his paintings in a fury of self-loathing, he was driven by a compulsion to annihilate his own creation.

Carlo remained in his stronghold for the next three years, tormented by his demons and submitting himself to daily bouts of flagellation. Though his days were spent in a half-mad haze of self-destruction, he continued to attend to his duties as feudal overlord and as father to Emmanuele, whom one of his men had fetched and brought to the castle two days after the murders. Finally his madness spent itself and his thoughts turned more and more to the fate of his immortal soul. Remorse began to wash over him at last, and as he could experience nothing without seeking a means to act out the drama of it, his terror and anguish at what he had done was expressed in an act of atonement. In 1592, two years after the murders, he built in the town of Gesualdo a Capuchin monastery with a chapel he entitled Santa Maria delle Grazie.

Carlo might have stayed hidden in his gloomy castle for the remainder of his life, battling his demons and writing stylish madrigals impregnated with love, death and guilt, music soon to be forgotten perhaps, had not a situation arisen in the far north of Italy that resulted in his marriage into one of its great noble houses and, more significantly, his exposure to one of the most splendid and enlightened courts in all of Europe, one famed for the brilliance and progressive taste of its music: Ferrara. Not only had Heaven forgiven him, it seemed, but destiny had conspired to ensure that the Prince of Venosa would become one of the immortals. If there was one place on earth that Carlo Gesualdo the composer truly belonged, it was Ferrara, the centre of the musical avant-garde.

Carlo himself took no part in the political machinations that led to his marriage and two-year sojourn in Ferrara; he was indeed entirely ignorant of what was taking place there. The aged Duke of Ferrara, Alfonso II, was childless, and he was plagued by the knowledge that on his death, having no heir, his kingdom would pass into the hands of the popes. In order to combat this—and the ensuing eclipse of the great house of d'Este—he sought the favour of powerful Cardinal Alfonso Gesualdo to plead with the papacy on his behalf, hoping for the issuing of a bull that would sanction his nephew inheriting the kingdom. Cardinal Alfonso was of course Carlo's uncle. Knowing that he must offer a powerful incentive in order to obtain such a favour, Duke Alfonso offered the hand of his niece, the noble Leonora d'Este, to Carlo. No stranger to murder himself, Duke Alfonso was undeterred by the fact that Carlo had murdered his first wife.

And so, in February 1594, Gesualdo, accompanied by prized members of his *camerata* and a train of one hundred and thirty-four laden mules, journeyed to the dazzling city of Ferrara to marry Leanora, a sister of Cesare d'Este, heir presumptive to the throne of Ferrara and later Duke of Modena. Carlo also took with him his first two books of madrigals and his handsome friend, the Count of Saponara, a young man noted for his jousting abilities, whom the Ferrarese noted was greatly devoted to Carlo.

Carlo had little interest in his devout bride; it was Ferrara he was enamoured with. During the sumptuous, five-day-long wedding celebration with its round of concerts, ballets and theatrical performances, he paid little attention to Leonora. He behaved erratically, poking fun at the few musicians who did not meet his high standards and running off during the course of a banquet. He redeemed himself, however, when he sang and played his own music, for even the Ferrarese found it daring and imaginative, albeit strange. 'His art is infinite,' commented an emissary. 'But it is full of attitudes and moves in an extraordinary way.'

Carlo never stopped singing the praises of Ferrara. He devoted the weeks after his wedding to absorbing its rich musical environment. Here, even the nunneries were centres of music. He listened daily to highly polished performances by these extraordinary nuns as well as those by Ferrara's three famed singing ladies and other virtuosi; he heard the luxuriant compositions of its celebrated resident maestro, Luzzasco Luzzaschi, and he studied the contents of the d'Este court's renowned music library.

Then, three months after the wedding, he left, ostensibly to attend to business at Gesualdo, but with something else on his mind entirely. His new wife did not accompany him. He stopped for several days at

Venice, which also delighted him, though it did nothing to temper his love of solitude and impatience with civilities and formalities. He ambled the labyrinthine streets of the city alone and incognito, eccentrically muffled in a coat as long as a nightgown, so noted the Ferrarese emissary sent to accompany him. Though he had an express commission from his uncle Cardinal Alfonso to give his compliments to the Patriarch of Venice, Carlo visited him only with displeasure. The quality of the music there so appalled him he withdrew from the room, summoned the director and cembalist to him and sharply reproved them.

Ferrara had offered Carlo no specific musical influence; he had always been sure of his own course. What its avant-garde environment did teach him, however, was that anything was possible. It liberated him. His state of mind in Venice was therefore highly sensitive: his reinvigoration at Ferrara so excited him that his senses were alive with music, his own, and he composed constantly during these days, just as he did on his return to Gesualdo. In the process of conquering unfamiliar musical territory he was embarking on a new style, one which introduced a greater melodic virtuosity into the upper registers, and a heightened expressiveness through establishing a new intimacy between word and music. As no other composer before him, Gesualdo, like a poet, began to focus on the meaning and nuances of these words. He even rewrote the verses, dramatising their emotion. In so doing he intensified the feeling in his music. He also began to develop his signature chromaticism, introducing a far wider use of sharps and flats, which previously had been used rather sparely. Gesualdo had hit on the style that in the ensuing years he would develop into miracles of composition. So thickly textured was this music, so complex the interrelation of voices, so exquisite his artifices and flights of fancy, so daring its harmonies, dissonances and chromatic richness, so moving its bitter-sweetness, that he eschewed instrumentation. By and large, he composed only for the voice—for unaccompanied choir and vocal groupings—and steadfastly continued to do so even when it became unfashionable. The voices *were* the instruments. With five voices Gesualdo could achieve effects that were equivalent to a full orchestra.

His sustained burst of creativity was interrupted only by the occasional hunting trip and a visit to Naples. Four years after the murders, he was compelled to face the city at last. Courtesy required him to play host to members of the Ferrarese court who wished to visit there, a courtesy even he could not fail to honour. In any case, what better way to make his re-entrance into the city that had so reviled him, his power and status now increased through his marriage to a d'Este and in the company of members of its court? He treated them to a whirl of musical concerts performed by members of his academy at various palaces. Even though many Neapolitans gave him a wide berth, others were pleased to renew their acquaintance with him, especially those who were keen to strike up a new one with a d'Este courtier. Carlo smiled to himself sardonically. Still, he didn't feel safe in Naples. The Carafas and the d'Avaloses had not taken their revenge as he'd once expected, but that was doubtless due to the remoteness of Gesualdo Castle. After a few days he informed the Ferrarese that business recalled him back to Gesualdo, where the discovery of himself as an artist kept him occupied for six months. It then came time to seek fresh inspiration from Ferrara's world of music, so he returned there, and to his marriage.

Carlo's ensuing two years in Ferrara, where he rented a spacious palace in the Strada degli Angeli, was one of the most productive musical periods of his life. There he composed one of his rare keyboard pieces, the thrilling *Canzon Francese del Principe*. His wife Leonora, a connoisseur of music herself having grown up constantly amidst the best of it, and now being treated by Carlo a little more kindly as she was pregnant with their child, considered it an extraordinary work, and it was indeed one of the most remarkable keyboard pieces of its own or any time. Like no other composition, it gave Leonora a profound insight into Gesualdo's erratic temperament. A work of the highest individualism and complexity, its opening phrases are elegant and measured, with subtle dissonances. Suddenly the mood, the tempo, shifts to contemplative, then darkly moody, then to joyous skipping rhythms followed by sombre cadences, and then it shifts again, and again, throughout the piece: the listener has no inkling of where Gesualdo will all of a sudden fly to next. It is as if a mischievous angel of music is sporting with the myriad possibilities of musical surface and emotional intent. The emotions are replaced by others before they can reach anything approaching resolution, yet they are all there, profoundly felt and perfectly expressed: gaiety, melancholy, playfulness, black depression, excitement, contemplation, joy, morbidity, and a strange mood that lingers on as an aftertaste when the playing is finished, a kind of yearning for ecstasy.

Leonora bore Gesualdo a son, Alfonsino, during this period in Ferrara. The men in Leonora's life had shown her only love and deep respect; her half-brother Alessandro in fact adored her, so she was ill equipped for marriage to a man as neurotic and evil-tempered as Gesualdo. Leonora had neither the striking beauty and charismatic charm of Maria d'Avalos, nor her dilettantish gifts and aesthetic interests, so there was little about her that Carlo found attractive. He soon came to despise her.

What she did have, regrettably, was a strong streak of the martyr, and her dutiful forbearance provoked Carlo's dark side, his cruelty. He was rude to her in public. He ignored her in public. He humiliated her. He struck her. He verbally abused her. He made her life a misery. His maltreatment of her soon became a subject of gossip in Ferrara, as did his amorous affairs, although the nature of these was never publicly disclosed. The Ferrarese became disgusted with him. For his part, Carlo began to long for his own territory and the solitude it offered him, and so he quit the city and returned to Gesualdo. Again Leonora did not accompany him. Neapolitan tongues, too, began to wag, for they had now been married three years and Leonora had not been introduced into Neapolitan society.

After several months of delays and claims of ill health on Carlo's part, he eventually summoned Leonora to Gesualdo in late 1597. And like the obedient fool a wife was expected to be, she went. She took with her a lady companion, Aurelia d'Errico, who was beautiful and far younger than she. Whether this was through naivety, aristocratic hauteur or sheer stupidity is difficult to say. Music aside, from here on it was all down hill.

Shortly before Leonora took up residence at Gesualdo Castle, the Duke of Ferrara died, and with him his hopes for the d'Este family's continuing governance of Ferrara. Cardinal Alfonso Gesualdo had recently been appointed Archbishop of Naples. To champion the d'Este cause would, he considered, involve putting the weight of his new position behind him and he was not prepared to take the risk. So Ferrara fell into the hands of the papacy. With the passing of Alfonso II, Ferrara's epoch as one of the great centres of humanist culture drew to a close. With it, the glorious Italian Renaissance itself died out, giving way to the repressions of the Counter-Reformation.

Gesualdo aficionados came to term these years of his life as the period of the Four Great Misfortunes. His remorse over the murders continued to dwell in his heart like a worm in a corpse. The severity of his masochistic rituals escalated, and he kept a dedicated band of servants whose duty it was to perform them. He submitted himself to painful floggings up to three times a day. His body ceased to function adequately; it became clogged with its own waste, and he found it increasingly difficult to breathe. The flagellations were part masochism and in part served a medical function, for Gesualdo believed that they cleared the intestinal blockages to which he attributed his chronic constipation.

His costive rages were spent on Leonora. He was occasionally physically violent with her. Now that she was isolated at Gesualdo Castle, far away from her protective brothers, Gesualdo's humiliation of her increased. He had a new companion, Castelvietro of Modena, who kept his back warm on the nights that Aurelia d'Errico did not share his bed. Leonora became ill and hysterical and began to suffer epileptic attacks. Gesualdo's doctor diagnosed her condition as black humour, or melancholy, caused by an excessive secretion of black bile from her liver, but in truth her sickness was called Carlo Gesualdo. Leonora's only solace was her constant correspondence with her brothers, who became increasingly concerned for her welfare. Alessandro suggested that the pope be petitioned for a divorce. In consideration of her son, little Alfonsino, Leonora refused to take such an extreme step.

Then, in 1600, a tragedy befell the couple. Gesualdo expressed his grief in a letter to Leonora's brother, Cesare.

It has pleased the Divine Majesty to call unto himself my Don Alfonsino, after an illness of seventeen days of fever and fluxes, and, indeed, in this world I could not experience a greater torment. My sorrow, however, is somewhat mitigated when I think that, surely, he now must enjoy the extreme glory of Heaven.

To the volatile mix of Gesualdo's tormentedness and masochism, and his terror at the bisexuality he was secretly unable to deny—an unspeakable transgression according to the doctrines of his faith—was now added morbidity at the death of Alfonsino and a constant anxiety about the very real possibility of the extinction of the Gesualdo male line. He placed all his hopes in Emmanuele, his heir and son by Maria d'Avalos, and although the boy was but thirteen, began planning to find him a suitable wife.

The memory of Maria's and Fabrizio's wounds haunted him; his asthma attacks became ever more frequent. He devised another masochistic ritual: bundles of rags were placed over his temples and other parts of his body and he was then given blows to these areas. He found it soothing.

These psychic and physical agonies Gesualdo expressed in the madrigals of books V and VI, with their agitated evocations of death, their lacerating ecstasies of pain and pleasure, their laborious *respiro*s (I breathe) and plummeting *sospiro*s (I sigh). The exuberant *gioia*s (joy), soaring *volo*s (I fly) and lugubrious *io moro*s (I die) he suffused with eroticism. Oxymoronic phrases like *dolcissima il languire* (sweetest languish) resonate with the bitter-sweetness that finds its fullest expression in these last madrigals. In *Resta di darmi noia* all frivolity is put aside in tortured harmonies to verses Gesualdo found deeply moving. This overwhelmingly affecting madrigal is resonant with autobiographical confession, haunted by Maria d'Avalos and Gesualdo's awareness that his murder of her ruined his life:

> *Cease now, no longer plague me,*
> *Deceitful thought and cruel,*
> *For I can never be what you desire.*
> *Dead is for me all joy,*
> *And never may I hope*
> *To know what gladness is.*

All of those in Gesualdo's domestic sphere were tainted by the tragedy of his personal life. Emmanuele grew up a divided soul. He'd felt loved by his father as a child and did his duty by him, obediently learning Carlo's lessons in the management of the estate and other princely duties, but he knew his father had murdered his mother and he could not but hate him for it. Carlo's treatment of Leonora d'Este he watched from the sidelines, assuming that his mother had been treated with the same violence and contempt. The ones who might have told him otherwise had long since disappeared from his life. Sylvia, after giving evidence at Carlo's trial, had returned to Messina and found employment in the house of a minor Sicilian nobleman, whose coachman she eventually married. Laura had turned up distraught at Palazzo Diomede Carafa the day after the murders and was taken in by Maddelena.

The death of her five-year-old son robbed Leonora of all power and consideration as a married woman. She lost all desire to live. Her two brothers again beseeched her to petition the pope for a divorce, Cesare, now Duke of Modena, going so far as to draw up a document. This time she considered it, but in the end she put her faith first. They insisted on restraining Gesualdo by appealing to his uncle, the Archbishop of Naples. Leonora begged them not to do so. The misery of her life with Gesualdo was relieved only by occasional visits to her brothers in Modena. When she was away, Carlo longed for her return and wrote beseeching letters to her. 'I will return home a willing martyr,' she wrote on one of these occasions, 'to suffer Purgatory in this life, so that I might enjoy Paradise in the next.' When she did return, Carlo paid scant attention to her.

In 1603 a scandal erupted in the community of Gesualdo. Aurelia d'Errico, insecure in her role as concubine and jealous of Leanora, wished to have greater sexual power over Carlo. Magic was her only means. She sought the aid of a local witch, Polisandra, and a sorcerer-priest, Antony Paulella. The rituals and paraphernalia the pair concocted for capturing the waning passion of the prince were bizarre: incantations, conjurations, the Eucharist, holy water, a crucifix, and the homeopathic magic of wax, key, lock and a special preparation. The key, lock and crucifix, together with a large loaf of bread, were buried under a passageway frequented by Carlo. Other ligatures were two little statues of Carlo and Aurelia transfixed by pins; coins and a locket containing the hair and toenails of dead persons, which were secreted in niches in the castle walls; and a spirit, captured by the sorcerer Paulella and put into a carafe given to Aurelia so that she could know the prince's thoughts and doings. Aurelia took a slice of bread especially prepared by Paulella and lubricated it with a mixture of her virginal humours, menstrual blood and Carlo's sperm. She then gave it to Carlo to eat.

'The princess is served,' boasted Aurelia to the village. 'The prince will be mine and only mine from the waist down. From the waist up he will belong to the princess, who can be served only with kisses.'

Aurelia's remarks were brought to the attention of the local bishop, and the entire affair was soon uncovered. Carlo had become ill with a fever after eating the bread. Within a few days he was dangerously ill, his condition worsened by the fact that Aurelia's doings had become public knowledge. Once again, his honour was gravely compromised; although this time he was not the guilty party, the offence to the still powerful d'Este family was immeasurable.

Honour required that Aurelia and Polisandra be sentenced to death. The baronial judge duly called for a trial and death by hanging if the parties were found guilty. The affair exploded into a violent conflict between Church and State. The Holy Office of Rome intervened: the women must be tried by the episcopal court of the local bishop; the judge was threatened with excommunication if he proceeded with the hangings. He handed the decision over to the Viceroy of Naples. In the course of all this, the sorcerer-priest slipped through the cracks. Only the two women were held culpable.

Throughout that autumn, Carlo hovered between life and death. Church and State finally reached a compromise. The guilty parties were tried and found guilty by Gesualdo's baronial court, but Carlo was forced to renounce his vengeance of the death penalty. Aurelia and Polisandra were tortured and imprisoned in the lower regions of Gesualdo Castle, where they remained until they died of illness and suffering.

Two years later, at the age of seventeen, Emmanuele married the German princess, Polissena von Furstenburg. Though he clashed with feisty Polissena, Carlo handed over the management of his estates to his son and concentrated entirely on his music. From the Gesualdos' point of view Emmanuele's marriage proved to be a disaster. No sons were born of it, only two daughters.

In 1608, eighteen years to the month after the murders, Fabrizio's wife, Maria Carafa, retreated into a Dominican convent. She had suffered in silence for all of those intervening years, ensuring that her and Fabrizio's sons attained high positions in the Church and that their daughters were well married. The sisters of the nunnery soon noted 'the inflamed condition of her soul'. Her continuous sighs and shouts disturbed the other inhabitants and she was consequently given a private cell. Punishing herself with the most extreme austerity, she lived on in agony for a further seven years until her death at the age of forty-nine.

Carlo became increasingly morbid at the prospect of his own death. He yearned for redemption from his 'infinite wickedness', as he described it. In 1609, he commissioned an altar painting for the chapel of Santa Maria delle Grazie, *Pala per perdona*, which, in its plea for heavenly forgiveness, dramatised the torment of his soul. He worked closely with his friend, the painter Giovanni Balducci, in developing its choice of figures, its meaning and iconography, and like the many works of art that Carlo directed throughout his life, it was a deeply personal expression of who he was and what he felt. His uncle Carlo Borromeo—who figured prominently in the painting—had, when he'd been Archbishop of Milan, issued an injunction for clarity in painting and representation of figures: angels must have wings, saints must have halos and be depicted with their particular attributes or, if they were really obscure, it might be necessary to write their names below them to avoid confusion. Carlo followed this closely: the Magdalene, for example, was depicted with her traditional jar of perfume, and all of the saints—Saint Francis, Saint Dominic, and so forth—were named.

Gesualdo, fear-struck, kneels positioned between Heaven and Hell. Carlo Borromeo in his red robes stands with his hand protectively on his nephew's shoulder, interceding on his behalf with Christ the Panocrator enthroned in the heavens. Carlo could not have chosen a more effective intercessor, for in the following year Carlo Borromeo was indeed made a saint. A host of angels and saints, as well as Carlo's sister, the nun, Sister Corona, echo this gesturing upwards with their long, Mannerist fingers, as if the very dynamic of their imploring for forgiveness on Carlo's behalf might lift him up to the golden radiance of Heaven. The most interesting and moving part of the picture, however, is Hell. Gesualdo deserves forgiveness, implies this infernal region, because he has confessed his sin and has forgiven those who sinned against him. Of the five figures here, two of them are being lifted out by angels: Maria d'Avalos, her naked form firmly in the embrace of a sweet-faced angel, is almost clear of the flames; while Fabrizio Carafa is still engulfed by them, his angel having just at that moment touched his outstretched hand. At the bottom right of the picture is a handsome woman who, gesturing toward Carlo, looks out of the picture as if pleading with the viewer, too, to forgive him. This woman is his unhappy second wife, Leonora d'Este, who remained a martyr to the end.

Carlo also expressed the torment of his soul in sacred music of unimaginable desperation. He composed the *Responsoria* cycle for Holy Week, the most important celebration of the Church calendar. The music follows the stages of Christ's Passion: the arrest, judgement, way of the cross, crucifixion and death. The Jesuit injunction that the composer must be able to sense the horrors of the Passion in order to be able to convey them, was a modest requirement indeed in light of the extent to which Gesualdo identified with Christ's sufferings. He fully unleashed his creativity in music of terror. As he developed the cycle, Christ's torments imperceptibly became subsumed by Carlo's own, so much so that the last movement, the Requiem *Morti, moriamo ancora* (Dead, we are still dying) contorts into an agony of self-flagellation. Dark chords, extreme rhythmic fragmentation, and vibrating dissonances rent with harrowing cries evoke an intensely visual Purgatorial pit. Metallic notes like bloody stilettos pierce the crystalline gloom. Sonorous solo lamentations erupt into a deafening chorus of panic. This was the mental landscape of the damned. No one had ever composed music of such terrible beauty. People came to refer to Carlo Gesualdo as the new Apollo.

In the late summer of 1613, at the age of twenty-five, Emmanuele Gesualdo died. He had lived to adulthood, just as Maria had always known her son by Carlo would. The loss was too much for Carlo to bear. Emmanuele was his only legitimate son and heir. Carlo's always precarious health deteriorated rapidly. Ever assiduous in business matters he rewrote sections of his will. Gesualdo did have another son, one that his imprisoned mistress Aurelia d'Errico had borne him. Although he provided a generous, lifelong stipend for this boy, he could not bring himself to name his illegitimate child by the troublesome Aurelia d'Errico as his principal inheritor. Things may have turned out better if he had.

Carlo Gesualdo died a month after Emmanuele, in September 1613, from a combination of asthma, grief and infections to wounds incurred during flagellation. He was forty-seven.

Mercifully, he did not live to see that the worst was to come.

To ensure that the principality of Venosa and the state of Gesualdo remained in the hands of his descendants, Carlo had stipulated in his will that his eldest grandchild, the Princess of Venosa, was to marry within the Gesualdo family. This did not happen. Polissena, outraged at being excluded from the principal beneficiaries of Gesualdo's will—which she unsuccessfully contested—married her eldest daughter to Prince Nicolino Ludovisio, the nephew of Pope Gregory XV. The young couple took up residence in Bologna, thereby forfeiting any claim to the Prince of Venosa's estate. The state of Gesualdo, which had been in the Gesualdo family for six hundred years, and the principality of Venosa passed into the hands of the papacy. The house of Gesualdo, descended from ancient Norman kings, was thus extinguished.

EPILOGUE

In the painting in Santa Maria delle Grazie, Gesualdo anticipated what posterity had in store for him. For centuries he remained suspended between Heaven and Hell, Heaven in this instance being the beauty of his music and his eventual reputation as a composer of genius, and Hell the horrifying stories that were circulated about him after the murders, which over the centuries took on legendary proportions. Maria d'Avalos was consistently referred to as virtuous. Gesualdo was the Devil. To this day certain inhabitants of the town of Gesualdo refer to him as *Il Diavolo*.

The first of these stories may contain some truth. It was claimed that in 1589, Maria gave birth to a daughter, Isabella. This was the year after Maria began her affair with Fabrizio Carafa, and it was said that Carlo recognised in the infant a resemblance to Fabrizio. At the inquest, Sylvia Albana recalled having cried out on the night of the murder, 'For the love of God, do not harm the baby.' As Emmanuele was three years old at this time, it is unlikely that she was referring to him. The story claims that after committing the murders, Carlo seized the baby and took her back with him to Gesualdo Castle. There he put her in a cradle, which was then attached by straps to one of the balconies in the castle courtyard. To the strains of the castle choir repeatedly singing one of Gesualdo's madrigals about the beauty of death, the infant was then rocked violently in her cradle for three days, presumably by a rotation of servants, until the violence of the movements eventually brought about her death. This child, it is claimed, is depicted in the *Pala per perdona*. She is the angel with outspread arms who hovers centrally above the flames of hell, and to whom Maria d'Avalos looks and gestures in prayer as she is raised out of the flames. That this angel might be Alfonsino is cast into doubt by the infancy of the form: Alfonsino was five years old at his death. Another explanation is that it is compositionally desirable to have a third angel at this point in the painting. Nevertheless, the angel's prominence and the significance of Maria's relation to it remains a mystery, especially in a work where the role and identity of all the other protagonists is clear.

The second and most persistent story concerns the fate of Maria's and Fabrizio's corpses after the murder. Carlo, it is claimed, had their mutilated bodies flung on the front steps of Palazzo San Severo for all of Naples to see. While the city still slept, a monk came along and defiled Maria's body. The bodies of the lovers remained exposed throughout the following day, and the people of Naples flocked to see the pitiful sight. At the hour of vespers the bodies were removed for burial amidst the lamentations of the entire city.

Gesualdo did wish it to be publicly known that he had avenged his honour; his careful orchestration of events and witnesses on the night of the murder makes that abundantly clear. But to publicly display the corpses was not only unnecessary, it would have gone against the grain of Gesualdo's almost pathological reserve in private matters. In any case, numerous witnesses at the inquest testified to having seen the bodies in the bedroom the following morning. However, in its dramatisation of the impact of the murders on the populace of Naples, this story sits in a similar category to the many poems written after the event.

The third version of events after the murder is the most gruesome. Here, the character of Gesualdo reaches the pitch of demonic antihero. It is riveting, as far as stories go, and displays a commendable feat of imaginative flair on the part of whoever originally dreamed it up, for it fuses two separate events, a hundred and fifty years apart, both of which took place in Palazzo San Severo.

Carlo, so the fable tells, was an alchemist. His particular gifts were anatomy and methods of preserving human corpses. After the murders, he had Maria's and Fabrizio's bodies taken down to the cellar of Palazzo

San Severo and there he set about working on them. This task occupied him for several days as it involved flaying the bodies, inserting a metalicising substance into their veins, along with various other mysterious processes known only to him. When he had completed his macabre works of alchemical art, he had them placed in glass showcases and put on display in the San Severo chapel, which faces the side of the palace in Via Francesco de Sanctis. Thus, it is said, the corpses of Maria d'Avalos and Fabrizio Carafa are on public display in Naples to this day.

There are two such remarkable corpses displayed in showcases with ornate gilt frames in the San Severo chapel, but they are not those of Maria and Fabrizio as they were preserved in the 1750s, not 1590. They are remarkable for the extent to which their arterial systems and main organs, which seem to spout from their branching veins, have been preserved. Their architect was the so-called Sorcerer Prince, Raimondo di Sangro, Prince of Torremaggiore and descendant of Carlo's friend, Prince Giovanni di Sangro, from whom the Gesualdo family rented Palazzo San Severo. Raimondo di Sangro was an inventor and alchemist, and it was he who used the basement of Palazzo San Severo as a laboratory, causing the emission of strange-coloured vapours and infernal smells that terrified superstitious Neapolitans. To this day, it is not known how he managed to inject the metalicising substance into the veins of the corpses, for to do so would have required a hypodermic syringe, which was not invented until a century later.

Although Gesualdo has no links with them whatsoever, there is nevertheless a poetic association between his murder of the lovers and these two startling anatomical figures. The woman is pregnant. In her open belly the placenta is clearly visible; the umbilical chord spills from it and joins the foetus. The unborn baby's skull can be opened to see the complex network of blood vessels inside. The woman has her right arm raised as if warding off a blow. Her eyeballs are still intact, almost shiny, and her expression is one of sheer terror. She is the very picture of terror. The male figure is in a defensive stance; his large penis, which appears to have been mummified, seems strangely alive. In viewing this pair of *vanitas* lovers, it seems as if the ongoing rhythm of their lives, the cycle of birth, life, sex and procreation, has suddenly been arrested by a surprise encounter with death. They are staring it right in the face. Their terror in the face of death is like a representation of the unimaginable terror Maria d'Avalos experienced when she saw Fabrizio Carafa die, saw Carlo come into the room and loom over her and experienced the white-hot agony of steel as his stiletto plunged into her vagina. Di Sangro's preserved corpses serve as reminders of the horrific nature of Carlo's crime.

The drama of Gesualdo's music—and the carefully constructed drama of the night of the murders—prefigured the rise of opera, which shortly after his death became the chief musical mode in Italy. But Gesualdo's music itself was forgotten for four centuries. The Baroque soon replaced his period of late Mannerism and, after a fleeting period of glory as the master of his age, Gesualdo's idiosyncratic creations, his adherence to composing mainly for the voice, were seen as a dead end. He had established no ongoing musical legacy. He was remembered as an illustrious dilettante. Worse, he was dismissed as the 'crank of chromaticism'.

It was not until the mid-twentieth century that his music was revived and came to be properly understood and appreciated, for Gesualdo's tortured expressionism anticipated the emotional sensibilities of the modern age. His champion was Igor Stravinsky, who devoted considerable scholarship to him and composed his *Monumentum pro Gesualdo* in admiration of him. It is now acknowledged that Gesualdo was a genius who anticipated the music of Richard Wagner by three centuries. As a consequence musicologists consistently make valiant attempts to disassociate the intense expressiveness of his music with his horrendous act.

In spite of this, however, Carlo Gesualdo lives on as the murderer of Maria d'Avalos, the most beautiful woman in Naples, and Fabrizio Carafa, its handsomest and most accomplished nobleman.

LETTERS FROM ST PETERSBURG

Victoria Hammond

'I know no one. I don't speak the language. The city has a reputation for being dangerous. I've become addicted to this scenario, to the thrill of travelling alone and watching how I deal with the terrors of a strange place. But this time it's different: Ada, a curator at the Russian Museum in St Petersburg, is meeting me. At least I hope to god she's meeting me.'

With its shimmering palaces and decaying mansions, enchanted forests and basements crammed full of Soviet art, St Petersburg is a city of ghosts and illusions where past and present, and reality and fiction are inextricably fused.

In this city blasted by history it is not the grand events but the intimate details that Victoria Hammond is drawn to: a walk through Dostoeveky's streets on a white night; the friendship between a mafia boss and a Siberian tiger; a swim in the warmth of a moonlit Russian lake; stories of struggling artists and dignified intellectuals eking out existences in single rooms.

Beautifully written, strange and evocative, *Letters from St Petersburg* is a compelling account of one woman's journey to the mysterious and surprising heart of Russia.

'The most vividly rendered and engaging memoir I have read this year.'
San Francisco Chronicle

'This candid, easy tale deftly weaves in history and art to create a lively picture of post-communist life in an extraordinary city.'
Sunday Age

'This book is so beautifully written that St Peterburg comes to life before the reader's eyes.'
Vacations and Travel

ISBN: 978 1 74175 055 3